LUTHER'S WORKS

American Edition

VOLUME 45

Published by Concordia Publishing House

and Fortress Press in 55 volumes.

General Editors are Jaroslav Pelikan (for vols. 1-30)

and Helmut T. Lehmann (for vols. 31-55)

LUTHER'S WORKS

VOLUME 45

The Christian in Society

II

EDITED BY

WALTHER I. BRANDT

GENERAL EDITOR

HELMUT T. LEHMANN

FORTRESS PRESS / PHILADELPHIA

GENERAL EDITORS'
PREFACE

The first editions of Luther's collected works appeared in the sixteenth century, and so did the first efforts to make him "speak English." In America serious attempts in these directions were made for the first time in the nineteenth century. The Saint Louis edition of Luther was the first endeavor on American soil to publish a collected edition of his works, and the Henkel Press in Newmarket, Virginia, was the first to publish some of Luther's writings in an English translation. During the first decade of the twentieth century, J. N. Lenker produced translations of Luther's sermons and commentaries in thirteen volumes. A few years later the first of the six volumes in the Philadelphia (or Holman) edition of the Works of Martin Luther appeared. But a growing recognition of the need for more of Luther's works in English has resulted in this American edition of Luther's works.

The edition is intended primarily for the reader whose knowledge of late medieval Latin and sixteenth-century German is too small to permit him to work with Luther in the original languages. Those who can will continue to read Luther in his original words as these have been assembled in the monumental Weimar edition (*D. Martin Luthers Werke.* Kritische Gesamtausgabe, Weimar, 1883-   ). Its texts and helps have formed a basis for this edition, though in certain places we have felt constrained to depart from its readings and findings. We have tried throughout to translate Luther as he thought translating should be done. That is, we have striven for faithfulness on the basis of the best lexicographical materials available. But where literal accuracy and clarity have conflicted, it is clarity that we have preferred, so that sometimes paraphrase seemed more faithful than literal fidelity. We have proceeded in a similar way in the matter of Bible versions, translating Luther's translations. Where this could be done by the use of an existing English version—King James, Douay, or Revised Standard—we have done so. Where it could not, we have supplied our own. To indicate this in each specific instance would have been pedantic; to adopt a uniform procedure would have been artificial—especially in view of Luther's own inconsistency in this regard. In each volume the translator will be responsible primarily for matters of text and language, while the responsibility of the editor will extend principally to the historical and theological matters reflected in the introductions and notes.

Although the edition as planned will include fifty-five volumes, Luther's writings are not being translated in their entirety. Nor should they be. As he was the first to insist, much of what he wrote and said was not that important. Thus the edition is a selection of works that have proved their importance for the faith, life, and history of the Christian church. The first thirty volumes contain Luther's expositions of various biblical books, while the remaining volumes include what are usually called his "Reformation writings" and other occasional pieces. The final volume of the set will be an index volume; in addition to an index of quotations, proper names, and topics, and a list of corrections and changes, it will contain a glossary of many of the technical terms that recur in Luther's works and that cannot be defined each time they appear. Obviously Luther cannot be forced into any neat set of rubrics. He can provide his reader with bits of autobiography or with political observations as he expounds a psalm, and he can speak tenderly about the meaning of the faith in the midst of polemics against his opponents. It is the hope of publishers, editors, and translators that through this edition the message of Luther's faith will speak more clearly to the modern church.

J.P.
H.T.L.

CONTENTS

ACW — *Ancient Christian Writers,* edited by Johannes Quasten and Joseph C. Plumpe (Westminster, Md., 1949-   ).

ANF — *The Ante-Nicene Fathers,* edited by Alexander Roberts and James Donaldson (Buffalo and New York, 1885-1896, American reprint of the Edinburgh edition).

BG — *Luthers Werke für das christliche Haus,* edited by Georg Buchwald, *et al.* (Braunschweig, 1889-1892).

Br A — *Luthers Werke für das christliche Haus,* edited by Georg Buchwald, *et al.,* 4th edition (Leipzig, 1924).

CL — *Luthers Werke in Auswahl,* edited by Otto Clemen, *et al.* (Bonn, 1912-1933; Berlin, 1955-1956).

C. R. — *Huldreich Zwinglis sämmtliche Werke,* vols. 88 ff. of the *Corpus Reformatorum,* edited by Emil Egli, Georg Finsler, *et al.* (Leipzig, 1905-   ).

EA — *D. Martin Luthers sämmtliche Werke* (Frankfurt and Erlangen, 1826-1857).

FC — *Fathers of the Church,* edited by Ludwig Schopp (New York, 1947-   ).

LCC — *Library of Christian Classics,* John T. McNeill and Henry P. van Dusen, General Editors (Philadelphia, 1953-   ).

LE — *The Precious and Sacred Writings of Martin Luther,* edited by John Nicholas Lenker (Minneapolis, 1904-1909).

LW — American Edition of *Luther's Works* (Philadelphia and St. Louis, 1955-   ).

LWZ — *The Latin Works of Huldreich Zwingli,* 3 vols., translated and edited by S. M. Jackson, *et al.* (New York, 1912; Philadelphia, 1922, 1929).

MA³ — *Martin Luther.* Ausgewählte Werke, edited by H. H. Borcherdt and Georg Merz.
3rd edition (München, 1948-   ).

MA,³ Er — *Martin Luther.* Ergänzungsbände Werke
(München, 1954-   ).

MPG — *Patrologia, Series Graeca,* 161 vols., edited by J. P. Migne
(Paris, 1857-1866).

MPL — *Patrologia, Series Latina,* 221 vols. in 222, edited by J. P. Migne
(Paris, 1844-1904).

PE — *Works of Martin Luther*
(Philadelphia, 1915-1943).

PNF¹ — *The Nicene and Post-Nicene Fathers of the Christian Church* (First Series), edited by Philip Schaff
(New York, 1886-1900).

St. L. — *D. Martin Luthers sämmtliche Schriften,* edited by Johann Georg Walch. Edited and published in modern German, 23 vols. in 25
(St. Louis, 1880-1910).

S-J — *Luther's Correspondence,* 2 vols., edited by Preserved Smith and Charles M. Jacobs
(Philadelphia, 1913-1918).

WA — *D. Martin Luthers Werke.* Kritische Gesamtausgabe
(Weimar, 1883-   ).

WA, Br — *D. Martin Luthers Werke.* Briefwechsel
(Weimar, 1930-1948).

WA, TR — *D. Martin Luthers Werke.* Tischreden
(Weimar, 1912-1921).

WA, DB — *D. Martin Luthers Werke.* Deutsche Bibel
(Weimar, 1906-   ).

INTRODUCTION TO VOLUME 45

As a parish priest, and later as a religious leader of wide reputation and influence, Luther was constantly being called upon to give advice and counsel for the guidance of Christians in the problems of everyday life. As the chief initiator of the Reformation, he felt a certain measure of responsibility for the reformatory acts of those who were at least nominally his followers. He was ever ready to comfort and encourage the fainthearted, and to caution and restrain the overbold. Keenly aware of the power of the printed word, he frequently issued his statements in the form of printed pamphlets in order to give them the widest possible publicity. Though printers found a ready sale for these pamphlets, Luther received no royalties on them.

Of the eleven treatises included in the present volume, all of which appeared during the years 1522-1524, three are particularly concerned with marriage problems. From the days of the apostles to the present, such problems have occupied much of the time of spiritual advisers, and Luther's age was no exception. He complained that as a parish priest he had to deal with such problems daily. He began preaching and writing about marriage as early as 1519 and dealt with the subject on numerous occasions thereafter. In the first two and last treatises of the present volume, all translated here for the first time into English, Luther discusses such matters as prohibited marriages, God's ordinance of creation and those who are exempt from it, the eighteen canonical impediments to marriage, divorce, the mutual obligations of husband and wife, the joys and blessings of married life, and the extent of parental authority in the matter of arranging their children's marriages.

The related matter of clerical celibacy is dealt with in *An Exhortation to the Knights of the Teutonic Order That They Lay Aside False Chastity and Assume the True Chastity of Wedlock.*

Grand Master Albert of the Teutonic Order had become a secret convert to Lutheranism during a stay at Nürnberg to attend the diets of 1522-1523. At that time he was being urged by the pope to undertake a much-needed reform of the order. He sought Luther's advice, at first through emissaries, and finally in a personal conference at Wittenberg in November, 1523. The address to the knights called for courageous public obedience to God's command and ordinance without regard to the commands of men and without waiting for the decision of a fallible council. In less than two years the order did dissolve, and Prussia became a secular state.

While Luther was primarily a religious leader, he was by no means indifferent to the economic conditions under which the German people lived. The age was one of commercial expansion and rising prices. Monopolistic trading companies were amassing huge profits, and possessors of capital sought profitable investments. The peasant, the small landholder, and the small businessman were preyed upon by money lenders, who readily found ways of evading the usury laws of church and state. The capitalists themselves, troubled in conscience, were occasionally desirous of Christian counsel. In 1519 Luther had published a brief tract on usury, which he reissued in expanded form the next year. In 1524 he published a tract on trading, to which he added the 1520 tract on usury. In this 1524 publication known as *Trade and Usury*, the longest treatise in the present volume, Luther sharply criticizes certain current financial and merchandising practices, the avarice which motivated them, and the ecclesiastical casuistry which justified them; he also sets forth the Christian attitude toward material goods.

Another problem involving economics to some degree was that of poor relief and parish reorganization. In common with other reformers, Luther strongly opposed the practice of begging; the alternative was some organized system of poor relief. Furthermore, if the local parish were to throw off the yoke of ecclesiastical domination, there must be a thorough reorganization of parish finances. One of the early experiments of this sort occurred at Leisnig, where the parish drew up a formal ordinance or plan of reorganization which was to center all parish finances in a "common chest." This plan was submitted to Luther, who gave it his immediate and warm approval. In 1523 he published the ordinance itself together with a preface he had written for it, both of which are translated in the present volume as *Ordinance of a Common Chest, Preface,* and *Fraternal Agreement on the Common Chest of the Entire Assembly at Leisnig.*

A serious problem which faced the Lutheran Christian of that day was the question of what his attitude should be toward temporal authority. The emperor and many of the German princes were determined to enforce the provisions of the Edict of Worms (1521). Luther and his followers were under the ban of both the church and the empire; the possession or reading of his books, including his German New Testament, were prohibited by Catholic princes. On his secret visit to Wittenberg during the period of his Wartburg exile, Luther was seriously disturbed by the evidence he saw of widespread unrest among the people. There were mutterings and threats of violence against the lords, both lay and ecclesiastical. Student riots had occurred at Wittenberg and at Erfurt. Clerics had been subjected to physical violence, and some churches and monasteries had been plundered. In 1522, before his final return from the Wartburg, *A Sincere Admonition by Martin Luther to All Christians to Guard Against Insurrection and Rebellion* came from the press. In it he urges his adherents to refrain from actual violence, on the grounds that God has chosen to avenge himself in more appropriate and severe ways; insurrection harms the innocent more than the guilty, brings reproach upon the whole evangelical cause, and involves a usurpation of functions belonging properly to the temporal government. He boasts that he has done more harm to the papacy by his pen than was ever accomplished by the violent acts of emperors, kings, and princes.

In his 1523 treatise on *Temporal Authority: To What Extent it Should be Obeyed* Luther faces squarely the question of what a Christian should do when the secular power seeks to coerce him in religious matters. In brief, his position is this: temporal authority is of divine origin, instituted for the restraining of evildoers; the Christian has no need of it but is subject to it out of love for his neighbor. In temporal matters the temporal authority is supreme, and must be obeyed; but when that authority attempts to hinder the gospel or coerce the conscience it should be met with passive disobedience. Active resistance is contrary to Scripture, which forbids us to resist evil (Matt. 5:38-41); instead the Christian should confess the truth, and not so much as lift a little finger to aid the government in enforcing an evil decree. Rulers in turn are to govern—on the basis of human wisdom—in the best interests of their subjects, not for their own glory and benefit. As the government, independently of the church, has a divine function, so the Christian has a duty to participate actively in governmental affairs.

Existing schools, especially those conducted by religious foundations, were under attack from several quarters. The humanists attacked their curricula as out-of-date, poorly taught, and at best very wasteful of the pupil's time. Luther denounced such schools in vigorous language as a tool of the devil by which he kept the German youth from a knowledge of the saving gospel. Extremists like Karlstadt and Münzer opposed all education, on the ground that the "inner spirit" was far superior to any sort of formal education. Moreover, the spirit of materialism was widespread; since Luther had discouraged parents from having their sons trained for the priesthood or the monastery, of what use was education? Let a boy learn some trade, they said, whereby he can earn a livelihood, and perhaps wealth.

Although he opposed the old-fashioned type of school Luther was a warm and consistent advocate of good schools. Since 1520 he had been pleading in general terms for the establishment of adequate schools. The nobility and the princes proved to be indifferent, or were occupied with other matters; parents lacked both time and ability to educate their children. Who then should assume the responsibility? In 1524 Luther issued his ringing appeal *To the Councilmen of All Cities in Germany*, urging that it was their duty to establish schools lest the German youth sink into brutish ignorance. Although he emphasized the need of schools to provide religious training, he placed equal emphasis on the necessity of providing an intelligent, trained, and capable citizenry. Both objectives, he contended, could be achieved only through the establishment of adequate schools in every city in the land.

Despite the fact that he was a busy man, Luther often took time to visit various areas in order to give personal encouragement to people attracted to the evangelical cause. In 1522 he received an appeal from far-off Riga, requesting him to encourage the Lutheran group in Livonia by sending them a letter or some devotional treatise. After delaying for well over a year, he responded in 1524 by sending them the *Exposition of Psalm 127*. Aside from the dedication, "For the Christians at Riga in Livonia," the treatise makes no mention of religious conditions there, for Luther had no first-hand knowledge of their affairs. Written at a time when the need for adequate schools, and the money to finance them, was so prominent in Luther's thinking, it deals rather with the Christian attitude toward the accumulation and ownership of material goods.

Finally there is included in this volume the 1523 treatise, *That Jesus Christ Was Born a Jew*, which must be classified as a reply to specific charges by his opponents. During the diets at Nürnberg Luther and his doctrines were a subject of controversy at the sessions, and also a matter of common gossip. It was rumored that Luther taught that "Jesus was conceived of the seed of Joseph, and that Mary was not a virgin, but had many sons after Christ." These charges were repeated publicly by no less a person than Archduke Ferdinand himself, then the ruler of the empire during the absence of Charles V in Spain. In his refutation of the charges, Luther firmly upholds the orthodox view, namely, that Jesus was a Jew, born of the seed of Abraham, but begotten by means of a miracle, and that Mary was a virgin when Jesus was born and, there being no scriptural evidence to the contrary, remained so thereafter. He then proceeds with a lengthy and sometimes labored argument to confute the Jewish denial of the messiahship of Jesus. Luther has often been charged with anti-Semitism; however, there is no evidence of it in this treatise. On the contrary, he scolds his fellow Christians for their hostile attitude toward the Jews, urging them to abandon their policy of discrimination and to receive them as equals, socially and otherwise.

W.I.B.

Note on Scriptural References

In quoting Scripture, Luther cites only chapter, not verse, since chapters were not yet customarily divided into verses at that time. In the present translation Luther's own citations have been retained—except in the case of the Psalms—and supplemented or corrected as need be in brackets to conform to the versification in the RSV.

Citations from the Psalms present a special problem. Luther had not yet translated the Old Testament when he composed the treatises included in the present volume; his citations are from the Vulgate. In the Vulgate—and in the modern Roman Catholic English versions based upon it—the Psalms are numbered differently than in the AV and RSV, though in both cases the total number of Psalms is 150. The difference parallels that between the Septuagint and the Hebrew in that for the greater part of the Psalter the numeration of the former is one behind that of the latter; only for Psalms 1-8 and 148-150 is the numeration identical. Further confusion arises from the fact that in modern Latin and German Bibles—following Hebrew precedent—the title or introductory statement attached to many of the Psalms is frequently given a verse number, a practice not followed in the RSV. In the present volume Luther's Psalms citations, if they were correct in terms of the Vulgate of his time, have been altered directly in the process of translation to conform to the chapter numbers of the RSV. In the few cases where it seemed advisable explanation has been made in a footnote.

LUTHER'S WORKS

VOLUME 45

THE PERSONS RELATED BY CONSANGUINITY AND AFFINITY WHO ARE FORBIDDEN TO MARRY ACCORDING TO THE SCRIPTURES, LEVITICUS 18

1522

Translated by Walther I. Brandt

INTRODUCTION

In the summer of 1522 the suffragan bishop of Meissen[1] announced
that he was coming to Zwickau to confirm the children there. He
accompanied his announcement with a public statement on the
virtue and grace of the sacrament of confirmation. Luther was
informed of the coming visitation by his friend Nicholas Hausmann,
who had become pastor at Zwickau the previous year. On August
3, 1522, Luther wrote Hausmann urging him to confront the
bishop, on his arrival, with evidence from Scripture on the non-
sacramental character of the rite of confirmation. If "the episcopal
idol" (*episcopale idolum*) were unable to justify his position from
Scripture, Hausmann ought to warn the children of the parish
against trusting in such a sacrament.[2]

In his letter Luther mentions a "*scedula,*" by which he
probably means the present little tract in its printed form.[3] It
occupied the two inner pages of a half sheet, with no printing
on the outside. A previous letter to Hausmann dated June 30
of the same year makes no mention of the subject.[4] Although
direct evidence is lacking, it seems reasonable to assume that
Luther wrote the tract and had it printed shortly after receiving
Hausmann's letter about the impending visitation, and that the
seemingly irrelevant paragraph on confirmation was included
because of the bishop's public statement. Judging from the language of the letter of August 3, with its reference to "this other"
(*hanc aliam*), a copy of the printed tract was probably sent with

[1] *WA* 10^{II}, 263, names the bishop of Meissen though, according to *WA*, Br
2, 585, n. 1, Zwickau belonged to the diocese of Naumburg-Zeitz.
[2] See the text of the letter in *WA*, Br 2, 584-585.
[3] In the absence of other means of duplication, Luther often had his tracts and
articles—and sometimes even letters of importance—printed, and sent them
to their destination in that form. Apparently the printers found a ready
market for anything from Luther's pen; some of his treatises went through
as many as ten printings within a single year. Sometimes the first sheets of
a treatise were set up in type and printed before the treatise was completed.
Occasionally they were pirated by unauthorized printers who sought to profit
from the demand.
[4] See this letter in *WA*, Br 2, 572.

the letter. For the relation of this brief tract to the treatise on *The Estate of Marriage,* see below, p. 15.

The following translation, the first into English, is based on the text published by Johann Grünenberg in Wittenberg, *"WIlche person verpoten sind tzu ehlichen ynn der heyligenn schrifft beyde der freundschafft und Mogschafft. Leuit. 18,"* as it has been reprinted with annotations in *WA* 10$^{\text{II},}$ 265-266.

THE PERSONS RELATED BY CONSANGUINITY AND AFFINITY WHO ARE FORBIDDEN TO MARRY ACCORDING TO THE SCRIPTURES, LEVITICUS 18

I am forbidden to marry the following persons related to me by consanguinity:

1. Father[1]
2. Mother
3. Stepmother
4. Sister
5. Stepsister
6. Son's daughter
7. Father's sister
8. Mother's sister

From this it follows[2] that with a good conscience before God I may marry the child of my brother or sister,[3] or my stepmother's sister.

I am forbidden to marry the following persons related to me by affinity:

1. Father's brother's wife
2. Son's wife
3. Brother's wife
4. Stepdaughter
5. The child of my stepson or stepdaughter[4]
6. My wife's sister, while my wife is still alive.

---

[1] Luther's 1520 *Babylonian Captivity* had omitted this category while listing the other "twelve persons a man is prohibited from marrying." *LW* 36, 99.
[2] Cf. p. 23.
[3] According to canon law this was a forbidden relationship of the second degree. See the "trees" of relationship diagrammed in Aemilius Friedberg (ed.), *Corpus Iuris Canonici* (Graz., 1955), I, cols. 1425-1432.
[4] Luther's 1520 *Babylonian Captivity* had omitted this category also.

From this it follows[5] that I may marry the sister of my deceased wife or fiancée,[6] as well as the widow of my deceased brother, as was commanded in the law, Matthew 22 [:24].

As to other forbidden persons or degrees of relationship, our clerical tyrants have forbidden them for the sake of money. This is evident from the fact that, for money, they turn right around and sell permission for a prohibited marriage, and if no money is forthcoming they break up the marriage, contrary to God and every sense of justice.

In addition they have also concocted new degrees of relationship, namely, the godparents, godchildren, and their children and brothers or sisters. It was really the devil who taught them that, for if the sacrament of baptism is supposed to create an impediment then no Christian man could take a Christian wife, since all baptized women are in a spiritual sense the sisters of all baptized men. They have in common the sacrament, the Spirit, faith, and spiritual gifts and blessings, by reason of which they are more closely related in Spirit than through the outward act of sponsorship.

Especially to be rejected is confirmation, that deceitful mumbo-jumbo of the episcopal idols.[7] It has no foundation in Scripture. The bishops are only deceiving people with their lies when they say that grace, a character, a mark are conferred in confirmation.[8]

---

[5] Cf. p. 23.

[6] Cf. Lev. 18:18. Later in a letter to the Zwickau pastor Leonhard Beyer, dated January 18, 1535, Luther joined Justus Jonas and Philip Melanchthon in declaring against the marriage of a man to his deceased wife's sister, on the grounds that by virtue of the one-flesh relationship established in marriage the wife's sister was already his sister as well and hence related in the first degree of affinity, a decree clearly forbidden by Leviticus 18. Such a union, Luther pointed out, was forbidden also by the imperial law of the land, and could only result in distress of conscience. See the text of the letter in WA, Br 7, 152-153, and St. L. 10, 704-705.

[7] Luther is not condemning the rite of confirmation, but its elevation to the status of a sacrament (cf. LW 36, 91-92). For an explanation of the inclusion of this comment on confirmation in a treatise on marriage, see the Introduction, p. 5.

[8] The Council of Florence, following Thomas Aquinas' "On the Articles of Faith and the Sacraments of the Church" almost word for word, had declared on November 22, 1439, "Among these sacraments there are three, baptism, confirmation, and orders, which imprint an indelible sign on the soul, that is, a certain character distinctive from the others. Hence they should not be repeated in the same person." Roy J. Defarrari (trans.), Henry Denzinger's The Sources of Catholic Dogma (St. Louis: Herder, 1957), p. 221. For the

It is rather the character of the beast, Revelation 13 [:16-17]. A Christian should not, at the peril of his soul, base his faith on human fantasy, which will surely betray and deceive him, but only on the Word of God, who does not lie.

MARTIN LUTHER

---

history of the distinction between sacramental grace and the sacramental character, see *The Catholic Encyclopedia* (16 vols.; New York, 1907-1914), III, 586-588, "Character."

THE ESTATE OF MARRIAGE

1522

Translated by Walther I. Brandt

INTRODUCTION

Luther left the Wartburg on March 1, 1522, arriving at Wittenberg on March 6. One of the first things he did was to preach a series of eight sermons, during the week beginning March 9, in an effort to counteract the extreme reforms which had been forced through by Karlstadt and Gabriel Zwilling.[1] Luther was by no means opposed to reform measures, but he held that they should be brought about by persuasion, not compulsion.

The events which had transpired during his year of seclusion at the Wartburg convinced him that writing was not enough; his personal influence and spoken word were needed to prevent the reform movement he had begun from degenerating into riot and disorder. The hesitant elector and the scholarly but irresolute Melanchthon were unable to cope with the fiery zeal of Karlstadt and Zwilling. Luther's letter of March 12, 1522, to the Elector Frederick gave his specific reasons for returning to Wittenberg contrary to the elector's desire, one reason being that "Satan has fallen upon my flock at Wittenberg."[2] Following the eight Wittenberg sermons, Karlstadt was for the time being reduced to an unwilling silence; Zwilling was persuaded that his extreme measures were a mistake, and became reconciled with Luther.[3]

If the "true gospel," as Luther understood it, fared so ill at Wittenberg in the presence of his most intimate colleagues, what was the situation elsewhere? He was determined to see for himself, particularly since the bishops of Meissen and Merseburg had suddenly begun a visitation of the churches. Despite the fact that he was now under both papal and imperial ban Luther undertook a short preaching tour. Leaving Wittenberg on April 26, 1522, he visited Borna, Altenburg, Zwickau, Eilenburg, and Torgau.[4]

---

[1] See the text of the *Eight Sermons at Wittenberg*. LW 51, 67-97. Cf. also LW 36, 233-235.
[2] See the text of the letter in S-J 2, 98-101; WA, Br 2, 467-470.
[3] Luther even recommended Zwilling's appointment as evangelical preacher at Altenburg, but was overruled by the cautious elector. G. Schwiebert, *Luther and His Times* (St. Louis: Concordia, 1950), p. 543.
[4] Ten sermons from this trip have survived; see the texts in WA 10III, 86-124.

Among the practical problems with which every priest, pastor, and confessor had to deal were those involving the marriage relationship. Since marriage was numbered among the sacraments, it was hedged about with numerous rules and restrictions.[5] Luther had for years been a parish priest and confessor to his flock in Wittenberg. In 1519 he published *A Sermon on the Estate of Marriage*,[6] his first on the subject. In his 1520 *Babylonian Captivity of the Church* he treated the matter at some length.[7] In his 1521 *Of Monastic Vows*,[8] he declared the vow of celibacy no longer binding, and encouraged monks and nuns to leave the cloister. It is reasonable to suppose that numerous instances of marriage problems and bad moral conditions came to his attention also during his preaching tour in the spring of 1522.

Unfortunately, the sources are virtually silent on the specific reasons which called forth the treatise here translated, as well as on the time of its composition and its appearance in print. That it appeared before the end of the year 1522 is established by the fact that Dietrich von Werthern, Duke George's representative at the diet, had a copy by December 19; Duke George himself had a copy of it by New Year's Day.[9] Beyond that, we must be content with inference and conjecture. We possess only a few extracts from Luther's afternoon sermon of April 30, 1522, at Zwickau, but we know that its fifth part dealt with the scriptural passages concerning married life which are basic in this treatise.[10] In a sermon of August 10, 1522, he discussed a marriage problem in terms almost identical with those used in the present treatise,[11] which suggests the possibility of a simultaneous origin for the two documents.

---

[5] Part II of Gratian's *Decretum*, a twelfth-century attempt to codify canon law, consists of a detailed analysis of thirty-six hypothetical cases, of which cases 27-36 deal directly with marriage. *Corpus Iuris Canonici*, I, cols. 1046-1292. The problem was also treated in the 1234 decretals of Gregory IX (*Corpus Iuris Canonici*, II, cols. 661-732) and other medieval collections of canon law (*Corpus Iuris Canonici*, II, cols. 1065-1068, 1177-1178). See p. 7, n. 3, and cf. *LW* 36, 96-106.

[6] See the text in *WA* 2, 166-171.

[7] See *LW* 36, 92-106.

[8] See the text in *WA* 8, 573-669.

[9] Felician Gess, *Akten und Briefe zur Kirchenpolitik Herzog Georgs von Sachsen* (2 vols.; Leipzig: Teubner, 1905-1917), I, 402, 415.

[10] See the text in *WA* 10III, 108.

[11] Cf. *WA* 10III, 265, ll. 15-18, with p. 26.

There is a close relationship between the brief tract on forbidden marriages, translated as the first document in this volume, and this longer treatise on *The Estate of Marriage*. One must have been the basis for the other. In both, the lists of persons forbidden to marry because of relationship through blood or marriage are identical; both reject impediments based on spiritual relationship. The longer treatise even retains the warning against the sacrament of confirmation, a warning which had its legitimate place only in the brief tract intended for Hausmann.[12] Had the longer treatise been available, it is unlikely that the Basel printers in the fall of 1522 would have appended the shorter tract to their printings of Luther's *Avoiding the Doctrines of Men* and *Against the So-called Spiritual Estate of Popes and Bishops* where it does not really belong, rather than to *The Estate of Marriage* where it would have been most appropriate. This would suggest that the longer treatise arrived in Basel later than the shorter tract. Since communications between the Wittenberg and Basel printers were very prompt at the time, we are justified in concluding that the treatise was originally published later than the tract. Since the tract was published not later than August 3, this would place the probable time for the composition of the treatise in the middle of August, 1522. Having written the tract first, Luther presumably worked its contents into the treatise on marriage, forgetting to blue-pencil the paragraph on confirmation. The treatise was probably published by the end of September since a reprinting in Basel appeared in December.[13]

In his introduction to the treatise Luther refers to it as a sermon, but says he dreads preaching on the subject. Luther's introductory remarks are appropriate only to a treatise intended for the press, not to a sermon. If its original form was a sermon delivered from the pulpit, it must have been greatly expanded before publication. No corresponding sermon text is known to us, much less a particular Sunday or occasion for its delivery.

The following translation, the first into English, is based on the text published by Johann Grünenberg in Wittenberg, *Uom Eelichen Leben*, as reprinted with annotations in WA 10[II], 275-304.

---

[12] See p. 5.
[13] *WA* 10[II], 267.

THE ESTATE OF MARRIAGE

Jesus

How I dread preaching on the estate of marriage! I am reluctant to do it because I am afraid if I once get really involved in the subject it will make a lot of work for me and for others. The shameful confusion wrought by the accursed papal law has occasioned so much distress, and the lax authority of both the spiritual and the temporal swords has given rise to so many dreadful abuses and false situations, that I would much prefer neither to look into the matter nor to hear of it. But timidity is no help in an emergency;[1] I must proceed. I must try to instruct poor bewildered consciences, and take up the matter boldly. This sermon is divided into three parts.

Part One

In the first part we shall consider which persons may enter into marriage with one another. In order to proceed aright let us direct our attention to Genesis 1 [:27], "So God created man . . . male and female he created them." From this passage we may be assured that God divided mankind into two classes, namely, male and female, or a he and a she. This was so pleasing to him that he himself called it a good creation [Gen. 1:31]. Therefore, each one of us must have the kind of body God has created for us. I cannot make myself a woman, nor can you make yourself a man; we do not have that power. But we are exactly as he created us: I a man and you a woman. Moreover, he wills to have his excellent handiwork honored as his divine creation, and not despised. The man is not to despise or scoff at the woman or her body, nor the woman the man. But each should honor the other's image and

---

[1] *Fur nott hilfft keyn schewhen.* Karl F. Wander (ed.), *Deutsches Sprich-wörter-Lexikon* (5 vols.; Leipzig: Brockhaus, 1867-1880), III, 1047, "*Noth*," No. 65.

body as a divine and good creation that is well-pleasing unto God himself.

In the second place, after God had made man and woman he blessed them and said to them, "Be fruitful and multiply" [Gen. 1:28]. From this passage we may be assured that man and woman should and must come together in order to multiply. Now this [ordinance] is just as inflexible as the first, and no more to be despised and made fun of than the other, since God gives it his blessing and does something over and above the act of creation. Hence, as it is not within my power not to be a man, so it is not my prerogative to be without a woman. Again, as it is not in your power not to be a woman, so it is not your prerogative to be without a man. For it is not a matter of free choice or decision but a natural and necessary thing, that whatever is a man must have a woman and whatever is a woman must have a man.

For this word which God speaks, "Be fruitful and multiply," is not a command. It is more than a command, namely, a divine ordinance [werck] which it is not our prerogative to hinder or ignore. Rather, it is just as necessary as the fact that I am a man, and more necessary than sleeping and waking, eating and drinking, and emptying the bowels and bladder. It is a nature and disposition just as innate as the organs involved in it. Therefore, just as God does not command anyone to be a man or a woman but creates them the way they have to be, so he does not command them to multiply but creates them so that they have to multiply. And wherever men try to resist this, it remains irresistible nonetheless and goes its way through fornication, adultery, and secret sins, for this is a matter of nature and not of choice.

In the third place, from this ordinance of creation God has himself exempted three categories of men, saying in Matthew 19 [:12], "There are eunuchs who have been so from birth, and there are eunuchs who have been made eunuchs by men, and there are eunuchs who have made themselves eunuchs for the sake of the kingdom of heaven." Apart from these three groups, let no man presume to be without a spouse. And whoever does not fall within one of these three categories should not consider

18

anything except the estate of marriage. Otherwise it is simply impossible for you to remain righteous. For the Word of God which created you and said, "Be fruitful and multiply," abides and rules within you; you can by no means ignore it, or you will be bound to commit heinous sins without end.

Don't let yourself be fooled on this score, even if you should make ten oaths, vows, covenants, and adamantine or ironclad pledges. For as you cannot solemnly promise that you will not be a man or a woman (and if you should make such a promise it would be foolishness and of no avail since you cannot make yourself something other than what you are), so you cannot promise that you will not produce seed or multiply, unless you belong to one of the three categories mentioned above. And should you make such a promise, it too would be foolishness and of no avail, for to produce seed and to multiply is a matter of God's ordinance [geschöpffe], not your power.

From this you can now see the extent of the validity of all cloister vows. No vow of any youth or maiden is valid before God, except that of a person in one of the three categories which God alone has himself excepted. Therefore, priests, monks, and nuns are duty-bound to forsake their vows whenever they find that God's ordinance to produce seed and to multiply is powerful and strong within them. They have no power by any authority, law, command, or vow to hinder this which God has created within them. If they do hinder it, however, you may be sure that they will not remain pure but inevitably besmirch themselves with secret sins or fornication. For they are simply incapable of resisting the word and ordinance of God within them. Matters will take their course as God has ordained.

As to the first category, which Christ calls "eunuchs who have been so from birth," these are the ones whom men call impotent, who are by nature not equipped to produce seed and multiply because they are physically frigid or weak or have some other bodily deficiency which makes them unfit for the estate of marriage. Such cases occur among both men and women. These we need not take into account, for God has himself exempted them and so formed them that the blessing of being able to multiply has not come to them. The injunction, "Be fruitful and

THE CHRISTIAN IN SOCIETY

multiply," does not apply to them; just as when God creates a person crippled or blind, that person is not obligated to walk or see, because he cannot.

I once wrote down some advice concerning such persons for those who hear confession.[2] It related to those cases where a husband or wife comes and wants to learn what he should do: his spouse is unable to fulfil the conjugal duty, yet he cannot get along without it because he finds that God's ordinance to multiply is still in force within him. Here they have accused me of teaching that when a husband is unable to satisfy his wife's sexual desire she should run to somebody else. Let the topsy-turvy liars spread their lies. The words of Christ and his apostles were turned upside down; should they not also turn my words topsy-turvy? To whose detriment it will be they shall surely find out.

What I said was this: if a woman who is fit for marriage has a husband who is not, and she is unable openly to take unto herself another—and unwilling, too, to do anything dishonorable—since the pope in such a case demands without cause abundant testimony and evidence, she should say to her husband, "Look, my dear husband, you are unable to fulfil your conjugal duty toward me; you have cheated me out of my maidenhood and even imperiled my honor and my soul's salvation; in the sight of God there is no real marriage between us. Grant me the privilege of contracting a secret marriage with your brother or closest relative, and you retain the title of husband so that your property will not fall to strangers. Consent to being betrayed voluntarily by me, as you have betrayed me without my consent."

I stated further that the husband is obligated to consent to such an arrangement and thus to provide for her the conjugal duty and children, and that if he refuses to do so she should secretly flee from him to some other country and there contract a marriage. I gave this advice at a time when I was still timid. However, I should like now to give sounder advice in the matter, and take a firmer grip on the wool[3] of a man who thus makes a

---

[2] See *The Babylonian Captivity of the Church.* LW 36, 103-105.
[3] *Bass ynn die wolle greyffen.* The expression occurs also in Luther's letter to Hans von der Planitz, February 4, 1523. WA, Br 3, 27, No. 581; S-J 2, 168, No. 573.

fool of[4] his wife. The same principle would apply if the circumstances were reversed, although this happens less frequently in the case of wives than of husbands. It will not do to lead one's fellow-man around by the nose[5] so wantonly in matters of such great import involving his body, goods, honor, and salvation. He has to be told to make it right.

The second category, those who Christ says "have been made eunuchs by men" [Matt. 19:12], the castrates, are an unhappy lot, for though they are not equipped for marriage, they are nevertheless not free from evil desire. They seek the company of women more than before and are quite effeminate. It is with them as the proverb says, "He who cannot sing always insists upon singing."[6] Thus, they are plagued with a desire for women, but are unable to consummate their desire. Let us pass them by also; for they too are set apart from the natural ordinance to be fruitful and multiply, though only by an act of violence.

The third category consists of those spiritually rich and exalted persons, bridled by the grace of God, who are equipped for marriage by nature and physical capacity and nevertheless voluntarily remain celibate. These put it this way, "I could marry if I wish, I am capable of it. But it does not attract me. I would rather work on the kingdom of heaven, i.e., the gospel, and beget spiritual children." Such persons are rare, not one in a thousand, for they are a special miracle of God. No one should venture on such a life unless he be especially called by God, like Jeremiah [16:2], or unless he finds God's grace to be so powerful within him that the divine injunction, "Be fruitful and multiply," has no place in him.

Beyond these three categories, however, the devil working

---

[4] *Auffs narrn seyll furet.* The *Narrenseil* was originally the rope with which a fool formerly was bound and so led about, like a monkey on a leash. Wander (ed.), *Sprichwörter-Lexikon,* III, 941, "*Narrenseil,*" Nos. 5, 6. Jacob Grimm and Wilhelm Grimm (eds.), *Deutsches Wörterbuch* (16 vols.; Leipzig: Hirzel, 1854-1954), VII, 379-380.

[5] *Mit der nassen umbfuren.* The expression parallels the preceding one about the *Narrenseil* with the added connotation of deliberately arousing vain hopes and expectations in a person by means of pleasant but deceptive words. Wander (ed.), *Sprichwörter-Lexikon,* III, 952, 956, "*Nase,*" Nos. 126, 133, and especially 220.

[6] See Ernst Thiele, *Luthers Sprichwörtersammlung* (Weimar: Böhlau, 1900), No. 157.

through men has been smarter than God, and found more people whom he has withdrawn from the divine and natural ordinance, namely, those who are enmeshed in a spiderweb of human commands and vows and are then locked up behind a mass of iron bolts and bars. This is a fourth way of resisting nature so that, contrary to God's implanted ordinance and disposition, it does not produce seed and multiply—as if it were within our power and discretion to possess' virginity as we do shoes and clothing! If men are really able to resist God's word and creation with iron bars and bolts, I should hope that we would also set up iron bars so thick and massive that women would turn into men or people into sticks and stones. It is the devil who thus perpetrates his monkey-tricks on the poor creature, and so gives vent to his wrath.

In the fourth place, let us now consider which persons may enter into marriage with one another, so that you may see it is not my pleasure or desire that a marriage be broken and husband and wife separated. The pope in his canon law has thought up eighteen distinct reasons[7] for preventing or dissolving a marriage, nearly all of which I reject and condemn. Indeed, the pope himself does not adhere to them so strictly or firmly but what one can rescind any of them with gold and silver. Actually, they were only invented in order to be a net for gold and a noose for the soul, II Peter 2 [:14]. In order to expose their folly we will take a look at all eighteen of them in turn.

The first impediment is blood relationship. Here they have forbidden marriage up to the third and fourth degrees of consanguinity. If in this situation you have no money, then even though God freely permits it you must nevertheless not take in marriage your female relative within the third and fourth degrees, or you must put her away if you have already married her. But if you have the money, such a marriage is permitted. Those hucksters offer for sale women who never have been their own. So that you can defend yourself against this tyranny, I will now

---

[7] Luther drew this list from the so-called "Summa angelica" of Angelo Carletti di Chivasso (1411-1495), an authority on canon and civil law whose handbook on casuistry, listing eighteen impediments to marriage, went through thirty-one editions between 1476 and 1520. LW 36, 96, n. 166.

list for you the persons whom God has forbidden, Leviticus 18 [:6-13], namely, my mother, my stepmother; my sister, my stepsister; my child's daughter or stepdaughter; my father's sister; my mother's sister. I am forbidden to marry any of these persons.

From this it follows[8] that first cousins may contract a godly and Christian marriage, and that I may marry my stepmother's sister, my father's stepsister, or my mother's stepsister. Further, I may marry the daughter of my brother or sister, just as Abraham married Sarah.[9] None of these persons is forbidden by God, for God does not calculate according to degrees, as the jurists do, but enumerates directly specific persons. Otherwise, since my father's sister and my brother's daughter are related to me in the same degree, I would have to say either that I cannot marry my brother's daughter or that I may also marry my father's sister. Now God has forbidden my father's sister, but he has not forbidden my brother's daughter, although both are related to me in the same degree. We also find in Scripture that with respect to various stepsisters there were not such strict prohibitions. For Tamar, Absalom's sister, thought she could have married her stepbrother Amnon, II Samuel 13 [:13].

The second impediment is affinity or relationship through marriage. Here too they have set up four degrees, so that after my wife's death I may not marry into her blood relationship, where my marriage extends up to the third and fourth degrees— unless money comes to my rescue! But God has forbidden only these persons, namely, my father's brother's wife; my son's wife; my brother's wife; my stepdaughter; the child of my stepson or stepdaughter; my wife's sister while my wife is yet alive [Lev. 18:14-18]. I may not marry any of these persons; but I may marry any others, and without putting up any money for the privilege. For example,[10] I may marry the sister of my deceased wife or fiancée;[11] the daughter of my wife's brother; the daughter

---

[8] Cf. p. 7.
[9] Tradition had long falsely identified Sarah with the Iscah of Gen. 11:29, thus making both Abraham and Nahor marry daughters of their deceased brother Haran (Josephus, *Antiquities* I, vi, 5; *Targum of Jonathan*, Jerome, Rashi), despite Gen. 20:12 which makes Sarah the stepsister of Abraham.
[10] Cf. p. 8.
[11] See p. 8, n. 6.

of my wife's cousin; and any of my wife's nieces, aunts, or cousins. In the Old Testament, if a brother died without leaving an heir, his widow was required to marry his closest relative in order to provide her deceased husband with an heir [Deut. 25:5-9]. This is no longer commanded, but neither is it forbidden.

The third impediment is spiritual relationship. If I sponsor a girl at baptism or confirmation, then neither I nor my son may marry her, or her mother, or her sister—unless an appropriate and substantial sum of money is forthcoming! This is nothing but pure farce and foolishness, concocted for the sake of money and to befuddle consciences. Just tell me this: isn't it a greater thing for me to be baptized myself than merely to act as sponsor to another? Then I must be forbidden to marry any Christian woman,[12] since all baptized women are the spiritual sisters of all baptized men by virtue of their common baptism, sacrament, faith, Spirit, Lord, God, and eternal heritage [Eph. 4:4-6].

Why does not the pope also forbid a man to retain his wife if he teaches her the gospel? For whoever teaches another becomes that person's spiritual father. St. Paul boasts in I Corinthians 4 [:15] that he is the father of all of them, saying, "I became your father in Christ Jesus through the gospel." According to this he could not have taken a wife in Corinth; neither could any apostle in the whole world have taken a wife from among those whom he taught and baptized.[13]

So away with this foolishness; take as your spouse whomsoever you please, whether it be godparent, godchild, or the daughter or sister of a sponsor, or whoever it may be, and disregard these artificial, money-seeking impediments. If you are not prevented from marrying a girl by the fact that she is a Christian, then do not let yourself be prevented by the fact that you baptized her, taught her, or acted as her sponsor. In particular, avoid that monkey business, confirmation, which is really a fanciful deception.[14] I would permit confirmation as long as it is understood that God knows nothing of it, and has said nothing about it, and

---

[12] This was Luther's position already in *The Babylonian Captivity* of 1520. *LW* 36, 99.

[13] Cf. *LW* 36, 100.

[14] See p. 8, n. 7, and the Introduction, p. 5.

that what the bishops claim for it is untrue. They mock our God when they say that it is one of God's sacraments, for it is a purely human contrivance.

The fourth impediment is legal kinship; that is, when an unrelated child is adopted as son or daughter it may not later marry a child born of its adoptive parents, that is, one who is by law its own brother or sister. This is another worthless human invention. Therefore, if you so desire, go ahead and marry anyway. In the sight of God this adopted person is neither your mother nor your sister, since there is no blood relationship. She does work in the kitchen, however, and supplements the income; this is why she has been placed on the forbidden list!

The fifth impediment is unbelief; that is, I may not marry a Turk, a Jew, or a heretic. I marvel that the blasphemous tyrants are not in their hearts ashamed to place themselves in such direct contradiction to the clear text of Paul in I Corinthians 7 [:12-13], where he says, "If a heathen wife or husband consents to live with a Christian spouse, the Christian should not get a divorce." And St. Peter, in I Peter 3 [:1], says that Christian wives should behave so well that they thereby convert their non-Christian husbands; as did Monica, the mother of St. Augustine.[15]

Know therefore that marriage is an outward, bodily thing, like any other worldly undertaking. Just as I may eat, drink, sleep, walk, ride with, buy from, speak to, and deal with a heathen, Jew, Turk, or heretic, so I may also marry and continue in wedlock with him. Pay no attention to the precepts of those fools who forbid it. You will find plenty of Christians—and indeed the greater part of them—who are worse in their secret unbelief than any Jew, heathen, Turk, or heretic. A heathen is just as much a man or a woman—God's good creation—as St. Peter, St. Paul, and St. Lucy,[16] not to speak of a slack and spurious Christian.

The sixth impediment is crime. They are not in agreement as to how many instances of this impediment they should devise.

---

[15] *Confessions* IX, ix, 22. Cf. *LW* 36, 100; *WA* 41, 321.

[16] A virgin of Syracuse, Lucy was martyred about the year 304 after having first been miraculously saved by God from the sentence of enforced prostitution. The traditional background for her festival, celebrated December 13, is recorded in *The Golden Legend of Jacobus de Voragine*. See the text as it has been translated from the Latin by Granger Ryan and Helmut Ripperger (New York: Longman's, Green, 1941), I, 34-37.

However, there are actually these three:[17] if someone lies with a girl, he may not thereafter marry her sister or her aunt, niece, or cousin; again, whoever commits adultery with a woman may not marry her after her husband's death; again, if a wife (or husband) should murder her spouse for love of another, she may not subsequently marry the loved one. Here it rains fools upon fools. Don't you believe them, and don't be taken in by them; they are under the devil's whip. Sins and crimes should be punished, but with other penalties, not by forbidding marriage. Therefore, no sin or crime is an impediment to marriage. David committed adultery with Bathsheba, Uriah's wife, and had her husband killed besides. He was guilty of both crimes; still he took her to wife and begot King Solomon by her [II Samuel 11]—and without giving any money to the pope!

I must pursue this subject a bit further. These wise guys posit the hypothetical case of a man who sins with his wife's mother or sister. Had this happened before the marriage it would have been a crime which would prevent and break up the proposed marriage. Since it happened subsequent to the marriage, however, for the sake of the wife—who is innocent in the matter—the marriage may not be dissolved. Nevertheless, the husband's punishment is to be that he shall lie with his wife but have no power to demand of her the conjugal duty. See what the devil through his fools does with the estate of marriage! He puts husband and wife together, and then says, "Be neither man nor woman." As well put fire and straw together and bid them not to burn![18] If one were to impose upon the pope a command one-tenth as hard as this, how he would rage and storm, and howl about unlawful authority! Away with the big fools. You just let marriage remain free, as God instituted it. Punish sins and crimes with other penalties, not through marriage and fresh sins.

The seventh impediment they call public decorum, respectability. For example, if my fiancée should die before we consummate the marriage, I may not marry any relative of hers up

---

[17] The first of the three was not cited in Luther's 1520 *Babylonian Captivity.* LW 36, 100.

[18] Luther used the same illustration almost verbatim in a sermon of August 10, 1522. WA 10III, 265. Cf. also has 1521 *Misuse of the Mass.* LW 36, 206; and his 1520 *Open Letter to the Christian Nobility.* PE 2, 122.

to the fourth degree, since the pope thinks and obviously dreams that it is decent and respectable for me to refrain from so doing—unless I put up the money, in which case the impediment of public decorum vanishes. Now you have heard a moment ago[19] that after my wife's death I may marry her sister or any of her relatives except for her mother and her daughter. You stick to this, and let the fools go their way.

The eighth impediment is a solemn vow,[20] for example where someone has taken the vow of chastity, either in or out of the cloister. Here I offer this advice: if you would like to take a wise vow, then vow not to bite off your own nose; you can keep that vow. If you have already taken the monastic vow, however, then, as you have just heard,[21] you should yourself consider whether you belong in those three categories which God has singled out. If you do not feel that you belong there, then let the vows and the cloister go. Renew your natural companionships without delay and get married, for your vow is contrary to God and has no validity, and say, "I have promised that which I do not have and which is not mine."

The ninth impediment is error, as if I had been wed to Catherine[22] but Barbara lay down with me, as happened to Jacob with Leah and Rachel [Gen. 29:23-25]. One may have such a marriage dissolved and take the other to wife.

The tenth impediment is condition of servitude. When I marry one who is supposed to be free and it turns out later that she is a serf, this marriage too is null and void. However, I hold that if there were Christian love the husband could easily adjust both of these impediments so that no great distress would be occasioned. Furthermore, such cases never occur today, or only rarely, and both might well be combined in one category: error.

---

[19] See p. 23. Cf. also p. 8, n. 6, and LW 36, 102.

[20] Luther had discussed vows at length in his 1521 De votis monasticis. WA 8, (564) 573-669, and briefly in his 1520 Babylonian Captivity. LW 36, 74-81. Cf. LW 36, 102.

[21] See pp. 19-22.

[22] At the time this treatise was composed, Luther was still a bachelor. His future wife, Katherine von Bora, was still a nun in the Cistercian convent at Nimbschen in Saxony. Luther did not meet her until the next year when she and several other nuns fled the convent early in April, 1523. They were married on June 13, 1525.

The eleventh impediment is holy orders, namely, that the tonsure and sacred oil are so potent that they devour marriage and unsex a man. For this reason a subdeacon, a deacon,[23] and a priest have to forego marriage, although St. Paul commanded that they may and should be married, II Timothy 3 [I Tim. 3:2, 12], Titus 1 [:6]. But I have elsewhere written so much about this [24] that there is no need to repeat it here. Their folly has been sufficiently exposed; how much help this impediment has been to those in holy orders is obvious to all.

The twelfth impediment is coercion, that is, when I have to take Grete to be my wife and am coerced into it either by parents or by governmental authority. That is to be sure no marriage in the sight of God. However, such a person should not admit the coercion and leave the country on account of it, thus betraying the girl or making a fool of her,[25] for you are not excused by the fact that you were coerced into it. You should not allow yourself to be coerced into injuring your neighbor but should yield your life rather than act contrary to love. You would not want anybody to injure you, whether he was acting under coercion or not. For this reason I could not declare safe in the sight of God a man who leaves his wife for such a cause. My dear fellow, if someone should compel you to rob me or kill me, would it therefore be right? Why do you yield to a coercion which compels you to violate God's commandment and harm your neighbor? I would freely absolve the girl however, for, as we will hear later,[26] you would be leaving her through no fault of her own.

How about a situation where a man is so attached to a girl that she is bestowed upon him at the point of a gun?[27] Does the principle of coercion apply here? It does not, because the girl understands that coercion is involved, and is therefore not

---

[23] *Epistoler, Euangelier* were those orders of the clergy responsible for chanting the epistle and the gospel respectively during the mass.

[24] See Luther's *Open Letter to the Christian Nobility* (1520). PE 2, 118-123; *Ad schedulam inhibitionis sub nomine episcopi Misnensis editam . . . responsio* (1520). WA 6, 147; *The Babylonian Captivity* (1520). LW 36, 101-102; and *Avoiding the Doctrines of Men* (1522). LW 35, 138.

[25] See p. 21, n. 4.

[26] See p. 29.

[27] *Yhm mit der axt gibt* is a colloquial expression referring to a forced marriage accomplished under threat of an "axe" literally.

being deceived. In this case it is indeed proper that he be compelled to keep her, because of the fact that he has ruined her. For Moses wrote that whoever lies with a girl shall keep her or, in the event that her father is unwilling, pay money in accordance with her father's demand, Exodus 22 [:16-17].

The thirteenth impediment is betrothal, that is, if I am engaged to one girl but then take another to wife. This is a widespread and common practice in which many different solutions have also been attempted. In the first place, if such an engagement occurs without the knowledge and consent of the father and mother, or of the guardians, then let the [fiancée's] father decide which girl is to remain as the wife. If she is betrayed it is her own fault, for she should know that a child is supposed to be subordinate and obedient to its father, and not become engaged without his knowledge. In this way, obedience to parental authority will put a stop to all these secret engagements which occasion such great unhappiness. Where this course is not followed, however, I am of the opinion that the man should stick to the first girl. For having given himself to her he no longer belongs to himself. He was therefore incapable of promising to the second girl something that already belonged to the first and was not his own.[28]

If he does so nonetheless and carries on to the point where he begets children by her, then he should stick with her. For she too has been betrayed, and would suffer even greater injury than the first girl were he to leave her. He has therefore sinned against them both. The first girl, however, is able to recover from the injury done her because she is yet without children. She should therefore out of love yield to the second girl and marry someone else; she is free from the man because he jilted her and gave himself to another. The man himself though should be made to suffer punishment and make amends to the first girl, for what he gave away really belonged to her.

The fourteenth impediment is the one touched on already, when a husband or wife is unfit for marriage.[29] Among these

---

[28] This was Luther's view also in *The Babylonian Captivity* (1520). *LW* 36, 100-101.

[29] Luther already had discussed impotence; see pp. 19-21.

eighteen impediments this one is the only sound reason for dissolving a marriage. Yet it is hedged about by so many laws that it is difficult to accomplish with the ecclesiastical tyrants.

There are still four more impediments, such as episcopal prohibition, restricted times, custom, and defective eyesight and hearing. It is needless to discuss them here. It is a dirty rotten business that a bishop should forbid me a wife or specify the times when I may marry, or that a blind and dumb person should not be allowed to enter into wedlock. So much then for this foolishness at present in the first part.

Part Two

In the second part, we shall consider which persons may be divorced. I know of three grounds for divorce. The first, which has just been mentioned and was discussed above,[30] is the situation in which the husband or wife is not equipped for marriage because of bodily or natural deficiencies of any sort. Of this enough has already been said.

The second ground is adultery. The popes have kept silent about this; therefore we must hear Christ, Matthew 19 [:3-9]. When the Jews asked him whether a husband might divorce his wife for any reason, he answered, "'Have you not read that he who made them from the beginning made them male and female, and said, "For this reason a man shall leave his father and mother and be joined to his wife, and the two shall become one"? What therefore God has joined together, let no man put asunder.' They said to him, 'Why then did Moses command one to give a certificate of divorce, and to put her away?' He said to them, 'For your hardness of heart Moses allowed you to divorce your wives, but from the beginning it was not so. And I say to you: whoever divorces his wife, except for unchastity, and marries another, commits adultery; and he who marries a divorced woman commits adultery.'"

Here you see that in the case of adultery Christ permits the divorce of husband and wife, so that the innocent person may

---

[30] See pp. 29 and 19-21. Cf. also Luther's sermon of May 8, 1524, on the subject of divorce. WA 15, 558-562.

remarry. For in saying that he commits adultery who marries another after divorcing his wife, "except for unchastity," Christ is making it quite clear that he who divorces his wife on account of unchastity and then marries another does not commit adultery.

The Jews, however, were divorcing their wives for all kinds of reasons whenever they saw fit, even though no unchastity was involved. That covers so much ground that they themselves thought it was going too far. They therefore inquired of Christ whether it was right; they were tempting him to see what he would say concerning the law of Moses.

Now in the law of Moses God established two types of governments; he gave two types of commandments. Some are spiritual, teaching righteousness in the sight of God, such as love and obedience; people who obeyed these commandments did not thrust away their wives and never made use of certificates of divorce, but tolerated and endured their wives' conduct. Others are worldly, however, drawn up for the sake of those who do not live up to the spiritual commandments, in order to place a limit upon their misbehavior and prevent them from doing worse and acting wholly on the basis of their own maliciousness. Accordingly, he commanded them, if they could not endure their wives, that they should not put them to death or harm them too severely, but rather dismiss them with a certificate of divorce. This law, therefore, does not apply to Christians, who are supposed to live in the spiritual government. In the case of some who live with their wives in an un-Christian fashion, however, it would still be a good thing to permit them to use this law, just so they are no longer regarded as Christians, which after all they really are not.

Thus it is that on the grounds of adultery one person may leave the other, as Solomon also says in Proverbs 18, "He that keepeth an adulteress is a fool."[31] We have an example of this in Joseph too. In Matthew 1 [:19] the gospel writer praises him as just because he did not put his wife to shame when he found that she was with child, but was minded to divorce her quietly. By this we are told plainly enough that it is praiseworthy to divorce

---

[31] Luther is referring to a portion of Prov. 18:22 in the Vulgate, which we have here cited according to the Douay version.

an adulterous wife. If the adultery is clandestine, of course, the husband has the right to follow either of two courses. First, he may rebuke his wife privately and in a brotherly fashion, and keep her if she will mend her ways. Second, he may divorce her, as Joseph wished to do. The same principle applies in the case of a wife with an adulterous husband. These two types of discipline are both Christian and laudable.

But a public divorce, whereby one [the innocent party] is enabled to remarry, must take place through the investigation and decision of the civil authority so that the adultery may be manifest to all—or, if the civil authority refuses to act, with the knowledge of the congregation, again in order that it may not be left to each one to allege anything he pleases as a ground for divorce.

You may ask: What is to become of the other [the guilty party] if he too is perhaps unable to lead a chaste life? Answer: It was for this reason that God commanded in the law [Deut. 22: 22-24] that adulterers be stoned, that they might not have to face this question. The temporal sword and government should therefore still put adulterers to death, for whoever commits adultery has in fact himself already departed[32] and is considered as one dead. Therefore, the other [the innocent party] may remarry just as though his spouse had died, if it is his intention to insist on his rights and not show mercy to the guilty party. Where the government is negligent and lax, however, and fails to inflict the death penalty, the adulterer may betake himself to a far country and there remarry if he is unable to remain continent. But it would be better to put him to death, lest a bad example be set.

Some may find fault with this solution and contend that thereby license and opportunity is afforded all wicked husbands and wives to desert their spouses and remarry in a foreign country. Answer: Can I help it? The blame rests with the government.

---

[32] *Wer seyn ehe bricht, der hatt sich schon selbst gescheyden.* The significance of this sentence turns on the fact that the one German word (*scheiden*) has two distinct meanings—"to separate" either in the sense of dissolving a marriage or in the sense of departing this life—both of which are involved here. Luther's point is that whoever destroys his own marriage has really left not only his wife but also his life; he has achieved not only his divorce but also his own death.

Why do they not put adulterers to death? Then I would not need to give such advice. Between two evils one is always the lesser,[33] in this case allowing the adulterer to remarry in a distant land in order to avoid fornication. And I think he would be safer also in the sight of God, because he has been allowed to live and yet is unable to remain continent. If others also, however, following this example desert their spouses, let them go. They have no excuse such as the adulterer has, for they are neither driven nor compelled. God and their own conscience will catch up to them in due time. Who can prevent all wickedness?

Where the government fails to inflict the death penalty and the one spouse wishes to retain the other, the guilty one should still in Christian fashion be publicly rebuked and caused to make amends according to the gospel, after the manner provided for the rebuking of all other manifest sins, Matthew 18 [:15-17]. For there are no more than these three forms of discipline on earth among men: private and brotherly, in public before the congregation according to the gospel, and that inflicted by the civil government.

The third case for divorce is that in which one of the parties deprives and avoids the other, refusing to fulfil the conjugal duty or to live with the other person. For example, one finds many a stubborn wife like that who will not give in, and who cares not a whit whether her husband falls into the sin of unchastity ten times over. Here it is time for the husband to say, "If you will not, another will; the maid will come if the wife will not."[34] Only first the husband should admonish and warn his wife two or

---

[33] *Es ist jhe unter tzwey boszen eyns besser.* Cf. Wander (ed.), *Sprichwörter-Lexikon,* V, 1036-1037, "*Böse (das),*" Nos. 95, 96, 113.

[34] "*Wiltu nicht, szo will eyn andere, wil fraw nicht, szo kum die magd.*" Cf. two similar proverbial expressions, both deriving ultimately from the Latin, in Wander (ed.), *Sprichwörter-Lexikon,* V, 392, "*Wollen,*" No. 120; and I, 1138, "*Frau,*" No. 714. In a letter of January 1, 1523, to Dietrich von Werthern, his representative at the Diet of Nürnberg, Duke George of Saxony cited this phrase out of context to discredit Luther. He sarcastically suggested that Dietrich make sure his maidservants were comely. Gess, *op. cit.,* I, 415. A charitable explanation of Luther's use of the phrase is found in Wilhelm Walther, *Für Luther wider Rom* (Halle: Niemeyer, 1906), pp. 693-695. He suggests that Luther deliberately put these proverbial expressions into the mouth of the offended husband in order that the offending wife might know that her husband's feelings in the matter were not peculiar to him but represented a generally accepted point of view.

three times, and let the situation be known to others so that her stubbornness becomes a matter of common knowledge and is rebuked before the congregation. If she still refuses, get rid of her; take an Esther and let Vashti go, as King Ahasuerus did [Esther 1:12–2:17].

Here you should be guided by the words of St. Paul, I Corinthians 7 [:4-5], "The husband does not rule over his own body, but the wife does; likewise the wife does not rule over her own body, but the husband does. Do not deprive each other, except by agreement," etc. Notice that St. Paul forbids either party to deprive the other, for by the marriage vow each submits his body to the other in conjugal duty. When one resists the other and refuses the conjugal duty she is robbing the other of the body she had bestowed upon him. This is really contrary to marriage, and dissolves the marriage. For this reason the civil government must compel the wife, or put her to death. If the government fails to act, the husband must reason that his wife has been stolen away and slain by robbers; he must seek another. We would certainly have to accept it if someone's life were taken from him. Why then should we not also accept it if a wife steals herself away from her husband, or is stolen away by others?

In addition to these three grounds for divorce there is one more which would justify the sundering of husband and wife, but only in such a way that they must both refrain from remarrying or else become reconciled. This is the case where husband and wife cannot get along together for some reason other than the matter of the conjugal duty. St. Paul speaks of this in I Corinthians 7 [:10-11], "Not I but the Lord gives charge to the married that the wife should not separate from her husband. But if she does, let her remain single, or else be reconciled to her husband. Likewise, the husband should not divorce his wife." Solomon complains much in the Proverbs about such wives, and says he has found a woman more bitter than death [Eccles. 7:26]. One may also find a rude, brutal, and unbearable husband.

Now if one of the parties were endowed with Christian fortitude and could endure the other's ill behavior, that would doubtless be a wonderfully blessed cross and a right way to heaven. For an evil spouse, in a manner of speaking, fulfils the devil's function

34

and sweeps clean him who is able to recognize and bear it. If he cannot, however, let him divorce her before he does anything worse, and remain unmarried for the rest of his days. Should he try to say that the blame rests not upon him but upon his spouse, and therefore try to marry another, this will not do, for he is under obligation to endure evil, or to be released from his cross only by God, since the conjugal duty has not been denied him. Here the proverb applies, "He who wants a fire must endure the smoke." [35]

What about a situation where one's wife is an invalid and has therefore become incapable of fulfilling the conjugal duty? May he not take another to wife? By no means. Let him serve the Lord in the person of the invalid and await His good pleasure. Consider that in this invalid God has provided your household with a healing balm by which you are to gain heaven. Blessed and twice blessed are you when you recognize such a gift of grace and therefore serve your invalid wife for God's sake.

But you may say: I am unable to remain continent. That is a lie. If you will earnestly serve your invalid wife, recognize that God has placed this burden upon you, and give thanks to him, then you may leave matters in his care. He will surely grant you grace, that you will not have to bear more than you are able. He is far too faithful to deprive you of your wife through illness without at the same time subduing your carnal desire, if you will but faithfully serve your invalid wife.

Part Three

In the third part, in order that we may say something about the estate of marriage which will be conducive toward the soul's salvation, we shall now consider how to live a Christian and godly life in that estate. I will pass over in silence the matter of the conjugal duty, the granting and the withholding of it, since some filth-preachers have been shameless enough in this matter to rouse our disgust. Some of them designate special times for this, and exclude holy nights and women who are pregnant. I will leave

[35] *"Wer des fewers haben will, muss den rauch auch leyden."* Wander (ed.), *Sprichwörter-Lexikon,* I, 1002, *"Feuer,"* Nos. 261, 267.

this as St. Paul left it when he said in I Corinthians 7 [:9], "It is better to marry than to burn"; and again [in v. 2], "To avoid immorality, each man should have his own wife, and each woman her own husband." Although Christian married folk should not permit themselves to be governed by their bodies in the passion of lust, as Paul writes to the Thessalonians [I Thess. 4:5], nevertheless each one must examine himself so that by his abstention he does not expose himself to the danger of fornication and other sins. Neither should he pay any attention to holy days or work days, or other physical considerations.

What we would speak most of is the fact that the estate of marriage has universally fallen into such awful disrepute. There are many pagan books which treat of nothing but the depravity of womankind and the unhappiness of the estate of marriage, such that some have thought that even if Wisdom itself were a woman one should not marry. A Roman official was once supposed to encourage young men to take wives (because the country was in need of a large population on account of its incessant wars). Among other things he said to them, "My dear young men, if we could only live without women we would be spared a great deal of annoyance; but since we cannot do without them, take to yourselves wives," etc. He was criticized by some on the ground that his words were ill-considered and would only serve to discourage the young men. Others, on the contrary, said that because Metellus was a brave man he had spoken rightly, for an honorable man should speak the truth without fear or hypocrisy.[36]

So they concluded that woman is a necessary evil, and that no household can be without such an evil. These are the words of blind heathen, who are ignorant of the fact that man and woman are God's creation. They blaspheme his work, as if man and woman just came into being spontaneously! I imagine that if women were to write books they would say exactly the same thing about men. What they have failed to set down in writing, however, they express with their grumbling and complaining whenever they get together.

Every day one encounters parents who forget their former

---

[36] This story, referred to frequently by Luther, is from the *Attic Nights* of Aulus Gellius, I, vi, 1-6. Metellus Numidieus was a Roman censor in 102 B.C.

misery because, like the mouse, they have now had their fill.[37] They deter their children from marriage but entice them into priesthood and nunnery, citing the trials and troubles of married life. Thus do they bring their own children home to the devil, as we daily observe; they provide them with ease for the body and hell for the soul.

Since God had to suffer such disdain of his work from the pagans, he therefore also gave them their reward, of which Paul writes in Romans 1 [:24-28], and allowed them to fall into immorality and a stream of uncleanness until they henceforth carnally abused not women but boys and dumb beasts. Even their women carnally abused themselves and each other. Because they blasphemed the work of God, he gave them up to a base mind, of which the books of the pagans are full, most shamelessly crammed full.

In order that we may not proceed as blindly, but rather conduct ourselves in a Christian manner, hold fast first of all to this, that man and woman are the work of God. Keep a tight rein on your heart and your lips; do not criticize his work, or call that evil which he himself has called good. He knows better than you yourself what is good and to your benefit, as he says in Genesis 1 [2:18], "It is not good that the man should be alone; I will make him a helper fit for him." There you see that he calls the woman good, a helper. If you deem it otherwise, it is certainly your own fault, you neither understand nor believe God's word and work. See, with this statement of God one stops the mouths of all those who criticize and censure marriage.

For this reason young men should be on their guard when they read pagan books and hear the common complaints about marriage, lest they inhale poison. For the estate of marriage does not set well with the devil, because it is God's good will and work. This is why the devil has contrived to have so much shouted and written in the world against the institution of marriage, to frighten men away from this godly life and entangle them in a web of fornication and secret sins. Indeed, it seems to me that

---

[37] *Des melhs, wie die mauss nu satt sind.* Luther's variation of the old proverb about the sated mouse may be paraphrased in English, "To a full belly all meat is bad." See Wander (ed.), *Sprichwörter-Lexikon*, III, 541-542, *"Maus,"* Nos. 177, 195.

even Solomon, although he amply censures evil women, was speaking against just such blasphemers when he said in Proverbs 18 [:22], "He who finds a wife finds a good thing, and obtains favor from the Lord." What is this good thing and this favor? Let us see.

The world says of marriage, "Brief is the joy, lasting the bitterness." [38] Let them say what they please; what God wills and creates is bound to be a laughingstock to them. The kind of joy and pleasure they have outside of wedlock they will be most acutely aware of, I suspect, in their consciences. To recognize the estate of marriage is something quite different from merely being married. He who is married but does not recognize the estate of marriage cannot continue in wedlock without bitterness, drudgery, and anguish; he will inevitably complain and blaspheme like the pagans and blind, irrational men. But he who recognizes the estate of marriage will find therein delight, love, and joy without end; as Solomon says, "He who finds a wife finds a good thing," etc. [Prov. 18:22].

Now the ones who recognize the estate of marriage are those who firmly believe that God himself instituted it, brought husband and wife together, and ordained that they should beget children and care for them. For this they have God's word, Genesis 1 [:28], and they can be certain that he does not lie. They can therefore also be certain that the estate of marriage and everything that goes with it in the way of conduct, works, and suffering is pleasing to God. Now tell me, how can the heart have greater good, joy, and delight than in God, when one is certain that his estate, conduct, and work is pleasing to God?

That is what it means to find a wife. Many *have* wives, but few *find* wives. Why? They are blind; they fail to see that their life and conduct with their wives is the work of God and pleasing in his sight. Could they but find that, then no wife would be so hateful, so ill-tempered, so ill-mannered, so poor, so sick that they would fail to find in her their heart's delight and would always be reproaching God for his work, creation, and will. And because they see that it is the good pleasure of their beloved Lord,

---

[38] *Eyn kurtze freud und lange unlust.* Cf. Wander (ed.), *Sprichwörter-Lexikon,* I, 1166, 1168, "*Freude,*" Nos. 40, 92.

they would be able to have peace in grief, joy in the midst of bitterness, happiness in the midst of tribulations, as the martyrs have in suffering.

We err in that we judge the work of God according to our own feelings, and regard not his will but our own desire. This is why we are unable to recognize his works and persist in making evil that which is good, and regarding as bitter that which is pleasant. Nothing is so bad, not even death itself, but what it becomes sweet and tolerable if only I know and am certain that it is pleasing to God. Then there follows immediately that of which Solomon speaks, "He obtains favor from the Lord" [Prov. 18:22].

Now observe that when that clever harlot, our natural reason (which the pagans followed in trying to be most clever), takes a look at married life, she turns up her nose and says, "Alas, must I rock the baby, wash its diapers, make its bed, smell its stench, stay up nights with it, take care of it when it cries, heal its rashes and sores, and on top of that care for my wife, provide for her, labor at my trade, take care of this and take care of that, do this and do that, endure this and endure that, and whatever else of bitterness and drudgery married life involves? What, should I make such a prisoner of myself? O you poor, wretched fellow, have you taken a wife? Fie, fie upon such wretchedness and bitterness! It is better to remain free and lead a peaceful, carefree life; I will become a priest or a nun and compel my children to do likewise."

What then does Christian faith say to this? It opens its eyes, looks upon all these insignificant, distasteful, and despised duties in the Spirit, and is aware that they are all adorned with divine approval as with the costliest gold and jewels. It says, "O God, because I am certain that thou hast created me as a man and hast from my body begotten this child, I also know for a certainty that it meets with thy perfect pleasure. I confess to thee that I am not worthy to rock the little babe or wash its diapers, or to be entrusted with the care of the child and its mother. How is it that I, without any merit, have come to this distinction of being certain that I am serving thy creature and thy most precious will? O how gladly will I do so, though the duties should be even more insignificant and despised. Neither frost nor heat, neither drudgery nor labor, will distress or dissuade me, for I am certain that it is thus pleasing in thy sight."

A wife too should regard her duties in the same light, as she suckles the child, rocks and bathes it, and cares for it in other ways; and as she busies herself with other duties and renders help and obedience to her husband. These are truly golden and noble works. This is also how to comfort and encourage a woman in the pangs of childbirth, not by repeating St. Margaret[39] legends and other silly old wives' tales but by speaking thus, "Dear Grete, remember that you are a woman, and that this work of God in you is pleasing to him. Trust joyfully in his will, and let him have his way with you. Work with all your might to bring forth the child. Should it mean your death, then depart happily, for you will die in a noble deed and in subservience to God. If you were not a woman you should now wish to be one for the sake of this very work alone, that you might thus gloriously suffer and even die in the performance of God's work and will. For here you have the word of God, who so created you and implanted within you this extremity." Tell me, is not this indeed (as Solomon says [Prov. 18:22]) "to obtain favor from the Lord," even in the midst of such extremity?

Now you tell me, when a father goes ahead and washes diapers or performs some other mean task for his child, and someone ridicules him as an effeminate fool—though that father is acting in the spirit just described and in Christian faith—my dear fellow you tell me, which of the two is most keenly ridiculing the other? God, with all his angels and creatures, is smiling—not because that father is washing diapers, but because he is doing so in Christian faith. Those who sneer at him and see only the task but not the faith are ridiculing God with all his creatures, as the

---

[39] For centuries Margaret of Pisidian Antioch was widely venerated as the patron saint of pregnant women. According to tradition, she suffered torture and martyrdom for refusing to renounce her faith and marry the Roman prefect, Olybrius. Her dates are uncertain though she may have died about the time of the Diocletian persecution (*ca.* 303-305). Among the legends of her martyrdom is the story of her prayer, just before being beheaded, that "whenever a woman in labor should call upon her name, the child might be brought forth without harm." Ryan and Ripperger, *op. cit.*, II, 354.

biggest fool on earth. Indeed, they are only ridiculing themselves; with all their cleverness they are nothing but devil's fools.

St. Cyprian, that great and admirable man and holy martyr, wrote that one should kiss the newborn infant, even before it is baptized, in honor of the hands of God here engaged in a brand new deed.[40] What do you suppose he would have said about a baptized infant? There was a true Christian, who correctly recognized and regarded God's work and creature. Therefore, I say that all nuns and monks who lack faith, and who trust in their own chastity and in their order, are not worthy of rocking a baptized child or preparing its pap, even if it were the child of a harlot. This is because their order and manner of life has no word of God as its warrant. They cannot boast that what they do is pleasing in God's sight, as can the woman in childbirth, even if her child is born out of wedlock.

I say these things in order that we may learn how honorable a thing it is to live in that estate which God has ordained. In it we find God's word and good pleasure, by which all the works, conduct, and sufferings of that estate become holy, godly, and precious so that Solomon even congratulates such a man and says in Proverbs 5 [:18], "Rejoice in the wife of your youth," and again in Ecclesiastes 11 [9:9], "Enjoy life with the wife whom you love all the days of your vain life." Doubtless, Solomon is not speaking here of carnal pleasure, since it is the Holy Spirit who speaks through him. He is rather offering godly comfort to those who find much drudgery in married life. This he does by way of defense against those who scoff at the divine ordinance and, like the pagans, seek but fail to find in marriage anything beyond a carnal and fleeting sensual pleasure.

Conversely, we learn how wretched is the spiritual estate of monks and nuns by its very nature, for it lacks the word and pleasure of God. All its works, conduct, and sufferings are un-

---

[40] Cyprian, Bishop of Carthage, martyred in A.D. 258, was the author of numerous letters, to one of which Luther is referring. In his letter to Fidus on the baptizing of infants (Ep. LXIV, 4) Cyprian writes, "In the kiss of an infant, each of us should, for very piety, think of the recent Hands of God, which we in a manner kiss, in the lately formed and recently born man, when we embrace that which God has made." *The Epistles of St. Cyprian* ("A Library of Fathers of the Holy Catholic Church Anterior to the Division of the East and West" [Oxford: Parker, 1844]), p. 197.

Christian, vain, and pernicious, so that Christ even says to their warning in Matthew 15 [:9], "In vain do they worship me according to the commandments of men." There is therefore no comparison between a married woman who lives in faith and in the recognition of her estate, and a cloistered nun who lives in unbelief and in the presumptuousness of her ecclesiastical estate, just as God's ways and man's ways are beyond compare, as He says in Isaiah 55 [:9], "As the heavens are higher than the earth, so are my ways higher than your ways." It is a great blessing for one to have God's word as his warrant, so that he can speak right up and say to God, "See, this thou hast spoken, it is thy good pleasure." What does such a man care if it seems to be displeasing and ridiculous to the whole world?

Small wonder that married folk for the most part experience little but bitterness and anguish. They have no knowledge of God's word and will concerning their estate, and are therefore just as wretched as monks and nuns since both lack the comfort and assurance of God's good pleasure. This is why it is impossible for them to endure outward bitterness and drudgery, for it is too much for a man to have to suffer both inward and outward bitterness. If they inwardly fail to realize that their estate is pleasing in the sight of God, bitterness is already there; if they then seek an outward pleasure therein, they fail to find it. Bitterness is joined with bitterness, and thence arises of necessity the loud outcry and the writings against women and the estate of marriage.

God's work and ordinance must and will be accepted and borne on the strength of God's word and assurance; otherwise they do damage and become unbearable. Therefore, St. Paul tempers his words nicely when he says, I Corinthians 7 [:28], "Those who marry will have worldly troubles," that is, outward bitterness. He is silent on the inner, spiritual delight, however, because outward bitterness is common to both believers and unbelievers; indeed, it is characteristic of the estate of marriage. No one can have real happiness in marriage who does not recognize in firm faith that this estate together with all its works, however insignificant, is pleasing to God and precious in his sight. These works are indeed insignificant and mean; yet it is from them that we all trace our origin, we have all had need of them. Without them no man would exist. For this reason they are pleasing to God who has so ordained them, and thereby graciously cares for us like a kind and loving mother.

Observe that thus far I have told you nothing of the estate of marriage except that which the world and reason in their blindness shrink from and sneer at as a mean, unhappy, troublesome mode of life. We have seen how all these shortcomings in fact comprise noble virtues and true delight if one but looks at God's word and will, and thereby recognizes its true nature. I will not mention the other advantages and delights implicit in a marriage that goes well—that husband and wife cherish one another, become one, serve one another, and other attendant blessings—lest somebody shut me up by saying that I am speaking about something I have not experienced,[41] and that there is more gall than honey in marriage. I base my remarks on Scripture, which to me is surer than all experience and cannot lie to me. He who finds still other good things in marriage profits all the more, and should give thanks to God. Whatever God calls good must of necessity always be good, unless men do not recognize it or perversely misuse it.

I therefore pass over the good or evil which experience offers, and confine myself to such good as Scripture and truth ascribe to marriage. It is no slight boon that in wedlock fornication and unchastity are checked and eliminated. This in itself is so great a good that it alone should be enough to induce men to marry forthwith, and for many reasons.

The first reason is that fornication destroys not only the soul but also body, property, honor, and family as well. For we see how a licentious and wicked life not only brings great disgrace but is also a spendthrift[42] life, more costly than wedlock, and that illicit partners necessarily occasion greater suffering for one another than do married folk. Beyond that it consumes the body, corrupts flesh and blood, nature, and physical constitution. Through such a variety of evil consequences God takes a rigid position, as though he would actually drive people away from

---

41 Luther was not yet married. See p. 27, n. 22.
42 *Unrhedlich.* CL 2, 355, n. 23, suggests the meaning *verschwenderisches.*

fornication and into marriage. However, few are thereby convinced or converted.

Some, however, have given the matter thought and so learned from their own experience that they have coined an excellent proverb, "Early to rise and early to wed; that should no one ever regret." [43] Why? Well because from that there come people who retain a sound body, a good conscience, property, and honor and family, all of which are so ruined and dissipated by fornication, that, once lost, it is well-nigh impossible to regain them— scarcely one in a hundred succeeds. This was the benefit cited by Paul in I Corinthians 7 [:2], "To avoid immorality, each man should have his own wife, and each woman her own husband."

The estate of marriage, however, redounds to the benefit not alone of the body, property, honor, and soul of an individual, but also to the benefit of whole cities and countries, in that they remain exempt from the plagues imposed by God. We know only too well that the most terrible plagues have befallen lands and people because of fornication. This was the sin cited as the reason why the world was drowned in the Deluge, Genesis 6 [:1-13], and Sodom and Gomorrah were buried in flames, Genesis 19 [:1-24]. Scripture also cites many other plagues, even in the case of holy men such as David [II Samuel 11–12], Solomon [I Kings 11:1-13], and Samson [Judg. 16:1-21]. We see before our very eyes that God even now sends more new plagues.[44]

Many think they can evade marriage by having their fling [auss bubenn] for a time, and then becoming righteous. My dear fellow, if one in a thousand succeeds in this, that would be doing very well. He who intends to lead a chaste life had better begin early, and attain it not with but without fornication, either by the grace of God or through marriage. We see only too well how they make out every day. It might well be called plunging into

---

[43] See Wander (ed.), Sprichwörter-Lexikon, I, 166, "Aufstehen," No. 16, cf. V, 842, No. 65.
[44] Syphilis was widespread in Luther's day. Its sudden upsurge late in the fifteenth century gave rise to the legend that it was brought from the New World by the sailors of Columbus. See Preserved Smith, The Age of the Reformation (New York: Holt, 1920), p. 512. An early treatise on the disease by Nicolaus Leonicenus was published in 1497. Cf. also Luther's reference to the Turkish menace in LW 35, 300, 404, 406-407, and in PE 5 (77), 79-123; and see in this volume, p. 116, n. 91.

immorality rather than growing to maturity.[45] It is the devil who has brought this about, and coined such damnable sayings as, "One has to play the fool at least once"; [46] or, "He who does it not in his youth does it in his old age";[47] or, "A young saint, an old devil." [48] Such are the sentiments of the poet Terence[49] and other pagans. This is heathenish; they speak like heathens, yea, like devils.

It is certainly a fact that he who refuses to marry must fall into immorality. How could it be otherwise, since God has created man and woman to produce seed and to multiply? Why should one not forestall immorality by means of marriage? For if special grace does not exempt a person, his nature must and will compel him to produce seed and to multiply. If this does not occur within marriage, how else can it occur except in fornication or secret sins? But, they say, suppose I am neither married nor immoral, and force myself to remain continent? Do you not hear that restraint is impossible without the special grace? For God's word does not admit of restraint; neither does it lie when it says, "Be fruitful and multiply" [Gen. 1:28]. You can neither escape nor restrain yourself from being fruitful and multiplying; it is God's ordinance and takes its course.

Physicians are not amiss when they say: If this natural function is forcibly restrained it necessarily strikes into the flesh and blood and becomes a poison, whence the body becomes unhealthy, enervated, sweaty, and foul-smelling. That which should have issued in fruitfulness and propagation has to be

---

[45] *Mehr eyngebubet denn aussgebubet.* Luther's play on words depends on the close similarity between the German words for "boy" (*Bube*) and "fornicate" (*buben*). *Ausbuben* in relation to *Bube* meant to put away childhood, grow up, reach maturity, and in this connection also to have one's fling or sow one's wild oats. However in relation to *buben,* the term also meant more literally to put away the unclean life, abandon immorality. Luther frequently used the term *hineinbuben* to express the very opposite. Both words thus carried overtones referring to age as well as to morality. See Grimm, *Deutsches Wörterbuch,* II, 457-462; I, 840; IV² 1416.

[46] Wander (ed.), *Sprichwörter-Lexikon,* III, 936, "*Narren,*" No. 3.

[47] See Wander (ed.), *Sprichwörter-Lexikon,* III, 936, "*Narren,*" No. 3; cf. also II, 1048-1050, "*Jugend,*" Nos. 190, 141, 166, 176, 193.

[48] Wander (ed.), *Sprichwörter-Lexikon,* I, 820, "*Engel,*" No. 7.

[49] Luther frequently cited this line from the Roman comic poet Terence (*ca.* 190-*ca.* 159 B.C.), "It is no crime, believe me, that a youth wenches" (*The Brothers,* I, ii, 21-22). See, e.g., *LW* 1, 166.

absorbed within the body itself. Unless there is terrific hunger or immense labor or the supreme grace, the body cannot take it; it necessarily becomes unhealthy and sickly. Hence, we see how weak and sickly barren women are. Those who are fruitful, however, are healthier, cleanlier, and happier. And even if they bear themselves weary—or ultimately bear themselves out—that does not hurt. Let them bear themselves out. This is the purpose for which they exist. It is better to have a brief life with good health than a long life in ill health.[50]

But the greatest good in married life, that which makes all suffering and labor worth while, is that God grants offspring and commands that they be brought up to worship and serve him. In all the world this is the noblest and most precious work, because to God there can be nothing dearer than the salvation of souls. Now since we are all duty bound to suffer death, if need be, that we might bring a single soul to God, you can see how rich the estate of marriage is in good works. God has entrusted to its bosom souls begotten of its own body, on whom it can lavish all manner of Christian works. Most certainly father and mother are apostles, bishops, and priests to their children, for it is they who make them acquainted with the gospel. In short, there is no greater or nobler authority on earth than that of parents over their children, for this authority is both spiritual and temporal. Whoever teaches the gospel to another is truly his apostle and bishop. Mitre and staff and great estates indeed produce idols, but teaching the gospel produces apostles and bishops. See therefore how good and great is God's work and ordinance!

Here I will let the matter rest and leave to others the task of searching out further benefits and advantages of the estate of marriage. My purpose was only to enumerate those which a Christian can have for conducting his married life in a Christian way, so that, as Solomon says, he may find his wife in the sight of God and obtain favor from the Lord [Prov. 18:22]. In saying this I do not wish to disparage virginity, or entice anyone away from virginity into marriage. Let each one act as he is able, and as he feels it has been given to him by God. I simply wanted

---

[50] Wander (ed.), *Sprichwörter-Lexikon*, I, 1634, *"Gesund,"* No. 6.

to check those scandalmongers who place marriage so far beneath virginity that they dare to say: Even if the children should become holy [I Cor. 7:14], celibacy would still be better. One should not regard any estate as better in the sight of God than the estate of marriage. In a worldly sense celibacy is probably better, since it has fewer cares and anxieties. This is true, however, not for its own sake but in order that the celibate may better be able to preach and care for God's word, as St. Paul says in I Corinthians 7 [:32-34]. It is God's word and the preaching which make celibacy—such as that of Christ and of Paul—better than the estate of marriage. In itself, however, the celibate life is far inferior.

Finally, we have before us one big, strong objection to answer. Yes, they say, it would be a fine thing to be married, but how will I support myself? I have nothing; take a wife and live on that, etc. Undoubtedly, this is the greatest obstacle to marriage; it is this above all which prevents and breaks up marriage and is the chief excuse for fornication. What shall I say to this objection? It shows lack of faith and doubt of God's goodness and truth. It is therefore no wonder that where faith is lacking, nothing but fornication and all manner of misfortune follow. They are lacking in this, that they want to be sure first of their material resources, where they are to get their food, drink, and clothing [Matt. 6:31]. Yes, they want to pull their head out of the noose of Genesis 3 [:19], "In the sweat of your face you shall eat bread." They want to be lazy, greedy rascals who do not need to work. Therefore, they will get married only if they can get wives who are rich, beautiful, pious, kind—indeed, wait, we'll have a picture of them drawn for you.

Let such heathen go their way; we will not argue with them. If they should be lucky enough to obtain such wives the marriages would still be un-Christian and without faith. They trust in God as long as they know that they do not need him, and that they are well supplied. He who would enter into wedlock as a Christian must not be ashamed of being poor and despised, and doing insignificant work. He should take satisfaction in this: first, that his status and occupation are pleasing to God; second, that God will most certainly provide for him if only he does his job to the

47

best of his ability, and that, if he cannot be a squire or a prince, he is a manservant or a maidservant.

God has promised in Matthew 6 [:25, 33], "Do not be anxious about what you shall eat, drink, and put on; seek first the kingdom of God and his righteousness, and all these things shall be yours as well." Again Psalm 37 [:25] says, "I have been young and now am old, yet I have not seen the righteous forsaken, or his children begging bread." If a man does not believe this, is it any wonder that he suffers hunger, thirst, and cold, and begs for bread? Look at Jacob, the holy patriarch, who in Syria had nothing and simply tended sheep; he received such possessions that he supported four wives with a large number of servants and children, and yet he had enough.[51] Abraham, Isaac, and Lot also became rich, as did many other holy men in the Old Teastment.

Indeed, God has shown sufficiently in the first chapter of Genesis how he provides for us. He first created and prepared all things in heaven and on earth, together with the beasts and all growing things, before he created man. Thereby he demonstrated how he has laid up for us at all times a sufficient store of food and clothing, even before we ask him for it. All we need to do is to work and avoid idleness; then we shall certainly be fed and clothed. But a pitiful unbelief refuses to admit this. The unbeliever sees, comprehends, and feels all the same that even if he worries himself to death over it, he can neither produce nor maintain a single grain of wheat in the field. He knows too that even though all his storehouses were full to overflowing, he could not make use of a single morsel or thread unless God sustains him in life and health and preserves to him his possessions. Yet this has no effect upon him.

To sum the matter up: whoever finds himself unsuited to the celibate life should see to it right away that he has something to do and to work at; then let him strike out in God's name and get married. A young man should marry at the age of twenty at the latest, a young woman at fifteen to eighteen; that's when they are still in good health and best suited for marriage. Let God worry about how they and their children are to be fed. God makes children; he will surely also feed them. Should he fail to

---

51 Genesis 28–33, especially 32:10.

exalt you and them here on earth, then take satisfaction in the fact that he has granted you a Christian marriage, and know that he will exalt you there; and be thankful to him for his gifts and favors.

With all this extolling of married life, however, I have not meant to ascribe to nature a condition of sinlessness. On the contrary, I say that flesh and blood, corrupted through Adam, is conceived and born in sin, as Psalm 51 [:5] says. Intercourse is never without sin; but God excuses it by his grace because the estate of marriage is his work, and he preserves in and through the sin all that good which he has implanted and blessed in marriage.

A SINCERE ADMONITION
BY MARTIN LUTHER
TO ALL CHRISTIANS TO
GUARD AGAINST INSURRECTION
AND REBELLION

1522

Translated by W. A. Lambert

Revised by Walther I. Brandt

INTRODUCTION

Luther remained in seclusion at the Wartburg from May 4, 1521, to March 1, 1522. During this time he kept in touch with his friends, principally through communication with Spalatin at the electoral court, where his hiding place was known to a few trusted counselors. During his absence from Wittenberg the leadership of the movement there was assumed by Andreas Karlstadt and Gabriel Zwilling, who introduced measures which went further and faster than Luther thought proper.[1] To be sure, Luther had taught that the sacrament ought to be distributed in both kinds;[2] he had suggested that mass, as then celebrated, was idolatry;[3] he had called for the abolition of monastic vows;[4] he had advocated clerical marriage.[5] But what Luther would permit, Karlstadt would compel; where Luther would introduce changes and innovations gradually, Karlstadt panted for direct action.

On June 21, 1521, Karlstadt proposed an academic disputation on celibacy, including the theses that priests should be married and that monks and nuns should be allowed to live in wedlock in the monastery.[6] On August 6, Luther wrote Spalatin, "Good God, will our Wittenbergers give wives even to the monks?"[7] Again, on August 15, he wrote, "I wish that Karlstadt had relied on more appropriate passages of Scripture in writing against celibacy.. . . . For what is more dangerous than to invite a great crowd of celibates to matrimony, with passages of Scripture so unreliable and so uncertain that those who marry will afterward be harassed with continual anguish of conscience worse than that which they now suffer?"[8]

---

[1] See *LW* 36, 129-130, 233, and *LW* 51, 69.
[2] See *The Babylonian Captivity of the Church* (1520). *LW* 36, 19-28.
[3] *LW* 36, 41-42.
[4] *LW* 36, 74-78.
[5] See *An Open Letter to the Christian Nobility*. *PE* 2, 118-123.
[6] Schwiebert, *Luther and His Times*, p. 524; Hermann Barge, *Andreas Bodenstein von Karlstadt* (2 vols.; Leipzig: Brandstetter, 1905), I, 265.
[7] *S-J* 2, 51; *WA*, Br 2, 377.
[8] *S-J* 2, 52-53; *WA*, Br 2, 380.

The question of clerical celibacy directly involved only a small proportion of society. It was different with such matters as the mass, communion in both kinds, and the use of images and other adornments in the churches. If it were wrong to celebrate mass, presumably mass ought to be abolished. After October 13, 1521, masses were no longer celebrated in the Augustinian monastery at Wittenberg; on October 17, Karlstadt presided at a disputation where it was proposed that all masses be abolished.[9] On other occasions he expressed himself about images, etc., in such phrases as: "Organs belong only to theatrical exhibitions and princes' palaces"; "Images in churches are wrong"; "Painted idols standing on altars are even more harmful and devilish." [10]

The impact of such ideas and sentiments upon a student body and a populace which had seen their famous professor publicly burn the volumes of canon law and even the papal bull which excommunicated him, inevitably led to demonstrations, some hilarious, others destructive. On October 5 and 6, 1521, a crowd of students jeered and threatened a monk of St. Anthony who had come to Wittenberg to collect alms for his order.[11] On November 12, the prior of the Augustinian cloister complained to the elector that some monks who had left the cloister had joined forces with citizens and students to stir up trouble for the monks who remained faithful, and that he himself hesitated to appear on the street for fear of being attacked.[12]

Reports of extreme measures and consequent unrest in Wittenberg gave Luther such concern that he determined to pay a secret visit to Wittenberg in his assumed character of "Junker Georg," wearing a beard and the trappings of a knight. Traveling by way of Leipzig, he arrived in Wittenberg on December 4, 1521, lodging at the home of his colleague, Amsdorf, where he was able to confer with a few of his most intimate friends. After a stay of three days, when rumors of his presence began to spread, he departed

---

[9] See the letter of Albert Burer to Beatus Rhenanus, dated October 19, 1521, in *Archiv für Reformationsgeschichte* (Leipzig: Heinsius), VI (1909), 192; S-J 2, 62.
[10] Schwiebert, *op. cit.*, p. 536.
[11] Gustav Kawerau (ed.), Julius Köstlin, *Martin Luther: sein Leben und seine Schriften* (5th ed., 2 vols.; Berlin: Duncker, 1903), I, 374.
[12] WA 8, 670.

as quietly as he had come, reaching the Wartburg by December 11.[13]

On December 3, the day before he arrived at Wittenberg on his secret visit, there were more disturbances. A mob of townspeople and students, the students with daggers concealed under their cloaks, invaded the parish church where early mass was being celebrated, seized the mass books, and drove the priests from the altar.[14] The following day a crowd of students rushed into the Franciscan monastery and disrupted the services with laughter and sneering remarks. Fearing further violence, the town council sent a guard to protect the monastery.[15] Later investigation showed that these December disturbances were instigated by unruly students from Erfurt.[16]

Because this present treatise appeared so soon after the events just mentioned, it would be natural to see in them the occasion for writing it. Several factors make this assumption doubtful. In the first place, Luther, who knew at first hand something of the ebullient nature of college students, laughed off these episodes as mere boyish pranks.[17] It is conceivable, too, that his friends did not fully inform him. While still in Wittenberg, sometime between December 4 and 9, Luther wrote Spalatin, "Everything that I see and hear pleases me very much."[18] The really serious disturbances at Wittenberg came later, after the arrival of the "Zwickau prophets" on December 27,[19] when Luther had already completed the treatise and sent it to Spalatin.

What really bothered Luther was not the rash acts of irresponsible students but rather the widespread feeling of unrest and smoldering resentment against the church, which he had sensed and observed on his journey to Wittenberg. Disguised as a knight,

---

[13] Köstlin, op. cit., I, 476-478.
[14] WA 8, 671. The episode is reported in a letter of Elector Frederick to Christian Beyer dated December 4, 1521; see the text in Archiv für Reformationsgeschichte, VI, 270-271.
[15] Its action is reported in a letter from the Wittenberg town council to the Elector Frederick dated December 5, 1521; see the text in Archiv für Reformationsgeschichte, VI, 272-273.
[16] Köstlin, op. cit., I, 477.
[17] Ibid., I, 476.
[18] S-J 2, 79; WA, Br 2, 410.
[19] Köstlin, op. cit., I, 486.

he was reasonably safe from recognition; doubtless he kept his ears open, and probably talked with people whom he met. We have a contemporary record of his stop at Leipzig on December 3.[20] He must have seen some of the violent pamphlets which were being circulated, for he refers in the treatise to one of them, the *Karsthans*.[21] The most direct evidence concerning the occasion of this treatise is found in the letter to Spalatin quoted above, where he writes, "I was worried on the way by various rumors about the violent conduct of some of our followers and have determined to issue a public exhortation on that subject as soon as I get back to my wilderness."[22] Our present treatise is the fulfilment of that expressed determination. While not occasioned specifically by the Wittenberg disturbances, it does provide an insight into the basis of Luther's views and actions with respect to such matters.

The completed manuscript was sent to Spalatin along with a letter which is undated but was probably written about the middle of December.[23] The exact publication date of the treatise is not known. It may have already appeared in January. The earliest extant mention of a printed copy is in a letter from Albert Burer to Beatus Rhenanus dated March 27, 1522.[24]

The following translation is a revision of the one in *PE* 3, 206-222, and is based on the original German edition printed by Melchior Lotther at Wittenberg, *Eyn trew vormanung Martini Luther tzu allen Christen. Sich tzu vorhuten fur auffruhr unnd Emporung*, as that has been reprinted with annotations in WA 8, (670) 676-687.

---

[20] *Ibid.*, I, 476.
[21] See p. 57.
[22] See p. 55, n. 18.
[23] Ernst Ludwig Enders, *D. Martin Luthers Briefwechsel* (Frankfurt-am-Main, 1884-1932), III, 254, No. 471, dates it "the middle of December." WA, Br 2, 411, dates it about December 12, 1521.
[24] *Archiv für Reformationsgeschichte*, VI, 467-469.

A SINCERE ADMONITION BY MARTIN LUTHER TO ALL CHRISTIANS TO GUARD AGAINST INSURRECTION AND REBELLION

Jesus

May God grant grace and peace to all Christians who read this pamphlet or hear it read.

By the grace of God the blessed light of Christian truth, hitherto suppressed by the pope and his adherents, has risen again in our day. Their manifold harmful and scandalous deceits and all manner of misdeeds and tyranny have thereby been publicly exposed and brought to shame. It seems likely that this may result in an insurrection, and that priests, monks, bishops, and the entire clerical estate may be murdered or driven into exile unless they themselves demonstrate some serious and significant improvement. For the common man seems to be discontented and brooding over the damage he has suffered in property, body, and soul. Apparently they have tried him too far, with utter lack of scruple burdening him beyond all measure. He seems to be neither able nor willing to endure it any longer, and to have good reason to lay about him with flail and cudgel, as *Karsthans*[1] threatens to do.

---

[1] Literally, "the man with the hoe," *Karsthans* here is probably not an allusion to the peasantry in general—to whom the name had been contemptuously applied in southwest Germany—but to a specific pamphlet bearing the same name as a title of honor for an aroused and knowledgeable peasantry. Written in 1521 by Joachim von Watt (Vadianus) of St. Gall, the pamphlet portrays Karsthans as simply an upright evangelical farmer ready to take up arms against his recognized enemy, the pope. Luther is introduced into the dialogue to caution the peasant against violence, and the tone of moderation prevails. See brief excerpts from the text of the pamphlet in *PE* 3, 204-205. The complete text is given in Herbert Burckhardt (ed.), *Karsthans*

I am not at all displeased to hear that the clergy are in such a state of fear and anxiety; perhaps they will come to their senses and moderate their mad tyranny. Would to God that their terror and fear were even greater! Nevertheless, I think—indeed I am sure and have no fear whatever on this score—that there will not be any insurrection or rebellion, at least none that would be general and affect the entire pack.[2] I have this confidence because I neither can nor ought to doubt that God will keep watch over his word, and will let heaven and earth pass away long before a single jot or tittle of his word shall fail, as he himself says in Matthew 5 [:18] and 24 [:35]. Therefore, I would allow anyone who can and will, to threaten and frighten them that the Scripture may be fulfilled which says of such clerical evildoers in Psalm 36, "Their iniquity is made manifest, that men may hate them";[3] and in Psalm 14, "They tremble for fear, where there is no fear";[4] and again in Proverbs 27 [28:1], "The wicked flee when no one pursues"; and yet again in Leviticus 26 [:36], "The sound of a rustling leaf shall terrify them"; and finally in Deuteronomy 28

(1521) (Otto Clemen [gen. ed.], "Flugschriften aus den ersten Jahren der Reformation" Vol. IV [4 vols.; Leipzig: Rudolf Haupt, 1907-1911]), pp. 75-120; and in Arnold E. Berger (ed.), Die Sturmtruppen der Reformation (Heinz Kindermann [gen. ed.], Deutsche Literatur: Sammlung literarischer Kunst-und Kulturdenkmäler in Entwicklungsreihen, Vol. II of "Reformation" [Leipzig: Philipp Reclam jun., 1931]), pp. 100-124. Later in the same year, between July and September of 1521, appeared the Neukarsthans written by Ulrich von Hutten. It portrays Franz von Sickingen trying to win the religiously aroused peasant for his own political program. It is more violent in tone, demanding an outright revolution. Cf. Clemen, op. cit., IV, 47-48; Berger, op. cit., pp. 50-51; and PE 3, 205. See the text of the "New Karsthans" in Eduard Bocking (ed.), Ulrich von Hutten's Opera (7 vols.; Leipzig: Teubner, 1859-1870), 4, 649-681.

2 That Luther's opinion in this regard soon changed is evident from his letter of March 7, 1522, to the Elector Frederick of Saxony, in which he justifies his second return from the Wartburg to his chaotic parish in Wittenberg by saying, "The third thing that moved me was that I fear—alas, I feel sure!— that there will be a great uprising in Germany, with which God will punish the German nation, for we see that the gospel pleases the common people greatly, and they receive it in a fleshly sense; they see that it is true, but will not use it rightly." WA, Br 2, 461 and 469; S-J 2, 100. See also his letter to Wenceslaus Link, March 19, 1522, "I greatly fear that if the princes continue to listen to that dull-witted Duke George there will be an uprising which will destroy the princes and rulers of all Germany and will involve all of the clergy; that is the way I see it." WA, Br 2, 479; S-J 2, 113.

3 Luther's citation of Ps. 36:2 is an interpretive paraphrase of the Vulgate.

4 Luther's citation of Ps. 14:5 closely follows the Vulgate.

[:65-67], "God will give you a trembling heart, that your life shall hang in doubt before you. In the morning you shall say, 'Would God that I may survive until evening'; and at evening you shall say, 'Would God that I may survive until morning'!" Scripture promises such terror and fear to all God's enemies as the beginning of their damnation. Therefore, it is right, and pleases me well, that such torment is beginning to appear among the papists, who persecute and condemn divine truth. Its bite will soon be sharper.

I will go further. If I had ten bodies and could acquire so much favor with God that he would chasten them with the gentle lash[5] of bodily death or insurrection, I would from the bottom of my heart most gladly offer them all in behalf of this wretched crew. Alas, no such mild chastisement awaits them; an inexpressible severity and limitless wrath has already begun to break upon them. The heaven is iron; the earth brass [Deut. 28:23]. No prayers can save them now. Wrath, as St. Paul says of the Jews [I Thess. 2:16], has come upon them at last. God's purposes demand far more than a mere insurrection. Since they are as a whole beyond the reach of help, would to God that we might extricate at least a few of them and save them from that horrible yawning abyss!

Scripture foretells for the pope and his adherents an end far worse than insurrection and bodily death. Daniel 8 [:25] says, "By no human hand he shall be broken," that is, by no sword or physical force. And St. Paul, in II Thessalonians 2 [:8], says of him, "Our Lord Jesus will slay him with the breath of his mouth and destroy him with the brightness of his coming." Artists portray Christ seated on a rainbow, with a sword and a twig proceeding out of his mouth,[6] a conception based on Isaiah 11 [:4], where he says, "He shall smite the earth with the rod of his mouth, and with the breath of his lips he shall slay the wicked."

---

5 *Fuchs schwantz,* the soft and bushy tail of a fox, is mentioned here by way of contrast with the harsh rod of discipline.

6 Luther had doubtless seen several such representations of Christ in Wittenberg: on the entrance to the cemetery, on the north tower entrance to the parish church, and on the old Wittenberg church seal. The conception was common in the fourteenth century. WA 8, 678, n. 1. A comparable woodcut representation may be found in Roland H. Bainton, *Here I Stand* (New York, 1950), p. 31. The artists presumably drew their inspiration from Rev. 1:16 and 19:15, 21.

But the artists depict a twig in blossom; that is not right. It should be a rod or staff, and both rod and sword should be on the same side, extending only over the damned.[7] Psalm 10 [:15] says, "Break thou the arm of the ungodly; seek out his wickedness, and his godlessness will not remain."

From these texts we learn how the pope and his anti-Christian regime[8] shall be destroyed. Through the word of Christ, which is the breath, the rod and the sword, of his mouth, the pope's villainy, deceit, rascality, tyranny, and beguilements shall be revealed and laid open to the world's derision. Lying and guile need only to be revealed and recognized to be undone. When once lying is recognized as such, it needs no second stroke; it falls of itself and vanishes in shame. That is the meaning of Psalm 10 [:15], "Only seek out his wickedness, and his godlessness is no more." It needs only to be sought out and recognized.

Now all that the pope is and has, his foundations, monasteries, universities, laws, and doctrines are mere lies, founded on nothing but lies. Only by pretense and a show of piety has the pope been able to deceive, beguile, and oppress the world, destroying men's bodies, property, and souls. It only needs to be recognized and made known, therefore, and pope, priests, and monks will end in shame and disgrace. For no man is crazy enough to follow rather than hate barefaced lies and dishonesty. Now when the papal villainy has been thus exposed and the breath of Christ's mouth prevails, so that men no longer esteem but despise the pope and his lies, then the Last Day will break in and, as Paul says [II Thess. 2:8], Christ will utterly destroy the pope by His coming.

The best feature of the whole business is that the pope and his adherents, hardened in heart, will not believe it, but will sneer at it, that they may fulfil the word of Paul, "*Cum dixerint pax;* when they shall feel secure and say, 'There is nothing to

---

[7] The "twig in blossom," to which Luther takes exception because he interprets it in terms of Isa. 11:4, is actually the stem of a lily, signifying innocence and purity; therefore, the sword of justice would be extended over the damned, and the lily over the blessed.

[8] The pretensions of the papacy suggested to Luther—as to Wyclif before him—that the pope was the Antichrist, the incarnation of all that is hostile to Christ and his kingdom, the wicked one whose appearance was prophesied in II Thess. 2:3-10; I John 2:18, 22; 4:3; and Revelation 13. *PE* 2, 73, n. 2; *MA*³ 2, 394, n. 91, 20. See in this volume, p. 144, n. 10.

worry about,' then sudden destruction will come upon them"
[I Thess. 5:3]. Now in order that the papists may not mend their
ways and look for mercy, they are not to believe this but are
rather to say, "O well, the Last Day is still a long way off"—until
in the twinkling of an eye, before they are aware of it, they lie
in a heap at the bottom of hell-fire.

As I have just said, these texts have convinced me that the
papacy and the clerical estate will not be destroyed by the hand
of men, or by insurrection. Their wickedness is so horrible that
no punishment is adequate except the wrath of God itself, without any intermediary. For this reason I have never yet let men
persuade me to oppose those who threaten to use fist and flail; I
know full well that they will never get that far. Even if a few
should get roughed up, there will be no general resort to violence.
Why, priests have been killed before this and probably in greater
number, quite apart from any tumult or insurrection, at a time
when men still feared their ban, and when the wrath of God had
not yet come upon them. Now that the wrath of God has come
upon them, however, and men no longer fear their ban, they
are to be afraid without cause, just as they formerly frightened us
without cause by means of their spurious ban, and took a pompous
pleasure in our fear.[9]

Although the hand, therefore, will not get far, and there is
hence no need for me to restrain it, I must nevertheless instruct
men's hearts a little. As regards the hand, I leave matters to the
temporal authorities and nobility.[10] They should, of course, take
action, each prince and lord in his own territory, by virtue of the
obligations incumbent upon such duly constituted authority; for
what is done by duly constituted authority cannot be regarded as
insurrection. However, at present they are just letting everything
go; one hinders the other, and some of them even support and
justify the cause of Antichrist. God will find them out and reward
them according to the manner in which they have used their
authority and power, whether to the deliverance or to the destruc-

---

[9] Cf. A Treatise Concerning the Ban (1520). WA 6, 63-75; PE 2, 37-54,
especially PE 2, 43-48, where Luther discusses that fear of the ban which led
people to do violence to those who imposed it.
[10] Cf. An Open Letter to the Christian Nobility of the German Nation Concerning the Reform of the Christian Estate (1520). PE 2, 61-164.

tion of the bodies, property, and souls of their subjects. But we must calm the mind of the common man, and tell him to abstain from the words and even the passions which lead to insurrection, and to do nothing in the matter apart from a command of his superiors or an action of the authorities. This course should commend itself to him for the following reasons.

First, as has been said, the threats of violence will not be implemented. All that men are saying and thinking on the subject is nothing but idle chatter and vain imagining.[11] As we have heard, God has reserved their punishment to himself; and they certainly do not deserve so light a punishment.[12] Besides, we see how the princes and nobles disagree among themselves, and evince no willingness whatsoever to improve matters. All this is ordained and decreed by God, so that he alone may pour out his wrath and punishment upon them. As has been said, the princes and lords are not thereby excused; they ought to do their part and use the power of their sword in the effort to ward off and moderate to the best of their ability at least some of God's wrath, as Moses did in Exodus 32 [:27-28]. At his command three thousand of the people were slain in order that the wrath of God might be turned away from the people as a whole. Scripture relates similar acts by Elijah [I Kings 18:40] and Phinehas [Num. 25:7-8]. Not that one should in our day kill the priests, for that is not necessary; but whatever they do beyond and contrary to the gospel should be forbidden in word only, and the command properly enforced. Words and edicts will more than suffice in dealing with them, so there will be no need of slashing or stabbing.

Second, even if insurrection were a practical possibility, and God were willing to impose so merciful a punishment upon them, it is still an unprofitable method of procedure. It never brings about the desired improvement. For insurrection lacks discern-

---

[11] The pre-Reformation background of the Peasants' War, whereby long before 1517 the class cleavages had almost reached the breaking point and a violent eruption was not only expected but actually predicted, is traced in Wilhelm Vogt, *Die Vorgeschichte des Bauernkrieges* (Halle: Verein für Reformationsgeschichte, 1887), see especially pp. 140-144. The actual attack of June 10-12, 1521, on the clergy at Erfurt is reported in a contemporary poem printed in Otto Clemen, *op cit.*, I, 365-370.

[12] The papacy and its adherents deserve a punishment more rigorous than mere death and insurrection. Cf. pp. 59-60, and p. 59, n. 5.

ment; it generally harms the innocent more than the guilty. Hence, no insurrection is ever right, no matter how right the cause it seeks to promote. It always results in more damage than improvement, and verifies the saying, "Things go from bad to worse."[13] For this reason governing authority and the sword have been established to punish the wicked and protect the upright, that insurrection may be prevented, as St. Paul says in Romans 13 [:1-4] and as we read in I Peter 2 [:13-14]. But when Sir Mob[14] breaks loose he cannot tell the wicked from the upright, or keep them apart; he lays about him at random, and great and horrible injustice is inevitable.

Therefore, keep your eye on the authorities; so long as they make no move and issue no instructions, you just keep hand, mouth, and heart quiet, and assume no responsibility. But if you can stir up the authorities to do something and to give commands, you may do so. If they are unwilling, you must also be unwilling. If you start anything on your own hook you are already in the wrong, and are much worse than your opponents. I am and always will be on the side of those against whom insurrection is directed, no matter how unjust their cause; I am opposed to those who rise in insurrection, no matter how just their cause, because there can be no insurrection without hurting the innocent and shedding their blood.

Third, God has forbidden insurrection, where he speaks through Moses, "*Quod iustum est, iuste exequaris;* Thou shalt follow justly after that which is just,"[15] and again, "Revenge is mine; I will repay."[16] Hence we have the true proverb, "He who strikes back is in the wrong,"[17] and again, "No one can be his own judge.[18] Now insurrection is nothing else than being one's own judge and avenger, and that is something God cannot tolerate. Therefore, insurrection cannot help but make matters much worse, because it is contrary to God; God is not on the side of insurrection.

Fourth, in this particular case insurrection is most certainly

13 Cf. Wander (ed.), *Sprichwörter-Lexikon* 4, 1387, "*Uebel,*" No. 29.
14 "*Er Omnes,*" literally, "Mr. Everybody."
15 Deut. 16:20 (Douay).
16 Deut. 32:35 (Douay); cf. Rom. 12:19.
17 See Wander (ed.), *Sprichwörter-Lexikon,* V, 226, "*Wiederschlagen,*" No. 2.
18 Cf. *ibid.,* III, 1675, "*Richter,*" Nos. 80-83.

a suggestion of the devil. He sees the bright light of the truth exposing his idols, the pope and the papists, before all the world; and he simply cannot cope with it. Its brilliant rays have so dazzled his eyes and blinded him that he can do nothing more than lie, blaspheme, and suggest errant nonsense. He even forgets to assume the hypocritical appearance of respectability he has usually shown hitherto, as exemplified in the bulls and pamphlets of those shameless liars, the pope, Eck, [19] Emser,[20] and the rest of them. Now he is at work trying to stir up an insurrection through those who glory in the gospel, hoping thereby to revile our teaching as if it came from the devil and not from God. Already some are boastfully making a point of this in their preaching as a result of the attack on the priests which he inspired at Erfurt.[21]

---

[19] Johann Eck (1486-1543), professor of theology at Ingolstadt, was Luther's adversary at the Leipzig Debate in 1519, and his inveterate opponent thereafter. He was largely responsible for procuring Luther's excommunication by the papal bull *Exsurge, Domine* at Rome in 1520. His anti-Lutheran defense of the papal position, *de primatu Petri,* was published at Paris in 1521.

[20] Hieronymus Emser (1478-1527), was secretary to Duke George of Saxony. In their war of letters and pamphlets Luther referred to him as "The Leipzig Goat," taking the name from the goat's head which appeared on his escutcheon. *PE* 3, 277-401.

[21] Luther's exact reference here is obscure since there was more than one such attack on the priests at Erfurt in the year 1521. Luther referred to such an attack in his letter of May 14 to Spalatin, "At Erfurt the students made a night attack on some of the priests' houses; it was at the time we came to Eisenach. They were indignant because the Dean of St. Severus [Johann Wiedemann], a great papist, seized Master [Johann] Draco, who is well disposed to us, by the robe and publicly dragged him out of the choir, alleging that he was under excommunication because he, along with others, had come to meet me when I entered Erfurt. Meanwhile, worse is feared; the city council is winking at the disorder; the priests there have a bad reputation, and it is said the young artisans are conspiring with the students. A little more and they will make the prophetic proverb true, 'Erfurt, a second Prague.'" *S-J* 2, 27, n. 1, dates the student riot on April 9, when Luther was on his way to Worms, and falsely refers a contemporary account of such a riot, *Ain neu Gedicht wie die gaystlichait zu Erffordt in Dhüringen Gesturmbt ist worden,* to this particular affair. Otto Clemen ascribes to the same affair a date of May 1 (*WA,* Br 2, 339, n. 9) and sees in *Ain neu Gedicht* a description of another *Pfaffensturm* which was far more significant, namely, the more general uprising of students, citizenry, and artisans, plus a few nobles and peasants, which ran its course without interference from the authorities on June 12. Clemen, *op. cit.,* I, 361-362; *MA*3 4, 324, n. 13, 35, erroneously dates this tumult in July rather than June. In a letter to Spalatin of sometime after July 15 Luther writes, "At Erfurt Satan has been plotting against us to give our friends a bad name, but he will

But God willing, he shall not succeed. We must bear his reviling; however, he will have to bear something in return which will amply repay him for it.

Those who read and rightly understand my teaching will not start an insurrection; they have not learned that from me. If some incite to insurrection, however, and make use of our name, what can we do about it? How much are the papists doing in the name of Christ that Christ has not only forbidden, but that tends to destroy Christ? Must we keep our company so pure that among us there may not even be a stumbling St. Peter? Why, among the papists there are none but Judases and Judas-like deceit—still they are not willing to have their teaching ascribed to the devil. But, as I say, the devil thus tries in ·every way to find an occasion for slandering our teaching. If there were anything worse he could do, he would do it. But he is checkmated, and, God willing, must take his punishment now that he has been reduced to such lame, futile, and rotten schemes. He will not and shall not succeed in stirring up the insurrection he so much desires.

Therefore, I beseech all who would glory in the name Christian to be guided by what St. Paul says in II Corinthians 3 [6:3] that we give our opponents no occasion to find fault with our teaching. For we see how apt the papists are to ignore the log in their own eyes, and how zealously they hunt and scratch to find a tiny speck in our eyes.[22] We are not supposed to reproach them with the fact that among them there is hardly anything good; but if even a single one of us is not wholly spiritual and a perfect angel, our entire cause is supposed to be wrong. Then they rejoice, then they dance, then they sing as if they had won the victory. Therefore, we must guard against giving them any occasion for slander, of which they are full to overflowing. This we must do not for their sake—since they shall have to slander anyway

---

accomplish nothing. It is not our friends who are doing these things. He is unable to resist the truth and seeks to bring it into ill-repute by inflaming against us the foolish jealousy of fools. I wonder that the city council puts up with it."

It may well be that Luther's two letters here cited have reference to two distinct episodes at Erfurt and that his mention of the city in this treatise has reference more to the later than to the earlier affair.

22 Cf. Matt. 7:3-5; Luke 6:41-42.

and let the mouth speak out of the abundance of the heart [Matt. 12:34], even if they should do it with lies, as we see them doing now—but for the sake of the holy gospel. We must protect it from reproach and put them to silence (as St. Peter bids us do),[23] that so far as it is within our power they may not be able to speak evil of us truthfully. For whatever evil they can say of us they immediately ascribe to our doctrine, and so God's holy word, from which we derive all the honor we have, must bear our shame. But their doctrine they regard as above reproach— these noble, tender, and innocent people—although they do nothing but evil.

Suppose you ask, "What are we to do if the authorities are unwilling to act? Are we to continue to put up with it and encourage their wantonness?" I answer: You are to do nothing of the kind. There are three things you should do. First, you are to acknowledge your own sins, because of which the strict justice of God has plagued you with this anti-Christian regime, as St. Paul foretold in II Thessalonians 2 [:11, 10], "God sends upon them false teaching and government because they refused to love the truth and so be saved." We alone are to blame for all that the pope and his adherents have done to our property, our bodies, and our souls. Therefore, you must first acknowledge your sins and put them from you before you try to escape the plague and punishment; otherwise you will only bring down judgment upon yourself,[24] and the stone you throw upward toward heaven will fall on your own head.[25]

Second. You should in all humility pray against the papal regime as Psalm 10 [:12-15] does and teaches us to do where it says, "Arise, O Lord God, and lift up thy hand; forget not thy poor. Why does the wicked blaspheme thee, Lord God, and say 'Thou wilt not call to account'? Thou dost see; yea, thou dost note his trouble and vexation, that thou mayest take it into thy hands. The hapless commits himself to thee; thou wilt be the

---

23 I Pet. 2:15; cf. 3:16 and Titus 1:11.
24 *Wydder den spiess tretten,* literally, "be treading on spear points," is thus paraphrased in *CL* 2, 305, n. 27.
25 I.e., the criticism you level against your superiors will rebound and strike you. Cf. Prov. 26:27.

helper of the fatherless. Break thou the arm of the ungodly; seek out his wickedness, and his godlessness will be no more," etc.

Third. You are to let your mouth become such a mouth of the Spirit of Christ as St. Paul speaks of in the text quoted above, "Our Lord Jesus will slay him with the mouth of his Spirit."[26] This we do when we boldly continue the work that has been begun, and by speaking and writing spread among the people a knowledge of the rascality and deceit of the pope and the papists until he is exposed, recognized, and brought into disrepute throughout the world. For he must first be slain with words; the mouth of Christ must do it. In that way he will be torn from the hearts of men, and his lies recognized and despised. When he is gone from men's hearts and so has lost their confidence, he is already destroyed. He can be handled better this way than with a hundred insurrections. By resort to violence we will do him no harm at all, but rather strengthen him, as many have experienced before.[27] But the light of truth hurts him; when we contrast him with Christ, and his teaching with the gospel, that brings him down and utterly destroys him without any effort and exertion on our part. See what I have done. Have I not, with the mouth alone, without a single stroke of the sword, done more harm to the pope, bishops, priests, and monks than all the emperors, kings, and princes with all their power ever did before? And why? Because Daniel 8 [:25] says, "By no human hand shall this king be broken"; and St. Paul says, "He will be destroyed by the mouth of Christ" [II Thess. 2:8]. Now every man—whether it be I or another—who speaks the word of Christ may boldly assert that his mouth is the mouth of Christ. I for my part am certain that my word is not mine, but the word of Christ; my mouth therefore must also be the mouth of him whose word it speaks.

Therefore, there is no need for you to demand an armed insurrection. Christ himself has already begun an insurrection with

---

[26] On p. 60 Luther had cited II Thess. 2:8 correctly, *"Geyst seynes munds."* His transposition here—*"Mund seynes geystes"*—makes sense in German because the word *"Geist"* may mean "spirit" as well as "breath."

[27] The attack on the papacy by the emperor Henry IV and his immediate successors in the eleventh and twelfth centuries ultimately strengthened the papacy; the Hohenstaufen attack in the thirteenth century left the papacy for the time being without a dangerous rival in Europe.

his mouth, one which will be more than the pope can bear. Let us follow that one, and carry on. What is now transpiring in the world is not our work. No mere man could possibly begin and carry on such an affair by himself. It has come thus far without my consideration and counsel; it will also be completed without my advice, and the gates of hell shall not stop it [Matt. 16:18]. A far different Man is the driving power;[28] the papists do not see Him but lay the blame on us. However, they shall see for themselves very soon. The devil has for a long time feared the coming of these years; he smelled the pot boiling a long way off. He even issued many prophecies against it, some of which point to me,[29] so I often stand amazed at his great cunning. Often he would have liked to kill me. Now he would like to see an armed insurrection develop which would hinder and bring into disrepute this spiritual insurrection. But, God willing, there should be and will be no such help for him. He must be destroyed "by no human hand" but "by the mouth" alone; nothing will prevent that.

Get busy now; spread the holy gospel, and help others spread it; teach, speak, write, and preach that man-made laws are nothing; urge people not to enter the priesthood, the monastery, or the convent, and hinder them from so doing; encourage those who have already entered to leave; give no more money for bulls,[30] candles, bells, tablets,[31] and churches; rather tell them that a Christian life consists of faith and love. Let us do this for two years, and you shall see what will become of pope, bishops, cardinals, priests, monks, nuns, bells, towers, masses, vigils, cowls, hoods, tonsures, monastic rules, statutes, and all the swarming vermin[32] of the papal regime; they will all vanish like smoke. But if we fail to teach and spread this truth among the people so their hearts will no

---

[28] *Der das redle treybt* means literally, "is making the wheel go round"; see *LW* 35, 262, n. 72.

[29] About a month earlier, in his 1521 *Misuse of the Mass,* Luther interpreted a prophecy he had heard as a child, to the effect that Emperor Frederick would deliver the Holy Sepulchre, in terms of its fulfilment in his own time in his own prince, Duke Frederick of Saxony, under whose enlightened rule the Holy Scriptures came once more into their own. See *LW* 36, 228-229.

[30] Fees were paid for papal bulls which conferred various privileges.

[31] *Tafeln* were decorative votive tablets or plaques placed in the churches in fulfilment of certain vows. *BG* 7, 216, n. 8; *MA*³ 4, 324, n. 16, 18.

[32] *Geschwurm unnd gewurm.*

longer cling to these things, we will still have the pope with us, though we were to start a thousand insurrections against him. Just see what has been accomplished in this one single year, during which we have been preaching and writing this truth! See how the papists' covers have shrunk in length and in breadth![33] The stationaries[34] complain that they are starving to death. What will be the result if the mouth of Christ continues to thresh by his Spirit for two more years? This is what the devil would like to prevent by stirring up an armed insurrection. But let us be wise, thank God for his holy word, and be bold with our mouths in the service of this blessed insurrection.

The ignorance of the papists has been revealed. Their hypocrisy has been revealed. The pernicious lies contained in their laws and monastic orders have been revealed. Their wicked and tyrannical use of the ban has been revealed. In short, everything with which they have hitherto bewitched, terrorized, and deceived the world has been exposed. Men see that these things were nothing but mumbo jumbo. They have nothing left with which to frighten men anymore except the meager expedient of power. Now that the external glitter is gone and they have to defend themselves by naked force, it is impossible for them to continue much longer. And whatever escapes the mouth of Christ, his coming will destroy, as St. Paul says [II Thess. 2:8]. Therefore, let us continue boldly, earnestly inculcating the word and driving

---

[33] Luther's figure of speech has reference to the blankets which warm, protect, and conceal a person in bed.

[34] The *Stationirer*, literally "stationed ones," were members of the mendicant orders assigned to certain "stations," the so-called "begging houses" (*Terminierhäuser*), in those cities where the orders had no cloisters. MA³ 4, 324, n. 16, 29; BG 7, 217, n. 10. In return for a donation these stationaries would exhibit real or supposed relics, or enrol the contributor in the list of beneficiaries of their patron saint, St. Anthony, St. Hubert, St. Cornelius, St. Valentine, etc. This was supposed to insure against disease, accident, and other adversities. Protests against the activities of the stationaries were included in the list of German grievances (Gravamina) presented at the Diets of Worms (1521) and of Nürnberg (1523); see the texts of these protests in A. Kluckhohn and A. Wrede (eds.), *Deutsche Reichstagsakten unter Karl V* (4 vols.; Gotha: Perthes, 1893-1905), II, 678 [23], and 688 [54]; III, 651 [4]. See Luther's complaint against them and the other beggars in his 1520 *Open Letter to the Christian Nobility. PE* 2, 135-136. A popular song of 1525 indicates that among the people generally they were not highly regarded; see this song in Oskar Schade, *Satiren und Pasquille aus der Reformationszeit* (2nd ed.; Hanover: Rümpler, 1863), I, 32.

THE CHRISTIAN IN SOCIETY

out the laws of men. Thus does Christ through us slay the papacy. Already it is singing, "Eloi, Eloi"; it has been stricken; soon the word will be *"Expiravit."* [35]

But in this very matter of inculcating the word and driving out the laws of men I must also admonish those who are causing wholesale defections from and denunciations of the holy gospel. There are some who, when they have read a page or two or have heard a sermon, go at it slam bang, and do no more than overwhelm others with reproach and find fault with them and their practices as being unevangelical, without stopping to consider that many of them are plain and simple folk who would soon learn the truth if it were told them. This also I have taught no one to do, and St. Paul has strictly forbidden it [Rom. 14:1–15:1, I Cor. 4:5-6]. Their only motive in doing it is the desire to come up with something new, and to be regarded as good Lutherans. But they are perverting the holy gospel to make it serve their own pride. You will never bring the gospel into the hearts of men in that way. You are much more apt to frighten them away from it, and then you will have to bear the awful responsibility of having driven them away from the truth. You fool, that's not the way; listen, and take some advice.

In the first place, I ask that men make no reference to my name; let them call themselves Christians, not Lutherans.[36] What is Luther? After all, the teaching is not mine [John 7:16]. Neither was I crucified for anyone [I Cor. 1:13]. St. Paul, in I Corinthians 3,[37] would not allow the Christians to call themselves Pauline or Petrine, but Christian. How then should I—poor stinking maggot-fodder[38] that I am—come to have men call the children of Christ by my wretched name? Not so, my dear friends; let us abolish all party names and call ourselves Christians, after

---

[35] Luther is here referring to the end of the papacy in the terms used in Mark 15:34, 37, to describe the death of Christ. Already mortally wounded, it utters the cry of the death struggle; soon it will "breathe its last."
[36] Just a few months later in his *Receiving Both Kinds in the Sacrament* (1522) Luther reiterated this position but with the important qualification that disavowal of the name Lutheran is tantamount to a disavowal of Christ "if you are convinced that Luther's teaching is in accord with the gospel." *LW* 36, 265, and n. 29 there.
[37] I Cor. 3:22; cf. 1:12 and 3:4.
[38] *Madensack*, literally, "bag of worms," was a favorite term of Luther for designating the perishable body, the mortal man.

him whose teaching we hold. The papists deservedly have a party name, because they are not content with the teaching and name of Christ, but want to be papist as well. Let them be papist then, since the pope is their master. I neither am nor want to be anyone's master. I hold, together with the universal church, the one universal teaching of Christ, who is our only master [Matt. 23:8].

In the second place, if you want to handle the gospel in a Christian way, you must take into account the people to whom you are speaking. These are of two kinds. On the one hand, there are those who are hardened and will not listen, and who, in addition, deceive and poison others with their lying mouths. Such are the pope, Eck, Emser, and some of our bishops, priests, and monks. You should not deal with them at all, but hold to the injunction of Christ in Matthew 7 [:6], "Do not give dogs what is holy, and do not throw pearls before swine, lest they trample them underfoot, and the dogs turn to attack you." Let them remain dogs and swine; they are a lost cause anyway. And Solomon says, "Where there is no hearing, pour not out words.[39] But when you see that these same liars pour their lies and poison into other people, then you should boldly take the offensive and fight against them, just as Paul in Acts 13 [:10-11] attacked Elymas with hard and sharp words, and as Christ called the Pharisees a "brood of vipers" [Matt. 23:33]. You should do this, not for their sake, for they will not listen, but for the sake of those whom they are poisoning. Just so does St. Paul command Titus to rebuke sharply such empty talkers and deceivers of souls [Titus 1:10-13].

On the other hand, there are some who have heretofore not yet heard the gospel, and who would be willing to learn if someone would tell it to them, or who are so weak that they cannot readily grasp it. These you should not bully or beat up, but instruct in a kindly and gentle manner, giving them a defense and explanation. If they are unable to grasp it at once, bear with

---

[39] Ecclus. 32:6 (Douay). Luther was mistakenly referring the quotation to some wisdom book traditionally ascribed to Solomon, perhaps Ecclesiastes; at any rate, he did not hold to Solomonic authorship of the apocryphal Ecclesiasticus. See *LW* 35, 347-348.

them for a time. St. Paul says of them in Romans 15,[40] "Welcome him who is weak in faith"; and Peter says in I Peter 3 [:15], "Always be prepared to give an answer to any one who desires a defense and explanation of the hope that is in you, yet do it with gentleness and fear." Here you see that we are to give instruction in our faith gently and in the fear of God to any man who desires or needs it.

If you only want to parade your vast learning before such people; if you pounce upon them with the bare assertion that their way of praying, fasting, and celebrating mass is wrong; if you insist upon eating meat, eggs, and other foods on Friday;[41] and if you do not, in addition, with gentleness and fear explain to them the why and wherefore—then these simple souls cannot help but think that you are a proud, impudent, and wicked man, and that is just what you are! They will get the impression that men are not to pray or do good, that the mass is nothing, and so on. You will be the cause of their error, and of their taking offense; you will be to blame. That is how it comes about that they disparage and belittle the holy gospel, and imagine that you have been taught some monstrous things. What do you gain by thus troubling your neighbor and hindering the gospel? When your inconsiderate ardor has cooled, they will say, "Ei, I will stick to my beliefs," and they will shut their hearts against the genuine truth.

You should rather tell them your reasons with fear and gentleness (as St. Peter teaches [I Pet. 3:15]), saying something like this, "My dear man, fasting and the eating of eggs, meat, and fish are matters of such a nature that salvation does not depend upon them. Both the doing of these things and the leaving of them undone may be for good or for evil; faith alone saves," etc., or, "The mass would be a good thing if it were properly celebrated," etc. In this way they would come to you and listen,

---

40 Rom. 14:1; cf. 15:1.
41 Friday had already degenerated as a fast day to the point where only certain foods (e.g., meat and eggs) were forbidden by canon law, while others (e.g., fish) were not. *BG* 7, 220, n. 3. See Luther's more extended discussion of fasting and other man-made regulations and his caution against overhasty reform in his *Avoiding the Doctrines of Men* of some eight months earlier. *LW* 35, (125) 131-153.

and ultimately learn what you know. But now that you are so insolent, priding yourself on your superior knowledge, acting like the Pharisee in the gospel [Luke 18:11-12], and basing your pride on the fact that they do not even know that which you know, you fall under the judgment of St. Paul in Romans 14, *"Iam non secundum caritatem ambulas"*; [42] you are despising your neighbor, whom you ought to be serving with gentleness and fear.

Take an analogous case: If an enemy had tied a rope around your brother's neck, endangering his life, and you like a fool were to fly into a rage at rope and enemy and frantically pull the rope toward you or slash at it with a knife, you would most likely either strangle or stab your brother, doing him more harm than either rope or enemy. If you really want to help your brother, this is what you must do: You may slash away at the enemy as vigorously as you please, but the rope you must handle gently and with caution until you get it off his neck, lest you strangle your brother.

In like manner you may deal harshly with the liars and hardened tyrants, and act boldly in opposition to their teachings and their works, for they will not listen. But the simple people, whom they have bound with the ropes of their teaching and whose lives are endangered, you must treat quite differently. You must with caution and gentleness undo the teachings of men, providing them a defense and explanation, and in this way gradually set them free. This is what St. Paul did when, in defiance of all the Jews, he would not permit Titus to be circumcised [Gal. 2:3], and yet he circumcised Timothy [Acts 16:3]. You must treat dogs and swine differently from men; wolves and lions differently from the weak sheep. With wolves you cannot be too severe; with weak sheep you cannot be too gentle. Living as we do among the papists today, we must act as though we were living among heathen. Indeed, they are heathen seven times over; we should therefore, as St. Peter teaches [I Pet. 2:12], maintain good conduct among the heathen, that they may not speak any evil of us truthfully, as they would like to do. They are delighted when they hear that you make a boast of this teaching

---

42 Rom. 14:15, "You are no longer walking in love."

and give offense to timid souls. This affords them a pretext for denouncing the whole teaching as offensive and harmful, for they have no other way of demolishing it; they have to admit that it is true.

God grant us all that we may practice what we preach, putting our words into deeds. There are many among us who say, "Lord, Lord" [Matt. 7:21], and praise the teaching, but the doing and following are simply not there.

Let this suffice for the present as a renewed[43] admonition to guard against insurrection and giving offense, so that we ourselves may not be the agents for the desecration of God's holy word. Amen.

---

[43] On July 13, 1520, the Wittenberg students had broken out in a riot, which Luther blamed on inflammatory remarks by the university rector, Peter Burkhard. Luther was present at the meeting addressed by the rector, but left when he saw "that Satan was presiding over the meeting." On July 15, he preached a sermon, no longer extant, warning against riot and insurrection. It is probably to this sermon that he refers in the present treatise. The riot and the sermon are mentioned in letters to Spalatin dated July 14 and 17. S-J 1, 339-341; WA, Br 2, 142-144. Rector Burkhard later returned to Ingolstadt, where he was among the seventeen members of the faculty who in 1523 issued articles denouncing Luther's teachings as heretical. Enders, *Briefwechsel*, 2, 440, n. 1.

CL 2, 310, n. 23, suggests the possibility that *newen* ("renewed") was intended actually as *trewen* ("sincere"), that this last sentence thus includes repetition of the title of the treatise in which a printer's error has crept in on one letter.

TEMPORAL AUTHORITY:
TO WHAT EXTENT
IT SHOULD BE OBEYED

1523

Translated by J. J. Schindel

Revised by Walther I. Brandt

INTRODUCTION

In 1520, in *An Open Letter to the Christian Nobility*, Luther denied that the spiritual authority (the church) is exempt from the jurisdiction of the temporal authority (the state).[1] Yet in 1521, at Worms, he himself refused to comply with the order of the highest temporal authority, the emperor, to recant the numerous books he had written and published. And following his excommunication, several rulers issued orders forbidding their subjects to own or read his books.[2]

Could a Christian recognize the validity of such decrees? Is he obligated to obey such orders emanating from the civil authority? Should he resist them? What of Christ's instructions on nonresistance in Matt. 5:38-41 and Rom. 12:19? Must the Christian's submission to "the governing authorities" (Rom. 13:1) be absolute? Many of Luther's sincere followers were perturbed about the scriptural injunction, "Do not resist evil" (Matt. 5:39). While at the Wartburg he sent to Melanchthon advice on this point, which they had frequently discussed,[3] to the effect that the gospel as such had nothing to do with the temporal sword, and that a truly Christian society had no need of it. His letter includes a number of statements and illustrations which reappear in our present treatise, such as John the Baptist's advice to soldiers (Luke 3:14), David's use of the sword,[4] and others.

By an edict of January 20, 1522, the Imperial Council of Regency in effect condemned such religious innovations as com-

---

[1] *PE* 2, 66-72; *WA* 6, 407-410.
[2] The Duke of Bavaria on March 5, 1522, had issued the first of a series of religious mandates posted throughout his realm, forbidding all his subjects to read or discuss Luther's books. Sigmund Riezler, *Geschichte Baierns* (8 vols.; Gotha, 1878-1914), IV, 79-80. Duke George of Saxony issued such an order to all his officials on February 10, 1522, the text of which may be seen in *S-J* 2, 86-88; Gess, *Akten und Briefe*, I, 269-271. See also in this volume, p. 284, n. 11, on Duke George's proscription of Luther's German New Testament.
[3] Luther's letter to Melanchthon of July 13, 1521, is obviously a reply to an earlier inquiry on the subject. *WA*, Br 2, 357-359.
[4] See pp. 87, 93.

77

munion in both kinds, clerical marriage, and the discarding of vestments. Copies of the edict were sent to secular and ecclesiastical princes, who were urged to impose severe penalties for infractions of the edict.[5] In the Netherlands his adherents were being arrested, jailed, and compelled to recant.[6] He also heard rumors that the princes were taking counsel together against his life, for which they had legal authorization in the Edict of Worms.[7] What should be the attitude of sincere, believing Christians? If they were to bow before the edicts of temporal authority, how could or should the gospel be preserved?

On the positive side, what were the duties of a Christian prince? While on his way back to Wittenberg from his Wartburg exile, Luther wrote Spalatin on May 5, 1522, that it was the elector's duty to provide for the "salvation" of his subjects and to keep the "wolves" from destroying them.[8] On September 21, 1522, in response to a number of questions, some of which concerned the relationship between the gospel and the worldly sword, Luther wrote Baron Schwarzenberg[9] that he intended soon to publish a special treatise on the subject.

---

[5] See the text of the edict in St. L. 15, 2194-2196, and in Gess, op. cit., I, 250-252; also Luther's bitter reaction to it in Receiving Both Kinds in the Sacrament (1522). LW 36, 246.

[6] Jakob Propst, prior of the Augustinian monastery at Antwerp and former student at Wittenberg, was arrested December 5, 1521, and brought before an ecclesiastical court. After harsh treatment, he recanted on February 9, 1522, in order to save his life. Later, however, he rescinded his recantation and managed to flee the country, in 1524 becoming pastor at Bremen, where he died in 1562. Samuel Macauley Jackson (ed.), The New Schaff-Herzog Encyclopedia of Religious Knowledge (12 vols.; Grand Rapids, Michigan: Baker Book House, 1949-1954), IX, 279.

[7] Kawerau (ed.), Köstlin's Martin Luther, I, 580.

[8] WA, Br 2, 515.

[9] Schwarzenberg, 1463-1528, was from a Frankish knightly family. He was noted as a warrior, and also for certain reforms in the criminal code of Bamberg which became the basis for the Carolina of Charles V in 1532. A warm supporter of Luther, he received and protected the Reformer's persecuted followers, and was a member of the Imperial Council of Regency at Nürnberg in 1522, and influential during its discussion of church matters. From 1501 on, he was chancellor under six successive bishops of Bamberg, but resigned his post in 1524 because of Bishop Weigand's intolerant attitude toward the evangelical movement. Thereupon he entered the service of the Margrave of Brandenburg, where he did much to further the Reformation. Luther's letter to the baron may be found in Wilhelm M. L. de Wette, Dr. Martin Luthers Briefe (Berlin: Reimer, 1826), II, 249, and WA, Br 2, 600-601.

When it became generally known that Luther had returned to Wittenberg and had succeeded in quelling the disturbances there, he was constantly urged to visit this place and that to settle questions of reformed church procedure and policy, especially in areas where the sectaries were active. From time to time he interrupted his busy schedule of activities at Wittenberg to go on preaching tours. In October, 1522, probably at the request of Duke John's court preacher, Wolfgang Stein, he undertook a tour which eventually brought him to Weimar. Here, with Duke John in the audience, he preached a series of six sermons, on October 19 and 24-26, the third and fourth of which are in effect a brief outline of this present treatise.[10]

The fourth sermon particularly is the direct forerunner of the treatise, being devoted almost entirely to a discussion of temporal authority—its divine origin, its limitations, and its proper exercise. Duke John, Wolfgang Stein, and others were so impressed by the ideas presented in it that they begged Luther to have it published.[11] But Luther had apparently spoken extemporaneously; he had neither transcript nor notes of the sermon.[12] Nevertheless, while elaborating his ideas into the form of a treatise, the fourth sermon was still so vivid in his mind that he repeated a number of quotations, proverbs, and historical allusions from it.

The treatise is divided into three parts. In the first part Luther upholds the divine origin of temporal authority; it is not needed for the true Christian, but was instituted by God so that evildoers might be restrained. In the second and major part he defines the limits within which the temporal power may act, pointing out that it has no power over faith or conscience, although it does have power over men's bodies and property. In the third part he discusses the manner in which a prince should exercise his power, a bit of pastoral advice that forms a remarkable contrast to the more famous document of just a decade later, Machiavelli's *The Prince*.

---

[10] The texts of these six sermons may be found in WA 10III, 341-352, 371-399, thanks to notes taken by some unidentified hearer which were first published in 1846. Enders, *Briefwechsel*, 4, 23, n. 1. The third and fourth sermons are on pp. 371-385.

[11] Köstlin, *op. cit.*, I, 581.

[12] See Luther's letter to Spalatin of November 3, 1522. WA, Br 2, 613-614.

The treatise is of more than religious significance. It is the first ethical defense of temporal government against the prevailing Roman Catholic concept that the church is the source of all earthly authority. The state, as well as the church, is of divine origin. Luther separates church and state, defines the sphere of each, but upholds the right of private judgment as against both authorities. The primary function of the state is to serve its people. The Christian has both the right and the duty to hold office under the state, even to the extent of serving as executioner if the need arises. Just as he opposed the Roman Catholic theory of the temporal power of the church, so Luther opposed the sectarian concept that a Christian should not participate actively in the affairs of government.

The composition of the treatise was begun shortly after Luther returned from his preaching tour near the end of October. It was completed by Christmas Day, 1522. We do not know just when it came from the press. Duke George, who was usually prompt to note any new product of Luther's pen, apparently had not yet heard of it when he wrote Count Albert of Mansfeld on March 12, 1523, about an insulting remark in one of Luther's published letters.[13] The first mention of the published treatise is in another letter from Duke George to Elector Frederick, March 21;[14] hence, it probably appeared early in March, 1523.

The following translation is a revision of the one that appeared in PE 3, 228-273, and is based on the first German edition printed by Nickel Schirlentz in Wittenberg, *Uon welltlicher uberkeytt wie weytt man yhr gehorsam schuldig sey*, as that has been reprinted with annotations in WA 11, (229) 245-280.

---

[13] See p. 85, n. 15.
[14] In this letter the duke calls upon the elector to take measures against the author, printer, and distributors of the treatise. See the text in Gess, *op. cit.*, I, 486-488.

TEMPORAL AUTHORITY: TO WHAT EXTENT IT SHOULD BE OBEYED

To the illustrious, highborn prince and lord, Lord John,[1] Duke of Saxony, Landgrave of Thuringia, Margrave of Meissen, my gracious lord.

Grace and peace in Christ. Again,[2] illustrious, highborn prince, gracious lord, necessity is laid upon me, and the entreaties of many, and above all your Princely Grace's wishes,[3] impel me to write about temporal authority and the sword it bears, how to use it in a Christian manner, and to what extent men are obligated to obey it. You are perturbed over Christ's injunction in Matthew 5 [:39, 25, 40], "Do not resist evil, but make friends with your accuser; and if any one would take your coat, let him have your cloak as well"; and Romans 12 [:19], "Vengeance is mine, I will repay, says the Lord." These very texts were used long ago against St. Augustine by the prince Volusian, who charged that Christian teaching permits the wicked to do evil, and is incompatible with the temporal sword.[4]

---

[1] John the Steadfast (1468-1532) was the brother of Frederick the Wise, whom he succeeded in the Electorate in 1525. Politically less sagacious than his brother, John nevertheless was a man of fearless courage and deep evangelical conviction. It was he who in the elector's absence refused to publish the bull directed against Luther. It was he who advised his brother to adopt the Reformer's cause more openly. It was he to whom Luther sent single sheets of the Wartburg New Testament as they became available, that John might be able daily to read the Scriptures.

[2] Luther had treated this same matter before in *A Sincere Admonition* (1522) (in this volume, pp. 51-74) and in *An Open Letter to the Christian Nobility* (1520). PE 2, 61-164. Cf. p. 83.

[3] Duke John himself was among those who requested Luther to write this treatise. See the Introduction, p. 79.

[4] Volusian was the brother of Albina to whom, with her daughter Melania and son-in-law Pirian, Augustine had dedicated his treatise *Contra Pelagium et Coelestium*. Volusian carried on some correspondence in the year A.D. 412 with Augustine, then Bishop of Hippo, on theological matters which troubled him (*Letters* 132, 135, 137). His doubts concerning the compatibility of

The sophists[5] in the universities have also been perplexed by these texts, because they could not reconcile the two things. In order not to make heathen of the princes, they taught that Christ did not command these things but merely offered them as advice or counsel to those who would be perfect.[6] So Christ had to become a liar and be in error in order that the princes might come off with honor, for they could not exalt the princes without degrading Christ—wretched, blind sophists that they are. And their poisonous error has spread thus through the whole world until everyone regards these teachings of Christ not as precepts binding on all Christians alike but as mere counsels for the perfect. It has gone so far that they have granted the imperfect estate of the sword and of temporal authority not only to the perfect estate of the bishops, but even to the pope, that most perfect estate of all; in fact, they have ascribed it to no one on earth so completely as to him! So thoroughly has the devil taken possession of the sophists and the universities that they themselves do not know what and how they speak or teach.

Christ's doctrine of nonresistance with the laws and customs of the state, however, was discussed in an exchange of letters between Augustine and Marcellinus that same year (*Letters* 136 and 138). Marcellinus, proconsul of Africa, was the tribune appointed by Emperor Honorius to preside over the June, 411, conference which put an end to the Donatist schism; to him Augustine dedicated the first two books of his *City of God*. The texts of these letters are in Sister Wilfrid Parsons (trans.), Roy J. Deferrari's (ed.), *Saint Augustine: Letters*, Vol. *III. FC* 20; see especially pp. 17, 41-48. *MPL* 33, 514-515 and 525-535.

[5] Luther often referred to the scholastic theologians as "*Sophisten.*"

[6] Cf. Luther's detailed treatment of the second table of the law, in which his dispute with the Paris theologians on this issue of command vs. counsel looms large, in his *Misuse of the Mass* (1521). *LW* 36, 204-210, especially p. 205, n. 66. The distinction between commands (*praecepta*) and counsels (*consilia*) was already discussed by Tertullian (*ca.* 160-*ca.* 220) in connection with Paul's own treatment of the subject in I Corinthians 7 (see Tertullian's *Second Book to His Wife*, par. 1). Thomas Aquinas (*ca.* 1225-1274) too distinguished between commandment and counsel in terms of obligation and option. It was held that the New Law—of liberty—fittingly added counsels to the commandments, as the Old Law—of bondage—did not. These "evangelical counsels" were to enable man more speedily to attain to eternal happiness through the renunciation of the things of the world, through poverty, chastity, and obedience in keeping with 1 John 2:16. They were not proposed for all, but for those who are fit to observe them, as in Matt. 19:12, 21. The same injunction of Christ, e.g., to love the enemy, is said to be a command, necessary to salvation, in the sense that we should be mentally prepared to do good; "but that anybody should actually and promptly behave thus toward an enemy when there is no

I hope, however, that I may instruct the princes and the temporal authorities in such a way that they will remain Christians —and Christ will remain Lord—and yet Christ's commands will not for their sake have to become mere counsels.

I do this as a humble service to your Princely Grace, for the benefit of everyone who may need it, and to the praise and glory of Christ our Lord. I commend your Princely Grace with all your kin to the grace of God. May he mercifully have you in his keeping.

At Wittenberg, New Year's Day,[7] 1523.

Your Princely Grace's obedient servant,

MARTIN LUTHER

Some time ago I addressed a little book to the German nobility,[8] setting forth their Christian office and functions. How far they acted on my suggestions is only too evident.[9] Hence, I must change my tactics and write them, this time, what they should omit and not do. I fear this new effort will have as little effect on them as the other, and that they will continue to be princes and never become Christians. For God the Almighty has made our rulers mad; they actually think they can do—and order their subjects to do—whatever they please. And the subjects make the mistake of believing that they, in turn, are bound to obey their rulers in everything. It has gone so far that the rulers have begun ordering the people to get rid of certain books,[10] and to

---

special need, is to be referred to the particular counsels." *Summa Theologica,* I, II, ques. 108, art. 4. *FC* 3, 319. Cf. *Summa Theologica,* 2, II, ques. 184, arts. 3 and 7, where the state of perfection is said to be most nearly realized in the monastic kind of life, and more so in the "episcopal" than in the "religious" state. Further bibliography on this question is given in *MA*³ 5, 395, n. 9, 21; see also *MA*³ 5, 421, n. 146, 32. See Luther's discussion of the question in this volume, pp. 87-88, 255-256, 275-276, 283, 289-290.

[7] Thinking of the new year as beginning with the day of Christ's birth, Luther undoubtedly meant here Christmas Day, December 25, 1522. Cf. the reference to New Year in the concluding line of his Christmas hymn, *"Vom himmel hoch"*: *"und singen uns solch neues Jahr,"* translated by Catherine Winkworth as "a glad new year to all the earth." *Service Book and Hymnal* (published by eight co-operating Lutheran churches), No. 22.

[8] *An Open Letter to the Christian Nobility* (1520). *PE* 2, 61-164; *WA* 6 (381), 404-469. See p. 81, n. 2.

[9] This is a reference to the Edict of Worms and its implementation; see the Introduction, p. 77.

[10] Luther's books. See p. 77, n. 2.

believe and conform to what the rulers prescribe. They are thereby presumptuously setting themselves in God's place, lording it over men's consciences and faith, and schooling the Holy Spirit according to their own crackbrained ideas. Nevertheless, they let it be known that they are not to be contradicted, and are to be called gracious lords all the same.

They issue public proclamations, and say that this is the emperor's command[11] and that they want to be obedient Christian princes, just as if they really meant it and no one noticed the scoundrel behind the mask. If the emperor were to take a castle or a city from them or command some other injustice, we should then see how quickly they would find themselves obliged to resist the emperor and disobey him. But when it comes to fleecing the poor or venting their spite on the word of God, it becomes a matter of "obedience to the imperial command." Such people were formerly called scoundrels; now they have to be called obedient Christians princes. Still they will not permit anyone to appear before them for a hearing or to defend himself, no matter how humbly he may petition. If the emperor or anyone else were to treat them this way, they would regard it as quite intolerable. Such are the princes who today rule the empire in the German lands.[12] This is also why things are necessarily going so well in all the lands, as we see!

Because the raging of such fools tends toward the suppression of the Christian faith, the denying of the divine word, and the blaspheming of the Divine Majesty, I can and will no longer just look at my ungracious lords and angry nobles; I shall have to

---

[11] A proclamation dated November 7, 1522, issued by Duke George of ducal Saxony and printed and posted at various places in his realm, reminds his subjects of previous prohibitions of buying or reading Luther's books, mentions that Luther has recently published the New Testament in a German translation adorned with disgraceful drawings of the pope, and commands all subjects to deliver up their copies to the duke's nearest representative and receive the purchase price in return. A time limit is set for this surrender; after that, failure to comply will be punished. See the text in Gess, *op. cit.*, I, 386-387. Cf. also Duke George's proclamation of February 10, 1522 (see p. 77, n. 2), in which he bases his "Christian duty" upon the imperial edict of Charles V which placed Luther under the ban and proscribed the reading and printing of his books.

[12] Luther is apparently thinking particularly of the Imperial Council of Regency set up by Charles V to act as a central government during his absence from the German nation. See the Introduction, p. 78, and n. 5 there.

resist them, at least with words. And since I have not been in terror of their idol, the pope,[13] who threatens to deprive me of soul and of heaven, I must show that I am not in terror of his lackeys[14] and bullies[15] who threaten to deprive me of body and of earth. God grant that they may have to rage until the gray coats[16] perish, and help us that we may not die of their threatenings. Amen.

First, we must provide a sound basis for the civil law and sword so no one will doubt that it is in the world by God's will and ordinance. The passages which do this are the following: Romans 12, "Let every soul [*seele*] be subject to the governing authority, for there is no authority except from God; the authority

---

[13] Luther's criticism is thus directed against the Catholic princes.

[14] *Schupen*, literally, "scales," is a favorite term of Luther for designating the adherents of the pope. He takes it from the figure in Job 41:15-17, where the devil is pictured as a dragon thickly covered with scales which stick close together. Grimm, *Deutsches Wörterbuch*, IX, 2014.

[15] *Wasserblassen* (literally, "water bubble") was a derogatory German rendering of the Latin term *bulla*, which was the common designation for an official papal mandate or "bull." The *bulla* (literally, "bubble") actually took its name from the leaden plate with which the document was authenticated in the middle ages, namely, a circular plate in form resembling an air bubble floating upon the water (*LW* 36, 77, n. 137). Luther delighted in recalling the etymology of the term as a way of deflating the ego of the bull's author (see his sarcastic *Bulla Coenae Domini* of 1522 in *WA* 8, 712-713). He used the term *Wasserblassen* also in a derived sense for such "blusterers" or "windbags" as were devotees and adherents of the pope and his bulls. This is the epithet which was applied to Duke George of Saxony in a letter from Luther to Hartmuth von Cronberg of March 26 or 27, 1522. It is possible that Luther did not actually mention Duke George by name and that in a printing not authorized by Luther the duke's name was inserted, though Otto Clemen believes the conjunction of name and epithet was original with Luther (*WA*, Br 2, 484-485). At any rate, when the letter was brought to his attention, Duke George wrote Luther on December 30, 1522, a dignified letter of protest inquiring as to Luther's part and purpose in the matter. Luther replied on January 3, 1523, in impolite terms, neither denying nor accepting responsibility but repeating the offensive term in a context where the reference to Duke George had to be unmistakable. See the text of the three letters in *S-J* 2, 104-110, 153-154, 158-159; *WA* 10^{II}, (42) 53-60; *WA*, Br 2, 642, and 3, 4.

[16] *Grawen röck* could have reference here to the plain and humble garb of the peasant, utterly unpretentious and, presumably, forever plentiful. *WA* 30^{II}, 711, n. 42, 19. Usually it has reference to the world-renunciation of monasticism, which people could hardly imagine ever passing away, as in *LW* 21, 254-255; *LW* 14, 24, n. 24. In view of Luther's own anticipation of monasticism's imminent decline (see, e.g., p. 143 in this volume), he may here be simply borrowing—imprecisely—a current expression for indicating a period without end. Grimm, *Deutsches Wörterbuch*, VIII, 1097.

which everywhere [*allenthalben*] exists has been ordained by God. He then who resists the governing authority resists the ordinance of God, and he who resists God's ordinance will incur judgment." [17] Again, in I Peter 2 [:13-14], "Be subject to every kind of human ordinance, whether it be to the king as supreme, or to governors,[18] as those who have been sent by him to punish the wicked and to praise the righteous."

The law of this temporal sword has existed from the beginning of the world. For when Cain slew his brother Abel, he was in such great terror of being killed in turn that God even placed a special prohibition on it and suspended the sword for his sake, so that no one was to slay him [Gen. 4:14-15]. He would not have had this fear if he had not seen and heard from Adam that murderers are to be slain. Moreover, after the Flood, God re-established and confirmed this in unmistakable terms when he said in Genesis 9 [:6], "Whoever sheds the blood of man, by man shall his blood be shed." This cannot be understood as a plague or punishment of God upon murderers, for many murderers who are punished in other ways or pardoned altogether[19] continue to live, and eventually die by means other than the sword. Rather, it is said of the law of the sword, that a murderer is guilty of death and in justice is to be slain by the sword. Now if justice should be hindered or the sword have become negligent so that the murderer dies a natural death, Scripture is not on that account false when it says, "Whoever sheds the blood of man, by man shall his blood be shed." The credit or blame belongs to men if this law instituted by God is not carried out; just as other commandments of God, too, are broken.

Afterward it was also confirmed by the law of Moses, Exodus 21 [:14], "If a man wilfully kills another, you shall take him from

---

[17] Luther's citation here of Rom. 13:1-2 differs slightly from his rendering of the same passage in his New Testament; cf *WA*, DB 7, 68-69. Emser approved heartily of the word *"seele,"* which Luther dropped from his 1522 Testament, and of the word *"allenthalben,"* which Luther dropped from his 1546 Testament. *WA*, DB 7, 569-570. Luther's chapter reference for the same passage is given correctly on other occasions in this same treatise.

[18] *Pflegern* could have reference to any kind of administrators, supervisors, trustees, guardians, or stewards; not simply to politically appointed executive officers. Grimm, *Deutsches Wörterbuch*, VII, 1748. Luther substituted the term *Heubtleuten* in his 1546 New Testament. *WA*, DB 7, 305.

[19] *Durch pusss oder gunst;* see MA³ 5, 396, n. 11, 32.

my altar, that he may die." And again, in the same chapter,[20] "A life for a life, an eye for an eye, a tooth for a tooth, a foot for a foot, a hand for a hand, a wound for a wound, a stripe for a stripe." In addition, Christ also confirms it when he says to Peter in the garden, "He that takes the sword will perish by the sword" [Matt. 26:52], which is to be interpreted exactly like the Genesis 9 [:6] passage, "Whoever sheds the blood of man," etc. Christ is undoubtedly referring in these words to that very passage which he thereby wishes to cite and to confirm. John the Baptist also teaches the same thing. When the soldiers asked him what they should do, he answered, "Do neither violence nor injustice to any one, and be content with your wages" [Luke 3:14]. If the sword were not a godly estate, he should have directed them to get out of it, since he was supposed to make the people perfect and instruct them in a proper Christian way.[21] Hence, it is certain and clear enough that it is God's will that the temporal sword and law be used for the punishment of the wicked and the protection of the upright.

Second. There appear to be powerful arguments to the contrary. Christ says in Matthew 5 [:38-41], "You have heard that it was said to them of old: An eye for an eye, a tooth for a tooth. But I say to you, Do not resist evil; but if anyone strikes you on the right cheek, turn to him the other also. And if anyone would sue you and take your coat, let him have your cloak as well. And if anyone forces you to go one mile, go with him two miles," etc. Likewise Paul in Romans 12 [:19], "Beloved, defend[22] not yourselves, but leave it to the wrath of God; for it is written, 'Vengeance is mine; I will repay, says the Lord.'" And in Matthew 5 [:44], "Love your enemies, do good to them that hate you." And again, in I Peter 2 [3:9], "Do not return evil for evil, or reviling for reviling," etc. These and similar passages would certainly make it appear as though in the New Testament Christians were to have no temporal sword.

Hence, the sophists also say that Christ has thereby abolished the law of Moses. Of such commandments they make "counsels"

---

[20] In the sequence of Exod. 21:23-25 Luther omits "a burn for a burn."
[21] Cf. Matt. 11:9-11.
[22] *Schützet* is closer to the Vulgate's *defendentes* than to the *Rechnet* (literally, "avenge") of Luther's 1522 New Testament. *WA*, DB 7, 68.

for the perfect. They divide Christian teaching and Christians into two classes. One part they call the perfect, and assign to it such counsels. The other they call the imperfect, and assign to it the commandments. This they do out of sheer wantonness and caprice, without any scriptural basis. They fail to see that in the same passage Christ lays such stress on his teaching that he is unwilling to have the least word of it set aside, and condemns to hell those who do not love their enemies.[23] Therefore, we must interpret these passages differently, so that Christ's words may apply to everyone alike, be he perfect or imperfect. For perfection and imperfection do not consist in works, and do not establish any distinct external order among Christians. They exist in the heart, in faith and love, so that those who believe and love the most are the perfect ones, whether they be outwardly male or female, prince or peasant, monk or layman. For love and faith produce no sects[24] or outward differences.

Third. Here we must divide the children of Adam and all mankind into two classes, the first belonging to the kingdom of God, the second to the kingdom of the world. Those who belong to the kingdom of God are all the true believers who are in Christ and under Christ, for Christ is King and Lord in the kingdom of God, as Psalm 2 [:6] and all of Scripture says. For this reason he came into the world, that he might begin God's kingdom and establish it in the world. Therefore, he says before Pilate, "My kingdom is not of the world, but every one who is of the truth hears my voice" [John 18:36-37]. In the gospel he continually refers to the kingdom of God, and says, "Amend your ways, the kingdom of God is at hand" [Matt. 4:17, 10:7]; again, "Seek first the kingdom of God and his righteousness" [Matt. 6:33]. He also calls the gospel a gospel of the kingdom of God;[25] because it teaches, governs, and upholds[26] God's kingdom.

---

23 Cf. Matt. 5:17-22.

24 Cf. Gal. 3:28; 5:6. By "sect" Luther means the divergences, rivalries, and jealousies between the various monastic orders and theological factions. Cf. LW 35, 80, and LW 36, 78, n. 138.

25 In Mark 1:14 the KJV phrase is more accurate than that of the RSV, which omits the term "kingdom." George Arthur Buttrick (commentary ed.), The Interpreter's Bible (New York: Abingdon-Cokesbury, 1951-1957), VII, 655.

26 Enthellt is here taken to mean erhält, following CL 2, 365, n. 6.

Now observe, these people need no temporal law or sword. If all the world were composed of real Christians, that is, true believers, there would be no need for or benefits from prince, king, lord, sword, or law. They would serve no purpose, since Christians have in their heart the Holy Spirit, who both teaches and makes them to do injustice to no one, to love everyone, and to suffer injustice and even death willingly and cheerfully at the hands of anyone. Where there is nothing but the unadulterated doing of right and bearing of wrong, there is no need for any suit, litigation, court, judge, penalty, law, or sword. For this reason it is impossible that the temporal sword and law should find any work to do among Christians, since they do of their own accord much more than all laws and teachings can demand, just as Paul says in I Timothy 1 [:9], "The law is not laid down for the just but for the lawless."

Why is this? It is because the righteous man of his own accord does all and more than the law demands. But the unrighteous do nothing that the law demands; therefore, they need the law to instruct, constrain, and compel them to do good. A good tree needs no instruction or law to bear good fruit;[27] its nature causes it to bear according to its kind without any law or instruction. I would take to be quite a fool any man who would make a book full of laws and statutes for an apple tree telling it how to bear apples and not thorns, when the tree is able by its own nature to do this better than the man with all his books can describe and demand. Just so, by the Spirit and by faith all Christians are so thoroughly disposed and conditioned in their very nature[28] that they do right and keep the law better than one can teach them with all manner of statutes; so far as they themselves are concerned, no statutes or laws are needed.

You ask: Why, then, did God give so many commandments to all mankind, and why does Christ prescribe in the gospel so many things for us to do? Of this I have written at length in the

---

[27] Cf. Matt. 7:17-18.
[28] *Aller ding genaturt;* cf. *MA*[3] 5, 396, n. 14, 3, *"durchaus von Natur geartet,"* and Grimm, *Deutsches Wörterbuch,* IV, 3347, *"die damalige form des sog. determinismus."*

Postils[29] and elsewhere. To put it here as briefly as possible, Paul says that the law has been laid down for the sake of the lawless [I Tim. 1:9], that is, so that those who are not Christians may through the law be restrained outwardly from evil deeds, as we shall hear later. Now since no one is by nature Christian or righteous, but altogether sinful and wicked, God through the law puts them all under restraint so they dare not wilfully implement their wickedness in actual deeds. In addition, Paul ascribes to the law another function in Romans 7 and Galatians 2,[30] that of teaching men to recognize sin in order that it may make them humble unto grace and unto faith in Christ. Christ does the same thing here in Matthew 5 [:39], where he teaches that we should not resist evil; by this he is interpreting the law and teaching what ought to be and must be the state and temper of a true Christian, as we shall hear further later on.[31]

Fourth. All who are not Christians belong to the kingdom of the world and are under the law. There are few true believers, and still fewer who live a Christian life, who do not resist evil and indeed themselves do no evil. For this reason God has provided for them a different government beyond the Christian estate and kingdom of God. He has subjected them to the sword so that, even though they would like to, they are unable to practice their wickedness, and if they do practice it they cannot do so without fear or with success and impunity. In the same way a savage wild beast is bound with chains and ropes so that it cannot bite and tear as it would normally do, even though it would like to; whereas a tame and gentle animal needs no restraint, but is harmless despite the lack of chains and ropes.

---

[29] The Postils were a collection of sermons expounding the Epistles and Gospels for the Sundays and festivals of the church year. Luther had published the Advent Postil in Latin in March of 1521 (see the text in WA 7 [458] 463-537). His German Postil, the so-called Wartburg Postil, began to appear in March, 1522, with the Christmas-Epiphany cycle, which preceded the German Advent sermons by more than a month (see the respective texts in WA 10I, 1, [vii] 1-728 and WA 10I, 2, [ix] 1-208). On the function of the law see especially WA 7, 476-477, and 504-505; see also in Luther's 1521 *A Brief Instruction on What to Look for and Expect in the Gospels*, originally intended as an introduction to the entire Wartburg Postil, "The fact that Christ and the apostles . . . explain the law is to be counted a benefit just like any other work of Christ." LW 35, 120.
[30] Rom. 7:7-13; Gal. 3:19, 24; cf. Rom. 3:20.
[31] See pp. 102-103.

If this were not so, men would devour one another, seeing that the whole world is evil and that among thousands there is scarcely a single true Christian. No one could support wife and child, feed himself, and serve God. The world would be reduced to chaos. For this reason God has ordained two governments: the spiritual, by which the Holy Spirit produces Christians and righteous people under Christ; and the temporal, which restrains the un-Christian and wicked so that—no thanks to them—they are obliged to keep still and to maintain an outward peace. Thus does St. Paul interpret the temporal sword in Romans 13 [:3], when he says it is not a terror to good conduct but to bad. And Peter says it is for the punishment of the wicked [I Pet. 2:14].

If anyone attempted to rule the world by the gospel and to abolish all temporal law and sword on the plea that all are baptized and Christian, and that, according to the gospel, there shall be among them no law or sword—or need for either—pray tell me, friend, what would he be doing? He would be loosing the ropes and chains of the savage wild beasts and letting them bite and mangle everyone, meanwhile insisting that they were harmless, tame, and gentle creatures; but I would have the proof in my wounds. Just so would the wicked under the name of Christian abuse evangelical freedom, carry on their rascality, and insist that they were Christians subject neither to law nor sword, as some are already raving and ranting.[32]

To such a one we must say: Certainly it is true that Christians, so far as they themselves are concerned, are subject neither to law nor sword, and have need of neither. But take heed and first fill the world with real Christians before you attempt to rule it in a Christian and evangelical manner. This you will never accomplish; for the world and the masses are and always will be un-Christian, even if they are all baptized and Christian in name. Christians are few and far between (as the saying is). Therefore, it is out of the question that there should be a common Christian government over the whole world, or indeed over a single country or any considerable body of people, for the wicked always outnumber the good. Hence, a man who would venture to govern

---

32 The allusion is to the Anabaptists.

an entire country or the world with the gospel would be like a shepherd who should put together in one fold wolves, lions, eagles, and sheep, and let them mingle freely with one another, saying, "Help yourselves, and be good and peaceful toward one another. The fold is open, there is plenty of food. You need have no fear of dogs and clubs." The sheep would doubtless keep the peace and allow themselves to be fed and governed peacefully, but they would not live long, nor would one beast survive another.

For this reason one must carefully distinguish between these two governments. Both must be permitted to remain; the one to produce righteousness, the other to bring about external peace and prevent evil deeds. Neither one is sufficient in the world without the other. No one can become righteous in the sight of God by means of the temporal government, without Christ's spiritual government. Christ's government does not extend over all men; rather, Christians are always a minority in the midst of non-Christians. Now where temporal government or law alone prevails, there sheer hypocrisy is inevitable, even though the commandments be God's very own. For without the Holy Spirit in the heart no one becomes truly righteous, no matter how fine the works he does. On the other hand, where the spiritual government alone prevails over land and people, there wickedness is given free rein and the door is open for all manner of rascality, for the world as a whole cannot receive or comprehend it.

Now you see the intent of Christ's words which we quoted above from Matthew 5,[33] that Christians should not go to law or use the temporal sword among themselves. Actually, he says this only to his beloved Christians, those who alone accept it and act accordingly, who do not make "counsels"[34] out of it as the sophists do, but in their heart are so disposed and conditioned [genaturt] by the Spirit that they do evil to no one and willingly endure evil at the hands of others. If now the whole world were Christian in this sense, then these words would apply to all, and all would act accordingly. Since the world is un-Christian, however, these words do not apply to all; and all do not act accordingly, but are under another government in which those who are

[33] See the quotation of Matt. 5:38-41 on p. 87.
[34] See p. 87, n. 6.

92

not Christian are kept under external constraint and compelled to keep the peace and do what is good.

This is also why Christ did not wield the sword, or give it a place in his kingdom.[35] For he is a king over Christians and rules by his Holy Spirit alone, without law. Although he sanctions the sword, he did not make use of it, for it serves no purpose in his kingdom, in which there are none but the upright. Hence, David of old was not permitted to build the temple [II Sam. 7:4-13], because he had wielded the sword and had shed much blood. Not that he had done wrong thereby, but because he could not be a type of Christ, who without the sword was to have a kingdom of peace. It had to be built instead by Solomon, whose name in German means "Friedrich" or "peaceful";[36] he had a peaceful kingdom, by which the truly peaceful kingdom of Christ, the real Friedrich and Solomon, could be represented. Again, "during the entire building of the temple no tool of iron was heard," as the text says [I Kings 6:7]; all for this reason, that Christ, without constraint and force, without law and sword, was to have a people who would serve him willingly.

That is what the prophets mean in Psalm 110 [:3], "Your people will act of their free volition"; and in Isaiah 11 [:9], "They shall not hurt or destroy in all my holy mountain"; and again in Isaiah 2 [:4], "They shall beat their swords into plowshares and their spears into pruning hooks, and no one shall lift up the sword against another, neither shall they put their efforts into war any more," etc. Whoever would extend the application of these and similar passages to wherever Christ's name is mentioned, would entirely pervert the Scripture; rather, they are spoken only of true Christians, who really do this among themselves.

Fifth. But you say: if Christians then do not need the temporal sword or law, why does Paul say to all Christians in Romans 13 [:1], "Let all souls be subject to the governing authority," and St. Peter, "Be subject to every human ordinance"

---

[35] Cf. Matt. 26:52-53; John 18:36.
[36] "Solomon" is derived from the Hebrew word for "peace," *shalom*. The equivalent German "Friedrich" means literally "one who is rich in peace." Cf. Jerome's *Liber de Nominibus Hebraicis*: "*Salomon, pacificus, sive pacatus erit.*" *MPL* 23, 843.

[I Pet. 2:13], etc., as quoted above?[37] Answer: I have just said that Christians, among themselves and by and for themselves, need no law or sword, since it is neither necessary nor useful for them. Since a true Christian lives and labors on earth not for himself alone but for his neighbor, he does by the very nature of his spirit even what he himself has no need of, but is needful and useful to his neighbor. Because the sword is most beneficial and necessary for the whole world in order to preserve peace, punish sin, and restrain the wicked, the Christian submits most willingly to the rule of the sword, pays his taxes, honors those in authority,[38] serves, helps, and does all he can to assist the governing authority, that it may continue to function and be held in honor and fear. Although he has no need of these things for himself—to him they are not essential—nevertheless, he concerns himself about what is serviceable and of benefit to others, as Paul teaches in Ephesians 5 [:21–6:9].

Just as he performs all other works of love which he himself does not need—he does not visit the sick in order that he himself may be made well, or feed others because he himself needs food—so he serves the governing authority not because he needs it but for the sake of others, that they may be protected and that the wicked may not become worse. He loses nothing by this; such service in no way harms him, yet it is of great benefit to the world. If he did not so serve he would be acting not as a Christian but even contrary to love; he would also be setting a bad example to others who in like manner would not submit to authority, even though they were not Christians. In this way the gospel would be brought into disrepute, as though it taught insurrection and produced self-willed people unwilling to benefit or serve others, when in fact it makes a Christian the servant of all.[39] Thus in Matthew 17 [:27] Christ paid the half-shekel tax that he might not offend them, although he had no need to do so.

Thus you observe in the words of Christ quoted above from

---

[37] See p. 86.
[38] Cf. Rom. 13:6-7.
[39] See Luther's 1520 *The Freedom of a Christian* where Romans 13 and Matthew 17 are also cited in illustration of the Christian's willing service to others. *LW* 31, 343-377, especially p. 369.

Matthew 5[40] that he clearly teaches that Christians among themselves should have no temporal sword or law. He does not,
however, forbid one to serve and be subject to those who do
have the secular sword and law. Rather, since you do not need
it and should not have it, you are to serve all the more those
who have not attained to such heights as you and who therefore
do still need it. Although you do not need to have your enemy
punished, your afflicted neighbor does. You should help him that
he may have peace and that his enemy may be curbed, but this is
not possible unless the governing authority is honored and feared.
Christ does not say, "You shall not serve the governing authority
or be subject to it," but rather, "Do not resist evil" [Matt. 5:39],
as much as to say, "Behave in such a way that you bear everything, so that you may not need the governing authority to help
you and serve you or be beneficial or essential for you, but that
you in turn may help and serve it, being beneficial and essential
to it. I would have you be too exalted and far too noble to have
any need of it; it should rather have need of you."

Sixth. You ask whether a Christian too may bear the temporal
sword and punish the wicked, since Christ's words, "Do not resist
evil," are so clear and definite that the sophists have had to make
of them a "counsel." Answer: You have now heard two propositions. One is that the sword can have no place among Christians;
therefore, you cannot bear it among Christians or hold it over
them, for they do not need it. The question, therefore, must be
referred to the other group, the non-Christians, whether you may
bear it there in a Christian manner. Here the other proposition
applies, that you are under obligation to serve and assist the sword
by whatever means you can, with body, goods, honor, and soul.
For it is something which you do not need, but which is very
beneficial and essential for the whole world and for your neighbor.
Therefore, if you see that there is a lack of hangmen, constables,
judges, lords, or princes, and you find that you are qualified, you
should offer your services and seek the position, that the essential
governmental authority may not be despised and become enfeebled
or perish. The world cannot and dare not dispense with it.

Here is the reason why you should do this: In such a case

---

[40] Matt. 5:38-41 was quoted on p. 87.

you would be entering entirely into the service and work of others, which would be of advantage neither to yourself nor your property or honor, but only to your neighbor and to others. You would be doing it not with the purpose of avenging yourself or returning evil for evil, but for the good of your neighbor and for the maintenance of the safety and peace of others. For yourself, you would abide by the gospel and govern yourself according to Christ's word [Matt. 5:39-40], gladly turning the other cheek and letting the cloak go with the coat when the matter concerned you and your cause.

In this way the two propositions are brought into harmony with one another: at one and the same time you satisfy God's kingdom inwardly and the kingdom of the world outwardly. You suffer evil and injustice, and yet at the same time you punish evil and injustice; you do not resist evil, and yet at the same time, you do resist it. In the one case, you consider yourself and what is yours; in the other, you consider your neighbor and what is his. In what concerns you and yours, you govern yourself by the gospel and suffer injustice toward yourself as a true Christian; in what concerns the person or property of others, you govern yourself according to love and tolerate no injustice toward your neighbor. The gospel does not forbid this; in fact, in other places it actually commands it.

From the beginning of the world all the saints have wielded the sword in this way: Adam and his descendants; Abraham when he rescued Lot, his brother's son, and routed the four kings as related in Genesis 14 [:8-16], although he was a thoroughly evangelical man. Thus did Samuel, the holy prophet, slay King Agag, as we read in I Samuel 15 [:33]; and Elijah slew the prophets of Baal, I Kings 18 [:40]. So too did Moses, Joshua, the children of Israel, Samson, David, and all the kings and princes in the Old Testament wield the sword; also Daniel and his associates, Hananiah, Azariah, and Mishael, in Babylon; and Joseph in Egypt, and so on.

Should anyone contend that the Old Testament is abrogated and no longer in effect, and that therefore such examples cannot be set before Christians, I answer: That is not so. St. Paul says in I Corinthians 10 [:3-4], "They ate the same spiritual food as we, and drank the same spiritual drink from the Rock, which is Christ." That is, they had the same Spirit and faith in Christ as we have, and were just as much Christians as we are. Therefore, wherein they did right, all Christians do right, from the beginning of the world unto the end. For time and external circumstances make no difference among Christians. Neither is it true that the Old Testament was abrogated in such a way that it must not be kept, or that whoever kept it fully would be doing wrong, as St. Jerome and many others[41] mistakenly held. Rather, it is abrogated in the sense that we are free to keep it or not to keep it, and it is no longer necessary to keep it on penalty of losing one's soul, as was the case at that time.

Paul says in I Corinthians 7 [:19] and Galatians 6 [:15] that neither uncircumcision nor circumcision counts for anything, but only a new creature in Christ. That is, it is not sin to be uncircumcised, as the Jews thought, nor is it sin to be circumcised, as the Gentiles thought. Either is right and permissible for him who does not think he will thereby become righteous or be saved. The same is true of all other parts of the Old Testament; it is not wrong to ignore them and it is not wrong to abide by them, but it is permissible and proper either to follow them or to omit them. Indeed, if it were necessary or profitable for the salvation of one's neighbor, it would be necessary to keep all of them. For everyone is under obligation to do what is for his neighbor's good, be it Old Testament or New, Jewish or Gentile, as Paul teaches

---

[41] Jerome (ca. 342-420), translator of the Vulgate and distinguished biblical commentator, had been attacked by Augustine (354-430) in 394 or 395 for his interpretation of Gal. 2:11-14. In the ensuing lively and sometimes bitter literary exchange between the Roman scholar and the North African bishop, Jerome had at one point crystallized the debate in these terms, admittedly derived from the philosophers, "To carry out the ceremonies of the Law cannot be an indifferent act; it is either bad or good. You say it is good; I insist that it is wrong." See Jerome's letter 112, 16, dated ca. A.D. 404 in MPL 22, 926; FC 20, 360.

Jerome enumerated among those who were his guides in the matter particularly Origen, and also Didymus the Blind, Apollinaris of Laodicea, Alexander ("the former heretic" who had ordained Origen), Eusebius of Emesa, Theodore of Heraclea, and John Chrysostom. FC 20, 345-348; cf. pp. 410-411.

Luther apparently sided with Augustine, whose rebuttal was that "these observances [circumcision, et al] were neither to be required as necessary, nor condemned as sacrilegious." FC 20, 399. On the whole issue, see Luther's How Christians Should Regard Moses (1525). LW 35, (155) 161-174.

in I Corinthians 12.[42] For love pervades all and transcends all; it considers only what is necessary and beneficial to others, and does not ask whether it is old or new. Hence, the precedents for the use of the sword also are matters of freedom, and you may follow them or not. But where you see that your neighbor needs it, there love constrains you to do as a matter of necessity that which would otherwise be optional and not necessary for you either to do or to leave undone. Only do not suppose that you will thereby become righteous or be saved—as the Jews presumed to be saved by their works—but leave this to faith, which without works makes you a new creature.

To prove our position also by the New Testament, the testimony of John the Baptist in Luke 3 [:14] stands unshaken on this point. There can be no doubt that it was his task to point to Christ, witness for him, and teach about him; that is to say, the teaching of the man who was to lead a truly perfected people to Christ had of necessity to be purely New Testament and evangelical. John confirms the soldiers' calling, saying they should be content with their wages. Now if it had been un-Christian to bear the sword, he ought to have censured them for it and told them to abandon both wages and sword, else he would not have been teaching them Christianity aright. So likewise, when St. Peter in Acts 10 [:34-43] preached Christ to Cornelius, he did not tell him to abandon his profession, which he would have had to do if it had prevented Cornelius from being a Christian. Moreover, before he was baptized the Holy Spirit came upon him [Acts 10:44-48]. St. Luke[43] also praises him as an upright man prior to St. Peter's sermon, and does not criticize him for being a soldier, the centurion of a pagan emperor [Acts 10:1-2]. It is only right that what the Holy Spirit permitted to remain and did not censure in the case of Cornelius, we too should permit and not censure.

A similar case is that of the Ethiopian captain, the eunuch in Acts 8 [:27-39], whom Philip the evangelist converted and baptized and permitted to return home and remain in office, although without the sword he could not possibly have been so high an official under the queen of Ethiopia. It was the same too

---

[42] I Cor. 12:13; cf. 9:19-22.
[43] Luther accepted the Lucan authorship of the book of Acts. LW 35, 363-364.

with the proconsul of Cyprus, Sergius Paulus, in Acts 13 [:7-12]; St. Paul converted him, and yet permitted him to remain proconsul over and among heathen. The same policy was followed by many holy martyrs who continued obedient to pagan Roman emperors, went into battle under them, and undoubtedly slew people for the sake of preserving peace, as is written of St. Maurice, St. Acacius, St. Gereon, and many others under the emperor Julian.[44]

Moreover, we have the clear and compelling text of St. Paul in Romans 13 [:1], where he says, "The governing authority has been ordained by God"; and further, "The governing authority does not bear the sword in vain. It is God's servant for your good, an avenger upon him who does evil" [Rom. 13:4]. Be not so wicked, my friend, as to say, "A Christian may not do that which is God's own peculiar work, ordinance, and creation." Else you must also say, "A Christian must not eat, drink, or be married," for these are also God's work and ordinance. If it is God's work and creation, then it is good, so good that everyone can use it in a Christian and salutary way, as Paul says in II Timothy 4 [I Tim. 4:4, 3], "Everything created by God is good, and nothing is to be rejected by those who believe and know the truth." Under "everything created by God" you must include not simply food and drink, clothing and shoes, but also authority and subjection, protection and punishment.

In short, since Paul says here that the governing authority is God's servant, we must allow it to be exercised not only by

---

[44] Maurice, the patron saint of Magdeburg, was commander of the Theban legion which, according to legend, was composed entirely of Christians, sixty-six thousand men from Thebes in North Africa. They were willing to "render unto Caesar" military service in a just war, but were massacred (ca. 287) on order of the emperor Maximian Herculius (285-310) when they refused to make the usual sacrifice to the pagan gods and aid in the extermination of the Christians in Gaul. See Ryan and Ripperger, *The Golden Legend of Jacobus de Voragine*, II, 566-569.

Acacius, a Cappadocian centurian in the Roman army stationed at Thrace, was tortured and beheaded at Byzantium (ca. 303) under Diocletian (284-305). The Benedictine Monks of St. Augustine's Abbey, Ramsgate, *The Book of the Saints* (New York: Macmillan, 1947), p. 4.

Gereon, according to unreliable tradition, was a member of the Theban legion, 319 of whom were martyred as a group near Cologne. *Ibid.*, p. 262.

Julian the Apostate was Roman emperor in 361-363. Luther probably confused him here with Diocletian and Maximian, under whom the specifically named saints were martyred. Julian's policy was to degrade Christianity and promote paganism, but without resort to force or persecution.

the heathen but by all men. What can be the meaning of the phrase, "It is God's servant," except that governing authority is by its very nature such that through it one may serve God? Now it would be quite un-Christian to say that there is any service of God in which a Christian should not or must not take part, when service of God is actually more characteristic[45] of Christians than of anyone else. It would even be fine and fitting if all princes were good, true Christians. For the sword and authority, as a particular service of God, belong more appropriately[46] to Christians than to any other men on earth. Therefore, you should esteem the sword or governmental authority as highly as the estate of marriage, or husbandry, or any other calling which God has instituted. Just as one can serve God in the estate of marriage, or in farming or a trade, for the benefit of others—and must so serve if his neighbor needs it—so one can serve God in government, and should there serve if the needs of his neighbor demand it. For those who punish evil and protect the good are God's servants and workmen. Only, one should also be free not to do it if there is no need for it, just as we are free not to marry or farm where there is no need for them.

You ask: Why did not Christ and the apostles bear the sword? Answer: You tell me, why did Christ not take a wife, or become a cobbler or a tailor. If an office or vocation were to be regarded as disreputable on the ground that Christ did not pursue it himself, what would become of all the offices and vocations other than the ministry, the one occupation he did follow? Christ pursued his own office and vocation, but he did not thereby reject any other. It was not incumbent upon him to bear the sword, for he was to exercise only that function by which his kingdom is governed and which properly serves his kingdom. Now, it is not essential to his kingdom that he be a married man, a cobbler, tailor, farmer, prince, hangman, or constable; neither is the temporal sword or law essential to it, but only God's Word and Spirit. It is by these that his people are ruled inwardly. This is the office which he also exercised then and still exercises now,

---

45 *So eben eygent.* Cf. MA³ 5, 397, n. 21, 13, "*So ganz zu seinem Wesen Gehört.*"
46 *Gepürt . . . zu eygen.* Cf. Grimm, *Deutsches Wörterbuch*, IV¹, 1893-1895.

always bestowing God's Word and Spirit. And in this office the apostles and all spiritual rulers had to follow him. For in order to do their job right they are so busily occupied with the spiritual sword, the Word of God, that they must perforce neglect the temporal sword and leave it to others who do not have to preach, although it is not contrary to their calling to use it, as I have said. For each one must attend to the duties of his own calling.

Therefore, although Christ did not bear or prescribe the sword, it is sufficient that he did not forbid or abolish it but actually confirmed it; just as it is sufficient that he did not abolish the estate of marriage but confirmed it, though without himself taking a wife or setting forth a teaching concerning it. He had to manifest himself wholly in connection with that estate and calling which alone expressly served his kingdom, lest from his example there should be deduced the justification or necessity of teaching and believing that the kingdom of God could not exist without matrimony and the sword and similar externals (since Christ's example is necessarily binding), when in fact it exists solely by God's Word and Spirit. This was and had to be Christ's peculiar function as the Supreme King in this kingdom. Since not all Christians, however, have this same function (although they are entitled to it), it is fitting that they should have some other external office by which God may also be served.

From all this we gain the true meaning of Christ's words in Matthew 5 [:39], "Do not resist evil," etc. It is this: A Christian should be so disposed that he will suffer every evil and injustice without avenging himself; neither will he seek legal redress in the courts but have utterly no need of temporal authority and law for his own sake. On behalf of others, however, he may and should seek vengeance, justice, protection, and help, and do as much as he can to achieve it. Likewise, the governing authority should, on its own initiative or through the instigation of others, help and protect him too, without any complaint, application, or instigation on his own part. If it fails to do this, he should permit himself to be despoiled and slandered; he should not resist evil, as Christ's words say.

Be certain too that this teaching of Christ is not a counsel for those who would be perfect, as our sophists blasphemously and falsely say,[47] but a universally obligatory command for all Christians. Then you will realize that all those who avenge themselves or go to law and wrangle in the courts over their property and honor are nothing but heathen masquerading under the name of Christians. It cannot be otherwise, I tell you. Do not be dissuaded by the multitude and common practice; for there are few Christians on earth—have no doubt about it—and God's word is something very different from the common practice.[48]

Here you see that Christ is not abrogating the law when he says, "You have heard that it was said to them of old, 'An eye for an eye'; but I say to you: Do not resist evil," etc. [Matt. 5:38-39]. On the contrary, he is expounding the meaning of the law as it is to be understood, as if he were to say, "You Jews think that it is right and proper in the sight of God to recover by law what is yours. You rely on what Moses said, 'An eye for an eye,' etc. But I say to you that Moses set this law over the wicked, who do not belong to God's kingdom, in order that they might not avenge themselves or do worse but be compelled by such outward law to desist from evil, in order that by outward law and rule they might be kept subordinate to the governing authority. You, however, should so conduct yourselves that you neither need nor resort to such law. Although the temporal authority must have such a law by which to judge unbelievers, and although you yourselves may also use it for judging others, still you should not invoke or use it for yourselves and in your own affairs. You have the kingdom of heaven; therefore, you should leave the kingdom of earth to anyone who wants to take it."

There you see that Christ does not interpret his words to mean that he is abrogating the law of Moses or prohibiting temporal authority. He is rather making an exception of his own people. They are not to use the secular authority for themselves but leave it to unbelievers. Yet they may also serve these unbelievers, even with their own law, since they are not Christians and no one can be forced into Christianity. That Christ's words apply only to his own is evident from the fact that later on he says they should love their enemies and be perfect like their

47 See p. 82, n. 6.
48 Cf. Tertullian, *De virginibus velandis*, chap. i, "Christ did not say, 'I am the common practice,' but, 'I am the truth.'" *MPL* 2, 889.

heavenly Father [Matt. 5:44, 48]. But he who loves his enemies and is perfect leaves the law alone and does not use it to demand an eye for an eye. Neither does he restrain the non-Christians, however, who do not love their enemies and who do wish to make use of the law; indeed, he lends his help that these laws may hinder the wicked from doing worse.

Thus the word of Christ is now reconciled, I believe, with the passages which establish the sword, and the meaning is this: No Christian shall wield or invoke the sword for himself and his cause. In behalf of another, however, he may and should wield it and invoke it to restrain wickedness and to defend godliness. Even as the Lord says in the same chapter [Matt. 5:34-37], "A Christian should not swear, but his word should be Yes, yes; No, no." That is, for himself and of his own volition and desire, he should not swear. When it is needful or necessary, however, and salvation or the honor of God demands it, he should swear. Thus, he uses the forbidden oath to serve another, just as he uses the forbidden sword to serve another. Christ and Paul often swore in order to make their teaching and testimony valuable and credible to others,[49] as men do and have the right to do in covenants and compacts, etc., of which Psalm 63 [:11] says, "They shall be praised who swear by his name."

Here you inquire further, whether constables, hangmen, jurists, lawyers, and others of similar function can also be Christians and in a state of salvation. Answer: If the governing authority and its sword are a divine service, as was proved above, then everything that is essential for the authority's bearing of the sword must also be divine service. There must be those who arrest, prosecute, execute, and destroy the wicked, and who protect, acquit, defend, and save the good. Therefore, when they perform their duties, not with the intention of seeking their own ends but only of helping the law and the governing authority function to coerce the wicked, there is no peril in that; they may use their office like anybody else would use his trade, as a means of livelihood. For, as has been said, love of neighbor is not concerned about its own; it considers not how great or humble, but how

---

[49] Cf., e.g., Christ's frequent use of the expression, "Truly, I say to you," and Paul's mentioning of God as his witness in II Cor. 11:31 and Gal. 1:20.

profitable and needful the works are for neighbor or community.

You may ask, "Why may I not use the sword for myself and for my own cause, so long as it is my intention not to seek my own advantage but to punish evil?" Answer: Such a miracle is not impossible, but very rare and hazardous. Where the Spirit is so richly present it may well happen. For we read thus of Samson in Judges 15 [:11], that he said, "As they did to me, so have I done to them," [50] even though Proverbs 24 [:29] says to the contrary, "Do not say, I will do to him as he has done to me," and Proverbs 20 [:22] adds, "Do not say, I will repay him his evil." Samson was called of God to harass the Philistines and deliver the children of Israel. Although he used them as an occasion to further his own cause, still he did not do so in order to avenge himself or to seek his own interests, but to serve others and to punish the Philistines [Judg. 14:4]. No one but a true Christian, filled with the Spirit, will follow this example. Where reason too tries to do likewise, it will probably contend that it is not trying to seek its own, but this will be basically untrue, for it cannot be done without grace. Therefore first become like Samson, and then you can also do as Samson did.

Part Two [51]

How Far Temporal Authority Extends

We come now to the main part of this treatise.[52] Having learned that there must be temporal authority on earth, and how it is to be exercised in a Christian and salutary manner, we must now learn how far its arm extends and how widely its hand stretches, lest it extend too far and encroach upon God's kingdom and government. It is essential for us to know this, for where it is given too wide a scope, intolerable and terrible injury follows; on the other hand, injury is also inevitable where it is restricted too narrowly. In the former case, the temporal authority punishes too much; in the latter case, it punishes too little. To err in this

---

[50] Luther had used this same verse to close his important 1520 statement on *Why the Books of the Pope and His Disciples Were Burned by Doctor Martin Luther.* LW 31, (379) 383-395.

[51] The main divisions of the treatise are suggested in Luther's dedication to Duke John; see p. 81; cf. also the Introduction, p. 79.

[52] *Sermon;* cf. the Introduction, p. 79.

direction, however, and punish too little is more tolerable, for it is always better to let a scoundrel live than to put a godly man to death. The world has plenty of scoundrels anyway and must continue to have them, but godly men are scarce.

It is to be noted first that the two classes of Adam's children— the one in God's kingdom under Christ and the other in the kingdom of the world under the governing authority, as was said above—have two kinds of law. For every kingdom must have its own laws and statutes; without law no kingdom or government can survive, as everyday experience amply shows. The temporal government has laws which extend no further than to life and property and external affairs on earth, for God cannot and will not permit anyone but himself to rule over the soul. Therefore, where the temporal authority presumes to prescribe laws for the soul, it encroaches upon God's government and only misleads souls and destroys them. We want to make this so clear that everyone will grasp it, and that our fine gentlemen, the princes and bishops, will see what fools they are when they seek to coerce the people with their laws and commandments into believing this or that.

When a man-made law is imposed upon the soul to make it believe this or that as its human author may prescribe, there is certainly no word of God for it. If there is no word of God for it, then we cannot be sure whether God wishes to have it so, for we cannot be certain that something which he does not command is pleasing to him. Indeed, we are sure that it does not please him, for he desires that our faith be based simply and entirely on his divine word alone. He says in Matthew 18 [16:18], "On this rock I will build my church"; and in John 10 [:27, 14, 5], "My sheep hear my voice and know me; however, they will not hear the voice of a stranger, but flee from him." From this it follows that with such a wicked command the temporal power is driving souls to eternal death. For it compels them to believe as right and certainly pleasing to God that which is in fact uncertain, indeed, certain to be displeasing to him since there is no clear word of God for it. Whoever believes something to be right which is wrong or uncertain is denying the truth, which is God himself. He is believing in lies and errors, and counting as right that which is wrong.

105

Hence, it is the height of folly when they command that one shall believe the Church,[53] the fathers, and the councils, though there be no word of God for it. It is not the church but the devil's apostles who command such things, for the church commands nothing unless it knows for certain that it is God's word. As St. Peter puts it, "Whoever speaks, let him speak as the word of God" [I Pet. 4:11]. It will be a long time, however, before they can ever prove that the decrees of the councils are God's word.[54] Still more foolish is it when they assert that kings, princes, and the mass of mankind believe thus and so. My dear man, we are not baptized into kings, or princes, or even into the mass of mankind, but into Christ and God himself. Neither are we called kings, princes, or common folk, but Christians. No one shall or can command the soul unless he is able to show it the way to heaven; but this no man can do, only God alone. Therefore, in matters which concern the salvation of souls nothing but God's word shall be taught and accepted.

Again, consummate fools though they are, they must confess that they have no power over souls. For no human being can kill a soul or give it life, or conduct it to heaven or hell. If they will not take our word for it, Christ himself will attend to it strongly enough where he says in the tenth chapter of Matthew, "Do not fear those who kill the body, and after that have nothing that they can do; rather fear him who after he has killed the body, has power to condemn to hell." [55] I think it is clear enough here that the soul is taken out of all human hands and is placed under the authority of God alone.

Now tell me: How much wit must there be in the head of a person who imposes commands in an area where he has no authority whatsoever? Would you not judge the person insane

---

[53] In this paragraph Luther uses the term *Kirche* in two different senses. Here, spelled with a capital "K" it signifies the external organization, which to his contemporaries meant the pope, cardinals, *et al.* In the next sentence, spelled with a lower case "k," it signifies the totality of true believers.
[54] This was a conviction which the Leipzig debate of 1519 with Johann Eck helped to bring into sharp focus for Luther. See Schwiebert, *Luther and His Times*, pp. 410-411, 416-417.
[55] Luther might even have strengthened his case had he actually quoted Matt. 10:28 ("who kill the body but cannot kill the soul," etc.) rather than its less specific parallel in Luke 12:4-5.

who commanded the moon to shine whenever he wanted it to? How well would it go if the Leipzigers were to impose laws on us Wittenbergers, or if, conversely, we in Wittenberg were to legislate for the people of Leipzig! [56] They would certainly send the lawmakers a thank-offering of hellebore[57] to purge their brains and cure their sniffles. Yet our emperor and clever princes are doing just that today. They are allowing pope, bishop, and sophists to lead them on—one blind man leading the other—[58] to command their subjects to believe, without God's word, whatever they please. And still they would be known as Christian princes,[59] God forbid!

Besides, we cannot conceive how an authority could or should act in a situation except where it can see, know, judge, condemn, change, and modify. What would I think of a judge who should blindly decide cases which he neither hears nor sees? Tell me then: How can a mere man see, know, judge, condemn, and change hearts? That is reserved for God alone, as Psalm 7 [:9] says, "God tries the hearts and reins"; and [v. 8], "The Lord judges the peoples." And Acts 10[60] says, "God knows the hearts"; and Jeremiah 1 [17:9-10], "Wicked and unsearchable is the human heart; who can understand it? I the Lord, who search the heart and reins." A court should and must be quite certain and clear about everything if it is to render judgment. But the thoughts and inclinations of the soul can be known to no one but God. Therefore, it is futile and impossible to command or compel anyone by force to believe this or that. The matter must be approached in a different way. Force will not accomplish it. And I am surprised at the big fools, for they themselves all say: *De*

---

[56] Leipzig was the capital of Albertine Saxony, ruled by the hostile Duke George the Bearded from 1500-1539 (see p. 77, n. 2), while Wittenberg was the capital of Ernestine Saxony, ruled by the friendly Elector Frederick the Wise from 1486-1525.

[57] *Nysse wortz* was a plant whose pulverized roots were used to induce sneezing, which since ancient times was thought to be a cure for various mental disorders including insanity and epilepsy. Grimm, *Deutsches Wörterbuch*, VII, 837.

[58] Cf. Matt. 15:14; Luke 6:39.

[59] See p. 77.

[60] Cf. Acts 1:24; 15:8.

occultis non iudicat Ecclesia,[61] the church does not judge secret matters. If the spiritual rule of the church governs only public matters, how dare the mad temporal authority judge and control such a secret, spiritual, hidden matter as faith?

Furthermore, every man runs his own risk in believing as he does, and he must see to it himself that he believes rightly. As nobody else can go to heaven or hell for me, so nobody else can believe or disbelieve for me; as nobody else can open or close heaven or hell to me, so nobody else can drive me to belief or unbelief. How he believes or disbelieves is a matter for the conscience of each individual, and since this takes nothing away from the temporal authority the latter should be content to attend to its own affairs and let men believe this or that as they are able and willing, and constrain no one by force. For faith is a free act, to which no one can be forced. Indeed, it is a work of God in the spirit, not something which outward authority should compel or create. Hence arises the common saying,[62] found also in Augustine,[63] "No one can or ought to be forced to believe."

Moreover, the blind, wretched fellows fail to see how utterly hopeless and impossible a thing they are attempting. For no matter how harshly they lay down the law, or how violently they rage, they can do no more than force an outward compliance of the mouth and the hand; the heart they cannot compel, though they work themselves to a frazzle. For the proverb is true: "Thoughts are tax-free." [64] Why do they persist in trying to force people to believe from the heart when they see that it is impossible? In so doing they only compel weak consciences to lie, to disavow, and to utter what is not in their hearts. They thereby load themselves down with dreadful alien sins,[65] for all the lies and false

---

61 This is a gloss to the canon *Erubescant impii*, dist. XXXII, C. XI, in the *Decreti Magistri Gratiani Prima Pars*, where the glossed phrase reads, *De manifestis quidem loquimur, secretorum autem cognitor et iudex est Deus* ("We indeed speak of open things, but God is the witness and judge of secret things"). *Corpus Iuris Canonici*, I, col. 120. This marginal gloss is found in *Decretum Gratiani emendatum et notationibus illustratum una cum glossis* (Paris, 1612), col. 175.

62 Cf. Wander (ed.), *Sprichwörter-Lexikon*, I, 1697, "*Glaube*," No. 36, and *ibid.*, V, 1352, No. 176.

63 See Augustine's *Contra litteras Petiliani*, II, 184. *MPL* 43, 315.

64 See Wander (ed.), *Sprichwörter-Lexikon*, I, 1395, "*Gedanke*," No. 44.

65 Scholastic theology had distinguished, among its many other classifications

confessions which such weak consciences utter fall back upon him who compels them. Even if their subjects were in error, it would be much easier simply to let them err than to compel them to lie and to utter what is not in their hearts. In addition, it is not right to prevent evil by something even worse.

Would you like to know why God ordains that the temporal princes must offend so frightfully? I will tell you. God has given them up to a base mind [Rom. 1:28] and will make an end of them just as he does of the spiritual nobility. For my ungracious lords, the pope and the bishops, are supposed to be bishops[66] and preach God's word. This they leave undone, and have become temporal princes who govern with laws which concern only life and property. How completely they have turned things topsy-turvy! They are supposed to be ruling souls inwardly by God's word; so they rule castles, cities, lands, and people outwardly, torturing souls with unspeakable outrages.

Similarly, the temporal lords are supposed to govern lands and people outwardly. This they leave undone. They can do no more than strip and fleece, heap tax upon tax and tribute upon tribute, letting loose here a bear and there a wolf.[67] Besides this, there is no justice, integrity, or truth to be found among them. They behave worse than any thief or scoundrel, and their temporal rule has sunk quite as low as that of the spiritual tyrants. For this reason God so perverts their minds also, that they rush on into the absurdity of trying to exercise a spiritual rule over souls, just as their counterparts try to establish a temporal rule. They blithely heap alien sins upon themselves and incur the hatred of God and man, until they come to ruin together with bishops, popes, and monks, one scoundrel with the other. Then they lay all the blame

---

of sin, nine so-called *peccata aliena* (see *PE* 1, 91; and 2, 364)—the term derives from the Vulgate rendering of I Tim. 5:22—such as commanding, counseling, consenting, approving, participating, co-operating, or simply failing to speak, hinder, punish, or expose where the sin of another party is involved. *Lexikon für Theologie und Kirche* (2nd ed.; 10 vols.; Freiburg im Breisgau: Herder, 1930-1938), IX, 900.

66 In the sense of the New Testament, bishops were to be overseers of Christ's flock.

67 Not only were the beasts which were set free for purposes of hunting a threat to the lives of the peasants, but the hunts themselves were destructive of their lands and property. *MA*³ 5, 398, n. 28, 22.

on the gospel, and instead of confessing their sin they blaspheme God and say that our preaching has brought about that which their perverse wickedness has deserved—and still unceasingly deserves—just as the Romans did when they were destroyed.[68] Here then you have God's decree concerning the high and mighty.[69] They are not to believe it, however, lest this stern decree of God be hindered by their repentance.

But, you say: Paul said in Romans 13 [:1] that every soul [*seele*] [70] should be subject to the governing authority; and Peter says that we should be subject to every human ordinance [I Pet. 2:13]. Answer: Now you are on the right track, for these passages are in my favor. St. Paul is speaking of the governing authority. Now you have just heard that no one but God can have authority over souls. Hence, St. Paul cannot possibly be speaking of any obedience except where there can be corresponding authority. From this it follows that he is not speaking of faith, to the effect that temporal authority should have the right to command faith. He is speaking rather of external things, that they should be ordered and governed on earth. His words too make this perfectly clear, where he prescribes limits for both authority and obedience, saying, "Pay all of them their dues, taxes to whom taxes are due, revenue to whom revenue is due, honor to whom honor is due, respect to whom respect is due" [Rom. 13:7]. Temporal obedience and authority, you see, apply only externally to taxes, revenue, honor, and respect. Again, where he says, "The governing authority is not a terror to good conduct, but to bad" [Rom. 13:3], he again so limits the governing authority that it is not to have the mastery over faith or the word of God, but over evil works.

This is also what St. Peter means by the phrase, "Human

---

68 When Rome was captured and sacked by the Goths in A.D. 410, the pagans blamed the disaster on the Christian desertion of the Roman gods. Augustine wrote *The City of God* to refute this charge. In dedicating his *Seven Books Against the Pagans* to Augustine, the early fifth century historian Paulus Orosius wrote, "You bade me reply to the empty chatter and perversity of those . . . pagans . . . [who] charge that the present times [*ca.* 417] are unusually beset with calamities for the sole reason that men believe in Christ and worship God while idols are increasingly neglected." Irving W. Raymond (trans.), *Seven Books of History Against the Pagans* (New York: Columbia University Press, 1936), p. 30.

69 *Grossen hanssen;* cf. WA 10II, 507, n. 21, 22, and WA, DB 3, 78, ll. 10-11.

70 See p. 86, n. 17.

ordinance" [I Pet. 2:13]. A human ordinance cannot possibly extend its authority into heaven and over souls; it is limited to the earth, to external dealings men have with one another, where they can see, know, judge, evaluate, punish, and acquit.

Christ himself made this distinction, and summed it all up very nicely when he said in Matthew 22 [:21], "Render to Caesar the things that are Caesar's and to God the things that are God's." Now, if the imperial power extended into God's kingdom and authority, and were not something separate, Christ would not have made this distinction. For, as has been said, the soul is not under the authority of Caesar; he can neither teach it nor guide it, neither kill it nor give it life, neither bind it nor loose it,[71] neither judge it nor condemn it, neither hold it fast nor release it. All this he would have to do, had he the authority to command it and to impose laws upon it. But with respect to body, property, and honor he has indeed to do these things, for such matters are under his authority.

David too summarized all this long ago in an excellent brief passage, when he said in Psalm 113 [115:16], "He has given heaven to the Lord of heaven, but the earth he has given to the sons of men." That is, over what is on earth and belongs to the temporal, earthly kingdom, man has authority from God; but whatever belongs to heaven and to the eternal kingdom is exclusively under the Lord of heaven. Neither did Moses forget this when he said in Genesis 1 [:26], "God said, 'Let us make man to have dominion over the beasts of the earth, the fish of the sea, and the birds of the air.'" There only external dominion is ascribed to man. In short, this is the meaning as St. Peter says in Acts 4 [5:29], "We must obey God rather than men." Thereby, he clearly sets a limit to the temporal authority, for if we had to do everything that the temporal authority wanted there would have been no point in saying, "We must obey God rather than men."

If your prince or temporal ruler commands you to side with the pope, to believe thus and so, or to get rid of certain books,[72]

---

[71] *Binden* and *lössen* have reference to the power of the keys derived from Matt. 16:19. See *LW* 35, 9-22.

[72] See p. 77, n. 2.

you should say, "It is not fitting that Lucifer[73] should sit at the side of God. Gracious sir, I owe you obedience in body and property; command me within the limits of your authority on earth, and I will obey. But if you command me to believe or to get rid of certain books, I will not obey; for then you are a tyrant and overreach yourself, commanding where you have neither the right nor the authority," etc. Should he seize your property on account of this and punish such disobedience, then blessed are you; thank God that you are worthy to suffer for the sake of the divine word. Let him rage, fool that he is; he will meet his judge. For I tell you, if you fail to withstand him, if you give in to him and let him take away your faith and your books, you have truly denied God.

Let me illustrate. In Meissen,[74] Bavaria,[75] the Mark,[76] and other places, the tyrants have issued an order that all copies of the New Testament are everywhere to be turned in to the officials.[77] This should be the response of their subjects: They should not turn in a single page, not even a letter, on pain of losing their salvation. Whoever does so is delivering Christ up into the hands of Herod, for these tyrants act as murderers of Christ just like Herod.[78] If their homes are ordered searched and books or property taken by force, they should suffer it to be done. Outrage is not to be resisted but endured; yet we should not sanction it, or lift a little finger to conform, or obey. For such tyrants are

---

[73] Since the third century, especially among the poets, the name Lucifer had been applied to Satan, the rebel angel hurled from heaven, on the grounds of an allegorical interpretation of Isa. 14:12 in terms of Luke 10:18.

[74] Duke George of Saxony was also the margrave of Meissen; see p. 84, n. 11.

[75] Bavaria was ruled at the time by Duke Wilhelm IV (1493-1550), a vigorous opponent of the Reformation; see p. 77, n. 2.

[76] Brandenburg was ruled at the time by Duke Joachim I (1484-1535), who remained an enemy of the Reformation despite his wife's espousal of it.

[77] Luther's German New Testament had appeared in September, 1522. On its prohibition in Meissen, see J. K. Seidemann, *Beiträge zur Reformationsgeschichte* (Dresden, 1846), I, 51; in Bavaria: Winter, *Schicksale der evangelischen Lehre*, II, 189; in the Mark: Paul Steinmüller, *Einführung der Reformation in die Kurmark Brandenburg* (Halle: Verein für Reformationsgeschichte, 1903), p. 22; and in Austria (the prohibition of November 6 and 17, 1522, by Ferdinand I): Johann Loserth, *Die Reformation und Gegenreformation in den innerösterreichischen Ländern im XVI Jahrhundert* (Stuttgart: Cotta, 1898), p. 23, n. 1.

[78] The reference is doubtless to Matt. 2:16 rather than Luke 23:7.

acting as worldly[79] princes are supposed to act, and worldly princes they surely are. But the world is God's enemy; hence, they too have to do what is antagonistic to God and agreeable to the world, that they may not be bereft of honor, but remain worldly princes. Do not wonder, therefore, that they rage and mock at the gospel; they have to live up to their name and title.

You must know that since the beginning of the world a wise prince is a mighty rare bird,[80] and an upright prince even rarer.[81] They are generally the biggest fools or the worst scoundrels on earth; therefore, one must constantly expect the worst from them and look for little good, especially in divine matters which concern the salvation of souls. They are God's executioners[82] and hangmen; his divine wrath uses them to punish the wicked and to maintain outward peace. Our God is a great lord and ruler; this is why he must also have such noble, highborn, and rich hangmen and constables. He desires that everyone shall copiously accord them riches, honor, and fear in abundance. It pleases his divine will that we call his hangmen gracious lords, fall at their feet, and be subject to them in all humility, so long as they do not ply their trade too far and try to become shepherds instead of hangmen. If a prince should happen to be wise, upright, or a Christian, that is one of the great miracles, the most precious token of divine grace upon that land. Ordinarily the course of events is in accordance with the passage from Isaiah 3 [:4], "I

---

[79] *Welltlich,* usually translated as "temporal," here is given its cognate rendering because of the play on words intended.

[80] *Seltzam vogel;* see Wander (ed.), *Sprichwörter-Lexikon,* I, 1285, *"Fürst,"* No. 61.

[81] Cf. *ibid.,* I, 1283, *"Fürst,"* No. 31.

[82] The term *stockmeyster,* meaning "jailer," is also used by Luther synonomously with *Zuchtmeister* for Paul's "custodian" of Gal. 3:24-25. See his exegesis of the Nunc Dimittis in a sermon preached on the Day of the Purification of Mary, February 2, 1526, where the term must mean more than merely a guard or warden; it refers actually to one who flogs or otherwise inflicts legal punishment in execution of a sentence. WA 20, 247. See also in the fourth of his Weimar sermons (on which this treatise is based; cf. the Introduction, p. 79) Luther's statement that "princes are the hangmen and *Stockblöcher* of Christ" (WA 10III, 381, l. 31), the latter term being a tautological construction of the two words for "stock" and "block" and signifying an instrument of torture or punishment. Grimm, *Deutsches Wörterbuch,* X3, 54.

will make boys their princes, and gaping fools[83] shall rule over them"; and in Hosea 13 [:11], "I will give you a king in my anger, and take him away in my wrath." The world is too wicked, and does not deserve to have many wise and upright princes. Frogs must have their storks.[84]

Again you say, "The temporal power is not forcing men to believe; it is simply seeing to it externally that no one deceives the people by false doctrine;[85] how could heretics otherwise be restrained?" Answer: This the bishops should do; it is a function entrusted to them[86] and not to the princes. Heresy can never be restrained by force. One will have to tackle the problem in some other way, for heresy must be opposed and dealt with otherwise than with the sword. Here God's word must do the fighting. If it does not succeed, certainly the temporal power will not succeed either, even if it were to drench the world in blood. Heresy is a spiritual matter which you cannot hack to pieces with iron, consume with fire, or drown in water. God's word alone avails here, as Paul says in II Corinthians 10 [:4-5], "Our weapons are not carnal, but mighty in God to destroy every argument and proud obstacle that exalts itself against the knowledge of God, and to take every thought captive in the service of Christ."

Moreover, faith and heresy are never so strong as when men oppose them by sheer force, without God's word. For men count it certain that such force is for a wrong cause and is directed against the right, since it proceeds without God's word and knows not how to further its cause except by naked force, as brute beasts do. Even in temporal affairs force can be used only after the wrong has been legally condemned. How much less possible it is

---

83 *Maulaffen* is literally an ape with a wide or open mouth. Grimm, *Deutsches Wörterbuch*, VI, 1796. In his 1522 *Wider den falsch genannten geistlichen stand* Luther defined the word in these terms, "They open their mouths up wide and preach of great things but there is nothing back of it." WA 10^{II}, 125. The various meanings of the term in Luther are discussed in WA 10^{II}, 510, n. 121, 22.

84 The proverb means in effect: "like people, like prince" according to Wander (ed.), *Sprichwörter-Lexikon*, I, 1230, "*Frosch*," No. 34. It derives from the Aesop fable about the frogs who insisted on having a king, and were finally granted a stork who devoured them all.

85 On Luther's approval in another connection of the position here rejected, see Kawerau (ed.), Köstlin's *Martin Luther*, I, 584.

86 Cf. Titus 1:9ff.

to act with force, without justice and God's word, in these lofty spiritual matters! See, therefore, what fine, clever nobles they are! They would drive out heresy, but set about it in such a way that they only strengthen the opposition, rousing suspicion against themselves and justifying the heretics. My friend, if you wish to drive out heresy, you must find some way to tear it first of all from the heart and completely turn men's wills away from it. With force you will not stop it, but only strengthen it. What do you gain by strengthening heresy in the heart, while weakening only its outward expression and forcing the tongue to lie? God's word, however, enlightens the heart, and so all heresies and errors vanish from the heart of their own accord.

This way of destroying heresy was proclaimed by Isaiah in his eleventh chapter where he says, "He shall smite the earth with the rod of his mouth, and with the breath of his lips he shall slay the wicked."[87] There you see that if the wicked are to be slain and converted, it will be accomplished with the mouth. In short, these princes and tyrants do not realize that to fight against heresy is to fight against the devil, who fills men's hearts with error, as Paul says in Ephesians 6 [:12], "We are not contending against flesh and blood, but against spiritual wickedness, against the principalities which rule this present darkness," etc. Therefore, so long as the devil is not repelled and driven from the heart, it is agreeable to him that I destroy his vessels[88] with fire or sword; it's as if I were to fight lightning with a straw. Job bore abundant witness to this when in his forty-first chapter he said that the devil counts iron as straw, and fears no power on earth.[89] We learn it also from experience, for even if all Jews and heretics were forcibly burned no one ever has been or will be convinced or converted thereby.

Nevertheless, such a world as this deserves such princes, none of whom attends to his duties. The bishops are to leave God's word alone and not use it to rule souls; instead they are to turn over to the worldly princes the job of ruling souls with the sword. The worldly princes, in turn, are to permit usury, robbery, adultery,

---

[87] See Luther's application of Isa. 11:4 on pages 59-60.
[88] *Gefesss;* cf. Rom. 9:22.
[89] Job 41:25-34, especially v. 27.

murder, and other evil deeds, and even commit these offenses themselves, and then allow the bishops to punish with letters of excommunication. Thus, they neatly put the shoe on the wrong foot: they rule the souls with iron and the bodies with letters, so that worldly princes rule in a spiritual way, and spiritual princes rule in a worldly way. What else does the devil have to do on earth than to masquerade[90] and play the fool with his people? These are our Christian princes, who defend the faith and devour the Turk![91] Fine fellows, indeed, whom we may well trust to accomplish something by such refined wisdom, namely, to break their necks and plunge land and people into misery and want.

I would in all good faith advise these blind fellows to take heed to a little phrase that occurs in Psalm 107: *"Effundit contemptum super principes."*[92] I swear to you by God that if you fail to see that this little text is applicable to you, then you are lost, even though each one of you be as mighty as the Turk; and your fuming and raging will avail you nothing. A goodly part of it has already come true. For there are very few princes who are not regarded as fools or scoundrels; that is because they show themselves to be so. The common man is learning to think, and the scourge of princes (that which God calls *contemptum*) is gathering force among the mob and with the common man.[93] I fear there will be no way to avert it, unless the princes conduct themselves in a princely manner and begin again to rule decently and reasonably. Men will not, men cannot, men refuse to endure your tyranny and wantonness much longer. Dear princes and lords be wise and guide yourselves accordingly. God will no longer tolerate it. The world is no longer what it once was, when you hunted and drove the people like game. Abandon therefore your

---

[90] *Fassnacht spiel treybe. Fastnacht,* literally "eve of the fast," was that period just prior to Lent which was observed with feasting, revelry, parades, masquerades, and mummery, and also simple dramatic episodes in which the people could anonymously mimic and ridicule their superiors.

[91] The Mohammedans were at that time a threat to all of Western Christendom; see *LW* 35, 300, n. 152. The very princes who were displaying their "Christianity" abroad by forcibly stemming the encroachment of the Turks were denying it at home, according to Luther, by presuming to rule souls with the sword. See p. 44, n. 44.

[92] Ps. 107:40, "He pours contempt upon princes."

[93] The smoldering dissatisfaction of the oppressed serfs was to erupt a couple years later in the Peasants' Revolt of 1524-1526. See p. 62, n. 11; cf. p. 57 n. 1.

wicked use of force, give thought to dealing justly, and let God's word have its way, as it will anyway and must and shall; you cannot prevent it. If there is heresy somewhere, let it be overcome, as is proper, with God's word. But if you continue to brandish the sword, take heed lest someone come and compel you to sheathe it—and not in God's name!

But you might say, "Since there is to be no temporal sword among Christians, how then are they to be ruled outwardly? There certainly must be authority even among Christians." Answer: Among Christians there shall and can be no authority; rather all are alike subject to one another, as Paul says in Romans 12: "Each shall consider the other his superior";[94] and Peter says in I Peter 5 [:5], "All of you be subject to one another." This is also what Christ means in Luke 14 [:10], "When you are invited to a wedding, go and sit in the lowest place." Among Christians there is no superior but Christ himself, and him alone. What kind of authority can there be where all are equal and have the same right, power, possession, and honor, and where no one desires to be the other's superior, but each the other's subordinate? Where there are such people, one could not establish authority even if he wanted to, since in the nature of things it is impossible to have superiors where no one is able or willing to be a superior. Where there are no such people, however, there are no real Christians either.

What, then, are the priests and bishops? Answer: Their government is not a matter of authority or power, but a service and an office, for they are neither higher nor better than other Christians.[95] Therefore, they should impose no law or decree on others without their will and consent. Their ruling is rather nothing more than the inculcating of God's word, by which they guide Christians and overcome heresy. As we have said, Christians can be ruled by nothing except God's word, for Christians must be ruled in faith, not with outward works. Faith, however, can come through no word of man, but only through the word of God, as Paul says in Romans 10 [:17], "Faith comes through hearing, and hear-

---

[94] Cf. Rom. 12:10.
[95] See Luther's comments on the sacrament of ordination in *The Babylonian Captivity of the Church* (1520). *LW* 36, 106-117.

ing through the word of God." Those who do not believe are not Christians; they do not belong to Christ's kingdom, but to the worldly kingdom where they are constrained and governed by the sword and by outward rule. Christians do every good thing of their own accord and without constraint, and find God's word alone sufficient for them. Of this I have written frequently and at length elsewhere.[96]

Part Three

Now that we know the limits of temporal authority, it is time to inquire also how a prince should use it. We do this for the sake of those very few who would also like very much to be Christian princes and lords, and who desire to enter into the life in heaven. Christ himself describes the nature of worldly princes in Luke 22 [:25], where he says, "The princes of this world exercise lordship, and those that are in authority proceed with force." For if they are lords by birth or by election they think it only right that they should be served and should rule by force. He who would be a Christian prince must certainly lay aside any intent to exercise lordship or to proceed with force. For cursed and condemned is every sort of life lived and sought for the benefit and good of self; cursed are all works not done in love. They are done in love, however, when they are directed wholeheartedly toward the benefit, honor, and salvation of others, and not toward the pleasure, benefit, honor, comfort, and salvation of self.

I will say nothing here of the temporal dealings and laws of the governing authority. That is a large subject, and there are too many lawbooks already, although if a prince is himself no wiser than his jurists and knows no more than what is in the lawbooks, he will surely rule according to the saying in Proverbs 28: "A prince who lacks understanding will oppress many with injustice."[97] For no matter how good and equitable[98] the laws

---

[96] See, for example, *A Treatise on Good Works* (1520). PE 1, 184-285; and *The Freedom of a Christian* (1520). LW 31, 343-377.
[97] Prov. 28:16 (Vulgate).
[98] *Billich* in this connection for Luther has reference to equity. See his 1526 treatise, *Whether Soldiers, Too, Can Be Saved,"* where he identifies *Billigkeit* with the latin *aequitas* and the Greek *epieikeia*. PE 5, 42.

are, they all make an exception in the case of necessity,[99] in the face of which they cannot insist upon being strictly enforced. Therefore, a prince must have the law as firmly in hand as the sword, and determine in his own mind when and where the law is to be applied strictly or with moderation, so that law may prevail at all times and in all cases, and reason may be the highest law and the master of all administration of law. To take an analogy, the head of a family fixes both the time and the amount when it comes to matters of work and of food for his servants and children; still, he must reserve the right to modify or suspend these regulations if his servants happen to be ill, imprisoned, detained, deceived, or otherwise hindered; he must not deal as severely with the sick as with the well. I say this in order that men may not think it sufficiently praiseworthy merely to follow the written law or the opinions of jurists. There is more to it than that.

What, then, is a prince to do if he lacks the requisite wisdom and has to be guided by the jurists and the lawbooks? Answer: This is why I said that the princely estate is a perilous one. If he be not wise enough himself to master both his laws and his advisers, then the maxim of Solomon applies, "Woe to the land whose prince is a child" [Eccles 10:16]. Solomon recognized this too. This is why he despaired of all law—even of that which Moses through God had prescribed for him—and of all his princes and counselors. He turned to God himself and besought him for an understanding heart to govern the people [I Kings 3:9]. A prince must follow this example and proceed in fear; he must depend neither upon dead books nor living heads, but cling solely to God, and be at him constantly, praying for a right understanding, beyond that of all books and teachers, to rule his subjects wisely. For this reason I know of no law to prescribe for a prince; instead, I will simply instruct his heart and mind on what his attitude should be toward all laws, counsels, judgments, and actions. If he governs himself accordingly, God will surely grant

---

[99] Cf. the proverb quoted frequently by Luther (see, e.g., *LW* 36, 255) and also by Thomas Aquinas (*Summa theologica*, 2, I, ques. 96, art. 6), "Necessity knows no law." Wander (ed.), *Sprichwörter-Lexikon*, III, 1051, "*Noth,*" No. 146.

him the ability to carry out all laws, counsels, and actions in a proper and godly way.

First. He must give consideration and attention to his subjects, and really devote himself to it. This he does when he directs his every thought to making himself useful and beneficial to them; when instead of thinking, "The land and people belong to me, I will do what best pleases me," he thinks rather, "I belong to the land and the people, I shall do what is useful and good for them. My concern will be not how to lord it over them and dominate them, but how to protect and maintain them in peace and plenty." He should picture Christ to himself, and say, "Behold, Christ, the supreme ruler, came to serve me; he did not seek to gain power, estate, and honor from me, but considered only my need, and directed all things to the end that I should gain power, estate, and honor from him and through him. I will do likewise, seeking from my subjects not my own advantage but theirs. I will use my office to serve and protect them, listen to their problems and defend them, and govern to the sole end that they, not I, may benefit and profit from my rule." In such manner should a prince in his heart empty himself of his power and authority, and take unto himself the needs of his subjects, dealing with them as though they were his own needs. For this is what Christ did to us [Phil. 2:7]; and these are the proper works of Christian love.

Now you will say, "Who would then want to be a prince? That would make the princely estate the worst on earth, full of trouble, labor, and sorrow. What would become of the princely amusements—dancing, hunting, racing, gaming, and similar worldly pleasures?"[100] I answer: We are not here teaching how a temporal prince is to live, but how a temporal prince is to be a Christian, such that he may also reach heaven. Who is not aware that a prince is a rare prize in heaven?[101] I do not speak with any hope that temporal princes will give heed, but on the chance that there

---

[100] See Luther's criticism of the rulers' preoccupation with amusements to the neglect of their office elsewhere in this volume, pp. 249-250 and 367-368.
[101] *Eyn furst wiltprett ym hymel ist.* Cf. p. 113, n. 80. This proverbial expression (cf. Wander [ed.]), *Sprichwörter-Lexikon*, I, 1288, *"Fürst,"* No. 119) was a favorite of Luther (cf. *PE* 2, 163; *LW* 21, 345). A *Wildbret* was a wild bird or beast hunted as game; the term came also to mean anything rare, precious, and desirable. Grimm, *Deutsches Wörterbuch*, XIV², 53.

might be one who would also like to be a Christian, and to know how he should act. Of this I am certain, that God's word will neither turn nor bend for princes, but princes must bend themselves to God's word.

I am satisfied simply to point out that it is not impossible for a prince to be a Christian, although it is a rare thing and beset with difficulties. If they would so manage that their dancing, hunting, and racing were done without injury to their subjects, and if they would otherwise conduct their office in love toward them, God would not be so harsh as to begrudge them their dancing and hunting and racing. But they would soon find out for themselves that if they gave their subjects the care and attention required by their office, many a fine dance, hunt, race, and game would have to be missed.

Second. He must beware of the high and mighty[102] and of his counselors, and so conduct himself toward them that he despises none, but also trusts none enough to leave everything to him.[103] God cannot tolerate either course. He once spoke through the mouth of an ass [Num. 22:28]; therefore, no man is to be despised, however humble he may be. On the other hand, he permitted the highest angel to fall from heaven;[104] therefore, no man is to be trusted, no matter how wise, holy, or great he may be. One should rather give a hearing to all, and wait to see through which one of them God will speak and act. The greatest harm is done at court when the prince gives his mind into the captivity of the high and mighty and of the flatterers, and does not look into things himself. When a prince fails and plays the fool, not just one person is affected, but land and people must bear the result of such foolishness.

Therefore, a prince should trust his officials and allow them to act, but only in such a way that he will still keep the reins of government in his own hands. He must not be overconfident but keep his eyes open and attend to things, and (like Jehoshaphat did [II Chron. 19:4-7]) ride through the land and observe everywhere how the government and the law are being administered.

---

102 See p. 110, n. 69.
103 Cf. Luther's earlier exposition of the *Magnificat*. LW 21, 357.
104 See p —, n. 73, on this reference to Isa. 14:12 and Luke 10:18.

In this way he will learn for himself that one cannot place complete trust in any man. You have no right to assume that somebody else will take as deep an interest in you and your land as you do yourself, unless he be a good Christian filled with the Spirit. The natural man will not. And since you cannot know whether he is a Christian or how long he will remain one, you cannot safely depend upon him.

Beware especially of those who say, "Oh, gracious lord, does your grace not have greater confidence in me? Who is so willing to serve your grace?" etc. Such a person is certainly not guileless; he wants to be lord in the land and make a monkey[105] of you. If he were a true and devout Christian he would be glad that you entrust nothing to him, and would praise and approve you for keeping so close a watch on him. Since he acts in accord with God's will, he is willing and content to have his actions brought to light by you or anyone else. As Christ says in John 8 [3:21], "He who does what is good comes to the light, that it may be clearly seen that his deeds have been wrought in God." The former, however, would blind your eyes, and act under cover of darkness; as Christ also says in the same place, "He who does evil shuns the light, lest his deeds should be exposed" [John 3:20]. Therefore, beware of him. And if he complains about it, say to him, "Friend, I do you no wrong; God is unwilling that I trust myself or any other man. Find fault with Him because He will have it so, or because He has not made you something more than a man. But even if you were an angel, I still would not fully trust you—Lucifer[106] was not to be trusted—for we should trust God alone."

Let no prince think that he will fare better than David, who is an example to all princes. He had so wise a counselor, Ahithophel by name, that the text says: The counsel which Ahithophel gave was as if one had consulted God himself [II Sam. 16:23]. Yet Ahithophel fell, and sank so low that he tried to betray, slay, and destroy David, his own lord [II Sam. 17:1-23]. Thus did David at that time have to learn that no man is to be trusted. Why do you suppose God permitted such a horrible incident to occur

---

105 *Maulaffen;* see p. 114, n. 83.
106 See p. 112, n. 73.

and be recorded? It could only be in order to warn princes and lords against putting their trust in any man, which is the most perilous misfortune that could befall them. For it is most deplorable when flatterers reign at court, or when the prince relies upon others and puts himself in their hands, and lets everyone do as he will.

Now you will say, "If no one is to be trusted, how can land and people be governed?" Answer: You are to take the risk of entrusting matters to others, but you are yourself to trust and rely upon God alone. You will certainly have to entrust duties to somebody else and take a chance on him, but you should trust him only as one who might fail you, whom you must continue to watch with unceasing vigilance. A coachman has confidence in the horses and wagon he drives; yet he does not let them proceed on their own, but holds rein and lash in his hands and keeps his eyes open. Remember the old proverbs—which are the sure fruit of experience—"The master's eye makes the horse fat"; and, "The master's footprints fertilize the soil best."[107] That is, if the master does not look after things himself but depends on advisers and servants, things never go right. God also wills it that way and causes it to be so in order that the lords may be driven of necessity to care for their office themselves, just as everyone has to fulfil his own calling and every creature do its own work. Otherwise, the lords will become fatted pigs and worthless fellows, of benefit to no one but themselves.

Third. He must take care to deal justly with evildoers. Here he must be very wise and prudent, so he can inflict punishment without injury to others. Again, I know of no better example of this than David. He had a commander, Joab by name, who committed two underhanded crimes when he treacherously murdered two upright commanders [II Sam. 3:27; 20:10], whereby

---

107 The first proverb may derive from the Greek Xenophon who wrote of a king's inquiry as to the best fodder for improving his horse, and of the wise man's answer, "Experience has taught me that the master's eye best feeds the horse." Both proverbs in various versions, and even in conjunction, are listed in Wander (ed.), *Sprichwörter-Lexikon*, II, 541-542, "Herr," Nos. 147-155, 158-161. The meaning is clear: the master must attend to things himself if they are to go well. *Ibid.*, I, 171, "Auge," No. 45. See WA 10^{III}, 384, ll. 4-7.

he justly merited death twice over. Yet David, during his own lifetime, did not have him put to death but commanded his son Solomon to do so without fail [I Kings 2:5-6], doubtless because he himself could not do it without causing even greater damage and tumult. A prince must punish the wicked in such a way that he does not step on the dish while picking up the spoon,[108] and for the sake of one man's head plunge country and people into want and fill the land with widows and orphans. Therefore, he must not follow the advice of those counselors and fire-eaters who would stir and incite him to start a war, saying, "What, must we suffer such insult and injustice?" He is a mighty poor Christian who for the sake of a single castle would put the whole land in jeopardy.

In short, here one must go by the proverb, "He cannot govern who cannot wink at faults."[109] Let this be his rule: Where wrong cannot be punished without greater wrong, there let him waive his rights, however just they may be. He should not have regard to his own injury, but to the wrong others must suffer in consequence of the penalty he imposes. What have the many women and children done to deserve being made widows and orphans in order that you may avenge yourself on a worthless tongue or an evil hand which has injured you?

Here you will ask: "Is a prince then not to go to war, and are his subjects not to follow him into battle?" Answer: This is a far-reaching question, but let me answer it very briefly. To act here as a Christian, I say, a prince should not go to war against his overlord—king, emperor, or other liege lord[110]—but let him who takes, take. For the governing authority must not be resisted by force, but only by confession of the truth. If it is influenced by this, well and good; if not, you are excused, you suffer wrong

---

[108] See *ibid.*, III, 224-226, *"Löffel,"* Nos. 55, 56, 73, 106. The proverb actually has reference to one who misses or neglects the big thing because he is too intent on that which is insignificant; cf. *LW* 21, 337, n. 35.

[109] See Wander (ed.), *Sprichwörter-Lexikon*, I, 1019, *"Finger,"* No. 77. Luther used the same figure in his fourth Weimar sermon (*WA* 10II, 383-384) and in his exposition of *The Magnificat* (*LW* 21, 337). In his 1526 lectures on Ecclesiastes he ascribed the saying to Emperor Frederick III (1415-1493); *WA* 20, 97-98.

[110] The *Lehen herrnn* was the feudal sovereign who actually owned a vassal's property. Grimm, *Deutsches Wörterbuch*, VI, 540.

for God's sake. If, however, the antagonist is your equal, your inferior, or of a foreign government, you should first offer him justice and peace, as Moses taught the children of Israel. If he refuses, then—mindful of what is best for you[111]—defend yourself against force by force, as Moses so well describes it in Deuteronomy 20 [:10-12]. But in doing this you must not consider your personal interests and how you may remain lord, but those of your subjects to whom you owe help and protection, that such action may proceed in love. Since your entire land is in peril you must make the venture, so that with God's help all may not be lost. If you cannot prevent some from becoming widows and orphans as a consequence, you must at least see that not everything goes to ruin until there is nothing left except widows and orphans.

In this matter subjects are in duty bound to follow, and to devote their life and property, for in such a case one must risk his goods and himself for the sake of others. In a war of this sort it is both Christian and an act of love to kill the enemy without hesitation, to plunder and burn and injure him by every method of warfare[112] until he is conquered (except that one must beware of sin, and not violate wives and virgins). And when victory has been achieved, one should offer mercy and peace to those who surrender and humble themselves. In such a case let the proverb apply, "God helps the strongest."[113] This is what Abraham did when he smote the four kings, Genesis 14; he certainly slaughtered many, and showed little mercy until he conquered them. Such a case must be regarded as sent by God as a means to cleanse the land for once and drive out the rascals.

What if a prince is in the wrong? Are his people bound to follow him then too? Answer: No, for it is no one's duty to do wrong; we must obey God (who desires the right) rather than men [Acts 5:29]. What if the subjects do not know whether their

---

111 *Gedenck deyn bestes;* see Berger, *Die Sturmtruppen der Reformation,* p. 109, n. 3; and MA³ 5, 399, n. 39, 14.

112 *Kriegs leufften* means simply "the wars," that is, war and everything that goes with it, including, as the context here demands though the syntax is somewhat ambiguous, the notion of usages, conventions, and rules of war. See Grimm, *Deutsches Wörterbuch,* V, 2280, and MA³ 5, 399, n. 39, 28.

113 See Wander (ed.), *Sprichwörter-Lexikon,* II, 30, "*Gott,*" No. 656.

prince is in the right or not? Answer: So long as they do not know, and cannot with all possible diligence find out, they may obey him without peril to their souls. For in such a case one must apply the law of Moses in Exodus 21,[114] where he writes that a murderer who has unknowingly and unintentionally killed a man shall through flight to a city of refuge and by judgment of a court be declared acquitted. Whichever side then suffers defeat, whether it be in the right or in the wrong, must accept it as a punishment from God. Whichever side fights and wins in such ignorance, however, must regard its battle as though someone fell from a roof and killed another, and leave the matter to God. It is all the same to God whether he deprives you of life and property by a just or by an unjust lord. You are His creature and He can do with you as He wills, just so your conscience is clear. Thus in Genesis 20 [:2-7] God himself excuses Abimelech for taking Abraham's wife; not because he had done right, but because he had not known that she was Abraham's wife.

Fourth. Here we come to what should really have been placed first, and of which we spoke above.[115] A prince must act in a Christian way toward his God also; that is, he must subject himself to him in entire confidence and pray for wisdom to rule well, as Solomon did [I Kings 3:9]. But of faith and trust in God I have written so much that it is not necessary to say more here. Therefore, we will close with this brief summation, that a prince's duty is fourfold: First, toward God there must be true confidence and earnest prayer; second, toward his subjects there must be love and Christian service; third, with respect to his counselors and officials he must maintain an untrammeled reason and unfettered judgment; fourth, with respect to evildoers he must manifest a restrained severity and firmness. Then the prince's job will be done right, both outwardly and inwardly; it will be pleasing to God and to the people. But he will have to expect much envy and sorrow on account of it; the cross will soon rest on the shoulders of such a prince.

Finally, I must add an appendix in answer to those who raise

---

[114] Exod. 21:13; Num. 35:10-25.
[115] See p. 118.

questions about restitution,[116] that is, about the return of goods wrongfully acquired. This is a matter about which the temporal sword is commonly concerned; much has been written about it, and many fantastically severe judgments have been sought in cases of this sort. I will put it all in a few words, however, and at one fell swoop dispose of all such laws and of the harsh judgments based upon them, thus: No surer law can be found in this matter than the law of love. In the first place, when a case of this sort is brought before you in which one is to make restitution to another, if they are both Christians the matter is soon settled; neither will withhold what belongs to the other, and neither will demand that it be returned. If only one of them is a Christian, namely, the one to whom restitution is due, it is again easy to settle, for he does not care whether restitution is ever made to him. The same is true if the one who is supposed to make restitution is a Christian, for he will do so.

But whether one be a Christian or not a Christian, you should decide the question of restitution as follows. If the debtor is poor and unable to make restitution, and the other party is not poor, then you should let the law of love prevail and acquit the debtor; for according to the law of love the other party is in any event obliged to relinquish the debt and, if necessary, to give him something besides. But if the debtor is not poor, then have him restore as much as he can, whether it be all, a half, a third, or a fourth of it, provided that you leave him enough to assure a house, food, and clothing for himself, his wife, and his children. This much you would owe him in any case, if you could afford it; so much the less ought you to take it away now, since you do not need it and he cannot get along without it.

If neither party is a Christian, or if one of them is unwilling to be judged by the law of love, then you may have them call in some other judge, and tell the obstinate one that they are acting contrary to God and natural law,[117] even if they obtain a

---

[116] The background of this specific question is not known. It may have been raised by Duke John of Saxony, to whom the treatise is dedicated. MA³ 5, 400, n. 40, 31.

[117] See the 1521 definition of "natural law" deduced by Melanchthon from Rom. 2:15, "A natural law is a common judgment to which all men alike assent, and therefore one which God has inscribed upon the soul of each

strict judgment in terms of human law. For nature teaches—as does love—that I should do as I would be done by [Luke 6:31]. Therefore, I cannot strip another of his possessions, no matter how clear a right I have, so long as I am unwilling myself to be stripped of my goods. Rather, just as I would that another, in such circumstances, should relinquish his right in my favor, even so should I relinquish my rights.

Thus should one deal with all property unlawfully held, whether in public or in private, that love and natural law may always prevail. For when you judge according to love you will easily decide and adjust matters without any lawbooks. But when you ignore love and natural law you will never hit upon the solution that pleases God, though you may have devoured all the lawbooks and jurists. Instead, the more you depend on them, the further they will lead you astray. A good and just decision must not and cannot be pronounced out of books, but must come from a free mind, as though there were no books. Such a free decision is given, however, by love and by natural law, with which all reason is filled; out of the books come extravagant and untenable judgments. Let me give you an example of this.

This story is told of Duke Charles of Burgundy.[118] A certain nobleman took an enemy prisoner. The prisoner's wife came to ransom her husband. The nobleman promised to give back the husband on condition that she would lie with him. The woman was virtuous, yet wished to set her husband free; so she goes and asks her husband whether she should do this thing in order

---

man." Charles Leander Hill (trans.), The "Loci Communes" of Philip Melanchthon (Boston: Meador, 1944), p. 112. Cf. LW 40, 97-98. Luther frequently cited Matt. 7:12 and Luke 6:31 when speaking of the natural law of love. See, e.g., in this volume, pp. 287, 292, 296. Cf. Karl Holl, Gesammelte Aufsätze zur Kirchengeschichte, Vol. I, Luther (6th ed.; Tübingen: Mohr, 1932), p. 265, n. 1.

[118] Charles the Bold, Duke of Burgundy in 1467-1477, had actually been involved in such a unique case at Vlissingen in 1469 according to the Dutch historian Pontus Heuter (1535-1602), Rerum Burgundicarum libri sex (Hagae-Comitis, 1639), pp. 393ff. In Luther's fourth sermon at Weimar, October 25, 1522, on which this treatise is based, he had referred to the wise ruler simply as a "king." WA 10III, 384. Melanchthon relates the same incident in C. R. 20, 531, No. XLII. Both accounts may derive from a contemporary lyrical poem. CL 2, 393, n. 32.

to set him free. The husband wished to be set free and to save his life, so he gives his wife permission. After the nobleman had lain with the wife, he had the husband beheaded the next day and gave him to her as a corpse. She laid the whole case before Duke Charles. He summoned the nobleman and commanded him to marry the woman. When the wedding day was over he had the nobleman beheaded, gave the woman possession of his property, and restored her to honor. Thus he punished the crime in a princely way.

Observe: No pope, no jurist, no lawbook could have given him such a decision. It sprang from untrammeled reason, above the law in all the books, and is so excellent that everyone must approve of it and find the justice of it written in his own heart. St. Augustine relates a similar story in *The Lord's Sermon on the Mount*.[119] Therefore, we should keep written laws subject to reason, from which they originally welled forth as from the spring of justice. We should not make the spring dependent on its rivulets, or make reason a captive of letters.

---

[119] *Sermon on the Mount* I, xvi, 50. An abridged version of Augustine's story, dealing with a similar deception involving a woman's fornication by consent of her husband who was imprisoned for defaulting on a debt to the public treasury, was appended to a German edition of the treatise already in 1523 (*WA* 11, 280-281). The full text of the original story is in Denis J. Kavanagh (trans.), *Saint Augustine: Commentary on the Lord's Sermon on the Mount. FC*, p. 71-73, *MPL* 34, 1254.

AN EXHORTATION TO THE
KNIGHTS OF THE
TEUTONIC ORDER
THAT THEY LAY ASIDE
FALSE CHASTITY AND ASSUME
THE TRUE CHASTITY
OF WEDLOCK

1523

Translated by W. A. Lambert

Revised by Walther I. Brandt

INTRODUCTION

The Teutonic Order, or Teutonic Knights of St. Mary's Hospital at Jerusalem, was the youngest of the three great military and religious orders which sprang from the Crusades.[1] Like the other two, it began with charity (in the operation of a field hospital begun in the winter of 1190-1191), developed into a military club (when it was made an order of Knights by Pope Innocent III in 1198), and ended as something of a chartered company, exercising rights of sovereignty on the troubled confines of Christendom. Unlike the Templars and Hospitallers, however, its membership was open only to Germans, specifically those of noble birth.

The Teutonic Knights never played an important role in Palestine. Reorganized by the fourth Grand Master, Hermann von Salza (1210-1239), the order embarked on its primary career of missionary and military activity on the eastern frontiers of Europe. In 1229 it was invited by the Polish Duke Conrad of Mazovia to assist him against the heathen Prussians, and was promised full sovereignty over such lands as it might conquer.

For nearly two centuries thereafter the Teutonic Knights were the pioneers of Germanism and Christianity in northeastern Europe. After converting or slaughtering the Prussians, they pushed on until they were masters of the whole south shore of the Baltic from the Vistula to the Gulf of Finland, attracting German colonists to settle on the lands wrested from the Slavs. In 1234 the order established its independence of all authorities except the papacy by surrendering its territories to the Holy See and receiving them back again as a fief. In 1263 Pope Urban IV granted them the right to trade, although not for profit, a proviso which was readily circumvented. The order became a military and commercial corporation of vast wealth and selfish aims, a serious

---

[1] See the article "Teutonic Order" in the Encyclopedia Britannica, XXI, 983-984. For a bibliography on the order see Rudolf ten Haaf, Kurze Bibliographie zur Geschichte des Deutschen Ordens, 1198-1561 (Kitzingen am Main: Holzner, 1949).

competitor to the very towns it had founded to consolidate its gains in the course of its expansion.[2] In 1309 the order moved its headquarters from Venice to Marienburg, and by the middle of the fourteenth century it had become a world power.

Toward the close of the century symptoms of decline became evident. Wealth brought with it corruption; the haughty knights made little effort to improve the lot of their German and Slavic subjects, whom they treated with disdain. The surviving Prussians were now Christians, and in 1386 the ruler of Lithuania married the Christian heiress to the Polish throne and converted his people en masse, thus leaving the Teutonic Knights with no more heathen to conquer.

Poland had long realized her error in sponsoring a power which cut off her access to the Baltic. In 1326 there began more than a century of intermittent warfare between Poland and the Teutonic Knights, in the course of which the Knights suffered a disastrous defeat by King Ladislaus at Tannenberg in 1410 which stimulated the elements of unrest in Prussia to fresh activity. In 1466 the order was compelled by the Peace of Thorn to give all of West Prussia to Poland and to acknowledge Poland's suzerainty over the territory which the order retained in East Prussia, with its headquarters at Königsberg.

To counterbalance the hostility of Poland and Lithuania, the Knights sought to gain allies by choosing powerfully connected German nobles as their Grand Masters. In 1511 Albert of Brandenburg[3] became head of the order. His chief adviser was Dietrich von Schönberg,[4] whose ambitious plans involved Albert

---

[2] Some eighty towns were founded by the order during the thirteenth century, including such notable ones as Kulm, Marienwerde, Memel, and Königsberg.

[3] Grand Master Albert is not to be confused with his cousin, also called Albert of Brandenburg, who became Archbishop of Mainz in 1514 and to whom Luther addressed the letter prefixed to the Ninety-five Theses. LW 31, 21-22.

[4] Dietrich von Schönberg was a German nobleman from Meissen, whose forebears had served the order. At one time he considered becoming a clergyman, but was attracted to a diplomatic career. After an apprenticeship under Duke Henry the Younger of Brunswick, he entered Albert's service in 1515, but did not join the order. During the Polish war of 1519 he was sent abroad as an envoy in a vain effort to gain the help of Charles V, the pope, the kings of England, Scotland, and France, as well as of the German princes. He was killed at the Battle of Pavia in 1525, while fighting

in a disastrous war with Poland in 1519. Dietrich's brother, Bishop Nicholas of Capua, was sent by Pope Leo X to Prussia to negotiate a peace. Dietrich suggested to his brother the advisability of a thorough reform of the order. The suggestion was passed on to Leo X, who approved; his successor, Adrian VI, pressed the idea vigorously.

During his diplomatic travels in search of allies during 1519-1521, Dietrich became acquainted with the Lutheran movement. On his return he brought to Prussia the first direct information about Luther, and proposed to Albert that the Knights' *Rule* be submitted to the now-famous Reformer for suggestions for improvement and reform. When Dietrich set out again for Germany on September 10, 1521, he had instructions to consult Elector Frederick on the advisability of seeking Luther's counsel. Dietrich conferred with Frederick in October or November, and apparently recommended to Albert that a copy of the *Rule* be sent to the electoral court for examination by Luther.[5] But on February 12, 1522, he wrote Albert advising against sending the *Rule* to Frederick because the disturbed conditions at Wittenberg made it difficult to keep such matters secret.[6]

In April, 1522, Grand Master Albert himself came to Germany to attend the Diet at Nürnberg. Here he saw the Lutheran movement at first hand, met Lazarus Spengler,[7] and listened to the

---

on the French side. Erich Joachim, *Die Politik des letzten Hochmeisters in Preussen, Albrecht von Brandenburg* (3 vols.; Leipzig: Hirzel, 1892-1895), I, 95, and III, 113; *idem*, "Des Hochmeisters Albrecht von Preussen erster Versuch einer Annäherung an Luther," in *Zeitschrift für Kirchengeschichte*, XII (1891), 116-122.

[5] Dietrich's report to Albert has been lost, but he had the habit of jotting down informal notes on official documents or elsewhere, some of which have survived. Joachim, "Des Hochmeisters . . . erster Versuch," pp. 120-121. Luther was probably not informed of this interview; at least his extant correspondence of that period nowhere refers to it. His first mention of Grand Master Albert, whom he mistakenly calls Frederick (Albert's predecessor as Grand Master, 1498-1510, the time of his death, was Frederick of Saxony), is in a letter to Wenceslaus Link of December 19, 1522, in which he praises the Grand Master for his reply to the papal envoys at Nürnberg, and remarks that he seems not unfavorable to the gospel. WA, Br 2, 633.

[6] Joachim, "Des Hochmeisters . . . erster Versuch," pp. 121-122.

[7] Lazarus Spengler (1479-1534) first met Luther on the latter's way to Augsburg in 1518, and became one of the leaders of the reform movement in Nürnberg. In 1519 he published a defense of Luther's doctrines, for which he was included in the bull *Exsurge, Domine*. He represented Nürnberg at the diets of Worms (1521) and Augsburg (1530).

sermons of Osiander[8] and became a convert to Lutheranism. His conversion was not openly acknowledged for some time; he had to feel his way carefully, since he was still seeking allies against Poland and could not afford to alienate such Catholic champions as his cousin Joachim I of Brandenburg and Duke George of Saxony. But there were signs of his growing adherence to Lutheran ideas. In a memorandum on the qualifications and duties of preachers which was being considered in the Reichstag in the summer of 1523, Albert with his own hand emended the provision that they should expound the holy gospel "according to the Scriptures and the interpretation of the four teachers, Jerome, Augustine, Gregory, and Ambrose"; he struck the "four teachers" and their names, substituting instead the phrase, "Christian interpretation." He further specified that priests who married or knights who left the order were to be subject only to ecclesiastical, not governmental, punishment.[9]

Prodded by Pope Adrian VI to reform the order, Albert proceeded to do so, but in a manner not at all in accord with the pope's intentions. On June 14, 1523, he sent his confidential agent, Johann Oeden of Heilbronn, to Wittenberg to confer with Luther. Oeden was provided with two documents. One was a letter to Luther from Albert in his own hand, stating that Oeden had a verbal message for him, and begging Luther in Christian love to make a confidential response. The other was a series of secret instructions to Oeden himself: he was to remain noncommittal until Luther should promise to keep the interview secret to the grave; then he was to show Luther the letter on Luther's promise to burn it as soon as it had been read; only then was he to turn

---

[8] Andreas Osiander (1498-1552) was ordained a priest in 1520 and called to Nürnberg as instructor in Hebrew, where he became a convert to Lutheranism. Called as preacher to the Church of St. Lawrence in Nürnberg in 1522, he exerted great influence in favor of Lutheranism and in opposition to the sectaries. Becoming involved in quarrels with his colleagues and with the Nürnberg city fathers, he left for Königsberg in 1549, where he was warmly received by Duke Albert (the former Grand Master, who honored Osiander as his spiritual father) and appointed as pastor and professor at the university. He broke with Luther ultimately on the doctrine of justification.
[9] Paul Tschackert, *Urkundenbuch zur Reformationsgeschichte des Herzogthums Preussen* ("Publicationen aus den K. Preussischen Staatsarchiven," Vols. XLIII-XLV [Leipzig: Hirzel, 1890]), II, 31-32, No. 118.

over the *Rule* and statutes of the order,[10] with the request that Luther examine them, point out what was Christian in their content, suggest any needful changes in the documents or in the order itself, and particularly in the clergy in its territory. These opinions were to be put in writing, either by Oeden or by Luther himself. "Then we will set to work." [11]

Unhappily, Oeden's report of the interview is lost. A Prussian chronicler, the Dominican Simon Grunau, has preserved the following rather unreliable and obscure report of Luther's reply to Oeden: In the beginning people of the order placed the gospel above their *Rule* and statutes, but later self-seekers got control and gave to their own statutes an authority equivalent to that of the gospel, so that now the most pious of the Knights is worse than a Turk, and though they swear ten oaths and sign a hundred briefs, they observe none.[12] Whether or not this was the substance of Luther's reply, the fact is certain that about this time Luther's friend Johann Briesmann accepted a call to preach in East Prussia, delivering his first sermon at Königsberg on September 27, 1523.[13]

Moreover, in November, 1523, Albert visited Wittenberg himself and had an interview with Luther on the 29th, at which Melanchthon was also present. When Albert asked Luther some questions about the *Rule,* Luther impulsively cried out that he

---

[10] The *Rule* of the order derives primarily from that of the Templars, which in turn was based on the Benedictine *Rule,* though chapters 4-7 are borrowed largely from the Hospitallers. The *Rule* provided in chapter 1 for the vows of poverty, chastity, and obedience common to all the monastic orders; it also dealt with matters affecting care of the sick and observance of communal living. The "statutes" included, in addition to the *Rule* itself, the so-called "laws" elaborating on various points in the *Rule,* and the "usages" which spoke of the organizational structure and duties of officers in peace and in war. Max Perlbach, *Die Statuten des deutschen Ordens* (Halle: Niemeyer, 1890), pp. xxx-xxxii and 29.

[11] Tschackert, *Urkundenbuch,* I, 23-24. The text of both documents is reproduced in *WA, Br* 3, 86-87, on the basis of a manuscript preserved in the state archives at Königsberg, possibly by Albert.

[12] Tschackert, *Urkundenbuch,* II, 30, No. 114a; *WA, Br* 3, 87, n. 3.

[13] Tschackert, *Urkundenbuch,* I, 24. John Briesmann (1488-1549), a Franciscan who became acquainted with Luther during a stay of six years at Wittenberg, 1513-1519, was present at the Leipzig Debate in 1519, following which he became a strong supporter of Luther. On his arrival at Königsberg he was appointed preacher and pastor at the cathedral by Bishop Polentz of Samland, who under the teaching and influence of Briesmann became the first Lutheran bishop.

should abandon his foolish and misleading *Rule*, take a wife, and make of Prussia a state, a principality or duchy. Melanchthon expressed the same opinion. Albert laughed, but said nothing.[14]

It was shortly after the November interview that Luther composed and published his *Exhortation to the Knights of the Teutonic Order*. All the early collected editions of Luther's writings give the date for this treatise as March 28, 1523, on the basis of an old note indicating the date of completion as "*Sabb. p. Concept. Mariae.*" The note, however, may well have been a mistake for "*Annunciat. Mariae*," which would fix the date as December 12, thus relating it directly to the November interview. Duke George of Saxony, who was generally prompt to note any fresh product from Luther's pen, wrote to Albert's brother Casimir, the Margrave of Brandenburg, on January 2, 1524, "Martin Luther has directed a little book to the Teutonic Order, which has been printed and is being given wide distribution"; he connected the treatise with Albert's visit to Wittenberg, warning that Albert had asked Luther to send preachers to Prussia.[15] Spalatin, then in attendance at the second Diet of Nürnberg, sent a copy of the address to Willibald Pirkheimer on January 19, 1524, as something new from Wittenberg.[16]

How decisive Luther's influence was in the secularization of the Teutonic Order is difficult to determine. One can hardly suppose that Albert first considered secularization as a consequence of his November interview with Luther. He had already become a secret convert to Lutheranism; Pope Adrian VI had urged him to reform the order; Poland and Lithuania were hostile, and he had failed in the effort to gain allies. The suzerainty of Poland over a secularized Prussia would be nothing new; it had been acknowledged since 1466. Albert's cousin Joachim I was hereditary ruler of Brandenburg. Why should Albert not found a

---

[14] Luther's account of the interview is in a letter to Briesmann dated July 4, 1524. *WA, Br* 3, 315. Otto Clemen suggests that Luther's account may have reference to a visit of Albert on November 14, which would correspondingly advance the date of this treatise. *WA, Br* 3, 195, No. 686, and *WA, Br* 3, 317, n. 8.

[15] See the text of the letter in Gess, *Akten und Briefe zur Kirchenpolitik Herzog Georgs von Sachsen*, I, 599.

[16] The arguments in favor of the December date are set forth in *WA* 12, 229-230.

hereditary dominion for himself if he could secure the approval of Poland, and thereby end their long conflict? Luther's treatise was perhaps in the nature of a trial balloon which would serve to bring to light the attitude of the Knights and the Prussian bishops, and prepare them for coming events. It seems fair to conclude that Luther's influence, and more particularly the present treatise, served to crystallize an idea that was already growing in Albert's mind as the necessary consequence of forces which had long been at work prior to and apart from those of religious reform.[17]

In 1525 the Teutonic Order was dissolved in Prussia and its possessions transformed into a hereditary duchy for Albert and his descendants[18] under the suzerainty of Poland. The Livonian holdings were annexed by Poland in 1561 and transformed into the Duchy of Courland.

The following translation is a revision of the one that appeared in *PE* 3, (405) 410-428, and is based on the first German edition printed by Johann Grünenberg in Wittenberg, *An die herrn Deutschs Ordens, das sie falsche keuscheyt meyden und zur rechten ehlichen keuscheyt greyffen Ermanung,* as that has been reprinted with annotations in *WA* 12, (228) 232-244.

---

[17] See Kurt Forstreuter, *Vom Ordensstaat zum Fürstentum: Geistige und politische Wandlungen in Deutschenordensstaate Preussen (1498-1525)* (Kitzingen am Main: Holzner, 1951), and Walter Hubatsch, "Die inneren Voraussetzungen der Säkularisation des deutschen Ordensstaates in Preussen," *Archiv für Reformationsgeschichte,* XLIII (1952), 145-171.

[18] On July 1, 1526, Albert married Dorothea, daughter of King Frederick I of Denmark, thus founding the evangelical house of the Hohenzollern.

AN EXHORTATION TO THE KNIGHTS OF THE TEUTONIC ORDER THAT THEY LAY ASIDE FALSE CHASTITY AND ASSUME THE TRUE CHASTITY OF WEDLOCK

Martin Luther

Grace and peace in Christ. Amen.

Marvel not, my dear Knights of the Teutonic Order, that I have made bold to write especially to you, and to advise you to give up your unchaste chastity in favor of marriage. My intentions are unquestionably good. Besides, many honest and intelligent men regard it as not only desirable, but even necessary, to look to you to do this, for your order is truly a unique order, primarily because it was founded for the purpose of making war on the infidel.[1] For this reason it must be temporal and wield the temporal sword, and yet at the same time it is also to be spiritual, taking and keeping the vows of chastity, poverty, and obedience like other monks.[2] Reason and daily experience teach us only too well how that combination works.

I have in other books[3] written quite enough about the

---

[1] See the Introduction, p. 133.
[2] See the Introduction, p. 137, n. 10.
[3] See *An Open Letter to the Christian Nobility* (1520). PE 2, 118-123; *The Babylonian Captivity of the Church* (1520). LW 36, 74-81; *Themata de Votis* (1521). WA 8, 323, 335; *De votis monasticis* (1521). WA 8, 573-669; *The Estate of Marriage* (1522), in this volume, pp. 17-22 and 27; and *Ursach und Antwort, dass Jungfrauen Klöster göttlich verlassen mögen* (1523). WA 11, 394-400.

abomination of clerical celibacy, and have consistently shown that such a vow is invalid and cannot be kept except by God's special grace, a grace that without any such vow or law can achieve not only chastity, but everything else as well. Nevertheless, I have been unable to refrain from addressing to the members of your order a special exhortation on the subject, in the firm conviction and fond hope that your order can establish an excellent and powerful example for all other orders if it should be the first to take this course. It might lead to a decrease of unchastity in other quarters as well, and to a more rapid increase of the fruits of the gospel.

In the first place, your order has the advantage of being provided with the temporal necessities of life. Its wealth can be divided up among the knights so that they can become land-holders or officeholders, or take up some other useful calling. You are not faced with the wretched poverty that keeps many a mendicant friar and other monk in the monastery for the sake of his belly. A secularized Teutonic knight could nonetheless be sent to war or on any service where he might be needed, and even more readily than in his present status. Out of it there would develop in the course of time a true and duly constituted knighthood which, free from hypocrisy and a false name, would be acceptable in the sight of God and of the world.

In the second place, hardly anyone doubts that the Teutonic Order would then be less burdensome and more acceptable to all its subjects than it is today. At present it is obvious that the order is of little benefit to either God or the world; besides, the knights are suspected and disliked also because everyone knows how rare chastity is, and every man must be afraid for his wife and daughter.[4] Single men cannot be trusted very far; even married men have all they can do to keep from falling, although among them there is more justification for hope and confidence. With single men one can have neither hope nor confidence, but only constant fear.

In the third place, we may confidently expect that the Teu-

---

[4] The flagrant immorality of the priesthood at this time is documented in Henry Charles Lea, *History of Sacerdotal Celibacy in the Christian Church* (3rd ed.; New York: Macmillan, 1907), II, 54-60.

tonic Order would prosper under such a change. There is no reason to fear that the knights would be attacked because of it, especially if the change grew out of a Christian understanding of the matter and had the approval and liking of your subjects (as was suggested above). Undoubtedly, there are many prominent knights who would welcome the change, inasmuch as they really want to live decent lives. If some of them made wry faces about it at first, that feeling would pass away by and by, or their dissatisfaction would at worst be harmless. It is to be hoped, at any rate, that from now on very few will become monks and religious any more, because the gospel is beginning to shine and to expose this false spirituality in such a way that those who today are the last and remain the last will be compelled to provide for themselves as best they can.

These are human considerations, of course, which carry weight only with the world. On account of them nothing should ever be done or left undone, begun or changed, which is to have validity in the sight of God. Nevertheless, they must be taken into account because they make this matter more tolerable in the eyes of the people. For we have stronger and more worthy arguments than these to prove that it is pleasing to God. With God we would soon be at one on this matter and reach a definite agreement; it is the world that is fastidious and hard to please in the things of God. For this reason we have to set the matter forth by way of giving that wretched devil's whore[5] at least a few reasons, thereby doing what we can to quiet and pacify her. If she accepts it, good; if not, we will bid her adieu, and despite her do the right and leave the wrong undone. It is enough that it pleases God.

We will therefore present some arguments now which are valid before God to prove that the estate of marriage is pleasing in his sight.[6] God says in Genesis 2 [:18], "It is not good that the man should be alone; I will make him a helper who shall be

---

[5] *Teuffels hurn,* frequently used elsewhere by Luther for natural human reason, here means the world.

[6] Luther had commented on marriage before, and at greater length. See *Ein Sermon von dem ehelichen Stand* (1519). WA 2, 166-171; *The Babylonian Captivity of the Church* (1520). LW 36, 92-106; and *The Estate of Marriage* (1522), in this volume, pp. 11-49.

with him," etc. These are God's words, which cannot be understood except by faith. Neither reason nor nature can comprehend that a wife is a help to her husband; rather, everyone scribbles and screeches about it, as we see and hear.[7] On this point the whole world must regard God as a liar. This is why even the pope in his canon law has put God to school, stipulating therein that a wife is not a help but a hindrance in serving God,[8] and that therefore he who would serve God must not have a wife.[9] And that is perfectly true, for the god whom the pope serves cannot be served by the work of our God.

The prophet Daniel said this of the pope a long time ago, stating in chapter 11, "He will know nothing of married women," or, "He will give no heed to married women." [10] To harlots, however, he was to give heed, and even worse. But whoever would be a true Christian must grant that this saying of God is true, and believe that God was not drunk when he spoke these words and instituted marriage. All right, if I had made a thousand vows, and if a hundred thousand angels—not to mention one or two miserable bags of maggot-fodder[11] like the pope—were to say that I should do without a helper and that it is good to be alone, what would such vows and commands be to me in comparison with these words of God, "It is not good that man should be

---

[7] Luther is referring to the current praises of monasticism, which implied that a wife is a hindrance to a man who would lead a spiritual life.

[8] *Decreti Magistri Gratiani Prima Pars*, dist. XXXI, can. 7, and dist. XXXII, can. 17, refer to the obstacle which intercourse represents to that prayer and wholehearted fellowship with God in which a priest is supposed to be engaged incessantly. *Corpus Iuris Canonici*, I, cols. 113 and 121. Cf. Luther's reference to this general question on pp. 46-47.

[9] *Decreti Magistri Gratiani Prima Pars*, dist. XXXI-XXXIII. *Corpus Iuris Canonici*, I, cols. 111-124; *Decretalium D. Gregorii Papae IX*, lib iii, tit. III: *De clericis conjugatis*, and lib iv, tit. VI: *qui clerici vel voventes matrimonium contrahere passunt. Corpus Iuris Canonici*, II, cols. 457-459 and 684-687.

[10] *"Er wird sich auff ehliche weyber nicht verstehen,"* oder *"er wird ehe weyber nicht achten."* Dan. 11:37. In his 1530 translation of Daniel Luther construed 11:36-45 as a part of chapter 12, the famous prophecy of the Antichrist, which already at this early date Luther saw to be fulfilled in the pope. *LW* 35, 303, n. 162; see also, in this volume, p. 60, n. 8. See in his accompanying *Preface to Daniel* his interpretation of this verse in terms of married love (*Frauenliebe*) rather than—as was suggested in the Vulgate's *concupiscentiis* and retained in Douay's "lust of women"—fornication or impure love. *LW* 35, 313.

[11] *Maden sack*; see p. 70, n. 38.

alone; I will make him a helper" [Gen. 2:18]? Unless, of course, God himself by a miracle should make an exception of me; as St. Paul says in I Corinthians 7 [:7], it must be a special gift.[12]

Just compare God and man! God says, "It is my will that you have a helper and not be alone; this seems good to me." Man replies, "Not so; you are mistaken; I vow to you to do without a helper; to be alone seems good to me." What is that but to correct God? And what is correcting God but to exalt oneself above him? How then can such a vow or command possibly be valid or binding? Indeed, how can such a vow possibly escape being worse than any act of adultery or unchastity? What kind of fortune must befall this vow and chastity which in the absence of a divine miracle is based solely on man's own wanton choice, and so blasphemously runs counter to God's word? If there be a miracle of God, the vow is unnecessary; if there be no miracle of God, the vow is against God and blasphemes his word and work.

But let us hear some of the things they say in their blind folly. Their favorite arguments, of which they loudly boast, are these, that this vow and estate of celibacy is an ancient tradition, taught and confirmed by many holy fathers and councils since the days of the apostles, and now accepted as such throughout the world, and that it is inconceivable that God would have permitted so many people to err over so long a period of time. Very good. But if I were to ask them whether they would be willing to die for their conviction that so ancient a practice is not wrong and that the councils and fathers have not erred, they would think twice when death drew near. Now that death seems far off, they boldly and bravely screech and scribble that men ought to believe what they themselves would then seriously doubt. Well, let them go, let them die in that faith; I will not.

What do they have to say to the fact that God is more ancient than all the councils and fathers? He is indeed also greater and higher than all the councils and fathers. Scripture, too, is higher and more ancient than all the councils and fathers. In addition, the angels are all on the side of God and Scripture.

---

[12] See *The Estate of Marriage* (1522), in this volume, p. 21.

Furthermore, the practice which existed from the time of Adam is also more ancient than the practice which originated with the popes.

If then age, longevity, greatness, number, and holiness are sufficient reason for believing anything, why do they believe men, whose history dates back only a short time, and refuse to believe God, who is the most ancient, the highest, the greatest, the holiest, the mightiest of all? Why do they not believe all the angels, when a single one of them counts for more than all the popes put together? Why do they not believe Scripture, when a single passage from it carries more weight than all the books in the world? Why do they not believe the physical nature [der Creatur] which has been created in us, since one work of God is mightier than all the words, thoughts, and dreams of all men and devils?

If we had any sense at all, we should really be heartily ashamed to harbor so much as a single doubt—to say nothing of setting up something contradictory—when we hear God's word, before which all the angels bow down and every creature stands in awe. Now here is God's word saying, "You shall not be alone but have a helper, unless I arrange it differently. We should stand in fear and terror of this word, which has the support of all angels and creatures from the beginning of the world. But we go right ahead and exalt high above it a vow we made but yesterday, and a dream which the pope has been having for a few years; we must even hear it said, "Such a vow cannot be in error; God has not permitted these fathers to make a mistake"! And so it is now supposed to be incredible that lowly men, who live and dream for a moment, can err; but it is supposedly credible that the eternal God does err in his word and works, and that all the angels and creatures make mistakes. Fie, fie, and again fie upon our unspeakable blindness, our mad and senseless blasphemy!

But so it must be: God's word has to be the most marvelous thing in heaven and on earth. That is why it must at one and the same time do two opposite things, namely, give perfect light and glory to those who believe it, and bring utter blindness and shame upon those who believe it not. To the former it must be the most certain and best known of all things; to the latter it must be the most unknown and obscure of all things. The former must extol and praise it above all things; the latter must blaspheme and slander it above all things. So does it operate to perfection and achieve in the hearts of men no insignificant works, but strange and terrible works. As St. Paul says in II Corinthians 4 [:3], if our gospel is veiled, it is veiled only to those who are perishing.

They also have yet another very neat way of proving their case, namely this. They yield to the point of conceding that it is true, God has indeed caused this to be said in the Scripture; but they claim that the church has altered and abrogated it and men therefore are not to do it unless it is again stipulated and authorized by a council, in order that the decree of the church and obedience to it may not be destroyed.[13] Ah me! May the good Lord bow down before you, my worthy gentlemen! It would be a fine thing, wouldn't it, for men to give you the honor they owe to God, exalt you above God, and say, "The thing is right and should be done because you authorize it; but even if God did command it and—as you yourselves admit—clearly wants it done, yet it would not be right and should not be done unless you also added your advice and consent!" Who gave you the right to change the word of God, to abrogate it, and to restore it again? So men are going to teach God his lessons and blue-pencil the mistakes of the Holy Ghost![14] Tell me, who ever heard of a more abominable abomination? And these are the pretensions of men who want to rule over souls!

We, on the contrary, state our position thus: Councils may

---

[13] Luther is referring to a polemical treatise, *Iohannis Fabri Constantiensis in spirtualibus vicarii opus adversus nova quaedam et a christiana religione prorsus aliena dogmata Martini Lutheri*, published at Rome, August 13, 1522, which gained considerable acclaim for its author, Johann Faber (1478-1541), later the bishop of Vienna. Faber had attacked Luther primarily on the issue of papal supremacy; in effect he claimed the right of the church to interpret and even modify biblical commands. See the text of his lengthy treatise in *Corpus Catholicorum* (28 vols.; Muenster im Westfalen: Aschendorff, 1919-1959), vols. XXIII-XXVI. Luther entrusted to Justus Jonas, then recently married, the task of writing a reply, but added a brief letter of his own (dating perhaps from early 1523) which Jonas included in his printed edition. See the text of Luther's letter in WA 12, (81) 85-87.
[14] *Gott zur schulen füren, und dem heyligen geyst die feddern streychen.*

make decisions and exact decrees in matters that are temporal or yet unclarified. But in matters where we can plainly see what is God's word and will, we will not wait for the decrees and decisions either of councils or of the church; we will rather fear God, and go right ahead and act accordingly before the question is even raised whether councils should be called or not. I refuse to wait until councils decide whether we are to believe in God the Father, Maker of heaven and earth, in his only Son, Jesus Christ our Lord, in the Holy Ghost, etc. The same applies as well to all other manifest, clear, and certain portions of Scripture which it is needful and profitable for me to believe. Suppose the councils should delay, and I should have to die before they could make up their minds. What would become of my soul, meanwhile, since it is not supposed to know what to believe but to await the decision of councils, when I need faith here on earth?

I will say further:[15] Suppose one, two, a hundred, a thousand, and even more councils should decree that clergy might marry, or anything else that God's word has already decreed shall be done or left undone. I would sooner overlook and trust to God's mercy the case of a man who all his life long had kept one, two, or three whores, than the case of a man who had married a wife in conformity with the decrees of such councils, and who otherwise would not have ventured to marry without such a decree. And I would in the name of God command and advise everybody that no one, on peril of his soul's salvation, take a wife on the strength of such a decree, but rather live in stricter chastity than before; or, if that be impossible for him, he should not despair in his weakness and sin, but call upon God's helping hand.

And I say this for this reason. Fornication or unchastity is certainly a great sin but it is a minor fault when compared with blasphemy. For even Christ himself says in Matthew 11 [:20-24] that it shall be more tolerable for Sodom and Gomorrah—whose unchastity exceeded the ordinary variety [Gen. 19:4-8]—than for Capernaum, Bethsaida, and all the great saints and Pharisees of

---

15 The following argument, repeated in virtually the same form only applied to the use of both elements in the Lord's Supper, occurs in a liturgical writing dating from almost the same time, Luther's *Formula of Mass and Communion at Wittenberg* (1523). PE 6, 96-97.

that time. And in Matthew 22[16] he also says that harlots and base fellows[17] shall enter the kingdom of heaven before the Pharisees and scribes, although they were pious, chaste, and respectable people. Why should that be? Because they opposed the word of God, the gospel; whereas the harlots and base fellows, although they sinned, did not strive against the gospel.

Now the matter stands thus: Whoever takes a wife on the authority of man-made statutes or the decrees of councils, when he would otherwise not do so, although he already has God's decree and word for it, is in his heart despising God's word and trampling it underfoot. For he is exalting man over God and is trusting more in the words and teachings of men than in the words and teachings of God. In so doing he is acting directly contrary to the faith, denying God himself, and setting up men as idols in the place of God. In this way his body becomes outwardly married and chaste, through human ingenuity, but his soul becomes inwardly before God a harlot and adulteress twice over, through unbelief, distrust, contempt of God, idolatry, denial of God's holy word; and who can enumerate all the other abominations of such an apostate heart? What a fine change in one's chastity, to become married outwardly and doubly unmarried inwardly! You see, therefore, how sincere these people are who would guide you in this matter by their councils and decrees, and do away with obedience to the word of God!

Don't you suppose that he who keeps a concubine is guilty of a lesser sin and is nearer to God's mercy than he who takes a wife under such conditions? Especially when that same fornicator would like very much to be married, and is compelled to sin by the weakness of his own nature while at the same time being forced into sin by the authority of men who forbid him to marry? Don't you suppose that God will regard the heart of such a man—a heart that would gladly act according to God's word, that confesses God's word and does not deny it, giving to God the honor due him in his word—and be gracious to him, the more so if he is disgraced in the eyes of the world? Actually, I think

---

16 Cf. Matt 21:31 and 22:10.
17 *Buben* is Luther's term for describing the kind of wickedness represented, e.g., in Judg. 19:22 where the KJV speaks of "sons of Belial."

such a case will never arise, for if God grants someone a knowledge of his word he will also either grant him chastity, or allow him to lead a married life secretly,[18] or strengthen him if he is persecuted and made to suffer on account of a public marriage.[19]

Therefore, if any ecclesiastic wishes to marry, he should hold before himself God's word, rely upon it, and in God's name marry, regardless of whether councils precede or follow. Let him say, "God's word says in Genesis 1 [:27-28] and 2 [:18-25] that I am a man and you are a woman, and that we shall and must come together to multiply; no one is to prevent us from doing that, nor can anyone forbid us to do it; neither do we have it in our power to vow otherwise. We dare to act upon the basis of that word, in sheer despite and contradiction of all councils, churches, all decrees of men, all vows, customs, and whatever else may be or has ever been opposed to it. Close eyes and ears, and simply lay hold of God's word in the heart! And if councils and men should allow and permit us to do so in the future, we do not want their permission; we will neither do a thing nor leave it undone because of their permission."

I will not be satisfied to have councils or the church (as they interpret it) permit or decree such a change; I refuse to be beholden to them for it, or to wheedle them out of it or beg them for it. They will simply have to do it, and not only that; they must first restore to God the honor due him, and confess openly before all the world that in forbidding marriage they have contradicted God and his holy word, like the soul-murderers they are, and have flooded the whole world with unchastity, condemned

---

[18] The secret marriage here proposed would simply be the regularizing of the relationship of fidelity already postulated between a pious fornicator and his private concubine. The two relationships would differ not so much in terms of legal status, something which was rarely Luther's concern, but in terms of their conformity to the will of God as understood and obeyed in their inmost conscience by the parties involved, something which was always Luther's concern. Legal proscriptions on concubinage had long been impossible to enforce; indeed, clerical concubines in the Middle Ages had even enjoyed a kind of ecclesiastical immunity. Lea, *op. cit.*, I, 420-423.

[19] The punishments being inflicted at this time for the crime of clerical marriage, though occasionally impeded by a sympathetic prince or populace, actually included all sorts of ecclesiastical and temporal measures ranging from banishment and excommunication to confiscation of property, imprisonment, and death. Examples are given in *ibid.*, II, 42-43 and 47-50.

the word of God, made the devil their false God, and exalted themselves above God, and that by sheer inspiration of the devil—instead of the Holy Spirit—they have been not bishops and teachers but wolves, thieves, murderers, and seducers.

They must first confess these abominations, repent of them, and make satisfaction for them by voluntarily humbling themselves before the whole world and once more honoring God's word, which they have so shamefully suppressed, blasphemed, and dishonored throughout the world. As soon as they do this—and no sooner—we will accept and abide by their permission and consent.

Yes, you say, and when will that be? When will they do that? All right, so they keep their councils and decrees; then let them live according to them themselves, we will not, nor will we either hear or heed them. I too know very well that they will never do what I propose, for they want to be admired and not be looked upon as men who have been in error until now. But we will yet succeed in teaching them that they must do it despite themselves. They shall be put to shame openly, as Paul says in II Timothy 2 [3:9] whether they will it or not; exactly that and nothing else, though they were ten times their number and each one had the power now possessed by all of them put together.

God's word will do it; even now it is shining forth and revealing their shame. That light they will never extinguish; the more they try to put it out by blowing on it, the brighter their blowing makes it burn. That is what is already happening now, no matter how much they worry and fume. It will not help them one bit to say, "Can a single impotent monk be wiser than the whole world?" True, the monk is impotent; but Another shall be omnipotent, and reduce them all to impotence. You can count on that. Would the true God let them turn up their nose at him as they please, and allow his eternal word, to which he has pledged himself, to avail only in case it should please those wretched filth-sacks? [20] I am willing to let them hope so, which is all they deserve; however, they will find out sure enough.

In olden times the Romans did the same thing. They had

---

[20] *Drecksack*, literally, "bag of dirt or dung," is here the equivalent of *Madensack* (see p. 70, n. 38). Grimm, *Deutsches Wörterbuch*, II, 1359.

brought together in their city gods from all over the world. But when they heard that some people regarded Jesus Christ as a God, they would not recognize him as a God, simply because the Roman senate had not yet authorized it and the belief had originated elsewhere. These arrogant men presumed that only he should be God whom they declared to be a god, and no one else. This was the same as saying, "We Roman senators are gods above all gods, and may make gods of whomsoever we will." And that is exactly what they did. This is why among them Christ could not be God. This is also what our fine gentlemen are doing today with their councils; God's word is to cool its heels in patience, and not be God's word until they grant it permission.

Yes, they are even worse than the Romans, for at least the Romans made to be God one who was regarded as a god. Our council devotees want to decree what is entirely their own, and then it is to be right merely because they decree it, no matter whether God has spoken before or not, or whether there was a God before or not. And they have the idea that if God should speak a word even in our day they would have the authority to judge and evaluate it, to legalize or abrogate it, to permit or forbid it. In every way they regard our God as a piece of soft wax which they can mold into a pig or a crow or whatever they please. Just so did the Jews turn God into a golden calf [Exod. 32:1-4]. These things are indeed horrible and abominable, enough to break a Christian's heart.

But it is my hope that Christ has preserved for himself, or will yet preserve, some bishops who will take serious thought and come to the true knowledge of God,[21] and either give up their horrible and abominable office or restore it to the position

---

21 This was a reference to George of Polentz (1478-1550), member of the Teutonic Order since 1511 and bishop of Samland since 1519. Luther's hope was fulfilled; on Christmas Day, 1523, Polentz preached a sermon in which he confessed his adherence to the evangelical teaching. As early as January 2, 1524, Duke George of Saxony wrote of him, "It is also said that the bishop of Samland . . . is quite infected with the Lutheran heresy." Gess, *op cit.*, I, 599. *WA* 12, 240, n. 1. The bishop's evangelical sympathies may perhaps have been of earlier date, but not publicized while his sovereign's conversion was yet being kept secret. See the Introduction, pp. 135-137, and p. 137, n. 13.

of a true episcopal office.[22] But even if none should be converted, or if the conversions are kept secret, we who have the clear word of God must not hold back on that account, or look behind us to see what they decide or whether they are following us. Christ would not allow St. Peter to question or concern himself about what John or anyone else would do, but said, "What is that to you? Follow me" [John 21:19-22], as much as to say, "Since you have my word, it is your duty to go forth and do its bidding; leave the others to me, whether they follow or do not follow."

For this reason everyone, though he be as hard as a stone, ought really to be terrified when he hears and perceives that his vow and celibacy (in the absence of a divine miracle) overstep and contradict this word of God, "It is my will that you should not be alone, but have a helper" [Gen. 2:18], and that they live under the horrible thunderbolt in which Daniel says, "He will give no heed to married women,"[23] as if to say, "It is true that he will shun married women, not because he loves chastity, however, or wants to serve God—as he will pretend in order to deceive the world—but that he may have an easy time of it and be spared the troubles and unhappiness of married life, and yet at the same time neither live chastely nor serve God, but carry on the more freely his fornication and other wickedness."

This is because he does not understand the words of God in which he says, "It is not good to be alone" [Gen. 2:18]. For, as has been said [John 6:63], these words are spirit and life as are all God's words, and must be understood in terms of faith. "Good" here does not mean good according to the flesh—indeed it is trouble (as St. Paul says[24])—but good according to the spirit. For in the sight of God it is a precious and noble good work to bring up children and train them, to rule your wife and servants in a godly manner, to support yourself by the sweat of your face

---

22 *Bischofflich amt;* see p. 109, n. 66.
23 Dan. 11:37; see p. 144, n. 10.
24 Compare Luther's exegesis of I Cor. 7:28 in *Das siebente Kapitel S. Pauli zu den Corinthern* published just a few months earlier, in which he distinguishes between "trouble in the flesh" (KJV) or "worldly troubles" (RSV), such as external work and unhappiness on the one hand, and "trouble in the spirit," such as sin and a bad conscience on the other hand. WA 12, 137.

[Gen. 3:19], and to endure much misfortune and unhappiness at the hands of your wife, children, servants, and others. Such good makes little show. "It is an evil (says the pope[25]) and a hindrance to the service of God," that is, to pleasurable, lazy living. But he who believes and rightly understands these words sees how good it is for the soul, even if it is an evil for the flesh and its lusts.

For this reason God has done marriage the honor of putting it into the Fourth Commandment, immediately after the honor due to himself,[26] where he commands, "Honor your father and your mother" [Exod. 20:12]. Just look! Show me an honor in heaven or on earth, apart from the honor of God, that can equal this honor! Neither the temporal nor the spiritual estate has been so highly honored. And if God had told us nothing more about married life than this Fourth Commandment, we should still have learned sufficiently from it alone that in the sight of God there is no higher office, estate, condition, or work (next to the gospel, which concerns God himself) than the estate of marriage.

But many still come with the old argument—and waste a lot of breath on it—that it is dishonorable to make a vow of celibacy to God and then not keep it, since even in the eyes of the world he who fails to keep his vow is branded as a faithless and dishonorable perjurer. Some of the nobility, in particular, work themselves blue in the face with such twaddle, most of all those who are supposed actually to have made many vows and who babble a lot about vows but have made little attempt to keep any, who have never in their lives thought seriously about trying to keep the least bit of what they so solemnly vowed to God in baptism, nor of acknowledging that they still owe it. The log in their own eye still blinds them so effectively, and they see so clearly the speck in other men's eyes! [Luke 6:41-42].

They are rude, hardened hearts, which neither perceive themselves nor allow others to tell them, like the smiths' anvils (as Job says[27]); they will have their mad way! How often must I say

---

[25] See p. 60, n. 8.
[26] The preceding commandments of the Decalogue have to do with God himself, his name, and his day. Exod. 20:2-11.
[27] Job 41:24 (Vulgate, 41:15).

that an unfulfillable vow, one that is contrary to God's word, is no vow at all and should be forsaken? It is like the man who says, "My mother vowed that I should be a bishop."[28] Is a man who vowed to commit adultery or to kill an innocent man supposed to keep his vow? Must I keep my vow if I have vowed to cling to the sky and to ride on sunbeams or float on the clouds? If I were to ask them that, I should think they would have to say: No, the first vow is wrong and must not be kept, the second is foolish and will fail of itself.

So I say in this case too: We were all created to do as our parents have done, to beget and rear children. This is a duty which God has laid upon us, commanded, and implanted in us, as is proved by our bodily members, our daily emotions, and the example of all mankind. Now unless God himself performs a miracle, if you vow celibacy and remain unmarried you do exactly the same as he who vows adultery or something else which God has forbidden. Since your vow is an impossible and foolish one, we can see and understand why it remains unfulfilled of itself, and why unchastity only becomes so much the more rampant and shameless that it is unspeakable. And yet those stubborn fellows want to compel the emotions: a man should not feel his masculine nature, nor a woman her feminine nature.

One more point remains to be considered. I have no doubt whatsoever that many a bishop, abbot, and other ecclesiastical lord would marry if only he would not be the first to do so, if the way had been smoothed in advance and such a marriage had become so much a matter of custom that it no longer brought disgrace or danger upon a man but was approved and honorable in the sight of the world. Indeed, my dear fellow, who wouldn't wish that? What shall we say to this objection? If you have God's word, which you can and ought to follow, but are concerned above all about whether others are going ahead, it is just as if I were to say, "I will not believe in God nor serve him until I see all the Turks and heathen and Jews believing in God and serving

---

[28] About half a year earlier Luther had written in his *Ursach und Antwort, dass Jungfrauen Klöster göttlich verlassen mögen*, "I once heard a learned man say of this: 'My mother had vowed that I should be a bishop. How can I fulfil such a vow?'" *WA* 11, 398.

him." Very well; but in the meantime with heathen and Jew you will be going to the devil, because you despise God's word and are willing to serve him, not for his own sake but because of others. In so doing, you are honoring and regarding men more than God and his word.

I may liken such people to Lot's wife, who looked back to see what the men of Sodom and Gomorrah were doing, and became a pillar of salt, Genesis 19 [:26]. She too had been commanded not to look back, but to follow the angel's instructions forthwith [Gen. 19:17]. Christ himself refers to this in Luke 17 [:31-32], where he speaks of the evil days to come, how there shall be great error and deception, and warns that no one shall think of what is behind him, or turn back into his house to get anything. "Remember Lot's wife," he says; as much as to say, as he said to Peter, "Follow me" [John 21:22]; let him who tarries, tarry; let him who waits, wait; do thou look upon no one, but upon my word alone, and then go forward boldly and cheerfully. That is just what we must do about marriage too in these perilous times. If you feel your nature and know now that God wishes you to be married, you ought to go right ahead, even though you should have to be the first and the only one to marry, and regardless of what all men—friend and foe—have to say[29] about it. If you are held up to shame and slandered for it, know this: God's mouth is greater, his praise mightier, his testimony more glorious than that of all men, though they filled a thousand worlds or more.

Moreover, if you abstain from marriage or put it off, not out of regard for God, but out of regard for men, you can readily see whom you are serving, and that all your celibate living is labor lost. He who would wait until the world speaks well of divine things, or is not offended in them, has a long wait ahead of him. What an abomination it is! The devil has brought things to such a pass that among Christians a man must be timid, fearful, and worried even about marrying, although marriage has

---

[29] *Singen oder sagen*, literally, "sing or say," was an alliterative formula deriving originally from the twofold form of the medieval poet's presentation, but in time coming to mean simply "make known" or "publish abroad" without specific reference to the mode of communication. Grimm, *Deutsches Wörterbuch*, VIII, 1659-1660; X[1], 1084-1089.

been from the beginning and still is free and honorable even among the heathen, and throughout the world. So completely has the devil, through the papal regime, destroyed that which is God's word and work that the question is first raised in Latin whether a man can and should be a man, and whether the vow is valid by which he vows not to be a man.

But that is the law and custom of the world; that is the way its god and prince, the devil, must rule it. For it does the same in all other things as well. Theft is the smallest sin in the eyes of God, because it involves only temporal goods; but the world punishes it most severely. Next comes adultery, a much graver sin; that goes unpunished in the world.[30] Then comes murder; in the world that brings honor to one bold and wicked enough to kill. But above all these, the most grievous sin on earth is the spiritual estate's appalling worship and service of God. Though contrary to God's majesty, honor, word, and work, it not only goes unpunished but has the greatest honor wealth, power, friends, and everything else on earth, as if it were a quite holy, heavenly, divine existence.

In order that this letter may not grow too lengthy, my dear knights, and since I have written so much on this subject,[31] I will stop here, humbly beseeching your graces and exhorting you kindly in God's name: Do not, as St. Paul says [II Cor. 6:1], accept grace in vain. For it is written in Isaiah 49 [:8], "At the acceptable time I have listened to you, and helped you on the day of salvation. Behold, now is the acceptable time; now is the day of salvation."[32] God's word is shining and calling; you have plenty of reason and opportunity to heed it, even as regards temporal wealth. The peril of conscience and of daily sins in the

---

[30] Cf. p. 33. In a later letter to Spalatin dated May 2, 1524, Luther, after referring to the Mosaic law on theft (Exod. 22:1-15), wrote, "Solomon, in the Proverbs [6:30-35], also approves this law where he says that a thief can redeem himself by returning what he has stolen, but an adulterer loses his soul. Would that this law were in force now!" WA, Br 3, 283. How statements of this sort were perverted is seen, e.g., in a letter from a Wittenberg student, Felix Ulscenius, to Wolfgang Capito dated July 20, 1522, "Martin and Melanchthon want adulterers and blasphemers to be beaten with rods, but not thieves." WA 12, 243, n. 2. S-J 2, 131.

[31] See p. 141, n. 3.

[32] II Cor. 6:2. The ascription of the entire quotation to Isaiah is Luther's.

weak flesh urge you to it. The impossibility of keeping a foolish vow compels you. The ecclesiastical estate and order in itself is worthless.

To wait upon or postpone action until a future council is wrong where there is the command and requirement of God's word. You are not to delay to see what others are doing; rather you—each one of you—ought to be the first to break a path and rush into the Jordan before King David [II Sam. 19:17-20], now that he is coming again into his kingdom and his son Absalom, the scoundrel, has been slain.

All things urge, compel, invite, and incite you to act at this time. In so doing you will be greatly honoring God and his word, and giving weak consciences a comforting example, whereby God's word may again prevail. There is nothing to hinder you from this course except the foolish opinion of the mad world, which will say, "What, are the Teutonic Knights doing that?" But since we know that even the prince of this world is judged [John 16:11], we ought not to doubt that this and every other opinion of the world is already condemned in the sight of God. Just go ahead boldly and confidently; set God before your eyes in true faith and turn your back on the world with its grumbling and noisy bluster, and neither listen nor look to see how Sodom and Gomorrah are sinking behind us, or what becomes of them!

May the God of mercy, who through Jesus Christ our Lord has again caused the light of his grace to shine upon us, enlighten, encourage, and strengthen your hearts with the power of his Holy Spirit in firm faith and fervent love, that in this and all things else you may do his fatherly and gracious will, to the honor and praise of his holy gospel, and to the comfort and benefit of all believers in Christ. To him be thanks, praise, and glory forever. Amen.

The grace of God be with you all. Amen.

ORDINANCE OF A COMMON CHEST

PREFACE

1523

Translated by Albert T. W. Steinhaeuser

Revised by Walther I. Brandt

FRATERNAL AGREEMENT ON THE COMMON CHEST OF THE ENTIRE ASSEMBLY AT LEISNIG

Translated by Walther I. Brandt

INTRODUCTION

The medieval church required financing at the local level as well as at the top. Church buildings, once erected, had to be kept in repair; clerical and lay personnel connected with them needed to be furnished a livelihood. Funds were required too for the church's efforts to deal, however inadequately, with the problem of widespread poverty among the masses. Normally the bulk of the local revenue for these purposes came from income-producing foundations or properties, endowments of altars at which special masses were celebrated, compulsory tithes, and fees for ministerial acts, especially those performed for the souls of the departed.

Some of these sources were already drying up before the Lutheran movement got under way. Others were condemned in principle by the reformers; private masses, for example, were frowned upon.[1] Secular princes, who had long coveted the wealth of the church, were on the point of confiscating the lands and property of church and monastery. Many laymen used the new "freedom" as a pretext for refusing to pay tithes. The burden of poor relief showed no signs of diminishing; estimates are that from 15 to 30 per cent of the population may have been paupers and vagrants in towns of that period.[2]

Begging, a common practice during the Middle Ages, one which had become almost respectable through the activities of the several mendicant orders, was condemned by the reformers. As early as 1520, in the *Long Sermon on Usury,* Luther denounced the practice on the basis of Deut. 15:4, 11; Christians were not to let anyone be in want or beg.[3] In his 1521 *Open Letter to the Christian Nobility* he suggested that every city should take care

---

[1] While at the Wartburg, Luther wrote to Melanchthon on August 1, 1521, that he would never again celebrate a private mass. WA, Br 2, 372; S-J 2, 50. Before his return to Wittenberg, his own monastery had ceased to celebrate mass in the accustomed fashion, according to a letter of unknown authorship dating from about December 4, 1521. S-J 2, 75-78.
[2] Smith, *The Age of the Reformation,* pp. 558-559.
[3] See pp. 281-282, 286-287.

of its own poor, and that an organized system of poor relief be set up to replace the current haphazard system.[4] All these circumstances made imperative a complete reorganization of the parish financial system.

The first attempt in this direction was made by Karlstadt in Wittenberg during Luther's stay at the Wartburg.[5] Other communities quickly followed suit, either on their own initiative or through the Wittenberg influence. Among these may be cited Augsburg, Nürnberg, and Altenburg in 1522; and Kitzingen, Strassburg, Breslau, and Regensburg in 1523.[6]

The Leisnig ordinance of 1523 is therefore by no means unique. It is included in the present volume because it was drawn up on Luther's direct advice, had his hearty approval, and was published by him together with a preface of his own. It was one of the most thoroughgoing of these ordinances, almost a rudimentary congregational constitution, and illustrates a number of the difficulties encountered in the complicated process of reorganizing parish finances in the sixteenth century.

The parish of Leisnig on the Mulde River in electoral Saxony was already in existence when in 1191 the Cistercians founded the monastery of Buch some distance up the river. In the same year Emperor Henry VI granted the parish of Leisnig to the monastery. Later, when a small city[7] grew up about the castle, and the church of St. Matthew was erected there and made the parish church, the bishop of Meissen decreed that the abbot of Buch should have the right to name the parish priest. This right was repeatedly confirmed; in 1419 it was specifically recognized by

---

[4] See *PE* 2, 134-135.

[5] Karlstadt's ordinance, which has many similarities with the later Leisnig ordinance, is summarized in Herrmann Barge, *Andreas Bodenstein von Karlstadt*, I, 378-382. See the complete text in Aemilius Ludwig Richter, *Die evangelischen Kirchenordnungen des sechzehnten Jahrhunderts* (2 vols. in 1; Weimar: Landes-Industriecomptoirs, 1846), II, 484-485; or in Hans Lietzmann, *Die Wittenberger und Leisniger Kastenordnung, 1522-23* ("Kleine Texte für theologische Vorlesungen und Uebungen," No. 21 [Bonn: Weber, 1907]), pp. 4-6.

[6] Detailed references to these instances are given in WA 12, 2. See also O. Winkelman, "Die Armenordnungen von Nürnberg (1522), Kitzingen (1523), Regensburg (1523), und Ypern (1525)." *Archiv für Reformationsgeschichte*, X (1912-1913), 242-280, and XI (1914), 1-18.

[7] In 1523 Leisnig had a population of about 1500. WA 12, 3, n. 1.

Pope Martin V. According to contemporary law, Leisnig was at once both a religious and a political community.[8]

Abbot Antoninus of Buch (d. 1526) was hostile to the Reformation. Nevertheless, the reform movement spread among the nobility, bourgeoisie, and peasantry of the parish, which then included eleven rural villages, until it seems to have become virtually unanimous.

In response to repeated requests from certain members of the Leisnig parish, Luther paid them a visit on September 25, 1522.[9] Presumably two items were discussed: first, the right of the parish to select its priest and preacher; second, the establishment of a common chest for the parish. It appears that Abbot Antoninus had appointed one of his monks, Heinrich Kind, as parish priest of Leisnig. After assuming the post, Kind embraced the evangelical cause, and was recalled by the abbot.[10] The Leisnig congregation, however, elected him as their priest, and Johann Gruner[11] as their preacher.[12] The two took office about the end of the year 1522.

Naturally, the abbot of Buch resented this usurpation of his well-established right of patronage, and instructed a new appointee to take over the parish. The bishop's appointee was notified by Sebastian von Kötteritzsch,[13] speaking on behalf of the parish, that they wanted Kind and Gruner, that they looked upon him as a

---

[8] MA[3] 5, 400.

[9] See Luther's letter to Spalatin dated September 25, 1522. WA, Br 2, 604.

[10] See Paul Kirn, *Friedrich der Weise und die Kirche* (Leipzig: Teubner, 1926), p. 116. Kind served as parish priest at Leisnig from 1523 until he was retired, for reasons of age and other considerations including his own request, by the visitors of 1529. WA 12, 7, n. 1. Cf., however, WA, Br 3, 22, n. 2.

[11] Johann Gruner is probably the "Johannes Gronigerus" or "Groner," former preacher in Oschatz, who in 1524 sought and obtained from Prince Wolfgang of Anhalt the appointment as parish priest in Zerbst, being installed there at Christmastime, 1524. He was the author of the treatise, *A Booklet to Comfort All Poor Consciences*, published at Wittenberg in 1524. WA 12, 7, n. 1.

[12] Their choice is reported in an undated letter from the Leisnig parish to Elector Frederick, quoted in WA 12, 3-4.

[13] With his brother Hans, Sebastian von Kötteritzsch (d. *ca.* 1575) held the fiefs of Sitten and Kroptowitz in the Leisnig parish. Having served as a magistrate in Altenburg, he was without office in 1523, but later became a magistrate in Bitterfeld and participated in the visitations of 1528-1530, 1533, 1534. At the Diet of Augsburg (1530) he was among those accompanying the Elector John of Saxony. WA, Br 3, 23, n. 3.

stranger not called by the congregation, and that they refused to recognize or accept him as their shepherd of souls. Thereupon the appointee departed.[14]

Official attempts at a compromise between the parish and the abbot failed. Hans von der Planitz[15] and Hans von Minkwitz, acting for the elector, proposed that the abbot name the priest and the citizens name the preacher. This was unsatisfactory to both parties. Next they proposed that the abbot yield up all his rights over the parish in return for an annual stipend. The abbot seems to have been willing, but most of his monks refused to accept this.[16] An agreement never was worked out between the parish and the monastery.[17] The independence of the parish never received formal recognition until it was confirmed by the visitation commission of 1529, and thus also by the temporal authority.[18] The Leisnig congregation protested to the elector that they had never granted the right of patronage to the abbot themselves, and that their right of choice was established by Christ fifteen hundred years before, namely, "that the whole congregation through the grace of God and by ordinance of divine Scripture has the right to call, choose, install, and depose one, two, or three persons from within its own company."[19]

---

[14] WA 12, 4; Kirn, op. cit., p. 116.

[15] Hans von der Planitz (d. 1535) was probably already in Elector Frederick's service when, together with Hans von Minkwitz, he visited Jerusalem in 1518. In 1521 he became chief magistrate in Grimma, where his work was frequently interrupted when he was sent on diplomatic errands by the elector. He was present at the Leipzig Debate in 1519, and represented the elector on the Council of Regency in 1521 where he worked to block implementation of the Edict of Worms. In 1530 he accompanied Elector John to the Diet at Augsburg. Allgemeine deutsche Biographie, XXVI 232-233. His reports from the diets of Nürnberg, an important source, have been edited by Ernst Wülcker and Hans Virck, Des kursächsischen Rathes Hans von der Planitz Berichte aus dem Reichsregiment in Nürnberg 1521-1523 (Leipzig: Teubner, 1899).

[16] See the letter from Antoninus to Von der Planitz dated October 4, 1524, and the text of the proposed agreement to a stipend in Kirn, op. cit., pp. 189-191.

[17] Ibid., p. 117.

[18] The visitation report stated, "Whereas the parish assembly at Leisnig on their own initiative conducted a common chest for some years according to their written and printed ordinance, it is to remain in force by authority of this visitation, as follows . . . ." Emil Sehling, Die evangelischen Kirchenordnungen des XVI. Jahrhunderts (6 vols.; Reisland, 1902-1957), I, 608.

[19] WA 12, 4.

The abbot, sensing the trend of the times and fearing more serious conflict, apparently failed to push his claims, or the Elector may have intervened on the side of the parish.[20] At any rate, the congregation proceeded with confidence in taking over all church properties within the parish and establishing an organization to administer them, to provide for divine worship and schools, and to assist the poor and needy. Luther's influence in the matter is seen by the fact that the town council and the congregation sent two representatives, Sebastian von Kötteritzsch and Franz Salbach, to Wittenberg with a formal letter dated January 25, 1523,[21] requesting his advice and counsel in the matter of their proposed ordinance, a copy of which they probably presented to him at that time. The ordinance itself may well have been the work of Kind and Gruner.

The delegation also presented two other requests to Luther: first, that he give them a written statement in approval of their procedure in calling Kind and Gruner to serve them; second, that he furnish them with an evangelical order of service. Luther replied promptly and briefly to the council in a letter of January 29, expressing his approval of their ordinance for the parish.[22] In the same letter he also promised to comply with their other two requests, a promise he fulfilled in the spring of that same year with the publication of two treatises: *The Right and Power of a Christian Congregation or Community to Judge All Teaching and to Call, Appoint, and Dismiss Teachers, Established and Proved from Scripture*,[23] and *Concerning the Ordering of Divine Worship in the Congregation*.[24] Luther's reply to the congregation came later in the form of a written preface to the ordinance; he had both preface and ordinance printed and published together.

Encouraged by the warm approval expressed in Luther's letter to the council, the Leisnig congregation proceeded to set up their common chest and to reform the order of service. On February 24 they elected the ten directors of the chest; on Sunday,

---

[20] WA 12, 4-5.
[21] See the text of this letter in WA, Br 3, 21-22.
[22] WA, Br 3, 23.
[23] WA 11, (401) 408-416; PE 4, (71) 75-85.
[24] WA 12, (31) 35-37; PE 6, 60-64.

March 8, they set aside the sacrifice of the mass, thereby abolishing the functions of the priests attached to the four side altars.[25] The report of the Saxon visitation of 1529, where it speaks of the changes that had to be undone, shows the thoroughness of their early reform of the service. Clerical vestments were abolished; the clergy consecrated the elements while garbed in lay attire; the three great festival periods of the church year were each reduced to a single day and celebrated in the "forenoon only, the afternoon being regarded as a work day . . . in order to avoid excessive drinking, carousing, and idleness."[26]

Unhappily, the administrators of the common chest encountered difficulties.[27] The city council was reluctant to transfer to the directors of the chest its existing right to dispose of endowments, bequests, etc., and maintained that it could not take such a step without the elector's express permission. The congregation appealed to the elector, who named the tax commissioner of Kolditz to hear the disputing parties. Negotiations dragged on for weeks.[28] A compromise was finally reached to the extent of having both parties agree to keep the peace and bring their differences to the elector for resolution as they might arise; on April 12 the elector wrote the congregation that he was happy over this agreement.[29]

In August, 1523, probably at the elector's request, Luther again visited Leisnig to look into the matter of the common chest. He found that the council was still withholding funds; despite his urging the council remained obdurate. Meanwhile, the congregation was running short of funds with which to pay its officials. On August 11 and again just eight days later, Luther wrote angrily to the elector, requesting confirmation of the Leisnig ordinance,[30] but the elector, as usual, hesitated and delayed. As late as November 24, 1524, Luther complained to Spalatin that the Leisnig

---

[25] WA 12, 6. On the altar priests, see p. 180.

[26] See the text of the 1529 visitation report in Emil Sehling, *op. cit.*, I, 605-606.

[27] For bibliographical references see Enders, *D. Martin Luthers Briefwechsel*, IV, 71, n. 1.

[28] Kawerau (ed.), Köstlin's *Martin Luther*, I, 551.

[29] WA 12, 6.

[30] See his letters in WA, Br 3, 124-125 and 128-129.

preacher, Tilemann Schnabel,[31] might soon have to leave for want of pay and sheer hunger. He deeply regretted that the Leisnig attempt, the first of its kind, which should have been such an example of success, had turned out to be such a miserable example of failure.[32]

There is no direct evidence to show when the preface with the appended ordinance came from the press. It has been held[33] on the basis of Luther's letters of August 11 and 19 that it did not appear until the time of Luther's second visit to Leisnig in August, 1523. Against this may be cited the fact that a copy of the first edition bears a marginal note by its original purchaser that he paid ten pfennig for it on July 6, 1523.[34] Furthermore, Luther was prompt in replying to the Leisnig request for a letter approving their method of choosing a preacher and for an order of service. These two documents came from the press between Easter and Pentecost, 1523; it would be strange if he then withheld the ordinance from the press for several months. Judging by his actions on other occasions, it is quite probable that he rushed the ordinance into print without consulting the elector, in order to give it the widest publicity and confront the elector with an accomplished fact. His very haste may have militated against the success of the Leisnig experiment, for in his sermon of December 26, 1523, where he suggested how a city parish might organize a system of poor relief, he added, "But we do not have the personnel for this, therefore I do not think we can put it into effect until God makes Christians."[35]

The translation of Luther's preface given here is a revision

---

[31] Tilemann Schnabel (d. 1559), an Augustinian monk, received his doctorate in theology at Wittenberg in 1515 and became a provincial of his order in Alsfeld shortly after 1520. There he preached evangelical sermons so eloquently that he won over the whole town by 1522, only to be forbidden to preach by the Landgrave Philip. Doffing his cowl, he remained for a time with Luther at Wittenberg until he accepted the office of preacher at Leisnig, succeeding Gruner. After Hesse embraced the evangelical cause, Philip granted the citizens of Alsfeld, as a reward for their faithfulness in the Peasants' War, their request to have Schnabel appointed as their priest. He served as superintendent of Alsfeld from 1531 to 1541, resigning on account of poor health. *Allgemeine deutsche Biographie*, XXXII, 81-82.
[32] See the letter to Spalatin in *WA*, Br 3, 390.
[33] This is the position, e.g., of De Wette, *Dr. Martin Luthers Briefe*, II, 382.
[34] *EA* 22, 106.
[35] *WA* 12, 693.

of the one that appeared in *PE* 4, 92-98. The ordinance itself is here translated for the first time in English. The translation of both documents is based on the first Wittenberg printing by Cranach and Döring: *Ordenung eyns gemeynen kastens. Radschlag wie die geystlichen gutter zu handeln sind* (1523), as that has been reprinted with annotations in *WA* 12, 11-30.

ORDINANCE OF A COMMON CHEST

PREFACE

Suggestions on how to deal with ecclesiastical property
Martin Luther, Ecclesiastic [1]

To all Christians in the congregation of Leisnig, my dear sirs and brethren in Christ: Grace and peace from God the Father and our Savior Jesus Christ.

Dear sirs and brethren. Since the Father of all mercies has called you as well as others to the fellowship of the gospel, and has caused his Son Jesus Christ to shine into your hearts; and since this richness of the knowledge of Christ is so active and powerful among you that you have set up a new order of service,[2] and a common fund after the example of the apostles [Acts 2:44-45; 4:32-35], I have seen fit to have this ordinance of yours printed, in the hope that God will so add his gracious blessing that it may become a public example to be followed by many other congregations, so that we, too, may boast of you, as St. Paul boasted of the Corinthians that their effort stirred up many others [II Cor. 9:2]. Nevertheless, you will have to expect and take comfort from the fact that if what you are undertaking is of God it will necessarily meet with vigorous opposition, for Satan never rests or takes a holiday.

We cherish the hope that this example of yours will come to be generally followed, and that as a result there will be a great decline in the existing foundations, monastic houses, chapels, and

---

[1] *Ecclesiastes* ("the preacher") is the Greek title for one of the Old Testament writings. Luther used it as a self-designation to assert his status as a man of the church after that dignity had been denied him by the papal bull and the Edict of Worms. *MA*³ 5, 401, n. 45, 1; *MA*³ 3, 374, n. 16, 2. See his defense of this title in his 1522 *Wider den falsch genannten geistlichen Stand des Papsts und der Bischöfe.* *WA* 10^{II}, 125-126. Cf. also the title of Emser's rebuttal: *Wider den falschgenannten Ecclesiasten und Wahrhaftigen Erzketzer Martinum Luther* (Leipzig, 1523).

[2] See the Introduction, pp. 165-166.

those horrible dregs[3] which have until now battened on the wealth of the whole world under the pretense of serving God. This decline is also being mightily facilitated by the holy gospel which is now bursting forth once more, and which reveals this blasphemous and damnable "service of God" in its true colors. Moreover, the clergy themselves are behaving in such a manner that goodness and integrity have vanished from their midst and will have nothing more to do with them. Things have everywhere come to such a pass that it seems both God and man have grown sick and tired of monkery and clericalism, and there has to be a change. At the same time for this very reason there is need of great care lest there be a mad scramble for the assets of such vacated foundations, and everyone makes off with whatever he can lay his hands on.

I have resolved, therefore, to the extent of my ability and duty to forestall such a catastrophe while there is still time, by offering Christian counsel and admonition. For since I have to take the blame whenever monasteries and foundations are vacated, when the number of monks and nuns decreases, and whenever anything else happens to diminish and damage the clerical estate, I refuse to accept any additional responsibility if some greedy bellies should grab these ecclesiastical possessions and claim as an excuse that I was the one who put them up to it.

If it comes to that, I fear that very few will be guided by my advice, for Greed is a disobedient and unbelieving scoundrel. I will nevertheless do my part, clear my own conscience, and place the burden upon theirs, so that no one can accuse me of remaining silent or speaking up too late. Let whoever will, then, follow my well-meant advice or reject it; I am not to blame. But first I want to warn sincerely, and kindly request, that no one heed or follow these suggestions of mine unless he realizes and thoroughly understands from the gospel that monkery and clericalism, as they have been for the past four hundred years, serve no useful purpose and are nothing but harmful error and deception. A weighty matter like this has to be tackled with a good and unshakeable Christian conscience; otherwise, things will

---

[3] *Grundsuppen* has reference to the priests who are at the bottom of it all. *MA³* 5, 401, n. 45, 22; *BG* 7, 111, n. 3.

go from bad to worse, and on our deathbed we will be overwhelmed by terrible remorse.

First. It would have been a good thing if no rural monasteries,[4] such as those of the Benedictines,[5] Cistercians,[6] Celestines,[7] and the like, had ever appeared on earth. But now that they are here, the best thing is to let them dwindle away, or, where it can properly be done, to assist them to disappear altogether. This can be done in either of two ways: first, by allowing the inmates, if they so desire, to leave of their own free will, as the gospel permits; second, by each governing authority arranging with the monasteries under its jurisdiction to admit no further applicants and, if there are too many inmates, to send the excess elsewhere and let the remainder die out.

Since no one is to be coerced into faith and the gospel, those who because of their age, their bellies, or their consciences elect to remain in the monastery should not be ejected or harshly dealt with, but should be supported for the rest of their days just as before. For the gospel teaches us to do good even to the unworthy, just as the heavenly Father sends rain and sunshine upon the good and the evil alike [Matt. 5:45]. We must remember, too, that these persons have drifted into this estate as a result of the blindness and error which prevailed generally, and have never learned a trade by which they could support themselves.

I would recommend that the governing authorities take over the property of such monasteries, and from it make provision for those inmates who choose to remain there, until they die. This provision should be even more ample and generous than what they may have had before, so that men may realize that this

---

[4] *Fellt kloster* was Luther's name for the monastic settlements which, to enable their monks to retire from the world, grew up outside of the cities and engaged primarily in agriculture. *BG* 7, 112, n. 7.

[5] The term Benedictines applied to a number of autonomous religious orders professing the *Rule* drawn up by St. Benedict of Nursia (*ca.* 480-*ca.* 550) for his monks at Monte Cassino.

[6] The Cistercians were a religious order founded in 1098 at Citeaux as an offshoot of the Benedictine Order, and given new life by the entry of St. Bernard of Clairvaux in 1112. For purposes of seclusion their houses were erected only in remote places, and hence frequently became important centers of pioneering agriculture.

[7] The Celestines were also an offshoot of the Benedictine Order, founded about 1250 by Peter of Murrone, who in 1294 became Pope Celestine V.

is not a case of greed opposing clerical possessions, but of Christian faith opposing monasticism. In carrying out this policy the permission of pope or bishop is not to be sought beforehand, neither is their ban or anathema to be feared; for I am writing this solely for those who understand the gospel and who have the authority to take such action in their own lands, cities, and jurisdictions.

Second. The property of those monasteries which are taken over by the governing authorities should be used in the following three ways. First, those inmates who choose to remain should be supported, as has just been said. Second, those who leave should be provided with sufficient funds to find a position and make a fresh start in life, even though they brought nothing with them when they entered the monastery. For when they depart, they are leaving at the same time their lifelong way of making a livelihood; and they have been defrauded, because the time they spent in the monastery might have been employed in learning something else. As for those who brought something with them when they entered, it is no more than right in the sight of God that they should have it returned to them, to each his own portion,[8] for here matters are to be determined by Christian love and not by strict human justice. If anyone is to suffer injury or loss, it should be the monastery and not the individual, for the monastery is the cause of their error. The third way is the best, however, to devote all the remaining property to the common fund of a common chest, out of which gifts and loans could be made in Christian love to all the needy in the land, be they nobles or commoners. In this way, too, the will and testament of the founders would be carried out. For although they erred and were misled when they gave this property to monasteries, their intention certainly was to give it for the glory and service of God; but their purpose was not realized. Now there is no greater service of God than Christian love which helps and serves the needy, as Christ himself will judge and testify at the Last Day, Matthew 25 [:31-46]. This is why the possessions of the church were formerly called *bona*

---

[8] *Yhe eyns teyls* is here taken to mean *"jeden sein Teil"* (*MA*[3] 5, n. 47, 15, and *CL* 2, 406, n. 20) rather than *"Jedem ein (gleiches) Thiel"* (*BG* 7, 114, n. 1 and Lietzmann, *op. cit.*, p. 8, n. 5).

ecclesiae, that is, common property, a common chest, as it were, for all who were needy among the Christians.[9]

If the heirs of the founder are impoverished and in want, however, it is fair and in harmony with Christian love that the foundation revert to them, at least a large portion of it, or the whole amount if their need be great enough to warrant it. It certainly was not the intention of their fathers—and should not have been—to take the bread out of the mouths of their children and heirs and bestow it elsewhere. And even if that was their intention, it is false and un-Christian, for fathers are in duty bound to provide for their own children first of all; that is the highest service they can render to God with their temporal goods. But if the heirs are not poor and in need of it, they should not take back their father's bequest, but let it go into the common chest.

But you might say, "That is opening the door too wide; on that basis the common chest will receive precious little, for everyone will claim the whole amount and say that his needs are so great, etc." Answer: This is why I said that Christian love must judge and act in this matter; it cannot be handled by laws and regulations. Besides, I am setting down this advice only in accordance with Christian love, and for Christians only. We have to expect that greed will creep in here and there. So what? We cannot just let things slide on that account. After all, it is better to have greed take too much in an orderly way than to have general plundering, as happened in Bohemia.[10] Let each one

---

[9] At least from the time of the investiture controversies and throughout the Middle Ages the church's legal rights to acquire, receive, hold, and dispose of property had been largely asserted and defended in terms of the rights of ecclesiastical personages over against persons not of the spiritual estate. The First Lateran Council of 1123, e.g., decided "that laymen . . . have no faculty for determining anything concerning ecclesiastical possessions . . . let the bishop have the care of all ecclesiastical business." Denzinger, *Sources of Catholic Dogma,* p. 147, No. 361. The Council of Constance of 1414-1418 asserted over against John Huss "that it is permissible for ecclesiastical personages to hold possessions and temporal goods" and that if the laity "lay hold on these ecclesiastical goods [*bona ipsa ecclesiastical*] they are to be punished as sacrilegious persons." *Ibid.,* p. 218, Nos. 684-685. Luther is using the term *ecclesia* in its etymological sense to underscore the communal aspect of such ecclesiastical property—in Greek *ekklesia* means "the assembly of people"—as belonging to laity as well as clergy. In Acts 2:44 and 4:32 the Vulgate term was *Omnia communia,* "all things in common."
[10] Luther is referring to the excesses of the radical Taborites during the Hussite Wars of 1420-1432. One of the "Four Prague Articles" set forth

examine himself to see what he should take for his own needs and what he should leave for the common chest.

Third. The same procedure should be followed in the case of bishoprics, foundations, and chapters which have under their control lands, cities, and other possessions. Such bishops and foundations are neither bishops nor foundations; they are in actual fact secular lords with ecclesiastical titles. Hence, they should be turned into secular lords, or else their possessions should be divided between the impoverished heirs and relatives, and the common chest. As for prebends and benefices, they should be left to their present incumbents; when these die no successors should be appointed, but the properties should be divided between the needy heirs and the common chest.

Fourth. The possessions of monasteries and foundations in part, and the prebends in large measure, are based on usury, which today is everywhere called "repurchase"[11] and which has in but a few years swallowed up the whole world.[12] The holdings thus derived would first of all have to be separated, like leprosy, from the property which consists of simple bequests. For the

---

by the Hussites in 1420 demanded that the clergy be divested of all worldly goods. The *Compactata* agreed upon by the Council of Basel in 1433 complied with this demand as regards all clergy bound by vows of poverty, allowing the church itself, however, to acquire and hold temporal goods, but merely as administrator.

[11] *Widderkauff* was known as early as the thirteenth century and was actually a type of sales contract in which the sale was conditional upon the seller's right to repurchase what he had sold. The two sales transactions together were the equivalent of a loan. A merchant would sell an article on credit for a given price, and immediately repurchase it from the buyer for cash in a smaller amount, the cash being then in effect a loan. The difference between the two prices became in effect an interest charge on the outstanding loan. See Herbert Heaton, *Economic History of Europe* (New York: Harper, 1936), p. 203; and Grimm, *Deutsches Wörterbuch*, XIV[1], 1063. The scholastics up through the fifteenth century condemned such contracts of sale and resale in the name of the whole medieval prohibition against usury—which was designed to protect the debtor—largely because of the unfair prices involved. The resale clause itself was not condemned, but incorporated into the fifteenth century *zinss* contract (see pp. 234-238) as a redeemability clause. John T. Noonan, *The Scholastic Analysis of Usury* (Cambridge: Harvard University Press, 1957), pp. 95-98. It is the mutually redeemable *zinss* contract—relatively recent (see p. 295, n. 141)—to which Luther here refers.

[12] Living in the "age of discovery," Luther saw in his lifetime a remarkable growth in trade and commerce, cities and the merchant class, and a consequent increase in the demand for capital which was accompanied by a sharp rise in prices and exorbitant "interest" rates. See *BG* 7, 494-513.

advice I gave above refers only to foundations established by true and honest bequests apart from "repurchase." Foundations established on the basis of "repurchase," however, may rightly be regarded as usury; for I have never yet seen or heard of a proper redeemable *zinss* contract.[13] In this matter, therefore, it is first necessary to make up for the usury by returning to each one what is his own before allowing such assets to go into the common chest, for God says, "I hate the offering that comes from robbery" [Isa. 61:8]. If it should prove impossible to find the persons who had suffered loss in the repurchase transaction, the common chest might then receive the property.

But the right and wrong of "repurchase" is too long a story for the present; I have dealt with it sufficiently in the treatise on usury,[14] from which one may learn what portion of such prebends and foundations should be restored to those who have been paying *zinss*. For there is no doubt that a good many prebends have long since received back the principal sum of their loans, yet they do not stop sucking the sweat and blood out of their creditors. Hence, this matter is decidedly one of the most pressing problems for consideration by emperor and kings, princes and lords, and everybody else.

Fifth. Mendicant houses located in cities[15] might be converted into good schools for boys and girls,[16] as they were before.[17] Other monasteries could be converted into dwellings if the city needed them. The fact that they were consecrated by bishops should raise no obstacle, for God knows nothing of such consecration. If this advice of mine were acted upon in a Christian way,

---

[13] *Zinsskauff auff Widderkauff.* For a discussion of the meaning of the mutually redeemable *zinss* contract, see Noonan, *op. cit.,* pp. 230-235.

[14] See the *Long Sermon on Usury* (1520) in this volume, pp. 273-308, esp. p. 295 ff.

[15] The monasteries of such mendicant orders as the Dominicans, Franciscans, and Augustinian Hermits were built mostly within the cities, in contrast to those rural orders mentioned on p. 171.

[16] Cf. Luther's 1521 *De votis monasticis.* WA 8, 615 and 641.

[17] The burden of lay education in the early Middle Ages was borne mainly by the monasteries, which conducted not only "internal" schools for future members of the order but also "external" schools to educate children of various classes for life in the community outside the monastery. The instruction was given gratuitously. *Catholic Encyclopedia,* XIII, 555-556. See in this volume, p. 341.

many other things would suggest themselves and be found feasible, and much would be learned by experience, more than can now be proposed in words, for various and extraordinary situations would arise where only Christian love can judge aright.

If God were to grant that these suggestions be carried out, not only would we have a well-filled common chest for every need, but three crying evils would diminish and eventually cease. The first of these is begging,[18] which does so much harm to land and people in soul and property. The second is the terrible misuse of the ban,[19] which serves no other purpose than to torture people in the interest of the possessions of priests and monks. If they had no possessions, there would be no need of this ban. The third is this cursed *zinss* contract,[20] the biggest usury on earth, which up to now has asserted its validity even in the matter of ecclesiastical properties—there above all.

If anyone does not care to follow these suggestions, and in so doing quench his greed, I wash my hands of him. Well do I know that few will accept such advice. I am content if only one or two follow me, or would at least like to follow me. The world must remain the world, and Satan its prince. I have done what I can, and what I am in duty bound to do. God help us all to do what is right and to stand firm. Amen.[21]

FRATERNAL AGREEMENT ON THE COMMON CHEST OF THE ENTIRE ASSEMBLY AT LEISNIG[22]

In the Name of the Holy undivided Trinity, Amen.

Since by the grace of the Omnipotent God, through the

---

18 Luther had previously denounced begging in *An Open Letter to the Christian Nobility* (1520). PE 2, 134-135; and in the *Long Sermon on Usury* (1520), in this volume, pp. 281-282, 286-287.

19 In 1520 Luther had written *A Treatise Concerning the Ban.* PE 2, (33) 37-54.

20 On the *zinsskauff*, see pp. 295-310; on its use in the churches, see especially p. 306.

21 Luther's own preface ends here. What follows is the Leisnig Ordinance itself, of which Luther is not the author, though he gave it his hearty approval and himself had it published. See the Introduction, pp. 162, 165.

22 Since no title at all appears in the Wittenberg printing at this point, we have supplied the title which appears on the cover of a very early original manuscript still extant at Leisnig, which is designated as "L" in WA 12, 9.

revelation of the Christian and evangelical Scriptures, we have been given not only firmly to believe but also profoundly to know that, according to the ordinance and precept of divine truth and not according to human opinion, all the internal and external possessions of Christian believers are to serve and contribute to the honor of God and the love of the fellow-Christian neighbor, we the nobility,[23] council, craft supervisors,[24] gentry,[25] and commoners dwelling in the city and villages[26] of the assembly and parish of Leisnig, by these presents confess and make known that we, for ourselves and our posterity, upon the considered and mature counsel of men learned in the divine Scriptures,[27] have drawn up and adopted the following fraternal agreement among ourselves as a community, and that both now and for the future it is to be held true and inviolable, namely:

Filling the pastoral office

In matters which relate to the filling of the pastoral office in our parish, including the calling, choosing, appointing, and dismissing of our pastor for the sole purpose of preaching God's word and administering the sacraments, we solemnly purpose and promise at all times to use, exercise, and employ our Christian liberty solely in conformity with the precept and ordinance of the divine biblical Scriptures; and in such a pre-eminently spiritual undertaking as the care of the poor and needy, to be obedient in true humility to the well-founded and proven instruction and counsel of those learned in the divine Scripture, submitting to it and following it by the grace of God, of which we have a clear

---

[23] The Erbar manne are named specifically in the last paragraph on p. 194.

[24] The Viertell meister (literally, "quarter master") exercised a certain supervisory authority in a particular quarter of the city. The term was also applied to the chief of any particular craft since shops of a given sort tended to be concentrated in a given area. Grimm, Deutsches Wörterbuch, XII², 331. The crafts in question are named in the last paragraph on p. 194.

[25] Eldesten is the equivalent of Honoratioren. CL 2, 408, n. 34.

[26] According to the report of the 1529 visitation, the parish included the eleven villages of Gorschmitz, Röda, Brösen, Tautendorf, Minckwitz, Meinitz, Neudörfchen, Vorwerf Hasenberg, Dölen, Lichtenhain, and Liebgens Mühle, the last three of which subsequently became part of Leisnig itself as the city expanded. WA 12, 3, n. 1; BG 7, 117, n. 3.

[27] This was probably a reference to Luther, who had visited Leisnig on September 25, 1522; see the Introduction, p. 163.

token in our midst in the administration given to our parish, which shall be retained intact.[28]

On hearing God's word

We solemnly purpose and promise that every master and mistress of a household within the confines of our parish shall be obliged themselves—and out of Christian love shall also hold their children and servants to it—to listen faithfully to God's saving and comforting word at the appointed days and hours and take it to heart for our own improvement, as God grants us grace.

Reverencing God and keeping his commandments

We solemnly purpose and promise that as masters and mistresses we shall diligently see to it—each one for himself and for his children and servants in his own home as God grants us grace— that God is reverenced, and we shall studiously avoid, guard against, and prevent open blasphemy, excessive drinking, fornication, ruinous dice games, and other sins and offenses which are known to be in direct conflict with God's commandments. If any member of our community is found to be negligent or lax in this regard, an assembly of the whole parish shall have the right and power to take up the matter and by proper means, with the aid and co-operation of the authorities, to secure appropriate punishment and salutary improvement.

Property, resources, and receipts for the common chest

In order that our Christian faith—in which all the temporal and eternal blessings won by our Lord and Savior Christ out of pure grace and mercy are granted unto us by the eternal God— may bear fruit in brotherly love, and this love truly express itself in deeds of tender kindness, we, the aforesaid general parish assembly, acting unanimously, for ourselves and our posterity have ordained, established, and set up a common chest, and by these presents we do now ordain, establish, and set up this same chest

---

28 This is probably a reference to Leisnig's priest and preacher, Kind and Gruner, whose appointments had been challenged by the erstwhile patron of the parish but successfully defended by the congregation itself. See the Introduction, pp. 163-164.

on the authority of this our fraternal agreement as to purpose, scope, and form, as follows.

The property and resources of the common chest shall consist of the following enumerated items: incomes [zinsse], properties, rights, moneys, and goods everywhere amassed, collected, brought, vested, and assigned in perpetuity.

Receipts from parish properties and rights

We, the parish assembly, by virtue of our universal priesthood,[29] have always had and should have had the full right and authority, which we reserve wholly to ourselves and in no way relinquish, to acquire all properties and rights, hereditary lands, quitrents, and supplementary rents,[30] proprietary rights, buildings, manor places, gardens, fields, pastures, stores, and chattels personal without exception, insofar as they were in every case granted and assigned by the original donors, and by those who later supplemented these bequests to the priestly and pastoral office here in our midst, and have in times past thereto belonged and therein been used—this was the substance of the negotiations and the decision reached between ourselves and the abbot of Buch in the chancellery of our most gracious lord, the Elector of Saxony[31]—which properties and rights are now on deposit in our common chest. Likewise, whatever belonged to the school and the sacristan's place[32] has been turned over to this chest.

Receipts from church property and rights

All property and rights, hereditary lands, quitrents and

---

[29] Luther had taught the priesthood of all believers three years earlier in *An Open Letter to the Christian Nobility*. PE 2, 66-73; and *The Babylonian Captivity*. LW 36, 112-117; and again in *The Misuse of the Mass* (1521). LW 36, 138-146.

[30] *Gatter zinse* were rents which had to be collected in person by the landlord or his agent, and only at the latticed gate (*gatter*) of the debtor. Grimm, *Deutsches Wörterbuch*, IV¹, 1511; 7, 237.

[31] See the Introduction, pp. 162-165. If the elector, Duke Frederick of Saxony, did intervene, as this sentence seems to suggest, no records of his disposition of the case are extant either at Weimar, Dresden, or Leisnig. WA 12, 5.

[32] *Kusterey* had reference to the office and holdings of the sacristan, who was usually attached to a certain benefice. His task was to care for the church property, particularly its sacred vessels and vestments (see p. 187). The term was also applied to that facility, in or near the church, in which the church's treasures were kept in custody (see p. 184).

supplementary rents, bridge tolls,[33] ready cash, silver and jewels,[34] stores, chattels personal, and thus everything that accrues to the church either regularly or from time to time, together with the written documents, lists, and records pertaining thereto, shall be included without exception in the common chest and there remain.

Receipts from the property and rights of the four beneficed altars[35] and other foundations

When the present beneficed altar priests die or the benefices otherwise become vacant,[36] the four beneficed altars in our church shall henceforth no longer be provided for. Instead, the four chapels, together with their properties, rents, revenues, usufructs, jewels, stores, and chattels personal, and the written archives, inventories, and records pertaining thereto, shall be put in the common chest. In addition, all their masses for the dead, perpetual memorials, indulgence weeks or octaves, and other one-time foundations[37] and alms for the hospital[38] or other objectives, shall be turned over to the common chest.

---

[33] The wooden toll bridge over the Moldau was church property until transferred to the state in 1847. WA 12, 18, n. 2.

[34] Silberwerg, Cleinod had reference to the costly materials used in decorating, and in such altarware as monstrances and shrines for relics. BG 7, 120, n. 3.

[35] The four side altars in the church at Leisnig, each separately endowed and served, were those of the Cross, the Annunciation of Mary, the Conception of Mary, and the Corpus Christi. WA 12, 18, n. 3. The most heavily endowed of the four according to the 1529 visitation report, the Corpus Christi, had an annual income of 32 gulden, 26 groschen, 6 pfennige, and 1 heller. Lietzmann, op. cit., p. 13, n. 11.

[36] One of the four altar priests died shortly after the ordinance went into effect. The other three continued to receive their stipends, although they had no functions to perform; the congregation had forbidden them to read mass, and they refused to celebrate an evangelical mass. WA 12, 6.

[37] Begengnus were "masses for the dead," including vigils and requiems, not the funeral itself. They were distinguished as being either einlitzige, "one-time," those held 8, 30, or 365 (the "anniversary" so-called) days after the death or burial, or "perpetual memorials," the Jare tage held annually on the anniversary of the death or burial. The "indulgence week or octave" is a memorial in which mass is held and prayers offered for the deceased over a period of one week, to procure indulgence for him. Each of these expressions can also stand, as here, for the fund endowed for the particular memorial in question. MA³ 5, 403, n. 52, 17. Luther had inveighed against such masses already in his 1520 Address to the Christian Nobility. PE 2, 125.

[38] The hospital, besides being a hospice for the lodging of strangers, was a charitable institution for the care of the aged, infirm, poor, sick, and dependent children.

Receipts from brotherhoods[39]

Whatever has hitherto been collected and is now available to the famous brotherhoods, the Calends,[40] St. Anne,[41] and the Cobblers,[42] in the way of ready cash, annuities [tzinsskauffen], jewels and silver, stores, and chattels personal, together with their written documents, lists, and records, shall without exception be turned over and assigned to the common chest, and there remain.

Receipts of donations to the church[43] by artisans and peasantry

Contributions, craft guild rights,[44] levies, penances, penalties, and fines, which as donations to the church were formerly collected, and in years to come will continue to be collected, within the city from the artisans and in the country villages outside the city from the peasants in our entire parish, into a reserve supply, are and in the future shall be all turned over to and deposited in the common chest.

Receipts of edible foodstuffs and money in the alms chests and coin boxes

It is ordered that in our church there shall at all times be kept two barrels or casks, not to be removed, in which bread,

---

[39] Brotherhoods were organizations, usually of laymen, formed for the purpose of performing devotional and charitable works for which the whole membership would receive spiritual credit. See Luther's own sharp critique of them dating from 1519 in The Blessed Sacrament of the Body of Christ. LW 35, 67-73.

[40] The Calend brotherhoods probably grew out of the priestly conferences held on the first day of each month (calendae). MA³ 5, 403, n. 52, 22. Their membership was restricted pretty largely to clergy, whose surfeiting at the common meal was almost proverbial. Albert Hauck (ed.), Realencyklopädie für protestantische Theologie und Kirche (3rd ed., 24 vol.; Leipzig: Hinrichs, 1896-1913), IX, 704. The Calends had endowed one of the four beneficed altars in Leisnig, the one to the Annunciation of Mary. Lietzmann, op. cit., p. 14, n. 5.

[41] The patron saint of the St. Anne brotherhood was Anne, according to tradition the mother of the Virgin Mary. Sodalities bearing her name spread "like an epidemic" after the fourteenth century. LW 35, 68, n. 44.

[42] The Cobblers brotherhood was composed of journeymen shoemakers united under church auspices for the purpose of aiding their deceased fellow craftsman through prayers and masses. BG 7, 121, n. 5.

[43] Gotsgabe (literally, "a gift to God") was the general term for a contractual endowment of a church institution, usually a benefice, a living, or a foundation involving gifts and benefits in cash or in kind made and administered "for God's sake." Grimm, Deutsches Wörterbuch, IV¹, 1240.

[44] Zunfftgerechtigkeitten has reference to legal claims of the church against craft guilds. MA³ 5, 403, n. 52, 29.

cheese, eggs, meat, and other foodstuffs and provisions may be placed, and a little box or two for coins, both for the maintenance of the common chest. Likewise, whenever our parish assembles in the church, two of our officials shall always be present to solicit each person for support of the poor, and the alms and love gifts thus received shall at once be contributed to and placed in these receptacles. Articles of food, being perishable, shall be distributed by the appointees among the poor as needed without delay, in accordance with their instructions hereinafter specified. Whatever is not perishable is to be kept until the following Sunday and then distributed as may be appropriate and beneficial for the poor.

Receipts of gifts made during days of good health, and by will at the time of death

Other voluntary gifts made during days of good health and by will at the time of death, insofar as they are made with a Christian intention, to the honor of God and love of neighbor, whether they consist of property, ready cash, jewels, stores, or chattels personal, shall be given wholly to this common chest and there remain. Faithful admonition thereto shall also be made by our pastor from the pulpit, and elsewhere in legitimate instances, even at the sickbed if the prospective heirs give their approval and the patient is still in possession of his faculties.

Setting up the administration of the common chest

The administration of the common chest shall be set up in the following manner: annually each year, on the Sunday following the octave of Epiphany,[45] at about eleven o'clock, a general assembly of the parish shall convene here in the town hall. There, by the grace of God united in true Christian faith, they shall elect from the entire assembly ten trustees or directors for the common chest who shall be without exception the best-qualified individuals; namely, two from the nobility, two from the incumbent city council; three from among the common citizens of the town; and three from the rural peasantry. The ten thus duly elected shall immediately assume the burden and responsibility

---

[45] Epiphany falls on January 6; therefore, the meeting was to convene on the first Sunday after January 13.

of administration and trusteeship of the common chest. They shall do so voluntarily and with a good Christian conscience, for the sake of God and the general welfare. They shall discharge their duties to the best of their ability, without regard to favor, animosity, personal advantage, fear, or any unseemly consideration, and shall be pledged and bound faithfully and honestly to handle the administration, receipts, and disbursements, according to the terms of our agreement herein described.

Locking the chest with four different keys

This common chest or receptacle shall be kept in that part of our church where it is safest, and shall be provided with four separate and distinct locks, each having its own key, so that the nobility shall have one of the keys, the council another, the town citizenry the third, and the rural peasantry the fourth.

The directors to meet together every Sunday

Every Sunday in the year, from eleven o'clock until two hours before vespers, the ten directors shall meet in the parsonage or in the town hall, there to care for and exercise diligently their trusteeship, making their decisions and acting in concert in order that deeds of honor to God and love to the fellow-Christian may be continued in an unbroken stream and be used for purposes of improvement. These decisions of theirs shall be kept in strictest confidence and not be divulged in unauthorized ways. If any of the directors are from time to time absent for good and sufficient reason, the majority shall have the power to go ahead anyway and transact business.

Three books, in which are recorded all properties, rights, and administrative acts

The ten directors at their regular Sunday meeting shall have on hand three record books, namely:

The primary documents. Herein shall be entered and preserved a transcription of this our fraternal agreement, an exact copy of the sealed original deposited in the chest; also, all written documents, deeds of conveyance, lists, and inheritance records having to do with all properties and rights which have ever been brought in and contributed to the common chest, as specified above, and which may come or be brought to it in the future.

The minutes. Herein shall be properly recorded and indexed all deliberations, conclusions, decisions, inquiries, investigations, and resolutions that have been undertaken, made, and completed, which in any way concern the administration, receipts, and disbursements of the common chest, so that the necessary information may be available at any time.

The annual accounts. Herein shall be transcribed at the outset a complete list or inventory of all items of stores, chattels personal, jewels, silver, and cash monies, each accurately described in terms of weight, quantity, and bulk, as they are handed over, item by item, to the aforementioned ten directors each year when they take office, as a balance and as the starting point for continued accounting. Herein shall also be entered every week on Sunday each and every receipt and disbursement, all in accordance with a customary accounting form agreed upon by the general parish assembly and modified from time to time as the assembly may see fit. From this then a definitive ledger, categorized under the necessary headings, shall always be prepared and drawn up by the outgoing directors, and turned over to the ten new directors on the day of their election, to forestall harmful errors and negligence. When these three books have been used in the manner described they shall at once be locked up again in the common chest.

Collecting all earnings and debts

The ten directors shall exercise all diligence in demanding and collecting for the common chest all rents, incomes, accounts, and obligations, both the recurrent and the occasional, to the fullest possible extent but without oppressing the poor; and in preserving inviolate all such sources of revenue.

The office of two building supervisors

The ten directors shall appoint from among their number two building supervisors. These two, with the advice and knowledge of the other eight, shall have charge of the church buildings, the bridge, the parsonage, the school, the sacristan's place, and the hospitals. Both of these men, equipped with two little bags or collection plates, shall also be on hand in the church whenever our parish is assembled, to solicit alms for the support of the poor. Such contributions shall at once be dumped into the two coin boxes provided for that purpose, the keys to which shall be kept in the common chest. Every Sunday the money shall be taken out of these boxes by the ten directors acting in a body, properly recorded in the annual accounts book, and placed in the common chest. Alms consisting of edible foodstuffs and other perishable stores shall be distributed daily among the poor whenever the ten directors, acting in concert on any particular Sunday, shall deem it necessary and proper. Nonperishable articles shall be removed from the alms chests and stored in appropriate places in the church until some Sunday when, at the judgment of the ten directors, they shall be distributed to the poor.

The burden of caring for nonresidents not assumed

With respect to the perceptible burden imposed in excessive measure upon the entire parish by nonresident, fictitious poor and idlers who are not really in need, a burden which only aggravates our own distressed condition and which men learned in the divine Scriptures have advised us to exclude and disavow, we, the nobility, council, craft supervisors, gentry, and commoners dwelling in the city and villages of our parish, by virtue of this our agreement have accordingly resolved for us and our posterity that this burden is and shall remain excluded and disavowed, namely:

Begging concessions[46] forbidden

No monks, of whatever order[47] they may be, shall henceforth have any sort of begging concession within our parish, either in the city or in the villages; their three houses,[48] therefore, shall

---

[46] *Termineyen* were the areas within which a mendicant order had the right to solicit alms. The term was also used to indicate the collection of such alms and the houses from which such begging monks operated as a headquarters away from their home cloister. Grimm, *Deutsches Wörterbuch*, XI[1], 260. Cf. p. 69, n. 34.

[47] See p. 175, n. 15.

[48] Of the three *Termineyheuser* in the parish of Leisnig at the time, the Frieberg cloister (Dominican) was granted in 1529 to the deacon for a

also be absorbed into the common chest, from which they shall be indemnified in accordance with a fair appraisal.

Begging by monks, stationaries,[49] and church beggars[50] abolished

No monk, *stationarius*, or church begger shall be permitted or allowed to beg or have others beg for him in our parish, either in the city or in the villages.

Begging by students from outside the parish forbidden

No student from outside the parish shall be permitted to beg in our parish, either in the city or in the villages. If anyone wants to attend our school he will have to provide his own board and keep.

Men and women beggars forbidden

No men or women beggars shall be tolerated in our parish, either in the city or in the villages, since anyone not incapacitated by reason of age or illness shall work or, with the aid of the authorities, be expelled from the parish, the city, and the villages. But those among us who are impoverished by force of circumstances, or are unable to work because of old age or illness, shall be supported in suitable fashion by the ten officials out of our common chest as follows:

Disbursements and assistance from the common chest

We, the members of this parish and our posterity, therefore solemnly purpose and promise henceforth to provide food, sustenance, and support through our ten elected directors out of our common chest, to the limit of our resources as God grants us grace, and as occasion demands to make the following disbursements, namely:

Disbursements for the pastoral office

To the pastor or priest called and elected by our congregation, and to a preacher similarly called by us and appointed to

residence, and the Oschatz cloister (Franciscan) became the archdiaconate. WA 12, 23, n. 1. Lietzmann, *op. cit.*, p. 17, n. 6.

[49] On the *stationirer*, see p. 69, n. 34, and p. 318, n. 7.

[50] *Kirchenbitter* were monks who did their begging on behalf of church construction. MA³ 5, 404, n. 56, 30.

assist the pastor[51] (though the pastor himself should be able and qualified to preach God's word and perform the other duties of his pastoral office), and also to a chaplain[52] if the need for one arises, the ten directors, on the unified resolution of the entire assembly, are to furnish annually each year a specified sum of money, together with certain consumable stores and lands and properties subject to usufruct, to support them and adequately meet their needs, one-fourth to be paid each quarter at the Ember fast[53] out of the common chest, in return for a proper receipt. They shall be content with such annual salary, stores, and usufruct, and shall by no means seek or accept anything more from the people of the parish, unless it be unsolicited, voluntary, free offerings and gifts. In this respect and in the administration of the pastoral office of the congregation, their conduct shall be in accordance with the ordinance and instructions of the men learned in the divine Scriptures,[54] which ordinance shall be kept in our common chest, and be considered and implemented by the ten directors every Sunday, so that no harm may come to the pastoral office.

Disbursements for the office of sacristan

The sacristan or custodian, to whom the assembly entrusts the locking up of the church and the suitable care of it, shall be given by the ten directors out of the common chest in quarterly instalments a specified annual salary and certain usable stores and usufructs, as may be determined by the assembly in accordance with the aforementioned scriptural ordinance for the pastoral office of the congregation, which embraces also the duties of the sacristan.

---

[51] The parish priest at the time was Heinrich Kind, the preacher was Johann Gruner. See the Introduction, p. 165.

[52] The *Cappellan* was a priest appointed to assist in the pastoral duties of the parish.

[53] *Quatemper*, derived from the Latin for "four times," had reference to the fast days with which each quarter of the church year began, namely, the Wednesday, Friday, and Saturday following December 13 (St. Lucy), Ash Wednesday, Pentecost, and September 14 (Holy Cross). For purposes of quarterly rents and payments the Wednesday in question was considered the terminal date. MA^3 5, 404, n. 57, 30; *CL* 2, 417, n. 2.

[54] See p. 177, n. 27.

Disbursements for the schools[55]

The ten designated directors, in the name of our general parish assembly, shall have the authority and duty, with the advice and approval of our elected pastor and preacher and others learned in the divine Scriptures,[56] to call, appoint and dismiss a schoolmaster for young boys, whereby a pious, irreproachable, and learned man may be made responsible for the honorable and upright Christian training and instruction of the youth, a most essential function. This schoolmaster shall be required to train, teach, govern, and live at all times in conformity with and hold unswervingly to the mandate of the aforementioned ordinance for the pastoral office of our congregation which is deposited in the coffers of our common chest. In accordance with a determination of the general assembly, the ten directors shall give the schoolmaster as compensation for his services a specified annual salary plus certain stores in quarterly instalments out of the common chest. He shall be content with this, and shall neither seek nor accept anything more from our parish assembly or any of its four groups as classified above.[57] But from pupils from outside the parish, who are permitted here only at their own expense without begging, the schoolmaster may, at the discretion of the priest and preacher, together with the ten directors, accept a suitable recompense, so that Christian training and instruction may be imparted to these outsiders too. Our pastor, preacher, and the ten directors shall maintain a constant and faithful supervision over this office of teaching school and governing the youth; every Sunday as need may arise they shall consider this matter, take action, and implement it with the utmost seriousness.

Likewise the ten directors shall grant to an upright, fully seasoned, irreproachable woman an annual stipend and certain

---

[55] *Zcucht schulen*, literally, "training schools," were so called because they were schools intended not simply for instruction of the mind in certain subjects but for training of the entire person in arts, skills, conduct, and the fear of God. Grimm, *Deutsches Wörterbuch*, XVI, 278; BG 7, 128, n. 6. In 1529 there were forty-five pupils in the Leisnig school. WA 12, 24, n. 1.

[56] In 1529 it was accordingly ordered that when next the post of schoolmaster became vacant, a qualified teacher, a graduate recommended by Melanchthon, should be called from Wittenberg. WA 12, 24, n. 2.

[57] The nobility, councilmen, townspeople, and peasants are categorized on p. 194.

stores out of our common chest for instructing young girls under twelve in true Christian discipline, honor, and virtue and, in accordance with the ordinance for our pastoral office, teaching them to read and write German, this teaching to be done during certain specified hours by the clear light of day and in a respectable place that is above suspicion. Beyond that she is neither to seek nor accept anything further from our assembly. But from girls outside the parish who might be sent hither to the German school this woman may, on recommendation of the ten directors, collect an appropriate fee. The ten directors shall also diligently supervise the training and governing of such German schools and young girls, so that Christian discipline, honor, and virtue may be maintained inviolate.

Disbursements for the poor who are aged and infirm

Those individuals in our parish and assembly who are impoverished by force of circumstances and left without assistance by their relatives, if they have any capable of helping, and those who are unable to work because of illness or old age and are so poor as to suffer real need, shall receive each week on Sunday, and at other times as occasion demands, maintenance and support from our common chest through the ten directors. This is to be done out of Christian love, to the honor and praise of God, so that their lives and health may be preserved from further deterioration, enfeeblement, and foreshortening through lack of shelter, clothing, nourishment, and care, and so that no impoverished person in our assembly need ever publicly cry out, lament,[58] or beg for such items of daily necessity. For this reason the ten directors shall constantly make diligent inquiry and investigation in order to have complete and reliable knowledge of all these poor—as above—in the city and villages within our entire parish, and they shall confer on this matter every Sunday. The names of the poor whom they have discovered and decided to help, together with the action taken, shall be legibly entered in the minutes so that the resources of our common chest are distributed in orderly fashion.

---

[58] Beggars customarily cried aloud in the streets and movingly pleaded their needs at the door of each home. BG 7, 130, n. 5.

Disbursements for the support of orphans and dependent children

Poor and neglected orphans within the city and villages of our entire parish shall, as occasion arises, be provided with training and physical necessities by the directors out of the common chest until such time as they can work and earn their bread. If there be found among such orphans, or the children of impoverished parents, young boys with an aptitude for schooling and a capacity for arts and letters, the directors should support and provide for them, like the other poor, out of the common chest; the other boys will be trained for labor, handicrafts, and other suitable occupations. The girls among the neglected orphans, and likewise the daughters of impoverished parents, shall be provided by the directors out of the common chest with a suitable dowry for marriage.

Disbursements for home relief[59]

To artisans and others suffering in private, whether married or widowers, who are residents of the city and villages within our parish and who are honestly unable to ply their trade or other urban or rural occupation, and have no other source of help, the directors shall advance an appropriate amount out of the common chest, to be repaid at some future date. In cases where despite honest and diligent toil they are unable to make repayment, the debt shall be forgiven for God's sake as a contribution to their need. Such circumstances shall be carefully investigated by the directors.

Disbursements for the relief of newcomers from without

In the case of newcomers to the parish of whatever estate, be they men or women, if they are in Christian and brotherly harmony with our general assembly and wish to seek their livelihood within the city or villages of our parish by their labor, toil, and industry, the ten directors shall encourage them, and even offer them help through loans and gifts out of our common chest,

---

[59] *Hawssarmer leutte* were those poor who, in contrast to the beggars, suffered their poverty privately and quietly at home, and also received such aid as came to them in the form of home relief rather than alms on the streets and in public places. *BG* 7, 131, n. 8; Grimm, *Deutsches Wörterbuch*, IV², 652.

as circumstances dictate, so that the strangers too may not be left without hope, and may be saved from shame and open sin.

Disbursements for the maintenance and construction of buildings

The directors shall provide for the daily maintenance and improvement of buildings, and for new buildings, at the following sites belonging to the common chest: the church, the Moldau bridge, the parsonage, the school, the sacristan's place, and the hospitals. With the advice of people skilled and experienced in construction they shall diligently and prudently arrive at decisions, place orders, and cause them to be executed, providing appropriately for supplies of the necessary materials and making the expenditures out of the common chest. They shall carry on the work through their two building supervisors, securing other hand labor, especially for the bridge, by calling on[60] men of the city and the country, as has been customary in the past.

Disbursements for the purchase of grain for the common stores

For the general welfare of our parish, the ten directors shall employ funds from the common chest, supplemented by grants from the town council out of the town treasury, to buy up and set aside a good quantity of grain and peas in storehouses which belong to the council and the entire parish. Such stores are not to be drawn upon in years when grain is plentiful and cheap, but by all means to be increased and supplemented. In this way the people of the whole parish everywhere in the city and villages may by the grace of God have recourse to these stores for bodily sustenance in times of imminent scarcity, through purchase, loans, or grants as the directors may deem fitting and appropriate. Whatever grain is bequeathed by will or given as gifts of love by farm laborers from the city or peasants in the country for the common good, and remains over after support of the poor as noted above, shall also be added to this common store and, as we have just heard, shall be used for the needs of the whole parish.

---

[60] *Bethe* referred to the notice given those volunteers who were next in line for the duty to report and take their turn. *MA*³ 405, n. 61, 16; *CL* 2, 420, n. 22.

Paying an annual tax to the common chest

Wherever the rents, collections, revenues, and contributions to the resources and stores of our common chest, as itemized above, should prove insufficient for the maintenance and support of our pastoral office, office of sacristan, schools, needy poor, and the buildings owned in common, as these have been duly set forth in orderly sequence, we the nobility, council, craft supervisors, gentry, and commoners dwelling in the city and villages of our whole parish, for ourselves and our posterity, and by virtue of this our fraternal agreement, have unitedly resolved and consented that every noble, townsman, and peasant living in the parish shall, according to his ability and means, remit in taxes for himself, his wife, and his children a certain sum of money to the chest each year, in order that the total amount can be arrived at and procured which the deliberations and decisions of the general parish assembly, on the basis of investigation in and experience with the annual statements, have determined to be necessary and sufficient.

To this end, throughout the entire extent of our parish, every householder, domestic servant, journeyman of the various handicrafts, and other persons who are not home owners but who share in the enjoyment and use of our parish rights shall individually contribute annually one silver groschen; that is, three new pennies, the fourth part of the groschen, every quarter at the Ember fast. Each master or mistress shall diligently collect this money and turn it over to the ten directors at each Ember fast.

The parish assembly solemnly purposes and promises that to the honor of God and the love of our fellow Christians we shall never spare ourselves this trifling annual contribution in view of the fact that hitherto, since time out of mind, both residents and nonresidents throughout our common parish have by many methods and devices been overburdened and fleeced incessantly the year round with exorbitant and intolerable impositions and assessments. By the grace of God these practices have now been restored to the true freedom of the Christian spirit. It is the duty of every Christian to see that such Christian liberty is not misused as a cover for shameful avarice [I Pet. 2:16].

Holding a general assembly three times a year

Three times a year, namely, on the Sunday following the octave of Epiphany,[61] the Sunday following St. Urban's Day,[62] and the Sunday following St. Michael's Day,[63] the whole general parish assembly shall convene at eleven o'clock in the town hall and remain in session there at least until two o'clock in the afternoon. First, this our fraternal agreement shall be read aloud; then our ten elected directors shall present their books of minutes and accounts, and make their report. Growing out of their report, and the ideas of us all, there shall be a discussion of the administration, receipts, and disbursements of our common chest, and of other matters generally which are needful and appropriate. Finally, by the grace of God, decisions shall also be made by which this fraternal agreement, according to the circumstances of the common stores and resources, may be maintained and not fall into decline. If anyone in the parish cannot be present on the three appointed days—and no one should absent himself without a manifestly good reason—the assembly shall nevertheless, as mentioned above,[64] legitimately proceed to transact business.

Directors to furnish a complete annual statement

Annually each year on the Sunday following the octave of Epiphany and on successive days thereafter, our ten elected directors shall make, deliver, and present their annual statement on the administration, receipts, and disbursements of our common chest, both through their books of minutes and accounts, and also by their oral report. This shall be done publicly, in the presence of our whole assembly or an appreciable number or committee acting on behalf of the whole assembly, as circumstances shall dictate, and according to the form and specifications for such a statement, as determined by action of the assembly and presented and turned over to the directors on the day they took office, as indicated above.[65] When this statement has been executed by the directors and accepted, then with a resolution of profound thanks on behalf of the assembly, the directors shall be declared

---

[61] See p. 182, n. 45.
[62] St. Urban's Day falls on May 25. *Catholic Encyclopedia*, XV, 209-210.
[63] September 29 was observed as the Feast of St. Michael. *Ibid.*, X, 276-277.
[64] See p. 183.   [65] See p. 184.

193

discharged, freed, and relieved of all responsibility. They shall then immediately entrust and turn over to our newly-elected ten directors the common chest together with all its written documents, lists, and records, as well as the three books, namely, the primary documents, minutes, and annual accounts, as many of them as exist. They shall also turn over all items of inventory which according to their final statement remain on hand and in storage, namely, grain, consumable stores, chattels personal, jewels, silver, cash monies, and all sorts of building supplies, all accurately described in terms of weight, quantity, and bulk. This transfer shall be duly recorded anew in a separate inventory or list which shall be sealed in the name of the whole assembly by the nobles, councilmen, and four craft supervisors, and deposited in the common chest as the starting point for continued accounting.

New directors to get help from their predecessors

The new directors, whenever they feel it necessary, may also consult with former directors. The former directors, for the sake of God and the common weal, shall not shirk this responsibility, but shall furnish reliable guidance and counsel.

In witness whereof, and so that all the articles, items, and provisions of this our fraternal agreement recorded above shall at all times be applied, used, and administered faithfully and without fraud by the parish here in Leisnig for no other purpose than the honor of God, the love of our fellow Christians, and hence for the common good, we the nobility, to wit, Balthasar von Arras, Sebastian von Kötteritzsch,[66] and Sigmund von Lausk, have affixed to this present document our family seals; and we, the council, the privy seal of our city; and we, the duly sworn craft supervisors of the four handicrafts, namely, clothmakers, bakers, cobblers, and coopers, our customary craft seals. This we have done on behalf of and at the request of each and every inhabitant of the city and villages of our parish, under legal public notarization, for ourselves and our future parish assembly. Done and given at Leisnig, in the one thousand five hundred and twenty-third year after the birth of Christ our dear Lord.

---

66 See p. 163, n. 13, and the Introduction, p. 165.

THAT JESUS CHRIST
WAS BORN A JEW

1523

Translated by Walther I. Brandt

INTRODUCTION

What to do about Luther was one of the major issues discussed at the Diet of Nürnberg (1522). Although under the ban of both church and empire, he was living openly at Wittenberg, his pen as active as ever. Among those in attendance at Nürnberg—Elector Frederick was not present—nearly all the princes were hostile toward Luther, but most of their own counselors were "good Lutherans."[1] Inevitably, there was much rumor and gossip about Luther's teaching. Hans von der Planitz, Elector Frederick's representative on the Council of Regency, reported some of this gossip to Frederick. It was charged among other things that Luther taught that "Jesus was conceived of the seed of Joseph, and that Mary was not a virgin, but had many sons after Christ."[2] In view of the current adoration of the Virgin Mary, these were serious charges.

When Luther learned through friends that even Archduke Ferdinand had publicly accused him in Nürnberg of teaching the new doctrine that Christ was through Joseph of the seed of Abraham, he could no longer regard such nonsense as a "joke," but realized that the charges were being made in earnest.[3] Idle gossip was one thing, but a public charge by the imperial regent was something quite different. Some sort of a reply had to be made, if for no other reason than to save the faces of his friends and supporters. Count John of Anhalt had urged Luther to clear himself of the charge,[4] and Luther's reply was the treatise here translated.

---

[1] This description of the state of affairs at Nürnberg was given in a letter from Hans von der Planitz (see p. 164, n. 15) to the Elector Frederick dated January 2, 1523. S-J 2, 158; Wülcker, *Des kursächsischen Rathes Hans von der Planitz Berichte aus dem Reichsregiment in Nürnberg 1521-1523*, p. 304.
[2] Smith, *The Age of the Reformation*, p. 156; Wülcker, *op. cit.*, p. 303. Cf. also the letter from Francis Chieregato, bishop of Teramo, to the Marquis of Mantua, dated January 10, 1523, in Nürnberg. Smith, *op. cit.*, p. 159.
[3] See Luther's letter to Spalatin of January 22, 1523. WA, Br 3, 19; S-J 2, 165.
[4] *Ibid.*

The treatise falls into two parts. In the first part Luther, on the basis of Scripture, demonstrates that Jesus was a Jew, born of the seed of Abraham, but begotten by means of a miracle; that Mary was a virgin when Jesus was born and, there being no scriptural evidence to the contrary, must have remained so thereafter. The second part is devoted to the Jews. It begins with an appeal to Christians to deal more kindly with the Jews in the hope of converting them, and ends with an elaborate argument from Scripture and history to convince the Jews of Christ's messiahship.

Luther probably began work on the treatise not long after his letter of January 22, 1523, to Spalatin.[5] We do not know just when the first (Wittenberg) edition came from the press, nor do the earliest letters which mention it bear a specific date. One of these, from Luther to Bernard, a converted Jew, mentions that a copy of the treatise was being sent him with the letter.[6] Since a second edition was in preparation at Strassburg in early June, it seems reasonable to assume that the first edition appeared in May.[7]

The following translation, the first into English, is based on the original Wittenberg printing by Cranach and Döring, *Das Jhesus Christus eyn geborner Jude sey*, as that has been reprinted with annotations in WA 11, (307) 314-336.

---

[5] *WA*, Br 3, 20, n. 18, credits Spalatin with being the prime mover in occasioning the treatise.

[6] *WA*, Br 3, 101-102, suggests as a possible date for this letter the latter part of June, 1523; S-J 2, 185-187, following Enders, *D. Martin Luthers Briefwechsel*, IV, 146-149, suggests the month of May.

[7] *WA* 11, 307; Enders, *op. cit.*, IV, 148, n. 1.

THAT JESUS CHRIST
WAS BORN A JEW

A new lie about me is being circulated.[1] I am supposed to have preached and written that Mary, the mother of God, was not a virgin either before or after the birth of Christ, but that she conceived Christ through Joseph, and had more children after that. Above and beyond all this, I am supposed to have preached a new heresy, namely, that Christ was [through Joseph] the seed of Abraham. How these lies tickle my good friends, the papists! Indeed, because they condemn the gospel it serves them right that they should have to satisfy and feed their heart's delight and joy with lies. I would venture to wager my neck that none of those very liars who allege such great things in honor of the mother of God believes in his heart a single one of these articles. Yet with their lies they pretend that they are greatly concerned about the Christian faith.

But after all, it is such a poor miserable lie that I despise it and would rather not reply to it. In these past three years I have grown quite accustomed to hearing lies, even from our nearest neighbors.[2] And they in turn have grown accustomed to the noble virtue of neither blushing nor feeling ashamed when they are publicly convicted of lying. They let themselves be chided as liars, yet continue their lying. Still they are the best Christians, striving with all that they have and are to devour the Turk[3] and to extirpate all heresy.

Since for the sake of others,[4] however, I am compelled to answer these lies, I thought I would also write something useful in addition, so that I do not vainly steal the reader's time with

---

[1] See the Introduction, pp. 197-198.
[2] This is probably an allusion to Duke George of ducal Saxony, a consistent opponent of Luther. See p. 33, n. 34; p. 84, n. 11; p. 85, n. 15; p. 107, n. 56.
[3] See p. 116, n. 91.
[4] See the Introduction, pp. 197-198.

such dirty rotten business. Therefore, I will cite from Scripture the reasons that move me to believe that Christ was a Jew born of a virgin, that I might perhaps also win some Jews to the Christian faith. Our fools, the popes, bishops, sophists,[5] and monks —the crude asses' heads—have hitherto so treated the Jews that anyone who wished to be a good Christian would almost have had to become a Jew. If I had been a Jew and had seen such dolts and blockheads govern and teach the Christian faith, I would sooner have become a hog than a Christian.

They have dealt with the Jews as if they were dogs rather than human beings; they have done little else than deride them and seize their property. When they baptize them they show them nothing of Christian doctrine or life, but only subject them to popishness and monkery. When the Jews then see that Judaism has such strong support in Scripture, and that Christianity has become a mere babble without reliance on Scripture, how can they possibly compose themselves and become right good Christians? I have myself heard from pious baptized Jews[6] that if they had not in our day heard the gospel they would have remained Jews under the cloak of Christianity for the rest of their days. For they acknowledge that they have never yet heard anything about Christ from those who baptized and taught them.

I hope that if one deals in a kindly way with the Jews and instructs them carefully from Holy Scripture, many of them will become genuine Christians and turn again to the faith of their fathers, the prophets and patriarchs.[7] They will only be frightened further away from it if their Judaism is so utterly rejected that nothing is allowed to remain, and they are treated only with arrogance and scorn. If the apostles, who also were Jews, had dealt with us Gentiles as we Gentiles deal with the Jews, there would never have been a Christian among the Gentiles. Since they dealt with us Gentiles in such brotherly fashion, we in our turn ought to treat the Jews in a brotherly manner in order that

---

[5] *Sophisten* was Luther's term for the scholastic theologians. See p. 82, n. 5.
[6] For an example of Luther's correspondence with converted Jews, see his 1523 letter to Bernard, who had married Karlstadt's maid the previous summer. S-J 2, 185-187; WA, Br 3, 101-102.
[7] Luther invariably refers to the righteous believers of the Old Testament as Christians. See pp. 96-97 and 203.

we might convert some of them.[8] For even we ourselves are not yet all very far along, not to speak of having arrived.[9]

When we are inclined to boast of our position we should remember that we are but Gentiles, while the Jews are of the lineage of Christ. We are aliens and in-laws; they are blood relatives, cousins, and brothers of our Lord. Therefore, if one is to boast of flesh and blood, the Jews are actually nearer to Christ than we are, as St. Paul says in Romans 9 [:5]. God has also demonstrated this by his acts, for to no nation among the Gentiles has he granted so high an honor as he has to the Jews. For from among the Gentiles there have been raised up no patriarchs, no apostles, no prophets, indeed, very few genuine Christians either. And although the gospel has been proclaimed to all the world, yet He committed the Holy Scriptures, that is, the law and the prophets, to no nation except the Jews, as Paul says in Romans 3 [:2] and Psalm 147 [:19-20], "He declares his word to Jacob, his statutes and ordinances to Israel. He has not dealt thus with any other nation; nor revealed his ordinances to them."

Accordingly, I beg my dear papists, should they be growing weary of denouncing me as a heretic, to seize the opportunity of denouncing me as a Jew. Perhaps I may yet turn out to be also a Turk, or whatever else my fine gentlemen may wish.

Christ is promised for the first time soon after Adam's fall, when God said to the serpent, "I will put enmity between you and the woman, and between your seed and her seed; he shall crush your head, and you shall bruise his heel" [Gen. 3:15]. Here I defer demonstrating that the serpent spoke possessed of the devil, for no dumb beast is so clever that it can utter or comprehend human speech, much less speak or inquire about such exalted matters as the commandment of God, as the serpent does here. Therefore, it must certainly have been a rational, highly intelligent, and mighty spirit which was able to utter human speech, deal so masterfully with God's commandments, and seize and employ human reason.

Since it is certain that a spirit is something higher than a

[8] Cf. I. Cor. 9:19-22.
[9] Cf. Phil. 3:12-14.

man, it is also certain that this is an evil spirit and an enemy of God, for it breaks God's commandment and acts contrary to his will. Therefore, it is undoubtedly the devil. And so the word of God which speaks of crushing the head must refer also to the devil's head; though not to the exclusion of the natural head of the serpent, for with a single word he speaks of both devil and serpent as of one thing. Therefore, he means both heads. But the devil's head is that power by which the devil rules, that is, sin and death, by means of which he has brought Adam and all Adam's descendants under his control.

This seed of the woman therefore, because he is to crush the devil's power, that is, sin and death, must not be an ordinary man, since all men have been brought under the devil through sin and death. So he must certainly be without sin. Now human nature does not produce such seed or fruit, as has been said, for with their sin they are all under the devil. How, then, can this be? The seed must be the natural child of a woman; otherwise, it could not be or be called the seed of the woman. On the other hand, as has been pointed out, human nature and birth does not produce such seed. Therefore, the solution must ultimately be that this seed is a true natural son of the woman; derived from the woman, however, not in the normal way but through a special act of God, in order that the Scripture might stand, that he is the seed only of a woman and not of a man. For the text [Gen. 3:15] clearly states that he will be the seed of woman.

This is thus the first passage in which the mother of this child is described as a virgin. She is his true natural mother; yet she is to conceive and bear supernaturally, by God, without a man, in order that her child may be a distinctive man, without sin, yet having ordinary flesh and blood like other men. This could not have been the case had he been begotten by a man like other men because the flesh is consumed and corrupted by evil lust, so that its natural act of procreation cannot occur without sin. Whatever conceives and bears through an act of the flesh produces also a carnal and sinful fruit. This is why St. Paul says in Ephesians 1 [2:3] that we are all by nature children of wrath.

Now this passage [Gen. 3:15] was the very first gospel message on earth. For when Adam and Eve, seduced by the devil, had fallen and were summoned for judgment before God, Genesis 3 [:9], they were in peril of death and the anguish of hell, for they saw that God was against them and condemned them; they would gladly have fled from him, but could not. Had God let them remain in their anguish, they would soon have despaired and perished. But when, after their terrible punishment, he let them hear his comforting promise to raise up from the woman's seed one who would tread upon the serpent's head, their spirits were quickened again. From that promise they drew comfort, believing firmly in that blessed seed of the woman which would come and crush the serpent's head, that is, sin and death, by which they had been crushed and corrupted.

The fathers, from Adam on, preached and inculcated this gospel, through which they acknowledged the promised seed of this woman and believed in him. And so they were sustained through faith in Christ just as we are; they were true Christians like ourselves. Only, in their day this gospel was not proclaimed publicly throughout the world, as it would be after the coming of Christ, but remained solely in the possession of the holy fathers and their descendants down to the time of Abraham.

The second promise of Christ was to Abraham, Genesis 22 [:18], where God said, "In your seed shall all the Gentiles be blessed." If all the Gentiles are to be blessed, then it is certain that otherwise, apart from this seed of Abraham, they were all unblessed and under a curse. From this it follows that human nature has nothing but cursed seed and bears nothing but unblessed fruit; otherwise, there would be no need for all of them to be blessed through this seed of Abraham. Whoever says "all" excludes no one; therefore, apart from Christ, all who are born of man must be under the devil, cursed in sin and death.

Here again the mother of God is proven to be a pure virgin. For since God cannot lie, it was inevitable that Christ should be the seed of Abraham, that is, his natural flesh and blood, like all of Abraham's descendants. On the other hand, because he was to be the blessed seed which should bless all others, he could not be begotten by man, since such children, as has been said, cannot be conceived without sin because of the corrupt and tainted flesh, which cannot perform its function without taint and sin.

Thus the word, by which God promises that Christ will be the seed of Abraham, requires that Christ be born of a woman and be her natural child. He does not come from the earth like Adam [Gen. 2:7]; neither is he from Adam's rib like Eve [Gen. 2:21-22]. He comes rather like any woman's child, from her seed. The earth was not the natural seed for Adam's body; neither was Adam's rib the natural seed for Eve's body. But the virgin's flesh and blood, from which children come in the case of all other women, was the natural seed of Christ's body. And she too was of the seed of Abraham.[10]

On the other hand, this word by which God promises his blessing upon all Gentiles in Christ requires that Christ may not come from a man, or by the act of a man; for work of the flesh (which is cursed) is incompatible with that which is blessed and is pure blessing. Therefore, this blessed fruit had to be the fruit of a woman's body only, not of a man, even though that very woman's body came from man, indeed, even from Abraham and Adam. So this mother is a virgin, and yet a true natural mother; not, however, by natural capacity or power, but solely through the Holy Spirit and divine power.

Now this passage [Gen. 22:18] was the gospel from the time of Abraham down to the time of David, even to the time of Christ. It is a short saying, to be sure, but a rich gospel, subsequently inculcated and used in marvelous fashion by the fathers both in writing and in preaching. Many thousands of sermons have been preached from this passage, and countless souls saved. For it is the living word of God, in which Abraham and his descendants believed, and by which they were redeemed and preserved from sin and death and the power of the devil. However, it too was not yet proclaimed publicly to all the world, as happened after the coming of Christ, but remained solely in the possession of the fathers and their descendants.

---

[10] In his 1543 *Vom Schem Hamphoras und vom Geschlecht Christi,* Luther dealt at length with the problem of the New Testament genealogies which seem to trace Jesus' lineage through Joseph rather than Mary. See the text in WA 53, 610-643.

Now just take a look at the perverse lauders of the mother of God. If you ask them why they hold so strongly to the virginity of Mary, they truly could not say. These stupid idolators do nothing more than to glorify only the mother of God; they extol her for her virginity and practically make a false deity of her. But Scripture does not praise this virginity at all for the sake of the mother; neither was she saved on account of her virginity. Indeed, cursed be this and every other virginity if it exists for its own sake, and accomplishes nothing better than its own profit and praise.

The Spirit extols this virginity, however, because it was needful for the conceiving and bearing of this blessed fruit. Because of the corruption of our flesh, such blessed fruit could not come, except through a virgin. Thus this tender virginity existed in the service of others to the glory of God, not to its own glory. If it had been possible for him to have come from a [married] woman, he would not have selected a virgin for this, since virginity is contrary to the physical nature within us, was condemned of old in the law,[11] and is extolled here solely because the flesh is tainted and its built-in physical nature cannot bestow her fruit except by means of an accursed act.

Hence we see that St. Paul nowhere calls the mother of God a virgin, but only a woman, as he says in Galatians 3 [4:4], "The Son of God was born of a woman." He did not mean to say she was not a virgin, but to extol her virginity to the highest with the praise that is proper to it, as much as to say: In this birth none but a woman was involved, no man participated; that is, everything connected with it was reserved to the woman, the conceiving, bearing, suckling, and nourishing of the child were functions no man can perform. It is therefore the child of a woman only; hence, she must certainly be a virgin. But a virgin may also be a man; a mother can be none other than a woman.

For this reason, too, Scripture does not quibble or speak about the virginity of Mary after the birth of Christ, a matter about which the hypocrites are greatly concerned, as if it were something of the utmost importance on which our whole salvation

---

[11] Cf., e.g., Isa. 4:1; Judg. 11:37-38.

depended. Actually, we should be satisfied simply to hold that she remained a virgin after the birth of Christ because Scripture does not state or indicate that she later lost her virginity. We certainly need not be so terribly afraid that someone will demonstrate, out of his own head apart from Scripture, that she did not remain a virgin. But the Scripture stops with this, that she was a virgin before and at the birth of Christ; for up to this point God had need of her virginity in order to give us the promised blessed seed without sin.

The third passage is addressed to David, II Samuel 7 [:12-14], "When your days are fulfilled, and you sleep with your fathers, I will raise up your seed after you, who shall come forth from your body, and I will establish his kingdom for ever. He shall build a house for my name, and I will establish the throne of his kingdom for ever. I will be his father, and he shall be my son." These words cannot have been spoken of Solomon, for Solomon was not a posthumous son of David raised up after his death. Neither did God after Solomon (who during David's lifetime was born and became king) ever designate anyone as His son, give him an everlasting kingdom, or have him build such a house. Consequently, the whole passage must refer to Christ. We will let this passage go for the present because it is too broad and requires so much in the way of exegesis; for one would have to show here that Christ accordingly had to be the son of a woman only in order to be called here God's child, who neither should nor could come out of an accursed act.

The fourth passage is Isaiah 7 [:14], "God himself will give you a sign. Behold, a virgin [*jungfrau*] is with child, and shall bear a son." [12] This could not have been said of a virgin who was about to be married. For what sort of a marvelous sign would that be if someone who is presently a virgin should bear a child within a year? Such is the ordinary course of nature, occurring daily before our eyes. If it is to be a sign from God, therefore, it must be something remarkable and marvelous not given by the

---

12 *Sihe eyne jungfraw ist schwanger und wirt eynen son gepern* was still Luther's rendering of Isa. 7:14 in his 1528 translation of Isaiah and in his 1545 German Bible. WA, DB 11[I], 42-43.

ordinary course of nature, as is commonly the case with all God's signs.

It is of no help for the Jews either to try to evade the issue here and come up with this way of getting around it, namely: the sign consists in the fact that Isaiah says flatly that the child shall be a son and not a daughter. By such an interpretation the sign would have nothing to do with the virgin but only with the prophet Isaiah, as the one who had divined so precisely that it would not[13] be a daughter. The text would then have to speak of Isaiah thus, "Behold, God himself will give you a sign, namely, that I, Isaiah, will divine that a young woman [*jung weyb*] is carrying a son, and not a daughter." Such an interpretation is disgraceful and childish.

Now the text forcefully refers the sign to the woman, and states clearly that it shall be a sign when a woman bears a son. Now it certainly is no sign when a woman who is no longer virgin bears a child, be it the mother of Hezekiah or whatever woman the Jews may point to.[14] The sign must be something new and different, a marvelous and unique work of God, that this woman is with child; her pregnancy is to be the sign. Now I do not deem any Jew so dense that he would not grant God sufficient power to create a child from a virgin, since they are compelled to acknowledge that he created Adam from the earth [Gen. 2:7] and Eve from Adam [Gen. 2:21-22], acts which require no less power.[15]

But then they contend that the Hebrew text does not read, "A virgin is with child," but, "Behold, an *almah* is with child."

---

[13] We have followed the lead of two early Basel printers in inserting the word "not" at this point. WA 11, 320, n. 33.
[14] The Jews interpreted the text to mean, "Behold, a young woman shall conceive and bear a son." The "woman" was frequently taken to be Abijah, mother of Hezekiah (II Kings 18:1-2; II Chron. 28:27–29:1), and the prophecy thus to refer to the birth of Ahaz's successor on the throne of Judah. See the *Dialogue with Trypho*, an Ephesian Jew, by the second century Christian apologist, Justin Martyr (chapters 43, 66-67, 71, 84), in Thomas B. Falls (trans.), *Writings of Saint Justin Martyr*. FC 6, 213, 254, 263, 281-282. Cf. also Tertullian's *Adversus Marcionem* III, 13, and *Adversus Judaeos* IX, 7-8, in *Tertulliani Opera. Corpus Christianorum, Series Latina* (Turnholti: Brepols, 1954), I, 524, and II, 1366.
[15] The point of this sentence was made in the same way by Justin Martyr in his *Dialogue with Trypho* (84), and followed immediately by the question Luther raises in his next sentence. FC 6, 281-282.

Almah, they say, does not denote a virgin; the word for virgin is *bethulah,* while *almah* is the term for young damsel [*dyrne*]. Presumably, a young damsel might very well have had intercourse and be the mother of a child.

Christians can readily answer this from St. Matthew and St. Luke, both of whom apply the passage from Isaiah [7:14] to Mary, and translate the word *almah* as "virgin." [16] They are more to be believed than the whole world, let alone the Jews. Even though an angel from heaven [Gal. 1:8] were to say that *almah* does not mean virgin, we should not believe it. For God the Holy Spirit speaks through St. Matthew and St. Luke; we can be sure that He understands Hebrew speech and expressions perfectly well.

But because the Jews do not accept the evangelists, we must confront them with other evidence. In the first place, we can say, as above, that there is no marvel or sign in the fact that a young woman conceives, otherwise, we would have a perfect right to sneer at the prophet Isaiah, and say, "What women would you expect to conceive if not the young ones? Are you drunk? Or is it in your experience a rare event for a young woman to bear a son?" For this reason that strained and farfetched answer of the Jews is just a vain and feeble excuse for not keeping silent altogether.

In the second place, grant that *bethulah* means virgin and not *almah,* and that Isaiah here uses *almah,* not *bethulah.* All this too is still nothing but a poor excuse. For they act as if they did not know that in all of Scripture *almah* nowhere designates a woman who has had intercourse (a fact of which they are perfectly well aware). On the contrary, in every instance [17] *almah* signifies a young damsel who has never known a man carnally or had intercourse. Such a person is always called a virgin, just as St. Matthew and St. Luke here translate Isaiah.

---

16 Matt. 1:23 and Luke 1:27, in referring to Mary, both use the Greek term *parthenos* with which the Septuagint had rendered *almah* in Isa. 7:14.

17 The term *almah* occurs in the singular in Gen. 24:43, Exod. 2:8, Prov. 30:19, and Isa. 7:14; in the plural in Ps. 68:25, Song of Sol. 1:3 and 6:8. Luther's distinction covers both groups, though he does distinguish between them in his 1543 *Vom Schem Hamphoras und vom Geschlecht Christi. WA* 53, 634-636.

Now since they are such literalists and like to argue about semantics, we will concede that *bethulah* is not the same word as *almah*. But the only point they have established thereby is that this young woman is not designated by the term "virgin." However, she is designated by another term which also means a young woman who has never had intercourse; call her by whatever term you please, in her person she is still a virgin. It is childish and disgraceful to take recourse to words when the meaning is one and the same.

Very well; to please the Jews we will not translate Isaiah thus: "Behold, a virgin [*jungfraw*] is with child," lest they be confused by the word "virgin," but rather, "Behold, a maiden [*Magd*] is with child." Now in German the word "maiden" denotes a woman who is still young, carries her crown[18] with honor, and wears her hair loose, so that it is said of her: She is still a maiden, not a wife (although "maiden" is not the same word as "virgin"). In like manner also, the Hebrew *elem* is a stripling who does not yet have a woman; and *almah* is a maiden who does not yet have a man, not a servant girl[19] but one who still carries a crown. Thus the sister of Moses is called an *almah* in Exodus 3 [2:8] as is Rebekah in Genesis 24,[20] when they were still virgins.

Suppose I say in German, "Hans is engaged to a maiden," and someone should comment, "Well, then he is not engaged to a virgin." Why, everyone would laugh at him for vainly disputing about words if he thinks that virgin and maiden are not the same thing because they are different words. This is true also in the Hebrew, when the Jews argue with respect to this passage in Isaiah [7:14] and say, "Isaiah does not say *bethulah*, but *almah*. I submit that among themselves their own conscience tells them this is so. Therefore, let them say what they please, *bethulah*

---

[18] The *krantz* was a decorative wreath or garland, worn on the head. Along with the flowing unbound tresses of the hair, it was in the Middle Ages an emblem of a girl's virginity. Grimm, *Deutsches Wörterbuch*, V², 2051-2053.

[19] The German words for servant girl and for young unmarried woman, as in English, are identical—*maid*.

[20] Gen. 24:43 calls Rebekah an *almah*—rendered as *parthenos* in the Septuagint—after she had been designated a *bethulah* in Gen. 24:16.

or *almah;* Isaiah means a damsel who is nubile but still wears her crown, whom in the truest German we call a maiden [*Magd*]. Hence, the mother of God is properly called the pure maiden, that is, the pure *almah.*

And if I should have had to tell Isaiah what to speak, I would have had him say exactly what he did say, not *bethulah,* but *almah,* for *almah* is even more appropriate here than *bethulah.* It is also more precise to say, "Behold, a maiden is with child," than to say, "A virgin is with child." For "virgin" is an all-embracing term which might also be applied to a woman of fifty or sixty who is no longer capable of childbearing. But "maiden" denotes specifically a young woman, nubile, capable of child-bearing, but still a virgin; it includes not only the virginity, but also the youthfulness and the potential for childbearing. Hence, in German too we commonly refer to young people as maidens or maidenfolk, not virginfolk.

Therefore, the text of Isaiah [7:14] is certainly most ac-curately translated, "Behold, a maiden is with child." No Jew who understands both German and Hebrew can deny that this is what is said in the Hebrew, for we Germans do not say "*con-cepit,* the woman has conceived"; the preachers have so rendered the Latin[21] into German. Rather, the German would say in his mother tongue, "The woman is with child," or, "is heavy with child," or, "is pregnant."

But here in the Hebrew it does not say, "Behold, a maiden shall be with child," as though she were not as yet. It says rather, "Behold, a maiden is with child," as though she has the fruit already in her womb and nevertheless is still a maiden, in order that you will have to notice how the prophet himself is amazed that there stands before him a maiden who is with child even before she knows a man carnally. She was of course going to have a husband, she was physically fit and mature enough for it; but even before she gets to that she is already a mother. This is indeed a rare and marvelous thing.

This is the way St. Matthew [1:18] construes this passage when he says, "When Mary the mother of Jesus had been

---

21 Jerome's Vulgate reads *concipiet,* which the Douay version renders as "shall conceive."

betrothed to Joseph, before they came together she was found to be with child of the Holy Spirit," etc. What does this mean other than that she was a young maiden who had not yet known a man although she was capable of it, but before she knew the man she was with child, and that this was an amazing thing since no maiden becomes pregnant prior to intercourse with a man? Thus, the evangelist regarded her in the same light as did the prophet, and set her forth as the sign and wonder.

Now this refutes also the false interpretation which some have drawn from the words of Matthew, where he says, "Before they came together she was found to be with child." They interpret this as though the evangelist meant to say, "Later she came together with Joseph like any other wife and lay with him, but before this occurred she was with child apart from Joseph," etc. Again, when he says, "And Joseph knew her not until she brought forth her first-born son" [Matt. 1:25], they interpret it as though the evangelist meant to say that he knew her, but not before she had brought forth her first-born son. This was the view of Helvidius[22] which was refuted by Jerome.[23]

Such carnal interpretations miss the meaning and purpose of the evangelist. As we have said, the evangelist, like the prophet Isaiah, wishes to set before our eyes this mighty wonder, and point out what an unheard-of thing it is for a maiden to be with child before her husband brings her home and lies with her; and further, that he does not know her carnally until she first has a son, which she should have had after first having been known

---

[22] Helvidius, disciple of the Arian bishop of Milan, Auxentius, was living in Rome at the time of Jerome's second sojourn there in 382-385. As a laymen he wrote a treatise against the generally accepted view of Mary's perpetual virginity, in which he attacked primarily the practical consequences drawn from the doctrine in terms of monasticism as a higher kind of Christian life. *Realencyklopädie*, VII, 654-655. His followers are included as No. 84 in Augustine's A.D. 428 list of 88 heresies (*De Haeresibus* I, lxxxiv). *MPL* 42, 46.

[23] The treatise of Helvidius is known only through its rebuttal by Jerome, who did not know him personally but who took up the debate at the urging of friends in order to promote and defend monasticism. *Realencyklopädie*, VII, 655. See the text of Jerome's *De perpetua virginitate B. Mariae, adversus Helvidium* in *MPL* 23, 183-206, and references to it by the author himself in *Epistola XXII ad Eustochium*, 22 (*MPL* 22, 409), *Epistola XLVIII ad Pammachium*, 18 (*MPL* 22, 508), and *Adversus Jovinianum* I, 13 (*MPL* 23, 230).

by him. Thus, the words of the evangelist do not refer to anything that occurred after the birth, but only to what took place before it. For the prophet and the evangelist, and St. Paul as well, do not treat of this virgin beyond the point where they have from her that fruit for whose sake she is a virgin and everything else. After the child is born they dismiss the mother and speak not about her, what became of her, but only about her offspring. Therefore, one cannot from these words [Matt. 1:18, 25] conclude that Mary, after the birth of Christ, became a wife in the usual sense; it is therefore neither to be asserted nor believed. All the words are merely indicative of the marvelous fact that she was with child and gave birth before she had lain with a man.

The form of expression used by Matthew is the common idiom, as if I were to say, "Pharaoh believed not Moses, until he was drowned in the Red Sea." Here it does not follow that Pharaoh believed later, after he had drowned; on the contrary, it means that he never did believe. Similarly when Matthew [1:25] says that Joseph did not know Mary carnally until she had brought forth her son, it does not follow that he knew her subsequently; on the contrary, it means that he never did know her. Again, the Red Sea overwhelmed Pharaoh before he got across. Here too it does not follow that Pharaoh got across later, after the Red Sea had overwhelmed him, but rather that he did not get across at all. In like manner, when Matthew [1:18] says, "She was found to be with child before they came together," it does not follow that Mary subsequently lay with Joseph, but rather that she did not lie with him.

Elsewhere in Scripture the same manner of speech is employed. Psalm 110 [:1] reads, "God says to my Lord: 'Sit at my right hand, till I make your enemies your footstool.'" Here it does not follow that Christ does not continue to sit there after his enemies are placed beneath his feet. Again, in Genesis 28 [:15], "I will not leave you until I have done all that of which I have spoken to you." Here God did not leave him after the fulfilment had taken place. Again, in Isaiah 42 [:4], "He shall not be sad, nor troublesome,[24] till he has established justice in the earth."

---

[24] Douay version.

There are many more similar expressions, so that this babble of Helvidius is without justification; in addition, he has neither noticed nor paid any attention to either Scripture or the common idiom.

This is enough for the present to have sufficiently proved that Mary was a pure maiden, and that Christ was a genuine Jew of Abraham's seed. Although more Scripture passages might be cited,[25] these are the clearest. Moreover, if anyone does not believe a clear saying of His Divine Majesty, it is reasonable to assume that he would not believe either any other more obscure passages. So certainly no one can doubt that it is possible for God to cause a maiden to be with child apart from a man, since he has also created all things from nothing. Therefore, the Jews have no ground for denying this, for they acknowledge God's omnipotence, and they have here the clear testimony of the prophet Isaiah.

While we are on the subject, however, we wish not only to answer the futile liars who publicly malign me in these matters but we would also like to do a service to the Jews on the chance that we might bring some of them back to their own true faith, the one which their fathers held. To this end we will deal with them further, and suggest for the benefit of those who want to work with them a method and some passages from Scripture which they should employ in dealing with them. For many, even of the sophists,[26] have also attempted this; but insofar as they have set about it in their own name, nothing has come of it. For they were trying to cast out the devil by means of the devil, and not by the finger of God [Luke 11:17-20].

In the first place, that the current belief of the Jews and their waiting upon the coming of the Messiah is erroneous is proved by the passage in Genesis 49 [:10-12] where the holy patriarch Jacob says: "The scepter shall not depart from Judah, nor a teacher from those at his feet, until the *Shiloh* comes; and to him shall be the gathering of the nations. He will bind his foal

---

25 In his 1543 *Vom Schem Hamphoras und vom Geschlecht Christi*, Luther treats these same passages plus Gen. 49:10, Luke 1:42, Ps. 22:10-11, Ps. 110:3, Jer. 31:22, and Luke 1:38 in discussing the Virgin Birth. WA 53, 634-644.
26 See p. 202, n. 5.

to the vine, and his ass to the choice vine. He will wash his garments with wine, and his mantle with the blood of grapes. His eyes are redder than wine, and his teeth whiter than milk." This passage is a divine promise, which cannot lie and must be fulfilled unless heaven and earth were first to pass away.[27] So the Jews cannot deny that for nearly fifteen hundred years now, since the fall of Jerusalem,[28] they have had no scepter, that is, neither kingdom nor king. Therefore, the *Shiloh*, or Messiah,[29] must have come before this fifteen hundred year period, and before the destruction of Jerusalem.

If they try to say that the scepter was also taken away from Judah at the time of the Babylonian captivity, when the Jews were transported to Babylon and remained captive for seventy years, and yet the Messiah did not come at that time, the answer is that this is not true. For during the whole period of captivity the royal line continued in the person of King Jechoniah, thereafter Zerubbabel[30] and other princes in turn until Herod became king. For "scepter" signifies not only a kingdom, but also a hegemony,[31] as the Jews are well aware. Furthermore, they still always had prophets. So the kingdom or hegemony never did disappear, even though for a time it existed outside of its territorial boundaries. Also, never during the captivity were all the inhabitants driven out of the land, as has happened during these

---

27 Cf. Matt. 5:18; 24:35.

28 See p. 222, n. 36.

29 The specific meaning of this passage has always been debated, though until recent times the Messianic reference was generally accepted by both Jewish and Christian commentators. In the Talmud *Sanhedrin* 98*b* reads, "Those of the school of R. Shila say, Shiloh is his [the Messiah's] name." The Targums Onkelos, Jerusalem, and Pseudo-Jonathan, as well as Raschi [d. 1104], identify Shiloh with the Messiah. On the pre-Reformation history of the exegesis of this passage see S. R. Driver, "Genesis XLIX. 10: An Exegetical Study," *The Journal of Philology*, XIV (1885), 1-28. In his German Bible Luther rendered the term *der Held* (the hero). See Luther's fuller discussion of the passage in his 1543 *Von den Juden und ihren Lügen.* WA 53, 450-462.

30 Jechoniah is a variant spelling of the name Jehoiachin. See Matt. 1:12 and I Chron. 3:16-19; also on Jechoniah, see Jer. 24:1, II Kings 24:6-15; II Chron. 36:9-10; and on Zerubbabel (also called Sheshbazzar by the Babylonians), see Ezra 1:8-11; 3:2-8, and Hag. 1:1; 2:23.

31 The Hebrew *shebet* referred in the Old Testament not simply to a king's scepter but also to the staff of office of a leader or chief, e.g., Judg. 5:14, Num. 21:18.

past fifteen hundred years when the Jews have had neither princes nor prophets.

It was for this reason that God provided them at that time with the prophets Jeremiah, Ezekiel, Haggai, and Zechariah, who proclaimed to them that they would again be freed from Babylon, in order that they would not think that this word of Jacob was false, or that the Messiah had come. But for these last fifteen hundred years they have had no prophet to proclaim that they should again be free. God would not have permitted this state of affairs to continue for such a long time, since he did not on that occasion permit it for such a short time. He thereby gives ample indication that this prophecy [Gen. 49:10-12] must have been fulfilled.

In addition, when Jacob says here that the scepter shall endure until the Messiah comes, it clearly follows that this scepter not only must not perish but also that it must become far more glorious than it ever was previously, before the Messiah's coming. For all the Jews know full well that the Messiah's kingdom will be the greatest and most glorious that has ever been on earth, as we read in Psalms 2, 72, and 89. For the promise is also made to David that his throne shall endure forever [Ps. 89:4, 29, 36-37]. Now the Jews will have to admit that today their scepter has now been nonexistent for fifteen hundred years, not to speak of its having become more glorious.

This prophecy can therefore be understood to refer to none other than Jesus Christ our Lord, who is of the tribe of Judah and of the royal lineage of David. He came when the scepter had fallen to Herod, the alien;[32] He has been king these fifteen hundred years, and will remain king on into eternity. For his kingdom has spread to the ends of the earth, as the prophets foretold [Ps. 2:8; 72:8-11]; and the nations have been gathered to him, as Jacob says here [Gen. 49:10]. And there could not possibly be a greater king on earth, whose name would be exalted among more nations, than this Jesus Christ.

It is true that some Jews do indeed feel how persuasive and

---

[32] Both parents of Herod the Great, who was king of Judea in 37–4 B.C., were Idumaeans; their people had been conquered by John Hyrcanus in 125 B.C. and under compulsion had nominally become Jews.

conclusive this passage really is. This is why they hunt up all sorts of weird ways of getting around it. But if you will notice, they only ensnare themselves. For example, they say that in this instance *shiloh* does not signify the Messiah or Christ, and that therefore this passage does not carry any weight with them. It matters not whether he is called Messiah or *shiloh;* we are concerned not with the name, but with the person, with the fact that he shall appear when the scepter is taken away from Judah. No such person can be found except Jesus Christ; otherwise, the passage is false. He will be no mere cobbler or tailor, but a lord to whom the nations will be gathered; that is, his kingdom will be more glorious than the scepter ever was before, as has been said.

Equally futile is another subterfuge, when they say: The nations which are gathered to him may well be only the Jewish nation, and *shiloh* means a lord. Be that as it may; I will not quarrel over what *shiloh* means, although it does seem to me that it signifies a man who is prosperous, well-to-do, has plenty, and is generous. From this comes the little word *salve,* which means *copia* [riches], *felicitas* [good fortune], *abundantia* [prosperity], an ample sufficiency of all good things, as it says in Psalm 122 [:7], *"Et abundantia in turribus suis"* ["and prosperity within your palaces"]; that is, everything is full and sufficient and prospering, so that in German I might call *shiloh* well-being.[33]

Now whether it signifies lord or whether it signifies well-being, *prosper* [prosperous], or *felix* [fortunate], at any rate it cannot be said to mean one of the former kings, princes, or teachers. For "the scepter of Judah" certainly comprises all those of the tribe of Judah who have been kings or princes with the exception of this *shiloh,* who here is singled out and preferred above all those who have wielded the scepter of Judah as some-

---

[33] *"Wollfart."* Luther evidently derives *shiloh* from the root *shalah,* meaning to be secure and at ease or rest, which in turn is related to the Hebrew greeting *shalom,* which corresponds to the Latin greeting *salve,* both meaning your health, peace, welfare, and prosperity. In his 1543 *Vom Schem Hamphoras,* Luther discusses the suggestion that *shiloh* may come from the root *shalah* meaning to draw out, from whence comes the term *shiljoh* ("afterbirth" in Deut. 28:57, RSV); but even in this derivation he still finds the personal and Messianic reference of the term to be unmistakeable. *WA* 53, 639-643.

one special, because Jacob says [Gen. 49:10] the scepter of Judah shall endure until *shiloh*. What kind of talk would that be for me, to try to make of *shiloh* one of them who have held the scepter of Judah and the nations, when the passage here means that the *shiloh* will come after all those others as a greater and more glorious king, and that he will have no successor. Why would he not otherwise have said, "The scepter of Judah shall endure forever, and not wait upon *shiloh*"?

Therefore, it is the kingdom of Christ which is here described in masterly fashion, namely, that before him many should wield the scepter of Judah until he should come himself and take it in his own hands forever, and that he would have no successor, nor would there ever be another king of the tribe of Judah. Thereby it is made clear that his kingdom would be a spiritual kingdom, following upon the temporal kingdom; for no person can have an eternal kingdom who is himself mortal and reigns temporally. Therefore, the scepter of Judah did indeed endure from David down to *shiloh* as something temporal, having a succession of mortal kings. But now that *shiloh* is come, the scepter remains forever in the hands of one person; no longer does it involve a succession of kings.

From this it necessarily follows that this *shiloh* must first die, and thereafter rise again from the dead. For since he is to come from the tribe of Judah [Gen. 49:10], he must be a true, natural man, mortal like all the children of Judah. On the other hand, because he is to be a special king, distinguished above all who have held the scepter of Judah before him, and he alone is to reign forever, he cannot be a mortal man, but must be an immortal man. Therefore, he must through death put off this mortal life, and by his resurrection take on immortal life, in order that he may fulfil this prophecy and become a *shiloh* to whom all the world shall be gathered. He is to be a truly living man, a king of the tribe of Judah, and yet immortal, eternal, and invisible, ruling spiritually in faith. But such sweet speech is still too exalted and difficult for the Jews.

But if they say: Well this Jesus of yours has never done what Jacob later says of this *shiloh*, namely, "He will bind his foal to the vine, and his ass to the choice vine; he will wash his garments in wine, and his mantle in the blood of grapes" [Gen. 49:11], then answer: A simpleton might perhaps take this to mean that this *shiloh* would be so rich a king that in his day wine would be as common as water, used for washing clothes, etc. From the foregoing, however, we have observed that this *shiloh* is to reign forever, a single person, and that he has no heirs to follow him. All the prophets too say this. Therefore, his kingdom cannot be a temporal one, consisting essentially of mortal and perishable goods.

And if this does not compel the interpretation that the wine and vine must be spiritual, then the very manner and nature of the words and language must compel it. For what sort of praise would it be to laud such a glorious kingdom above all kingdoms on these four grounds, namely, that its ruler binds his foal to the vine, his ass to the choice vine, and washes his garments with wine, and his mantle with the blood of grapes? Could Jacob find no other praise than that which has to do with drinking? Must such a king have nothing else than wine? Again, is there nothing else praiseworthy in him but the fact that his eyes are redder than wine and his teeth whiter than milk? [Gen. 49:12]. What does it benefit a kingdom that its ruler has white teeth, red eyes, and binds a foal to a vine?

Assuming for a moment that these things are said concerning superfluous riches, why doesn't Jacob say much more, such as: He will wash his garments in balsam and myrrh? That would be even more luxurious. Who ever heard of anyone longing to wash his clothes in wine? Again, why doesn't he say: He will pasture his horses in the wheat? Who ever heard of anyone wanting to tether his ass to a vine? What is the point of an ass at the vine, and clothes in the wine? The whole thing is sheer nonsense. Wine ruins clothes, and the ass is better off with thistles than with a vine. A vine would be better suited to a sheep; it could eat the leaves. This seemingly ridiculous talk therefore forcibly compels a spiritual interpretation.

Then too, why does he praise him for his red eyes and white teeth? Is there nothing else beautiful about his body than red eyes and white teeth? What kind of praise is that for so glorious and great a king? We usually praise great kings for their strong and splendid physique, and above all for their great spirit, wisdom, graciousness, fortitude, power, and glorious deeds and virtues. But in this case, only his eyes and teeth are praised; this sounds more like praise of a woman than of a man, let alone of such a king.

There can be no doubt that in these words the Spirit through Moses portrayed this person for us in the setting of a spiritual kingdom as it was to come into being and be governed. This is not the time, however, to discuss this at length. We have enough to do for the present in forcefully asserting against the Jews that the true *shiloh* or Christ must have come long ago, because they been long since bereft of the kingdom and hegemony, and of prophets as well. Here the clear text stands firm and testifies that the scepter shall remain with the tribe of Judah until the true king comes, when for the first time it shall really hold sway.

Thus, the kingdom of our Lord Jesus Christ squares perfectly with this prophecy. For there was a hegemony among the Jews until he came. After his coming, however, it was destroyed, and at the same time he began the eternal kingdom in which he still reigns forever. That he was of the tribe of Judah is unquestionable. Because as regards his person he was to be an eternal king, it could not be that he should govern in a temporal and secular sense, because what is temporal will pass away. Conversely, because he had to be David's natural seed, it could not be otherwise than that he should be a natural, mortal, temporal, perishable man.

Now to be temporal and to reign eternally are two mutually contradictory concepts. Therefore, it had to turn out that he died temporally and departed this life, and again that he arose from the dead and became alive in order that he might become an eternal king. For he had to be alive if he were to reign, because one who is dead cannot reign; and he had to die too if he were to shift from this mortal life, into which he necessarily had to enter to fulfil the Scripture which promised he would be the natural blood of David and Abraham.

So now he lives and reigns, and holds the exalted office of binding his foal to the vine and washing his garments in the red wine; that is, he governs our consciences with the holy gospel, which is a most gracious preachment of God's loving-kindness, the forgiveness of sins, and redemption from death and hell, by which all who from the heart believe it will be comforted, joyous, and, as it were, drowned in God with the overwhelming comfort of his mercy. The Jews, however, will not listen to this interpretation until they first accept and acknowledge the fact that Christ must have come in accordance with this prophecy. Therefore, we will let the matter rest until its own good time.

On the basis and testimony of this passage [Gen. 49:10-12], another sensible argument is also to be proved, namely, that this *shiloh* must have come at the time our Jesus Christ came, and that he can be none other than that selfsame Jesus. The prophecy says that nations shall be gathered to or be subject to this *shiloh*. Now I ask the Jews: When was there ever such a man of Jewish ancestry to whom so many nations were subject as this Jesus Christ? David was a great king, and so was Solomon; but their kingdom never extended beyond a small portion of the land of Syria. This Jesus, on the contrary, is accepted as a lord and king throughout the world, so that one may consider as fulfilled in him the prophecy from the second Psalm [v. 8], where God says to the Messiah, "I will give you the Gentiles for your possession, and the uttermost parts of the earth for your inheritance." This had indeed come true in the person of our Jesus since the time when the scepter was taken from the Jews; this is quite apparent and has never yet happened in the case of any other Jew. Because *shiloh* was to come when Judah's scepter was ended, and since that time no other has fulfilled these prophecies, this Jesus must certainly be the real *shiloh* whom Jacob intended.

The Jews will have to admit further that the Gentiles have never once yielded themselves so willingly to a Jew for their lord and king, as to this Jesus. For although Joseph was certainly a great man in Egypt, he was neither its lord nor its king [Gen. 41:40]. And even if he had been, Egypt was a mighty small thing compared to this kingdom which everybody ascribes to this Jesus.

Again, neither in Babylon nor in Persia was either Daniel [Dan. 5:29; 6:1-3] or Mordecai [Esther 10:3] a king, although they were men of power in the government.

It is amazing that the Jews are not moved to believe in this

Jesus, their own flesh and blood, with whom the prophecies of Scripture actually square so powerfully and exactly, when they see that we Gentiles cling to him so hard and fast and in such numbers that many thousands have shed their blood for his sake. They know perfectly well that the Gentiles have always shown greater hostility toward the Jews than toward any other nation, and have been unwilling to tolerate their dominion, laws, or government. How is it then that the Gentiles should now so reverse themselves as to willingly and steadfastly surrender themselves to this Jew, and with heart and soul confess him king of kings and lord of lords, unless it be that here is the true Messiah, to whom God by a great miracle has made the Gentiles friendly and submissive in accordance with this and numerous other prophecies?

The second[34] passage is Daniel 9 [:24-27], where the angel Gabriel speaks to Daniel in the plainest terms about Christ, saying, "Seventy weeks are determined concerning your people and your holy city, that transgression may be finished, forgiveness sealed, iniquity atoned for, and everlasting righteousness brought in, and vision and prophecy fulfilled, and the most holy anointed. Take notice therefore and know: from the going forth of the word to rebuild Jerusalem are seven weeks and sixty-two weeks until Messiah the prince; the streets and the wall shall be built again in a troubled time. And after sixty-two weeks Messiah shall be cut off, and they [who cut him off] shall not be his. But the people of the prince who is to come shall destroy the city and the sanctuary. Its end shall come with violence. And after the end of the war there shall remain the appointed desolation. And he shall confirm the covenant with many in one week; and in the middle of the week sacrifice and offering shall cease," etc.

God help us! This passage has been dealt with so variously by both Jews and Christians[35] that one might doubt whether anything certain can be derived from it! Well this much at least we

---

[34] Discussion of the first passage, Gen. 49:10-12, began on p. 213.
[35] Thirty-two major Christian and Jewish interpretations of this passage (which can, however, legitimately be grouped into a few main types) are distinguished by Franz Fraidl in his *Die Exegese der Siebzig Wochen Daniels in der Alten and Mittleren Zeit* (Graz: Lueschner, 1883).

will derive from it, namely, that the true Messiah must have come over one thousand and five hundred years ago, just as we hold that our Jesus Christ did. The computation and exegesis we will postpone to the last, and for the first simply say: Neither Jew nor anyone else can deny that the angel Gabriel is speaking here of the rebuilding of Jerusalem after the Babylonian captivity; this took place under Nehemiah.

In the second place, Gabriel can surely be referring only to that destruction of Jerusalem which subsequently took place under the Roman emperor Titus about the thirtieth[36] year after the ascension of our Lord. For after Jerusalem was rebuilt [by Nehemiah] there was no other destruction of the city, although it had been captured at the time of the Maccabees.[37] From this we draw the assured and incontrovertible conclusion that the Messiah of whom Gabriel here speaks must have come before the destruction [by Titus]. That, I think, is quite certain and sufficiently clear.

It is true that the Jews long ago began to feel the pressure of this mighty flood of evidence, and have anxiously defended their position with all manner of preposterous glosses. They make of this Messiah something other than the true Messiah, as for example King Cyrus of Persia, whom Isaiah in chapter 45 calls a Messiah,[38] and who was slain by Tomyris, the Scythian queen.[39]

---

[36] *Dreyssigst* in the original, a figure which is retained in the Latin translation by Justus Jonas, is changed by *EA* 29, 69, and *St. L.* 20, 1816, to read "fortieth," but without any indication of textual authority. Jerusalem was actually destroyed by the Romans under Titus in the year A.D. 70. In his 1541 *Suppotatio Annorum Mundi,* Luther dates it more accurately forty years after Christ's passion and seventy-four years after his nativity. *WA* 53, 127.

[37] After capturing Jerusalem in 170 B.C., Antiochus Epiphanes desecrated the temple, which was then purified by Judas when the Maccabees retook the city in 165 B.C.

[38] Luther translates the *mashiach* of Isa. 45:1 as *gesalbeten,* literally "anointed," in his 1528 and 1545 versions. *WA,* DB 11I, 136-137.

[39] Cyrus probably died a violent death in the year 529 B.C. The unreliable tradition that he was killed in battle against the forces of Tomyris, queen of the Massagetes, derives ultimately from *The History of Herodotus,* I, 214. Luther may have depended for his account of it on the *Summa historialis* (I, iv, 1) of Antoninus (Florentinus, 1389-1459), the archbishop of Florence. *WA* 23, 503, n. 2. The same tradition was accepted in another of Luther's chief historical sources, the *Breviarium de temporibus* ascribed to Philo of Alexandria. *WA* 53, 20, l. 3.

This and similar efforts are worthless excuses, capricious and unwarranted evasions, and therefore quickly disposed of as follows:

These seventy weeks (says Gabriel) are to extend to the time of a Messiah of such a sort that in his time, when the weeks have elapsed, sin and iniquity shall be finished, forgiveness and everlasting righteousness brought in, and vision and prophecy fulfilled. Now I ask them both, Jews and everyone else: Did such things come to pass in the days of Cyrus? In the time of Cyrus and after him no more special righteousness was brought upon earth than what existed before and since under other kings. Moreover, in the days of David and Solomon the level of righteousness was much higher than at the time of Cyrus, but Scripture does not designate this as everlasting righteousness. The righteousness of which Gabriel speaks must therefore be far superior to that which prevailed in the time of David, the most holy king, let alone to such righteousness as the pagan Cyrus had in his day.

And further, when Gabriel says here that the city of Jerusalem shall be rebuilt in seven weeks, and that afterward the Messiah shall be cut off after sixty-two weeks, how can that apply to King Cyrus, who was slain before the seven weeks began, or—if their calculation is correct—at any rate before Jerusalem was rebuilt? How can the Messiah be someone who was slain before the rebuilding of Jerusalem, and then was cut off sixty-two weeks later after Jerusalem was rebuilt?

So now we have it; their defense is fallacious, and the passage cannot be interpreted in terms of Cyrus. Since Scripture designates no one as Messiah after Cyrus except the only true one, and since such great and exalted qualities cannot be attributed to any temporal king, we conclude—and thus mightily overcome the error of the Jews—that the true Messiah came after the rebuilding of Jerusalem [by Nehemiah] and prior to its destruction [by Titus]. For no Messiah was put to death before the destruction of Jerusalem except our Lord Jesus Christ, whom we call Messiah, that is, Christ, or the Anointed One. For this reason we will now examine the text,[40] and see how exactly it conforms to our Lord Jesus Christ.

---

[40] Luther subsequently dealt with this text, and varied somewhat his calculation of the seventy years, in his sermon of November 20, 1524, on

I must address my remarks to those who are familiar with the histories of the kingdoms;[41] those who are unfamiliar with them will probably not understand me. The surest method in this exegesis is to reckon backward, namely, beginning with the time when Jesus was baptized and began to preach. Gabriel is referring to this time when he says, "Until Messiah the prince" [Dan. 9:25], as if he would say: I speak of matters prior not to the birth of Christ but to the hegemony of Christ, when he began to reign, to teach, to instruct, and to represent himself as a ruler to be followed. This is the position taken by the gospel writers, especially Mark [1:1-15], and by Peter in Acts [1:22]. They begin the activities of Christ after his baptism by John, as Luke [3:21-23] also does. That is when his work really began. But Christ was then about thirty years old.

Now among those who are well versed in Scripture there is no doubt whatever that Gabriel is speaking here not of the normal week of seven days, but of year-weeks, in which seven years comprise one week.[42] Scripture commonly employs such terminology.[43] Therefore, the seventy weeks [Dan. 9:24] amount altogether to four hundred and ninety years.

If we now reckon from Christ's thirtieth year [Luke 3:23] backward through the Greek and Persian kingdoms for four hun-

---

Matt. 24:15ff. (WA 15, 743-745), his 1530 *Preface to Daniel* (LW 35, 303-305) and its subsequent revisions (WA, DB 11ᴵᴵ, 18-31), his 1543 *Von den Juden und ihren Lügen* (WA 53, 492-510), a table talk of July, 1543 (WA, Tr 4, No. 4848), and his 1541-1545 *Suppotatio Annorum Mundi* (WA 53, 13-14, 25-27, 108-110, 125, 173-177).

[41] On Luther's chief historical sources, other than the Bible, for Old Testament history, and particularly for the chronology of the Persian kings customarily mentioned in the exegesis of Dan. 9:24-27, see WA, DB 11ᴵᴵ, xliii-xlv, and WA 53, 9-21. Among others, Luther relied heavily, as did Melanchthon and most of his non-Italian contemporaries, on a historical document which was presumed to be genuine but was actually quite spurious, in which the Italian Dominican John Annius of Viterbo (*ca.* 1432-1502) had compiled what purported to be chronologies of antiquity by various ancient authors. The two ancients from this spurious collection quoted most frequently by Luther were Metasthenes Persa, presumed author of the *Iudicium temporum et Annalium Persarum,* and Philo of Alexandria, the pseudonymous author of *Breviarum de Temporibus.* The pertinent passages from both authors are reprinted in WA 53, 17-21.

[42] In Dan. 9:24 the "seventy weeks" in the KJV is literal, the "seventy weeks of years" in the RSV represents the interpretation which Luther describes as universal. Luther's generalization is substantiated in Fraidl, *op. cit.*

[43] See, e.g., Lev. 25:8, Ezek. 4:4-5.

dred and ninety years, we arrive exactly at the twentieth [Neh. 2:1] and last year of Cambyses,[44] the third king or the second king in Persia[45] after Cyrus, that Cyrus who permitted the building of the temple at Jerusalem, II Chron. 36 [:22-23], and Ezra 1 [:1-3]. However, more than forty-six years[46] later Cambyses, and after him Darius Longimanus (who had previously vowed to do so [I Esd. 4:43]), permitted the building of the city of Jerusalem, which was done under Nehemiah. All this is set forth in the books of Nehemiah and Ezra. Thus, if we take the seventy weeks as beginning with Nehemiah's departure from Persia [Neh. 2:1-11], that is, about the seventh year of Darius Longimanus,[47] it corresponds exactly with our Christ.

Now Gabriel says [Dan. 9:24], "Seventy weeks (that is, four hundred and ninety years) are determined concerning your peo-

---

[44] Metasthenes (see p. 224, n. 41) fixed the reign of *"priscus Artaxerxes Assuerus,"* whom Luther identifies with the historical Cambyses, at "twenty-years." WA 53, 18, ll. 35-36.

[45] The first five kings of the Persian Empire were actually Cyrus (538-529), Cambyses (529-522), Darius I Hystapsis (522-486), Xerxes I (485-465), and Artaxerxes I Longimanus (464-424). W. O. E. Oesterley, *A History of Israel* (Oxford: Clarendon, 1932) II, 466. The comparable list of Archaemenid kings on which Luther based his calculation, derived from the inadequate information of his chief sources, Metasthenes and Pseudo-Philo (see p. 224, n. 41), was as follows: Darius Hystapsis reigned for two years along with Cyrus; Cyrus then reigned alone for twenty-two years; he was followed for twenty years by Priscus Artaxerxes Assuerus who is also called Arthahsastha and Cambyses and Ahasuerus (Ezra 4:6); and finally came Darius Longimanus who ruled for thirty-seven years. WA, DB 11[II], 19, n. 4. Luther noted the considerable discrepancies between the Bible and the various Greek and Latin histories with respect to the names, dates, and number of the Persian kings in his 1524 lectures on Haggai (WA 13, 511-512, 532-533) and his 1527 exposition of Zechariah (WA 23, 503).

Darius the Mede (Dan. 5:31; 6:28; 9:1) is here called Darius Hystapsis after the manner of Pseudo-Philo and the *Summa historialis* of Antoninus Florentinus (*op. cit.*, I, iv, 1, section 4). The Artaxerxes of Ezra and Nehemiah is really identical with the historical Artaxerxes I Longimanus (464-424). The Ahasuerus of Ezra 4:6 is really the historical Xerxes I (485-465). The epithet Longimanus ("long hand") belonged historically to Artaxerxes I (464-424); in ascribing it here to Darius, Luther is following the lead of Metasthenes and Pseudo-Philo (WA 53, 18, ll, 37-39, 20, l. 11).

[46] The forty-six years presumably included the two years of Darius Hystapsis and Cyrus, the twenty-two years of Cyrus, the twenty years of Cambyses, and two years of Darius Longimanus (cf. Ezra 4:24; Hag. 1:1; Zech. 1:1). Luther treats extensively of these forty-six years as related to John 2:20 in the preface to his 1545 *Suppotatio Annorum Mundi*. WA 53, 25-27.

[47] See p. 226, n. 49.

ple and your holy city." This is as if he were to say: Your nation of the Jews and the holy city of Jerusalem have yet four hundred and ninety years to go; then they will both come to an end. As to what shall actually transpire, he says that transgression will be finished and forgiveness sealed and iniquity atoned for and ever-lasting righteousness brought in, and vision and prophecy fulfilled, that is, that satisfaction will be made for all sins, forgiveness of sins proclaimed, and the righteousness of faith preached, that righteousness which is eternally valid before God. This it is to which all the prophets and the whole of Scripture bear witness, as Paul in Romans 1 [:17] and Peter in Acts 2 [:38-39] testify. For before it there has been nothing but sin and work-righteous-ness, which is temporal and invalid in the sight of God. I know of course that some invariably interpret the little Hebrew word "*Hathuth*" here as "sins"; I have taken it to mean "forgive-ness"—as Moses sometimes does, and as it is used in Psalm 51 [:7]—[48] not without reason.

Next he shows when the period of seventy weeks begins, say-ing [Dan. 9:25], "From the going forth of the word to rebuild Jerusalem (that is, at the time of Nehemiah, in the twentieth year of Cambyses), until Messiah the prince (that is, until the baptism of Christ in the Jordan), are seven weeks (that is, forty-nine years, during which Jerusalem was rebuilt in a troubled time, as the book of Nehemiah [2-6] teaches) and sixty-two weeks" (that is, 441[49] years after Jerusalem was rebuilt). This makes alto-

---

[48] The Hebrew root *chata* does mean to "sin" at most places in the Old Testament. In the *Piel* form, however, it occasionally has such contrasting meanings as "purge" (Ps. 51:7) and "cleanse" (e.g., Exod. 29:36; Lev. 14:52) and "purify" (Lev. 8:15; Num. 19:19), in which instances Luther usually rendered the term as *entsündigen* (literally to "de-sin"). In his Bible translations of 1530 and 1545, though, Luther rendered the *chattath* of Dan. 9:24 as *Sünde* ("sins").

[49] There are several obvious inconsistencies in Luther's calculations. Without citing any textual basis, *St. L.* 20, 1819, changes the figure from 441 to 434, presumably in order to correct an error and make the total of 49 plus 434 equal 483. However, an error is not necessarily involved; Luther is simply inconsistent in setting the time here as 483 years (sixty-nine weeks) after he had carefully calculated the years from Nehemiah's rebuilding to Christ's baptism as 490 years (seventy weeks; see pp. 224-225). He is also inconsistent here in starting Nehemiah's effort during "the twentieth year of Cambyses," while on p. 225 he started it in "the seventh year of Darius Longimanus." By 1530, in his *Preface to Daniel*, Luther had adopted the

gether sixty-nine weeks, that is 483 years. There is still lacking one week, that is, seven years, to make the total of seventy weeks, or 490 years. He then shows what is to happen in that selfsame week, saying [Dan. 9:26]:

"And after sixty-two weeks (note that this if after the first seven weeks of troubled rebuilding) Messiah shall be cut off (this did not happen at the beginning of the last week, but right in the middle of it,[50] for Christ preached for three and one-half years, and Gabriel uses the term 'cut off,'[51] that is, taken from this life into the immortal life through death and his resurrection). And they [who cut him off] shall not be his" (that is, those who crucify him and drive him from this world will no more belong to him and be his people, but he will take unto himself another people). Gabriel explains this and tells how they will not go unpunished for it, saying [Dan. 9:26]:

"And the people of a prince who is to come (that is, Titus, the Roman emperor) shall destroy the city and that which is holy, and its end shall come with violence (that is, it shall be destroyed with force and fury, as by a flood). And after the end of the war there shall remain the appointed desolation." (All of this happened just that way. Jerusalem and the temple were destroyed with frightful severity, and to this time have never come into the hands of the Jews or been restored to the former position of power despite the earnest efforts made in that direction. The

---

position he later firmly retained, namely, that the seventy years must have begun with the second year of Darius (LW 35, 303-304; see also WA 53, 173, ll. 4-8, and 26, ll. 37-39).

50 In placing Christ's death at the middle of the seventieth week Luther was following the lead of Nicholas of Lyra, Albertus Magnus, and others as far back as Eusebius of Caesarea. Fraidl, op. cit., pp. 156-158. In his 1541-1545 Suppotatio Annorum Mundi—though not yet in his 1530 Preface to Daniel (LW 35, 305)—Luther placed at the middle of the seventieth year the apostolic council of Jerusalem (Acts 15:1-35) where freedom from the law was first established. He did this in order to square his computation of the 70 years with his scheme of world history, according to which the time of the Messiah—the end of the 70 years—had to coincide with the beginning of the Fifth Millenium. WA 53, 13-14.

51 Ausgerottet, literally, "rooted out," eventually became Luther's rendering in his German Bible from 1543 on, though at first (1530) he chose to stick with the term getödtet, following the Vulgate's occideretur, "slain." WA, DB 11II, 170-171.

city today is still the ruin it was before,[52] so that no one can deny that this prophecy and the actual situation before our eyes coincide perfectly.)

"And he shall confirm the covenant with many in the one week" [Dan. 9:27]. (This is the period of three and one-half years during which Christ himself preached, plus the succeeding three and one-half years of apostolic activity). During these seven years the gospel (which is God's covenant with us, that through Christ he will be merciful toward us) received its greatest impetus. Since that time it has never been so pure and mighty, for shortly thereafter heresy and error came to be mingled with it. "And in the middle of the week the sacrifice and offering shall cease" [Dan. 9:27] (that is, the law of Moses will no longer prevail), because Christ, after preaching for three and one-half years, will fulfil all things through his suffering, and thereafter provide for the preaching of a new sacrifice, etc.

Now let someone tell me: Where will one find a prince, or Messiah, or king, with whom all this accords so perfectly, as with our Lord Jesus Christ? Scripture and history agree so perfectly with one another that the Jews have nothing they can say to the contrary. They certainly are painfully conscious of their destruction, which is immeasurably greater than any they have ever endured. They cannot point to any transgression so great that they would have merited such punishment (because they feel it is not a sin that they crucified Jesus, and that they committed greater sins before that but suffered less punishment). It would be unthinkable that God would leave them so long without prophets unless they were finished and all Scripture fulfilled.

But there are still more prophecies, as for example in Haggai 2 [:91],[53] where God says of the rebuilt temple, "The splendor of this latter house shall be greater than that of the former," which is also very conclusive; and Zechariah 8 [:23], "In those

---

[52] After Titus, Jerusalem was successively captured and occupied by various peoples through the centuries including Romans, Persians, Arabs, Seljuk Turks, European Crusaders, Egyptians, and others. In 1517 it was captured by the Ottoman Turks, who built the present walls in 1542.

[53] Luther discusses this passage in his 1524 lectures on Haggai (WA 13, 526, 541-542) and in his 1543 *Von den Juden und ihren Lügen* (WA 53, 487-492).

days ten men of all languages of the Gentiles shall take hold of the robe of a Jew, saying: We want to go with you; for we have heard that the Lord is with you," etc. There are many more, but it would take too long to discuss them all clearly and at length. For the present the two prophecies just cited[54] are enough for a beginning.

If the Jews should take offense because we confess our Jesus to be a man, and yet true God, we will deal forcefully with that from Scripture in due time. But this is too harsh for a beginning. Let them first be suckled with milk, and begin by recognizing this man Jesus as the true Messiah; after that they may drink wine, and learn also that he is true God. For they have been led astray so long and so far that one must deal gently with them, as people who have been all too strongly indoctrinated to believe that God cannot be man.

Therefore, I would request and advise that one deal gently with them and instruct them from Scripture; then some of them may come along. Instead of this we are trying only to drive them by force, slandering them, accusing them of having Christian blood if they don't stink, and I know not what other foolishness. So long as we thus treat them like dogs, how can we expect to work any good among them? Again, when we forbid them to labor and do business and have any human fellowship with us, thereby forcing them into usury, how is that supposed to do them any good?

If we really want to help them, we must be guided in our dealings with them not by papal law but by the law of Christian love. We must receive them cordially, and permit them to trade and work with us, that they may have occasion and opportunity to associate with us, hear our Christian teaching, and witness our Christian life. If some of them should prove stiff-necked, what of it? After all, we ourselves are not all good Christians either.

Here I will let the matter rest for the present, until I see what I have accomplished. God grant us all his mercy. Amen.

---

[54] Gen. 49:10-12 is treated on pp. 213-221; Dan. 9:24-27, on pp. 221-229. For Luther's expanded treatment of a more inclusive list of texts see his *Von den Juden und ihren Lügen* (1543). WA 53, (412) 417-552; and *Vom Schem Hamphoras und vom Geschlecht Christi* (1543). WA 53, (573) 579-648.

TRADE AND USURY

1524

Translated by Charles M. Jacobs

Revised by Walther I. Brandt

INTRODUCTION

Although by no means the most important of Luther's writings, this treatise is of considerable significance for understanding his ethics, and of great interest to the economic historian inasmuch as it includes keen observations on the business practices of the early sixteenth century. Luther's frame of reference was of course that of the Middle Ages. He held to the long scholastic tradition which, following Aristotle,[1] taught that money does not produce money. He agreed with the canonists, who for years had taught that usury is something evil.[2] In common with the vast majority of his learned contemporaries, he knew very little about economic laws. Of the far-reaching economic revolution which was gradually transforming Germany from a nation of peasant agriculturalists into a society with at least the beginnings of a capitalist economy, he had no conception whatsoever. Its obvious manifestations, high prices and growing disparity in wealth, were to him nothing more than the results of the greed and avarice of sinful men, a

---

[1] According to Aristotle money is simply a conventional medium for measuring demand, used to facilitate equality of exchange. *Nichomachean Ethics*, V, 5, 1133ab. "There are two sorts of wealth-getting . . . one is a part of household management, the other is retail trade: the former necessary and honourable, while that which consists in exchange is justly censured; for it is unnatural, and a mode by which men gain from one another. The most hated sort . . . is usury, which makes a gain out of money itself . . . money was intended to be used in exchange, but not to increase at interest." *Politics*, I, 10, 1258ab. Richard McKeon (ed.), *The Basic Works of Aristotle* (New York: Random House, 1941), p. 1141. This view of Aristotle is cited and espoused by Thomas Aquinas in his *Summa Theologica*, 2, II, ques. 78, art. 1, who also declares usury to be a sin.
[2] Canons 1-3 in *Decreti Secunda Pars*, causa XIV, ques. 3, cite Augustine, Jerome, and Ambrose to the effect that seeking or demanding in return more than what had originally been given constitutes usury and is condemned. Ambrose mentions specifically the prohibition in Deut. 23:19. *Corpus Iuris Canonici*, I, cols. 734-735. Numerous additional authorities are then cited (ques. 4) to show that usury is forbidden for both clergy and laity; here reference is made twice (in canons 4 and 8) to Ps. 15:5. *Corpus Iuris Canonici*, I, cols. 736-737. It is significant that the canonical proof proceeds initially from the premise of total poverty enjoined in Matt. 19:21 upon those who would be perfect (ques. 1). In the *Decretalium D. Gregorii Papae* IX, lib. v, tit. XIX, usury is dealt with in the context of murder, adultery, theft, and other crimes. *Corpus Iuris Canonici*, II, cols. 811-816.

judgment which was consistent with his own personal indifference to money and wealth, other than as a means of subsistence and something to be shared with less fortunate brethren, and with his generally pessimistic outlook on human affairs in the light of his expectation of Christ's impending return and the end of all things.

Within Luther's own lifetime the discovery of America and of an all-water route to the Indies gave a tremendous stimulus to trade, which had been on the increase ever since the Crusades, and especially to the foundation of great trading companies. Oriental goods, an Italian monopoly until about 1500, were shipped to the north by way of the Alpine passes. Northern cities fortunate enough to be situated along these trade routes prospered greatly. Augsburg is a typical example. Here large commercial organizations were formed, one of the best known being the Fuggers.[3] Expanding trade demanded larger supplies of precious metals, a demand which was met first by more intensive exploitation of European mines, and later by the influx of American treasure. Increased circulation of gold and silver was an important factor in the general rise in prices—in Germany amounting to 50 per cent in the first half of the sixteenth century[4]—with consequent economic distress for those having small or fixed incomes. The distressed, ignorant of economic laws, blamed their misfortunes on the moneylenders and especially on the great trading companies.

Trade on a large scale required capital, and capital accumulated in trade sought safe and profitable investment. Usury laws which hampered such investments were either evaded or ignored. The ethics of charging interest was publicly discussed. In 1514 Johann Eck drew up a series of theses justifying an interest rate of 5 per cent; he defended his position in a public disputation at Bologna in 1515.[5] Characteristic of the casuistry of the scholastics were his statements that a creditor is permitted to accept freewill

---

[3] On the Fuggers, see Mildred Hartsough (trans.), J. Strieder's *Jacob Fugger the Rich, 1459-1525* (New York, 1931); Götz Freiherr von Polnitz, *Jakob Fugger* (2 vols.; Tübingen: Mohr, 1949-1951).
[4] *BG* 7, 495.
[5] See the lengthy study by J. Schneid, "Dr. Johann Eck und das kirchliche Zinsverbot," *Historisch-politische Blätter für das katholische Deutschland*, CVIII (1891), 241-259, 321-335, 473-496, 570-589, 659-681, 789-810.

gifts if he has thereby no intention to commit usury, and that a creditor may exact interest from an enemy whom he is otherwise rightfully permitted to injure anyway.[6]

Luther's first public pronouncement on the subject was his *Short Sermon on Usury*,[7] published not later than November, 1519. Early in 1520 he brought out a greatly expanded version, known as *The Long Sermon on Usury*.[8] This was not, as the title would imply, an attack on usury as such, for usury was already condemned by church, state, and public opinion, and had been since at least the thirteenth century. His attack was directed at certain common financial practices of the day, which he contended were in fact usury, practices which the papal theologians were quite willing to justify and defend.[9]

The first part of the *Long Sermon on Usury* sets forth what Luther held should be the Christian attitude toward temporal goods.[10] The second part is devoted to a lengthy discussion and criticism of the current investment practice known as *"Zinskauf,"*[11] of which some explanation must here be given. The word *Zins*, which in its modern usage may be translated either as "tax" or as "interest," derived originally from the Latin cognate, *census*, particularly from that meaning of the term whereby *census* had reference to the tribute levied by Rome upon its subject provinces.[12] In medieval usage, however, and hence also in Luther's usage, the word had an additional meaning in the area of capitalist economics and financial contracts, a meaning which developed out of, and hence must be understood in terms of, the feudal system of the Middle Ages.

When a feudal landlord turned over a piece of land as a fief

---

[6] See *BG* 7, 501, and n. 2.

[7] *WA* 6, 3-8.

[8] See below, pp. 273-308. Luther himself made no distinction in the titles of these two works; the distinction was first made by the editors of the early Jena edition, and subsequent editors have followed their example. *WA* 6, 1.

[9] See Noonan, *The Scholastic Analysis of Usury*, and Karl Diehl (gen. ed.), Edmund Schreiber, *Die volkswirtschaftlichen Anschauungen der Scholastik seit Thomas v. Aquin.* ("Beiträge zür Geschichte der Nationalökonomie," I [Jena: Fischer, 1913]).

[10] See pp. 273-295.

[11] See pp. 295-308.

[12] Cf. Matt. 17:25; 22:17.

in perpetuity, he normally received from the tenant a specified, usually annual, return in the form of livestock or produce from that plot of ground. This return was called *Rente* (rent) and the contract, from the standpoint of the landlord, was called a *Rentenkauf* (the purchase of rent). Begun as early as the twelfth century, this basic transaction was varied in many ways as it became more widespread in the thirteenth and fourteenth centuries. Not only were the terms of the contract altered as periods and media for payment became highly differentiated but the very base of the contract itself was modified as properties other than acreage came to be chief security in the transaction. As the practice increased and became diversified, and particularly as money became the chief and then ultimately almost the sole factor both in the original exchange and in the method of payment, the terms *Zins* and *Zinskauf* came to be used increasingly until by the fourteenth century they were used interchangeably in this context with *Rente* and *Rentenkauf*.[13]

At the same time, it became increasingly important to distinguish this type of contract from the interest-bearing loan which was universally and earnestly condemned as usury. With the growth of cities and of commerce, and particularly with the huge impetus given to world trade in the age of discovery, the demand for money to support an expanding economy—not to speak of the very dependence of the church upon the regular receipts accruing to it from its vast income-producing properties—made urgent a theological analysis of such "loans" in terms that would justify their exemption from the ban on usury. This analysis by and large regarded the contract as a sale (*Kauf*) rather than a loan and the *Zins* or *Rente* as a delayed cash payment on a purchase made for credit rather than as an interest payment on a loan. Since the creditor, on this analysis, was actually nothing but a purchaser who bought (with money or property) a fixed and regular income or the right thereto, and the debtor was nothing but a seller who (for money or property) sold such income or right, the contract itself, the *Zinskauf,* was held to be not usurious.

---

[13] Grimm, *Deutsches Wörterbuch*, XV, 1475-1527; Max Neumann, *Geschichte des Wuchers in Deutschland* (Halle: Waisenhaus, 1865), pp. 212-292.

Provisions of a *zins* contract varied with time and place. In one variation the borrower retained the title to his land, but gave the produce to his creditor; in another the debtor paid his creditor a specified interest on the principal of the loan, with the land as security; in a third the entire property of the debtor was pledged for the interest due.[14] *Zins* contracts were distinguished according to whether the base on which they rested was real or personal, the payments fructuary or pecuniary, the time perpetual or for life or otherwise specifically delimited, whether the principal sum was redeemable or nonredeemable by the buyer and seller or either alone, and whether in terms of risk the contract was guaranteed or not guaranteed.[15]

Luther's usage of the terms *Zins* and *Zinskauf* must be seen in the light of both the economic practice of the period and the scholastic analysis of it. While in his opinion this contract was *in effect* an interest-bearing loan the terms "interest" and "loan" would be quite inaccurate as renderings in modern English. Though the modern "mortgage" and "annuity" have decided similarities to the ancient *Rentenkauf* and *Zinskauf*, the divergences between them would be so great as to make the use of these English terms as equivalents misleading. Charles M. Jacobs rendered the term as "annuity" in his translation of *An Open Letter to the Christian Nobility* (*PE* 2, 159), but adopted a revised rendering about sixteen years later when he translated the present treatise (*PE* 4, 10-11), namely, "purchase of income" or, "buying of income." While these circumlocutions may at times be illuminating they are hardly satisfactory renderings for a technical term which simply has no equivalent in modern English because the practice to which it refers no longer exists. We have therefore chosen in most instances to retain Luther's own term for the contract itself (*Zinskauf*) and also for the payment involved in it (*Zins*), which was both a tribute (from the standpoint of the debtor-seller) and an income (from the standpoint of the creditor-buyer).[16]

---

[14] *WA* 15, 322, note.
[15] Wilhelm Endemann, *Studien in der romanisch-kanonistischen Wirtschafts- und Rechtslehre bis gegen Ende des siebzehnten Jahrhunderts* (2 vols. in 1; Berlin: Guttentag, 1874-1883), II, 120.
[16] Both Nelson (Benjamin N. Nelson, *The Idea of Usury* [Princeton:

Although Luther in general roundly condemned the *Zinskauf* with its exaction of interest, he was realistic enough to concede that under certain circumstances an interest charge of 4 to 6 per cent might be tolerated, "if this can be done without violating canon law." [17] It is precisely these circumstances he proposes, however, which are the important thing to note, for they amount really to a reformation of the *Zins* contract as it was currently practiced. Luther would insist on specific collateral, an existent, real, and itemized base, in order that the entire person and property of the debtor may not be subject totally to the creditor's demands as in an "indiscriminate" contract. He would insist that the creditor share in the risk, that all risk should not be borne exclusively by the debtor. He would oppose the mutually redeemable contract and insist that prior repayment of the principal sum should be an option of the debtor alone, not of the creditor.[18] To the extent that he was responsible for it, the debtor would be obligated according to Luther's view to recompense to the creditor—whose equity was also of concern to Luther!—his *damnum emergens* and *lucram cessans;* interest thus became a guard against loss and damages for the creditor.[19]

Luther's great concern was for justice and equity in the economic sphere. Responsibility for the attainment of this end he assigned to those in authority. He differed from the early scholastics and the canonists in taking seriously—as commands not counsels—the rigorous prescriptions of the Sermon on the Mount regarding giving and lending to those in need; in positively affirming the validity and worth of private property, over against the ascetic ideal of monasticism, as a means to the end of implementing Christian charity; and in exposing and judging as

---

Princeton University Press, 1949], e.g., pp. 32-36) and Noonan (*op. cit.,* p. 155) retain the foreign term, making no attempt to establish a single English equivalent.

[17] See p. 305, especially n. 152.

[18] This was an essential feature of the old *Rentenkauf* in German law. Hermann Barge, *Luther und der Frühkapitalismus* ("Schriften des Vereins für Reformationsgeschichte," No. 168, Jahrgang 58, Heft 1 [Gütersloh: Bertelsmann, 1951]), p. 21.

[19] See particularly Luther's 1540 *Admonition to the Clergy that They Preach Against Usury.* WA 51, 343ff.

harshly the actual motives of self-seeking avarice as he did the actual intentions of the theological casuistry which sought to defend and justify what custom had already sanctified. At the same time Luther repudiated with equal vigor the radicals who would implement—by law if possible or even contrary to law if necessary—in a non-Christian society codes of behavior which were meant for and attainable by Christians only.

It is important to remember in evaluating Luther's statements in this treatise that his concern was religious in the first instance and only secondarily economic. His primary purpose was to instruct the Christian conscience, though the observations on and suggestions for the business procedures of his time are—if only a by-product—among the most significant that remain from that period. Luther distinguished clearly between the law and the gospel, and regarded himself as a servant of the gospel. Though his formulations may appear largely medieval and reactionary to the superficial observer, his faith certainly shattered the bonds of the past, freeing the economy from the false ideal of sanctimonious poverty, the state from the bondage of ecclesiastically prescribed laws, and the church from a soul-stultifying preoccupation with legalistic casuistry. In short, Luther was not the reactionary that some have interpreted him to be when they emphasize his critique of the rebellious peasants; nor was he by any means the prophetic protagonist of modern capitalism. He was the theologian and pastor who laid upon the heart of Christian hearers the uncomprising demands of God, and upon the hearts of statesmen and merchants the practical necessity for unselfishly seeking the ends of equity for all men. His views of economics, while temporally conditioned, were biblically determined, and must be seen in the light of his entire social ethics.[20]

---

[20] Penetrating interpretations of Luther's economic ethics in general and of this treatise in particular are given by S. Eck in BG 7, 494-513, by Werner Elert in *Morphologie des Luthertums* (2 vols.; München: Beck, 1932), II, 466-492, and by Herrmann Barge in *Luther und der Frühkapitalismus*. Barge, in refuting the interpretations of Wilhelm Roscher and Max Weber, also rejects completely the notion of any *Eigengesetzlichkeit* of the economy in Luther; see Barge, *op. cit.*, pp. 44-51. For a bibliography on Luther's view of usury extending somewhat beyond the works cited in this volume, see Nelson, *op. cit.*, p. 30, n. 1.

Luther published his treatise on trade in 1524,[21] adding to it a reprint of the *Long Sermon on Usury* of 1520,[22] supplemented with a few new paragraphs on the Mosaic tithe and jubilee year.[23] The whole is known as the treatise on *Trade and Usury*, a complete translation of which is here presented.

In the section on trade of 1524, he deals with business ethics and the monopolistic practices of the great trading companies, repeating again his basic understanding, derived from the Sermon on the Mount, of the Christian way to deal with temporal goods.[24] Valuable, as well as amusing, is his description of a number of tricks by which merchants took advantage of their customers.[25] Many of these tricks he had observed with his own eyes.

His determination to speak out on the evils of trade and at the same time to reissue his treatise on usury is traceable to two factors: first, the contention by certain evangelical preachers that the payment, as well as the exaction, of interest was sinful; second, the failure of the diets of Nürnberg in 1522 and 1524 to deal effectively with the monopolistic practices of the trading companies.

The two evangelical preachers involved were the Eisenach pastor Jacob Strauss,[26] and Wolfgang Stein,[27] Duke John's court preacher at Weimar. Both of them maintained that civil law, since it was of pagan origin, and canon law, since it was the product of papal legislation, must both give way to God's law,

---

[21] See pp. 245-273.

[22] See pp. 273-308.

[23] See pp. 308-310.

[24] See pp. 255-261.

[25] See pp. 261-270.

[26] Jacob Strauss (*ca.* 1480-*ca.* 1532), a native of Basel, had a rather stormy career, first as an evangelical preacher at Berchtesgaden in 1521; then in the Tyrol, where he got into difficulties with the Franciscans and was expelled in 1522. Making his way to Saxony, he became evangelical preacher in Eisenach about the end of 1522, and here took up his struggle against the *Zinskauf*, advocating a return to strict Mosaic law in that matter and other problems of the day. Enders, *Dr. Martin Luthers Briefwechsel*, IV, 248, n. 1; S-J 2, 304, n. 5. For a detailed study, see Herrmann Barge, *Jakob Strauss: ein Kämpfer für das Evangelium in Tirol, Thüringen und Süddeutschland* ("Schriften des Vereins für Reformationsgeschichte," No. 162 Jahrgang 54, Heft 2 [Leipzig: Heinsius, 1937]).

[27] Wolfgang Stein (d. *ca.* 1553) was a student at Erfurt in 1504. In 1508 he became provost of the Cistercian nuns at Eisenburg, and thereafter court preacher at Weimar. Enders, *Briefwechsel*, IV, 33, n. 1.

i.e., the precepts laid down by Moses in Deut. 15:1-11. Early in 1523 Strauss drew up fifty-one theses against the un-Christian practice of usury, in which he interpreted Deut. 15:7-11 and Luke 6:34-35 on lending to mean that not only the taking of interest but also the paying of it was sin; that a debtor is not obligated to pay his debt to the usurer, since he would thereby approve the usurer's act and share his guilt.[28]

On October 18, 1523, Luther wrote to Chancellor Brück condemning this point of view.[29] At about the same time he wrote also to Strauss in similar vein, expressing agreement with his condemnation of the usurious *census*, but denying that he (Luther) ever taught that it was sin to pay interest, since the masses cannot be ruled by the gospel.[30] · Some months later Melanchthon, happening to be in Eisenach, conferred with Strauss, and persuaded him to concede that if the exaction of interest must be suffered under the authority of civil law, then one might also with good conscience, while disapproving the tyranny, pay interest voluntarily.[31]

The second motive for publishing the present treatise was the failure of the diets of Nürnberg in 1522 and 1524 to take any effective action against monopolies.[32] As early as 1512, the Diet of Trier-Cologne had outlawed monopolies,[33] but for a decade no attempt was made to enforce the ban. At the Diet of Worms in 1521, monopolies were again discussed, but no effective action

---

[28] Most of these theses are summarized in Barge, *Jakob Strauss*, pp. 65-67.
[29] *WA*, Br 3, 176.
[30] *WA*, Br 3, 178-179.
[31] See Melanchthon's letter to either Luther or Spalatin, undated, about the middle of April, 1524. *C.R.* 1, 655-656. See also Luther's letter to Strauss of April 25. *WA*, Br 3, 278. To some extent the dispute was based on a popular misunderstanding of Strauss' position which was that the debtor should not voluntarily and uncompelled pay the interest of his own accord. *WA*, Br 3, 276, n. 1.
[32] The discussions of monopolies in the several diets from 1512 to 1530 are summarized in Clemens Bauer, "Conrad Peutingers Gutachten zur Monopolfrage: Eine Untersuchung zur Wandlung der Wirtschaftsanschauungen im Zeitalter der Reformation," *Archiv für Reformationsgeschichte*, XLV (1954), 1-42 and 145-195.
[33] The text of the 1512 decree is cited by the 1521 Diet of Worms in Adolf Wrede, *Deutsche Reichstagsakten unter Kaiser Karl V*, (second series, 7 vols.; Gotha: Perthes, 1893-1935), II, 351-352; also in J. Strieder, *Studien zur Geschichte kapitalischer Organisationsformen* (Munich and Leipzig, 1914), pp. 71-72.

was taken.[34] At the Nürnberg Diet of 1522-1523, an effort was made to revive the resolution of 1512.[35] In 1523 the imperial attorney-general haled the principal Augsburg capitalists before the Council of Regency and formally charged them with violating imperial law.[36] This attempt too came to naught, for company agents at the Spanish court were able to persuade Charles to order his official to drop the suits.[37]

The new diet opened at Nürnberg on January 16, 1524. Before the arrival of the imperial legate, Hannart, the Council of Regency declared that the anti-monopoly resolutions of the previous diet should be published throughout the empire.[38] When Hannart reached Nürnberg[39] the situation changed. Presumably acting on instructions from Charles, he made common cause with the Augsburg financiers. They protested so effectively against the proposed anti-monopoly legislation that in the recess of the diet, April 18, 1524, the resolution of 1512 once more failed of revival.[40] Charles, always short of funds, simply could not afford to antagonize the Augsburg financiers.[41]

On February 1, 1524, Luther wrote Spalatin, then at Nürnberg, expressing the hope that the diet would act on matters pertaining to the general welfare, by which he presumably referred to the pending anti-monopoly legislation.[42] From the general disappointment which followed the diet's failure to take decisive action probably arose the requests which caused Luther to express himself publicly on the financial evils of the day. Beyond his own statement[43] we have no evidence on these requests.

---

[34] *Deutsche Reichstagsakten*, II, 351-354.
[35] *Deutsche Reichstagsakten*, III, 554-571.
[36] Strieder, *Studien*, pp. 73ff.
[37] This was the Burgos decree of September 15, 1523. *Ibid.*, pp. 370-371.
[38] *Deutsche Reichstagsakten*, IV, 275.
[39] He arrived on January 31. *Ibid.*, IV, 92.
[40] See the text of the recess in *ibid.*, IV, 602-603.
[41] Early in 1523 Jakob Fugger wrote Charles V, reminding him of the vast sums lent him for his election, without which he could not have been victorious, and begging him politely to make repayment with interest. The letter is quoted in J. Strieder, *Das reiche Augsburg* (Munich, 1938), pp. 77-78.
[42] *WA*, Br 3, 241.
[43] See p. 245. Luther was no archivist; he took little pains to preserve the letters he received.

Until the recess was adopted by the diet on April 18 there was still some hope for anti-monopoly legislation. Hence, the requests for some statement from him would probably not have been made before the middle of that month. The composition of the first part of the present treatise could scarcely have been begun before May, 1524. Luther's letters to Capito of June 15[44] and to Prince John Frederick of June 18,[45] while speaking of the *census,* make no mention of the treatise. On June 24 the prince replied to Luther, expressing the wish that Luther would make a journey through the congregations, like St. Paul, and quiet extremists such as Strauss and others.[46] Had the treatise been available, John Frederick would scarcely have made this suggestion.

The printed treatise is first cited in the *Apology* of Thomas Münzer, which was printed at Nürnberg in October, 1524.[47] Because of pronounced similarities between the supplement (pp. 308-310) and the June 15 and June 18 letters, we may conclude with Otto Clemen[48] that the portion on trade was composed during the latter part of June, 1524, and that the whole treatise came from the press in the late summer of 1524, certainly not later than September.[49]

The following translation is a revision of the one that appeared in *PE* 4, 12-69, and is based on the original Wittenberg printing of Hans Lufft, *Von Kauffshandlung und wucher,* as that has been reprinted with annotations in *WA* 15, (279) 293-313 and 321-322. The second half of the treatise, which is a reprinting of the 1520 treatise on *Usury,* is given in WA 6, 36-60.

---

[44] *WA,* Br 3, 303.
[45] *WA,* Br 3, 307.
[46] *WA,* Br 3, 310.
[47] See the Münzer text in Ludwig Enders (ed.), *Neudrucke deutscher Litteraturwerke des 16 und 17 Jahrhunderts* (Halle: Niemeyer, 1876-1949), No. 118, p. 25.
[48] *CL* 3, 1.
[49] *WA* 15, 282.

TRADE AND USURY

The holy gospel, now that it has come to light, rebukes and reveals all the "works of darkness," as St. Paul calls them in Romans 13 [:12]. For it is a brilliant light, which illumines the whole world and teaches how evil are the works of the world, and shows the true works we ought to do for God and our neighbor. As a result even some of the merchants have been awakened and become aware that in their trading many a wicked trick and hurtful financial practice[1] is in use. It is to be feared that the words of Ecclesiasticus apply here, namely, that merchants can hardly be without sin [Ecclus. 26:29]. Indeed, I think St. Paul's saying in the last chapter of the first epistle to Timothy fits the case, "The love of money is the root of all evils" [I Tim. 6:10], and again, "Those who desire to be rich fall into the devil's snare and into many useless and hurtful desires that plunge men into ruin and perdition" [I Tim. 6:9].

I suppose that my writing will be quite in vain, because the mischief has gone so far and has completely gotten the upper hand in all lands; and because those who understand the gospel are probably able in such easy, external things to judge for themselves what is fair and what is not, on the basis of their own consciences. Nevertheless, I have been asked and urged[2] to touch upon these financial evils and expose some of them so that, even though the majority may not wish to do right, at least some people—however few they are—may be delivered from the gaping jaws of avarice. For it must be that among the merchants, as among other people, there are some who belong to Christ and would rather be poor with God than rich with the devil, as Psalm 37 [:16] says, "It is better for the righteous to have a little than

---

[1] *Fynantze* in the sixteenth century had not the neutral meaning of modern times but carried exclusively the evil connotations of usurious intrigue, fraud, and deception on the part of unscrupulous profit-minded dealers. Grimm, *Deutsches Wörterbuch*, III, 1639-1640.

[2] The specific source and nature of these requests is not known. See the Introduction, p. 242.

to have the great possessions of the wicked." For their sake, then, we must speak out.

It cannot be denied that buying and selling are necessary. They cannot be dispensed with, and can be practiced in a Christian manner, especially when the commodities serve a necessary and honorable purpose. For even the patriarchs bought and sold cattle, wool, grain, butter, milk, and other goods in this way. These are gifts of God, which he bestows out of the earth and distributes among mankind. But foreign trade, which brings from Calcutta and India and such places wares like costly silks, articles of gold, and spices[3]—which minister only to ostentation but serve no useful purpose, and which drain away the money of land and people—would not be permitted if we had [proper] government and princes.[4] But of this it is not my present purpose to write, for I expect that, like overdressing and overeating, it will have to stop of itself when we have no more money. Until then, neither writing nor teaching will do any good. We must first feel the pinch of want and poverty.

God has cast us Germans off[5] to such an extent that we have to fling our gold and silver into foreign lands and make the whole world rich, while we ourselves remain beggars.[6] England would have less gold if Germany let her keep her cloth;[7] the

---

[3] In the absence of any sort of refrigeration, spices served frequently as a food preservative.

[4] In his *Open Letter to the Christian Nobility* (1520), Luther had also blamed many of the economic ills of his day on the inactivity of the temporal government. See *PE* 2, 158-159. Like many of his contemporaries he deplored commercial imports, while largely overlooking the compensating value of the export trade. *BG* 7, 515, n. 1.

[5] Compare Luther's glowing account of God's blessing upon Germany in the provision of an abundance of scholars qualified to teach, in this volume, p. 532.

[6] The export of money and precious metals was generally assumed at that time to be a major factor contributing to the widespread poverty and rising prices. MA[3] 5, 415, n. 116, 6. Vigorous complaints were lodged at the Reichstag of 1522 against the merchants and trading companies that paid out gold, silver, and copper for their import goods. Gustav Schmoller, *Zur Geschichte der national-ökonomische Ansichten in Deutschland während der Reformations-Periode* ("Zeitschrift für die gesamte Staatswissenschaft" [Tübingen], vol. XVI [1860]), p. 637.

[7] Not many years later the general desire to protect the native textile industry led to official legislation both in England and Germany to restrict textile imports and wool exports. *Ibid.*, pp. 650-653.

king of Portugal would have less if we let him keep his spices.[8] Count up how much cash is taken out of Germany, without need or reason, from a single Frankfurt fair,[9] and you will wonder how it happens that there is still a heller[10] left in German lands. Frankfort is the gold and silver drain through which everything that springs and grows—or is minted or coined—here, flows out of Germany. If that hole were stopped up we should not now have to listen to the complaint that there are debts everywhere and no money, that all lands and cities are burdened with zinss[11] payments and milked dry by usury. But let that pass; it will go that way anyhow. We Germans must always be Germans; we never stop until we have to.

It is our purpose here to speak about the abuses and sins of trade, insofar as they concern the conscience. The matter of their detrimental effect on the purse we leave to the princes and lords, that they may do their duty in this regard.

First. Among themselves the merchants have a common rule which is their chief maxim and the basis of all their sharp practices, where they say: "I may sell my goods as dear as I can." [12] They think this is their right. Thus occasion is given for avarice, and every window and door to hell is opened. What else does it mean but this: I care nothing about my neighbor; so long as I have my profit and satisfy my greed, of what concern is it to me if it injures my neighbor in ten ways at once? There you see how shamelessly this maxim flies squarely in the face not only of Christian love but also of natural law.[13] How can there be anything good then in trade? How can it be without sin when

---

[8] Following Vasco de Gama's discovery of the Cape route to India in 1498, Portugal held a virtual monopoly on the lucrative spice trade. In a complaint lodged at the Reichstag of 1523 the knights decried Portugal's unwillingness to accept from Germany anything but money for its spices. *Ibid.*, p. 638.

[9] The Frankfort fair was perhaps the greatest of several important German fairs, at which merchants gathered even from distant lands to sell their wares.

[10] The heller was a small coin worth one-half pfennig.

[11] On the meaning of the term zinss, see the Introduction, pp. 234-238.

[12] Cf. Luther's *Large Catechism* of 1529, where in speaking of the Seventh Commandment he describes how every merchant at the market place thinks he has a perfect right to set any price he pleases on what is his. Theodore G. Tappert (ed.), *The Book of Concord* (Philadelphia, Muhlenberg Press, 1959), p. 397.

[13] On natural law, see p. 127, n. 117.

such injustice is the chief maxim and rule of the whole business? On such a basis trade can be nothing but robbing and stealing the property of others.

When once the rogue's eye and greedy belly of a merchant find that people must have his wares, or that the buyer is poor and needs them, he takes advantage of him and raises the price. He considers not the value of the goods, or what his own efforts and risk have deserved, but only the other man's want and need. He notes it not that he may relieve it but that he may use it to his own advantage by raising the price of his goods, which he would not have raised if it had not been for his neighbor's need. Because of his avarice, therefore, the goods must be priced as much higher as the greater need of the other fellow will allow, so that the neighbor's need becomes as it were the measure of the goods' worth and value. Tell me, isn't that an un-Christian and inhuman thing to do? Isn't that equivalent to selling a poor man his own need in the same transaction? When he has to buy his wares at a higher price because of his need, that is the same as having to buy his own need; for what is sold to him is not simply the wares as they are, but the wares plus the fact that he must have them. Observe that this and like abominations are the inevitable consequence when the rule is that I may sell my goods as dear as I can.

The rule ought to be, not, "I may sell my wares as dear as I can or will," but, "I may sell my wares as dear as I ought, or as is right and fair." [14] For your selling ought not to be an act that is entirely within your own power and discretion, without law or limit, as though you were a god and beholden to no one. Because your selling is an act performed toward your neighbor, it should rather be so governed by law and conscience that you do it without harm and injury to him, your concern being directed more toward doing him no injury than toward gaining profit for yourself. But where are there such merchants? How few merchants there would be, and how trade would decline, if they were

---

[14] The just price, a concept first employed by the Roman law, was considered by the scholastic theologians generally to be normally the market price. Noonan, *op. cit.*, pp. 82-99.

to amend this evil rule and put things on a fair and Christian basis!

You ask, then, "How dear may I sell? How am I to arrive at what is fair and right so I do not take increase from neighbor or overcharge him?" Answer: That is something that will never be governed either by writing or speaking; nor has anyone ever undertaken to fix the value of every commodity, and to raise or lower prices accordingly. The reason is this: wares are not all alike; one is transported a greater distance than another and one involves greater outlay than another. In this respect, therefore, everything is and must remain uncertain, and no fixed determination can be made, anymore than one can designate a certain city as the place from which all wares are to be brought, or establish a definite cost price for them. It may happen that the same wares, brought from the same city by the same road, cost vastly more in one year than they did the year before because the weather may be worse, or the road, or because something else happens that increases the expense at one time above that at another time. Now it is fair and right that a merchant take as much profit on his wares as will reimburse him for their cost and compensate him for his trouble, his labor, and his risk. Even a farmhand must have food and pay for his labor. Who can serve or labor for nothing? The gospel says, "The laborer deserves his wages" [Luke 10:7].

But in order not to leave the question entirely unanswered, the best and safest way would be to have the temporal authorities appoint in this matter wise and honest men to compute the costs of all sorts of wares and accordingly set prices which would enable the merchant to get along and provide for him an adequate living, as is being done at certain places with respect to wine, fish, bread, and the like.[15] But we Germans have too many other things to do; we are too busy drinking and dancing[16] to provide

---

[15] Public regulation of dealers in food goes back as far as ancient Egypt, Greece, and Rome. The Prefect of Constantinople set the price of fish each morning according to the size of the previous night's catch. By 1202 the king was fixing the price of bread in England. Bread and wine were controlled in price, weight, and quality in most of medieval Europe. Heaton, *Economic History of Europe* (rev. ed., 1948), pp. 194-195.

[16] See Luther's criticism of the rulers' preoccupation with amusements to the neglect of their office elsewhere in this volume, pp. 120-121, and 367-368.

for rules and regulations of this sort. Since this kind of ordinance therefore is not to be expected, the next best thing is to let goods be valued at the price for which they are bought and sold in the common market, or in the land generally. In this matter we can accept the proverb, "Follow the crowd and you won't get lost."[17] Any profit made in this way I consider honest and proper, because here there is always the risk involved of having to suffer loss in wares and outlay, and excessive profits are scarcely possible.

Where the price of goods is not fixed either by law or custom, and you must fix it yourself, here one can truly give you no instructions but only lay it on your conscience to be careful not to overcharge your neighbor, and to seek a modest living, not the goals of greed. Some have wished to place a ceiling on profits, with a limit of one-half on all wares; some say one-third; others something else. None of these measures is certain and safe unless it be so decreed by the temporal authorities and common law. What they determine in these matters would be safe. Therefore, you must make up your mind to seek in your trading only an adequate living. Accordingly, you should compute and count your costs, trouble, labor, and risk, and on that basis raise or lower the prices of your wares so that you set them where you will be repaid for your trouble and labor.

I would not have anyone's conscience be so overly scrupulous or so closely bound in this matter that he feels he must strike exactly the right measure of profit to the very heller. It is impossible for you to arrive at the exact amount that you have earned with your trouble and labor. It is enough that with a good conscience you make the effort to arrive at what is right, though the very nature of trade makes it impossible to determine this exactly. The saying of the Wise Man will hold good in your case too: "A merchant can hardly act without sin, and a tradesman will hardly keep his lips from evil" [Ecclus. 26:29]. If you take a trifle too much profit unwittingly and unintentionally, dismiss the matter in the Lord's Prayer where we pray, "Forgive us our trespasses" [Matt. 6:12]. After all, no man's life is without sin; besides, the time will come in turn when you get too little for

---

[17] *Thu wie ander leute, so narrestu nicht.* Wander (ed.), *Sprichwörter-Lexikon*, III, 93, *"Leute,"* No. 1148.

your trouble. Just throw the excess in the scale to counterbalance the losses you must similarly expect to take.[18]

For example, if you had a business amounting to a hundred gulden[19] a year, and you were to take—over and above all the costs and reasonable profit you had for your trouble, labor, and risk—an excessive profit of perhaps one or two or three gulden, that I would call a business error which could not well be avoided, especially in the course of a whole year's trading. Therefore, you should not burden your conscience with it, but bring it to God in the Lord's Prayer as another of those inevitable sins (which cling to all of us) and leave the matter to him. For it is not wickedness or greed, but the very nature and necessity of your occupation which forces you into this mistake. I am speaking now of goodhearted and God-fearing men, who would not willingly do wrong. It is like the marital obligation, which cannot be performed without sin; yet because of its necessity, God winks at it, for it cannot be otherwise.[20]

In determining how much profit you ought to take on your business and your labor, there is no better way to reckon it than by computing the amount of time and labor you have put into it, and comparing that with the effort of a day laborer who works at some other occupation and seeing how much he earns in a day. On that basis figure how many days you have spent in getting your wares and bringing them to your place of business, and how much labor and risk was involved; for a great amount of labor and time ought to have a correspondingly greater return. That is the most accurate, the best, and the most definite advice

---

[18] The rendering here of this obscure sentence is based on the suggestions of WA 15, 813, n. 297, 12/13, and CL 3, 5, n. 21.

[19] It is almost impossible to establish the value of money in the Reformation period, particularly since the value of the various coins in terms of gold and silver—and in terms of their relationship to one another—varied from one German land to another and from one period and mintage to another throughout the Middle Ages, as is evident from the variety of laws and decrees regulating and establishing the various types of coinage during the period. See, e.g., Johann C. Hirsch, *Münz-Archiv . . . von dem VIII. bis auf das XVIII Seculum* (Nürnberg: Felszecker, 1766), especially pp. 44-64 *passim*, on the fifteenth and early sixteenth century Saxon coins. Cf. Smith, *Age of the Reformation*, p. 463, and Schwiebert, *Luther and His Times*, p. 311.

[20] Cf. Luther's 1522 *The Estate of Marriage*, in this volume, pp. 11-49.

THE CHRISTIAN IN SOCIETY

and direction that can be given in this matter.[21] Let him who dislikes it, better it himself. I base my case (as I have said) on the gospel that the laborer deserves his wages [Luke 10:7]; and Paul also says in I Corinthians 9 [:7], "He who tends the flock should get some of the milk. Who can go to war at his own expense?" If you have a better ground than that, you are welcome to it.

Second. A common error, which has become a widespread custom not only among the merchants but throughout the world, is the practice of one person becoming surety for another.[22] Although this practice seems to be without sin, and looks like a virtue stemming from love, nevertheless it generally ruins a good many people and does them irreparable harm. King Solomon often forbade it, and condemned it in his proverbs. In Proverbs 6 [:1-5] he says, "My son, if you have become surety for your neighbor, you have given your hand on it; you are snared in the utterance of your lips, and caught in the words of your mouth. Then do

---

[21] Presumably Luther did not intend to imply that a merchant was entitled to no more than common day-labor wages. He was simply suggesting this as a starting point for calculating a just return for the merchant. Schmoller, op. cit., p. 495.

[22] Property insurance, a contract unknown in Roman law and the early Middle Ages, was first developed in the fourteenth-century Mediterranean ports as a means to secure risks in maritime commerce. The idea of an owner transferring the risks of his property to an insurer for a fee quickly became familiar in all the commercial cities, and was accepted by the scholastics as being nonusurious, except where it was used to guarantee a loan. In his 1485 Summa angelica de casibus conscientiae, Angelo Carletti di Chivasso, vicar-general of the Franciscans of the Observance, allowed for the insurance of capital invested in a partnership, but only with a third party. In his 1499 Tractatus de contractibus licitis atque illicitis, Conrad Summenhart, pupil of Gabriel Biel, allowed for such insurance with the partner himself, thus paving the way for Johann Eck's vigorous defense of the so-called "triple contract" (contractus trinus) or "5 per cent contract." Eck described the transaction—common in business finance for some forty years, he said— whereby the capitalist partner received a fixed 5 per cent return on his investment, in terms of three contracts instead of two: (1) the original partnership itself, (2) insurance of the principal given in return for assignment of future probable gain from the partnership, (3) sale of an uncertain future gain for a lesser certain gain. Noonan, op. cit., pp. 202-212.
Contracts of guaranty which transformed the most rigid real zinss contract into a personal obligation to pay, even though the zinss base should perish, were defended by Biel, Summenhart, and Sylvester de Prierio in such a way that the personal, guaranteed, and mutually redeemable zinss contract became quite acceptable to any lender wishing to extend credit, as well as legally nonusurious. Ibid., pp. 230-237.

this, my son, and save yourself, for you have come into your neighbor's power: Go, hasten and importune your neighbor. Give your eyes no sleep, and your eyelids no slumber. Save yourself like a gazelle from the hand, and like a bird from the hand of the fowler." Again, in the twentieth chapter, "Take a man's garment when he has given surety for another, and take a pledge from him for the stranger's sake" [Prov. 20:16]. Again, in the twenty-second chapter: "Be not one of those who give their hand on it and become surety for debts" [Prov. 22:26]. And he repeats in chapter twenty-seven: "Take a man's garment when he has given surety for another, and take a pledge from him for the stranger's sake" [Prov. 27:13].

See how strictly and vehemently the wise king in Holy Scripture forbids one's becoming surety for another.[23] The German proverb agrees with him, "Guarantors to the gallows;"[24] as much as to say: It serves the surety right when he is seized and has to pay, for he is acting rashly and foolishly in becoming surety. Hence, it is decreed according to Scripture that no one shall become surety for another, unless he is able and entirely willing to assume the debt and pay it himself. Now it does seem strange that this practice should be wrong and be condemned, although a good many have learned by experience that it is a foolish thing to do, and have had subsequent misgivings about it. Why, then, is it condemned? Let us see.

Standing surety is a work that is too lofty for a man; it is unseemly, for it is a presumptuous encroachment upon the work of God. In the first place, Scripture commands us not to put our trust and reliance in any man, but in God alone. For human nature is false, vain, deceitful, and unreliable, as Scripture says and experience daily teaches. He who becomes surety, however, is putting his trust in a man, and risking life and property on a

---

[23] See also Prov. 11:15; 17:18; but cf. Ecclus 29:14-20.
[24] *Burgen soll man wurgen* means that the bondsman or surety himself ought to be haled into court, in the manner of Matt. 18:28. The proverb is richly documented from German literature and law—most of the ancient laws holding the surety fully culpable eyen to the point of suffering death in the stead of the guilty person—in Wander (ed.), *Sprichwörter-Lexikon*, I, 513, "Burge," No. 4. Cf. the English, "He that is surety for another is never sure himself." *Ibid.*, V, 1084.

false and insecure foundation. It serves him right when he fails, falls, and is ruined.

In the second place, the surety is trusting in himself and making himself God (for whatever a man trusts in and relies upon is his god[25]). But his own life and property are never for a single moment any more secure or certain than those of the man for whom he becomes surety. Everything is in the hand of God alone. God will not allow us a hair's breadth of power or right over the future, nor will he let us for a single moment be sure or certain of it. Therefore, he who becomes surety acts in an un-Christian way; he deserves what he gets, because he pledges and promises what is not his and not in his power, but solely in God's hands.

Thus we read in Genesis 43 and 44, how the patriarch Judah became surety to his father Jacob for his brother Benjamin, promising to bring him home again or bear the blame forever [Gen. 43:8-9]. God nicely punished this presumption, and caused him to flounder and fail so that he could not bring Benjamin back until he gave himself up for him [Gen. 44:14-34] and then was barely freed by grace. The punishment served him right, for these sureties act as though they didn't even have to consult God on the matter or give thought to whether they are even sure of a tomorrow for their own life and property. They act without fear of God, as though they were themselves the source of life and property, and these were in their own power as long as they themselves willed it. This is nothing but a fruit of unbelief. It is what James in the fourth chapter of his epistle rebukes as arrogance, saying, "Come now, you who say: 'Today or tomorrow we will go into such and such a town and trade and get gain'; whereas you do not know about tomorrow. What is your life? It is but a mist that appears for a little time and then vanishes. Instead you ought to say: 'If we live, and God wills it, we shall do this or that.' As it is, you boast in your arrogance" [Jas. 4: 13-16].

Moreover, God has condemned this presumption about the

---

25 Cf. the similar statement made in Luther's *Large Catechism* of 1529 in connection with the First Commandment. Tappert, *The Book of Concord,* p. 365.

future and disregard for him in a number of other places. For example, in Luke 12 [:16-21], where the rich man had so much grain one year that he wanted to pull down his barns and build larger ones for storing his goods, and said to his soul: "Good soul, you have ample goods for many years; eat, drink, and be merry." But God said to him: "Fool! This night your soul is required of you; and the things you have gathered, whose will they be?" So it goes with all who are not rich in God. He answers similarly the disciples in Acts 1 [:7], "It is not for you to know the times or seasons which the Father has in his own power." And in Proverbs 27 [:1], "Do not boast about tomorrow, for you do not even know what today may bring forth." Therefore, he has bidden us to pray in the Lord's Prayer for no more than our daily bread today [Matt. 6:11], so that we may live and act in fear, and know that at no time are we sure of either life or property, but may await and receive everything from his hands, as a true faith does. And truly we see it every day in many of God's works, that things must work out a certain way whether we like it or not.

Solomon has devoted to this teaching nearly the whole of his book called Ecclesiastes. He points out that all man's undertakings and presumption are sheer vanity, and nothing but toil and evil, unless God is brought into them, so that man fears him and is content with the present and rejoices in it.[26] God is an enemy of that assured, unbelieving presumption which forgets him; therefore, he opposes it in all that he does, lets us fail and stumble, snatches away life and property when we least expect it, and comes at an hour we do no know [Matt. 24:50], so that the godless, as the Psalter says [Ps. 55:23], never live out half their days, but must always depart this life unexpectedly, just when they are getting under way, as Job also says in many places.[27]

Perhaps you will say, "How then are people to trade with one another if surety is improper? That way many would be left behind who might otherwise get ahead." Answer: There are four Christian ways of exchanging external goods with others, as I have

---

[26] Cf., e.g., Eccles. 1:2-3, 14; 2:11, 21, 24-25; 3:11-14, 22; 5:18-20; 12:13.
[27] Cf., e.g., Job 4:20; 15:32-33; 18:14; 20:11, 22; 24:24.

said elsewhere.[28] The first way[29] is to let them rob or steal our property, as Christ says in Matthew 5, "If anyone takes away your cloak, let him have your coat as well, and do not ask it of him again."[30] This way of dealing counts for nothing among the merchants; besides, it has not been held or preached as common teaching for all Christians, but merely as a counsel or a good idea for the clergy and the perfect,[31] though they observe it even less than do the merchants. But true Christians observe it, for they know that their Father in heaven has assuredly promised in Matthew 6 [:11] to give them this day their daily bread. If men were to act accordingly, not only would countless abuses in all kinds of business be avoided, but a great many people would not become merchants, because reason and human nature flee and shun to the uttermost risks and damages of this sort.

The second way[32] is to give freely to anyone who needs it, as Christ also teaches in the same passage [Matt. 5:42; Luke 6:30]. This too is a lofty Christian work, which is why it counts for little among the people. There would be fewer merchants and less trade if this were put into practice. For he who does this must truly hold fast to heaven and look always to the hands of God, and not to his own resources or wealth, knowing that God will support him even though every cupboard were bare, because he knows to be true what God said to Joshua, "I will not forsake you or withdraw my hand from you" [Josh. 1:5]; as the proverb has it, "God still has more than what he ever gave away."[33] But that takes a true Christian, and he is a rare animal on earth, to whom the world and nature pay no heed.

The third way[34] is lending. That is, I give away my prop-

---

28 In his *Short Sermon on Usury* of 1519 (*WA* 6, 3-6) and again in his *Long Sermon on Usury* of 1520 (see in this volume, p. 295) Luther had specifically limited the designation "Christian" to only the first three of the four ways here listed.

29 Cf. Luther's more extended statement of 1520 on pp. 273-280.

30 Luke 6:29-30; cf. Matt. 5:40.

31 On the scholastic teaching which distinguished between general commands for all men and counsels for those who would be perfect, see p. 82, especially n. 6.

32 Cf. Luther's more extended statement of 1520 on pp. 280-289.

33 See Wander (ed.), *Sprichwörter-Lexikon*, II, 28, *"Gott,"* No. 617.

34 Cf. Luther's 1520 statement on pp. 289-295.

erty, and take it back again if it is returned to me; but I must do without it if it is not returned. Christ himself defines this kind of transaction in what he says in Luke 6 [:35], "Lend, expecting nothing in return." That is, you should lend freely, and take your chances on getting it back or not. If it comes back, take it; if it does not, it is a gift. According to the gospel there is thus only one distinction between giving and lending, namely, a gift is not taken back, while a loan is taken back—if it is returned—but involves the risk that it may become a gift. He who lends expecting to get back something more or something better than he has loaned is nothing but an open and condemned usurer,[35] since even those who in lending demand or expect to get back exactly what they lend, and take no chances on whether they get it back or not, are not acting in a Christian way. This third way too (in my opinion) is a lofty Christian work; and a rare one, judging by the way things are going in the world. If it were to be practiced generally, trade of all sorts would greatly diminish and virtually cease.

These three ways of exchanging goods, then, observe in masterful fashion this matter of not presuming upon the future, and not trusting in any man or in oneself but clinging to God alone. Here all transactions are in cash,[36] and are accompanied by the word which James teaches, "If God wills, so be it" [Jas. 4:15]. For here we deal with people as with those who are unreliable and might fail; we give our money freely, or take our chances on losing what we lend.

Now someone will say, "Who can then be saved? And where shall we find these Christians? Why, in this way there would be no trade left in the world; everyone would have his property taken or borrowed away, and the door would be thrown open for

---

[35] This statement accords with the most primitive and universal understanding of the matter in both church and state. The first medieval definition of usury, in the Nyweger capitulary of 806, declares that usury is "where more is asked than is given." Noonan, op. cit., p. 15. Along with the bare definition there was always the assumption that usury occurs in loans. The usury prohibition was first extended in the twelfth century to a transaction which was explicitly in the form of a loan. Ibid., pp. 17, 19.

[36] Luther was generally opposed to all forms of credit; only cash transactions precluded the possibility of usury.

the wicked and idle gluttons—of whom the world is full—to take everything with their lying and cheating." Answer: I have already said that Christians are rare people on earth. This is why the world needs a strict, harsh temporal government which will compel and constrain the wicked to refrain from theft and robbery, and to return what they borrow (although a Christian ought neither to demand nor expect it). This is necessary in order that the world may not become a desert, peace vanish, and men's trade and society be utterly destroyed; all of which would happen if we were to rule the world according to the gospel, rather than driving and compelling the wicked by laws and the use of force to do and to allow what is right. For this reason we must keep the roads safe, preserve peace in the towns, enforce law in the land, and let the sword hew briskly and boldly against transgressors, as St. Paul teaches in Romans 13 [:4]. For it is God's will that people who are not Christian be held in check and kept from doing wrong, at least from doing it with impunity. Let no one think that the world can be ruled without bloodshed; the temporal sword must and shall be red and bloody, for the world will and must be evil, and the sword is God's rod and vengeance upon it. But of this I have said enough in my little book on *Temporal Authority*.[37]

Borrowing would be a fine thing if it were practiced between Christians, for every borrower would then willingly return what had been lent him, and the lender would willingly forego repayment if the borrower were unable to pay. Christians are brothers, and one does not forsake another; neither is any of them so lazy and shameless that he would not work but depend simply on another's wealth and labor, or consume in idleness another's goods. But where men are not Christians, the temporal authorities ought to compel them to repay what they have borrowed. If the temporal authorities are negligent and do not compel repayment, the Christian ought to tolerate the robbery, as Paul says in I Corinthians 6 [:7], "Why not rather suffer wrong?" But you may exhort, insist, and do what you will to the man who is not a

---

[37] See in this volume, pp. 75-129.

Christian; he pays no attention because he is not a Christian and has no regard for Christ's doctrine.

You still have a grain of comfort too in the fact that you are not obligated to make a loan except out of your surplus and what you can spare from your own needs, as Christ says of alms, "What you have left over,[38] that give in alms, and everything is clean for you." Now if someone wishes to borrow from you an amount so large that you would be ruined if it were not repaid, and you could not spare it from your own needs, then you are not bound to make the loan. Your first and greatest obligation is to provide for the needs of your wife and children and servants; you must not divert from them what you owe them. The best rule to follow is this: If the amount asked as a loan is too great, just go ahead and give something outright, or else lend as much as you would be willing to give, and take the risk of having to lose it. John the Baptist did not say, "He who has one coat, let him give it away"; but, "He who has two coats, let him give one to him who has none; and he who has food, let him do likewise" [Luke 3:11].

The fourth way[39] of exchanging goods is through buying and selling, but for hard cash or payment in kind. He who would use this method must make up his mind to rely not on something in the future but on God alone; also, that he will have to be dealing with men, men who will certainly fail and lie. Therefore, the best advice is this: whoever sells should not give credit or

---

[38] Luther is quoting Luke 11:41 according to the Vulgate, which translates the ambiguous Greek words *ta enonta* by the Latin words *quod superest*. The sole prevailing interpretation of this obscure passage in the Middle Ages—going back to Jerome and Augustine—suited the convenience of the reluctant giver and assigned an expiatory virtue to alms, "whatever is left beyond what is necessary for food and clothing, you owe to the poor." Gerhard Uhlhorn, *Christian Charity in the Ancient Church* (New York: Scribners, 1883), pp. 68-69, and p. 401, n. 4. In his own Bible translations, however, Luther had consistently avoided the traditional rendering, using *von ewr habe* in 1522 (cf. KJV's "of such things as ye have") and *von dem das da ist* from 1526 on (literally, "of what there is"). *WA*, DB 6, 266-267. Cf. his 1520 quotation of the verse on p. 306: *von dem das deyn ist* ("of that which is thine"). Thomas had declared the giving of alms *"de superfluo"* to be a matter of precept as over against counsel (see p. 82, n. 6). Karl Holl, "Der Neubau der Sittlichkeit," in *Gesammelte Aufsätze zur Kirchengeschichte,* Vol. I, Luther, p. 166, n. 1.
[39] Cf. Luther's 1520 statement on p. 295.

accept any security, but sell only for cash. If he wishes to lend, let him lend to Christians, or else take the risk of loss, and lend no more than he would be willing to give outright or can spare from his own needs. If the temporal government and regulations will not help him to recover his loan, let him lose it. Let him beware of becoming surety for anyone; let him much rather give what he can. Such a man would be a true Christian merchant; God would not forsake him, because he trusts properly in Him and cheerfully takes a chance in dealing with his untrustworthy neighbors.

If there were no such thing in this world as becoming surety, if the free lending portrayed in the gospel were the general practice, and if only hard cash or wares on hand were exchanged in trade, then the greatest and most harmful dangers and faults and failings of trade and commerce would be well out of the way. It would then be easy to engage in all sorts of business enterprises, and the other sinful faults of trade could the more readily be prevented. If there were none of this becoming surety and this lending without risk, many a man would have to maintain his humble status and be content with a modest living who now aspires day and night to reach an exalted position, relying on borrowing and standing surety. That is why everyone now wants to be a merchant and get rich. From this stem the countless dangerous and wicked devices and dirty tricks that have today become a joke among the merchants. There are so many of them that I have given up the hope that trade can be entirely corrected; it is so overburdened with all sorts of wickedness and deception that in the long run it will not be able to sustain itself, but will have to collapse inwardly of its own weight.

In what has been said I have wished to give a bit of warning and instruction to everyone about this great, filthy, widespread business of trade and commerce. If we were to tolerate and accept the principle that everyone may sell his wares as dear as he can, approving the practice of borrowing and forced lending and standing surety, and yet try to advise and teach men how to act the part of Christians and keep a good and clear conscience in the matter, that would be the same as trying to teach men how wrong could be right and bad good, how one could at the same time live and act in accordance with divine Scripture and contrary to divine Scripture. These three errors—that everyone may sell what is his as dear as he will, also borrowing and becoming surety—these are like three fountainheads from which the whole stream of abomination, injustice, low cunning, and trickery flows far and wide. To try to stem the flood without stopping up the source is a waste of effort and energy.

At this point, therefore, I wish to tell of some of these tricks and evil practices which I have myself observed, and which good and pious people have described to me. This I do in order that one may realize how necessary it is that the rules and principles which I have set forth above be established and put into practice, if consciences are to be counseled and aided in matters of trade, and also in order that all the other evil practices not specifically mentioned may be recognized and measured by these. How can one possibly enumerate them all? By the three errors mentioned above as the fountainheads of evil, door and window are opened wide to greed and to wicked, wily, self-seeking nature; breathing space and room is afforded them; opportunity and power is given them to practice unhindered all manner of wiles and trickery, and daily to think up more schemes, so that everything stinks of avarice, indeed, is submerged and steeped in avarice as in a great new Deluge.

First, there are some who have no conscientious scruples against selling their goods on time and credit for a higher price than if they were sold for cash. Indeed, there are some who will sell nothing for cash but everything on time, so they can make large profits on it. Observe that this way of dealing—which is grossly contrary to God's word, contrary to reason and every sense of justice, and springs from sheer wantonness and greed—is a sin against one's neighbor; for it does not consider his loss, but robs and steals from him that which is his. The seller is not trying to make a modest living, but to satisfy his lust for profits. According to divine law[40] he should not sell his goods at a higher price on the time payment plan than for cash.

---

[40] Cf. Lev. 25:36-37.

Again, there are some who sell their goods at a higher price than they command in the common market, or than is customary in the trade; they raise the price of their wares for no other reason than because they know that there is no more of that commodity in the country, or that the supply will shortly be exhausted, and people must have it. That is the rogue's eye of greed, which sees only the neighbor's need; not to relieve it, but to make the most of it and get rich at his expense. All such fellows are manifest thieves, robbers, and usurers.

Again, there are some who buy up the entire supply of certain goods or wares in a country or a city in order to have these goods entirely under their own control; they can then fix and raise the price and sell them as dear as they like or can. Now I have said above[41] that the rule by which a man may sell his goods as dear as he will or can if false and un-Christian. It is far more abominable that one should buy up a whole commodity for that purpose. Even the imperial and secular laws forbid this;[42] they call it *monopolia*, i.e., transactions for selfish profiteering, which are not to be tolerated in country or city. Princes and lords would punish it and put a stop to it if they really wanted to do their duty. For such merchants act as if God's creatures and God's goods were created and given for them alone, as if they could take them from others and set on them whatever price they chose.

If anyone wishes to cite the example of Joseph in Genesis 41 [:48-57; 47:13-26], how the holy man gathered up all the grain in the country and afterward, in a time of famine, bought with it for the king of Egypt all the money, cattle, land, and people—which certainly seems to have been a monopoly, or selfish

---

[41] See pp. 247-252.

[42] Monopolies were forbidden by Roman civil law; *Corpus juris civilis, Codex* IV, 59 *De monopoliis*. In Germany, the first statutory prohibition of monopolies was adopted by the Diet of Trier-Cologne in 1512. After decrying the practice of merchants who built up monopolies of certain commodities, and condemning it as contrary to the common imperial law and to decency, the diet specifically forbade the practice on pain of confiscation of the monopolist's goods. See the relevant text in Schmoller, *op. cit.*, pp. 500-501. The question of monopoly was a lively topic of current debate in the most recent Reichstags; see Clemens Bauer, "Conrad Peutingers Gutachten zur Monopolfrage: Eine Untersuchung zur Wandlung der Wirtschaftsanschauungen im Zeitalter der Reformation," *Archiv für Reformationsgeschichte*, XLV (1954), 146-157.

profiteering[43]—this is the answer: Joseph's transaction was no monopoly, but a common and honest purchase, such as was customary in that country. For he prevented no one else from buying during the good years, but it was his God-given wisdom that enabled him to gather in the king's grain during the seven years of plenty, while others were accumulating little or nothing. The text does not say that he alone bought up the grain, but that he gathered it into the king's cities [Gen. 41:48]. If others did not do likewise, the loss was their own. The common man usually consumes what he has without much concern for the future; and sometimes he has nothing to store up.

We still see the same thing today. Where neither princes nor cities provide a reserve supply for the benefit of the whole country, there is little or no reserve in the hands of the common man, who lives from year to year on his annual income. Accumulation of this sort is not self-interest or monopoly, but a good and proper Christian foresight for the good of the community and for others. It is not practiced in such a way that they seize everything for themselves, as these merchants do, but out of the yield of the common market, or the yearly income which everyone has, they set aside a store; others either will not or cannot accumulate anything, but get out of it only their daily living. Moreover, Scripture does not tell us that Joseph gathered grain in order to sell it as dearly as he pleased; the text clearly says [Gen. 41:36] that he did it not from greed but that land and people might not perish. But the greedy merchant sells as dearly as he pleases, seeking only his own profit, and regardless of whether land and people thereby perish.

The fact that Joseph by this means brought all the money and cattle—and all the land and people besides—into the king's possession, certainly does not seem to have been a Christian act, since he ought to have given to the needy without return, as the gospel [Matt. 5:42, Luke 6:30-31] and Christian love instruct us.

---

[43] Cf. Gabriel Biel's defense of Joseph, whose speculations in grain seemed to many writers of the time to need justification, on the grounds that the increase of his selling price over his purchase price was due to actual changes in the market price produced by scarcity. Robert B. Burke (trans.), *Treatise on the Power and Utility of Moneys* (Philadelphia: University of Pennsylvania Press, 1930), p. 33.

Yet he did right and well, for Joseph was administering the temporal government in the king's stead. I have often taught thus, that the world ought not and cannot be ruled according to the gospel and Christian love, but by strict laws and with sword and force, because the world is evil. It accepts neither gospel nor love, but lives and acts according to its own will unless compelled by force. Otherwise, if only love were applied, everyone would eat, drink, and live at ease at someone else's expense, and no one would work. Indeed, everyone would take from another what was his, and we would have such a state of affairs that no one could live because of the others.[44]

Joseph therefore did right because God so arranged it that he brought everything into his possession at a fair price equal to what prevailed at the time, and in keeping with temporal law allowed the people to remain under restraint and to sell themselves and all that they had. For in that country there was always a strict government, and it was customary to sell people like other goods. Besides, there can be no doubt that as a Christian[45] and a righteous man he let no poor man die of hunger, but, as the text states [Gen. 41:36], after he had been placed in charge of the king's temporal law and government he gathered, sold, and distributed the grain for the benefit and profit of the land and its people. Therefore, the example of the faithful Joseph is as remote from the conduct of the unfaithful, self-seeking merchants as heaven is far from earth. So much for this digression. We return now to the merchants' tricks.

Some of them, when they see that they cannot otherwise effect their selfish profiteering transactions and establish their monopolies because others have the same goods and wares, proceed to sell their goods so dirt cheap that the others cannot meet the competition, and are forced either to withhold their goods from sale, or to face ruin by selling them as cheaply as their competitors do. Thus, the greedy ones get their monopoly after all. Such fellows are not worthy to be called human beings or to live

---

[44] Luther expressed similar ideas in *Temporal Authority*, in this volume, pp. 89-92.
[45] On Luther's designation of Old Testament personages as "Christian," see p. 200.

among men; they are not even worth admonishing or instructing, for their envy and greed is so open and shameless that even at the cost of their own losses they cause loss to others, in order that they may have the whole place to themselves. The temporal authorities would do right if they took from such fellows everything they had, and drove them out of the country. It would scarcely have been necessary to tell of such practices, but I wanted to include them so that one might see what great villainy there is in trade and commerce, and to make evident to everyone what is going on in the world, in order that everyone may know how to protect himself against such a dangerous class.

Another fine bit of sharp practice is for one man to sell to another, on promise of future delivery, wares that the seller does not have. It works this way: A merchant from a distance comes to me and asks me if I have such and such goods for sale. Although I do not have them I say Yes anyway and sell them to him for ten or eleven gulden, when they could otherwise be bought for nine or less, promising delivery in two or three days. Meanwhile, I go out and buy the goods where I knew in advance that I could buy them cheaper than I am selling them to him. I deliver them, and he pays me for them. Thus I deal with his (the other man's) own money and property without any risk, trouble, or labor, and I get rich. That is appropriately called "living off the street" on someone else's money and goods, without having to travel over land or sea.[46]

Another practice called "living off the street" is this: When a merchant has a purseful of money and no longer cares to venture on land and sea with his goods, but to have a safe business, he settles down in a large commercial city. When he hears that some merchant is being pressed by his creditors and lacks the money he must have to satisfy them, but still has good wares, he gets someone to act for him in buying the wares, and offers eight gulden for what is otherwise worth ten. If this offer is turned down, he gets someone else to make an offer of six or seven gulden. The poor man begins to be afraid that his wares are depreciating, and

---

[46] The comparison is with the common beggar who manages to survive without any of the customary risks and effort.

is glad to accept the eight gulden so as to get hard cash and not have to suffer too great a loss and disgrace. It may also happen that needy merchants themselves seek out such tyrants and offer their goods for ready cash with which to pay their debts. These tyrants drive hard bargains, and eventually get the wares at a low enough price; afterward they sell them at their own price. Such financiers are known as "cutthroats,"[47] but they pass for distinguished and clever people.

Here is another piece of selfish profiteering: Three or four merchants have in their control one or two kinds of goods which others do not have, or do not have for sale. When these men see that the goods are valuable and are advancing in price all the time because of war or some disaster, they join forces and let it be known to others that the goods are much in demand, and that not many have them for sale. If they find any who have these goods for sale, they set up a dummy to buy up all such goods. When they have cornered the supply, they draw up an agreement to this effect: since there are no more of these goods to be had, we will hold them at such and such a price, and whoever sells cheaper shall forfeit so and so much.

This practice, I am told, is carried to the crudest lengths primarily by the English merchants, especially in the sale of English or London cloth. It is said that for this trade they have a special council, like a city council, and all Englishmen who sell English or London cloth must obey this council on penalty of a fine. The council decides at what price they are to sell their cloth, and at what day and hour they are to have it on sale, and when not. The head of this council is called the governor, and is regarded as little less than a prince.[48] See what avarice can and dares to do!

---

[47] *Gorgel stecher odder kelstecher.*

[48] The Fellowship of the Merchant Adventurers in London, organ of co-operation between the various dealers in English cloth, was formally recognized in 1486. Besides the original purpose of financing, equipping, and dispatching fleets from London to the quarterly marts, it soon extended its functions to include direction of the adventurers' mercantile policy and critical control of their finances. It determined when, if at all, the ships were to sail and to which marts. In 1518 the governor of the company was powerful enough to defy even the mayor of London and fine two city aldermen for disobedience to his directives. E M. Carus-Wilson, "The Origins and Early Development of the Merchant Adventurers' Organization in London

Again, I must report this little trick: I sell a man pepper or the like on six months' credit, knowing that he has to sell it again immediately to get ready money. Then I go to him myself, or send someone else, and buy the pepper back from him for cash, but on such terms that what he bought from me on six month's credit for twelve gulden I buy back for eight, while the market price is ten. Thus I buy it from him at two gulden less than the current market, while he bought it from me at two gulden above the market. So I make a profit going and coming, simply because he has to have the money to maintain his credit standing; otherwise, he might have to suffer the disgrace of having no one extend him credit in the future.

People who buy on credit more than they can pay for (for example, a man who is worth scarcely two hundred gulden and makes a deal involving five or six hundred gulden) practice or have to practice this sort of finance.[49] If those indebted to me cannot pay, then I cannot pay my creditors; so the mischief goes deeper and deeper, and one loss follows another the more I practice this kind of finance, until at last I see the shadow of the gallows and must either abscond or go to prison. So I keep my own counsel and give my creditors fair words, telling them I will pay my debts. Meanwhile, I go out and get as much goods as I can on credit and turn them into money, or get money otherwise on a promissory note, or borrow as much as I can. Then whenever it is most advantageous to me, or when my creditors give me no rest, I lock my house, get up and run away, hiding myself somewhere in a monastery,[50] where I am as free as a thief or murderer in a churchyard. Then my creditors are so glad I have not fled the country that they release me from a half or a third of my debts on condition that I pay the balance in two or three years, giving me letter and seal for it. Then I come back

---

as Shown in Their Own Medieval Records," *The Economic History Review,* IV² (1933), 147-176 (published for the Economic History Society by A. & C. Black, London).

[49] *Fynantzen,* see p. 245, n. 1.

[50] The church's right of sanctuary, recognized by the state since about the fourth century as a part of the church's ministry of charity (see Uhlhorn, *op. cit.,* pp. 365-367), proved to be a public liability when used for purposes of fraud and deception. MA³ 5, 417, n. 130, 28.

to my house and am a merchant who has made two or three thousand gulden by getting up and running away.[51] That is more than I could have made in three or four years if I knocked myself out hustling.

Or if this procedure seems disadvantageous, when I see that I have to abscond I simply go to the emperor's court or to his viceroy, where for one or two hundred gulden I can obtain a *quinquernell*,[52] that is, an imperial letter and seal granting me respite from all my creditors for two or three years on my plea that I have suffered great losses. So the *quinquernells* too make a pretense of being godly and right; actually, though, they are knaves' tricks.

Another little trick is customary in the trading companies. A citizen deposits with a merchant perhaps two thousand gulden for six years. The merchant is to trade with this and, win or lose, pay the citizen a fixed *zinse* of two hundred gulden a year. What the merchant makes over and above this is his own, but if he makes no profit he must still pay the *zinse*. In this way the citizen is doing the merchant a great service, for the latter anticipates a profit of at least three hundred gulden from the two thousand. On the other hand, the merchant is doing the citizen a great service, for his money would otherwise lie idle and bring him no return. That this common practice is wrong and is in fact usury, I have shown sufficiently in the treatise on usury.[53]

I must give one more illustration to show how this spurious borrowing and lending leads to misfortune. Some people, when they see that a buyer is unreliable and does not meet his payments, are able to repay themselves neatly in this way: I get a strange merchant to approach him and buy up his wares to the amount of a hundred gulden or so, and I say to the stranger, "When you

---

[51] As fraudulent bankruptcies increased in the early sixteenth century, penalties were made increasingly severe ranging from banishment or disfranchisement to death by hanging. Schmoller, *op. cit.*, pp. 591-592.

[52] The *Quinquernell*, providing for the debtor a five-year moratorium, was often granted—for good and sufficient financial reimbursement—by the emperor even in violation of agreements won by certain cities that their citizens should be exempt from its deleterious effects. Schmoller, *op. cit.*, p. 593.

[53] Luther's 1520 treatise on *Usury*, included as the second half of this composite 1524 treatise, deals in Part Two with the objectionable *zinss* contract. See pp. 234-238.

have bought up all his wares, promise him cash or refer him to a certain man who owes you money. When you have the goods, bring him to me as though I owed you money, and act as though you were unaware that he is in my debt. In that way I shall be repaid, and will give him nothing." That is really practicing finance![54] It ruins the poor man entirely, together with all those to whom he may be in debt. But that is the way it goes in this un-Christian borrowing and lending.

Again, they have learned to store their goods in places or under conditions where they will increase in bulk. They put pepper, ginger, and saffron in damp cellars or vaults where they will take on more weight. Woolen goods, silks, furs of marten or sable, they sell in dimly-lit vaults or shops, keeping them from the air. This custom is so general that almost every sort of commodity has its special kind of air. There are no goods but what some way is known of taking advantage of the buyer, whether it be in the measure or the count of the dimensions or the weight. They know, too, how to give them an artificial color; or the best-looking items are put at top and bottom and the worst in the middle. There is no end to such cheating; no merchant dare trust another out of his sight and reach.

Now the merchants raise a great cry about the nobles or robbers,[55] complaining that they have to transact business at great risk, and that for their trouble they are imprisoned, beaten, taxed, and robbed, etc. If they endured all this for righteousness' sake, the merchants would surely be saints because of their sufferings. To be sure, it may happen that one of them suffers something that is an injustice in the sight of God, in that he has to suffer for another in whose company he is found, and pay for another man's sins. But when such great injustice and un-Christian thievery and robbery is practiced by merchants all over the world, even against one another, what wonder is it that God causes this great wealth, wrongfully acquired, to be lost or taken by robbers, and the merchants themselves to be beaten over the head or imprisoned?

---

[54] *Fynantzen;* see p. 245, n. 1.
[55] In addition to actual robbery at sword's point, traveling merchants had to pay transit tolls when crossing the lands of a knight or baron. These tolls were often tantamount to robbery.

God simply has to administer justice, even as in Psalm 11 [:4-7] he has himself extolled as a righteous judge.

Not that I would thereby excuse the highwaymen and bushwhackers, or approve of their thievery! It is the fault of the princes; they are supposed to keep the roads safe for the benefit of the wicked as well as of the upright. It is also their duty to use their duly constituted authority in punishing the injustices of the merchants and preventing them from so shamefully skinning their subjects. Because the princes fail to do so, God uses the knights and robbers to punish the wrongdoing of the merchants; they must be His devils, just as He plagues the land of Egypt [Exod. 7–12] and the whole world with devils, or destroys it with enemies. Thus he uses one rascal to flog the other, but without thereby giving us to understand that the knights are any the less robbers than the merchants,[56] even though the merchants rob everybody every day, while a knight robs one or two people once or twice a year.

On the trading companies I ought to say a good deal, but the whole subject is such a bottomless pit of avarice and wrongdoing that there is nothing in it that can be discussed with a good conscience. Who is so stupid that he cannot see that the trading companies are nothing but pure monopolies? Even the temporal laws of the heathen forbid them[57] as openly harmful to the whole world, to say nothing of divine right and Christian law. They control all commodities, deal in them as they please, and practice without concealment all the tricks that have been mentioned. They raise or lower prices at their pleasure. They oppress and ruin all the small businessmen, like the pike the little fish in the water, just as if they were lords over God's creatures and immune from all the laws of faith and love.

So it happens that all over the world spices must be bought at whatever price they choose to set, and they vary it from time to time. This year they raise the price of ginger, next year that

---

[56] Cf. Hutten's 1521 dialogue, *"Praedones"* ("The Robbers"). Böcking (ed.), *Vlrichi Hvtteni Opera* 4, 363-406. Hutten said that of the four classes of robbers—free-booting knights, lawyers, priests, and merchants—the merchants were the worst. Smith, *Age of the Reformation,* p. 530.
[57] See p. 262, n. 42.

of saffron, or vice versa; so that in the end it all comes out the same:[58] they do not have to suffer any loss, injury, or risk. If the ginger spoils or they have to take a loss on it, they make it up on saffron, and vice versa, so that they make sure of their profit. All this is contrary to the nature, not only of merchandise, but of all temporal goods, which God wills should be subject to risk and uncertainty. But they have found a way to make safe, certain, and continual profit out of unsafe, uncertain, and perishable goods; though because of it all the world must be sucked dry and all the money sink and swim in their gullets.

How could it ever be right and according to God's will that a man in such a short time should grow so rich that he could buy out kings and emperors?[59] They have brought things to such a pass that everybody else has to do business at the risk of loss, winning this year and losing next year, while they themselves can always win, making up their losses by increased profits. It is no wonder that they quickly appropriate the wealth of the whole world, for a pfennig that is permanent and sure is better than a gulden that is temporary and uncertain. But these companies are always dealing with permanent and sure gulden for our temporary and uncertain pfennigs. Is it any wonder that they become kings and we beggars?

Kings and princes ought to look into this matter and forbid them by strict laws. But I hear that they have a finger in it themselves,[60] and the saying of Isaiah [1:23] is fulfilled, "Your princes

---

58 *Die krümme ynn die beuge kome* means literally, "the bend comes to the crook," things even themselves up.
59 Bartholomew Rem, for example, a bookkeeper in the Augsburg trading company of Ambrose Höchstetter, ran an investment of five hundred florins in the spice trade up to a fortune of thirty thousand florins in six years. August Kluckhohn, *Zur Geschichte der Handelsgesellschaften und Monopole im Zeitalter der Reformation* ("Historische Aufsätze dem Andenken an Georg Waitz gewidmet" [Hannover: Hohn, 1886]), p. 671. The most notable example of such hastily amassed fortunes, of course, was that of the Fugger family in Augsburg, which skyrocketed its fortune by 1634 per cent in one period of twenty-one years. *PE* 2, 160, n. 2. Having attained monopolies in mining, commerce, and finance over the period of a couple generations they were able, by means of enormous cash outlays running into the equivalent of millions of dollars, to secure the imperial election of 1519 for Charles V. Schwiebert, *op. cit.*, p. 41. G. F. von Pölnitz, *op. cit.*, I, 418-441.
60 Vigorous enforcement of the Trier-Cologne anti-monopoly legislation of 1512 (see p. 262, n. 42) did not begin until the imperial attorney proceeded

have become companions of thieves." They hang thieves who have stolen a gulden or half a gulden, but do business with those who rob the whole world and steal more than all the rest, so that the proverb remains true, "Big thieves hang little thieves."[61] As the Roman senator Cato said, "Simple thieves lie in dungeons and stocks; public thieves walk abroad in gold and silk."[62] What will God say to this at last? He will do as he says through Ezekiel: princes and merchants, one thief with the other, he will melt together like lead and bronze [Ezek. 22:20] as when a city burns to the ground, so that there shall be neither princes nor merchants any more. That time, I fear, is already at the door. We do not think of amending our lives, no matter how great our sin and wrong. So, too, He cannot leave wrong unpunished.

This is why no one need ask how he may with a good conscience be a member of a trading company. My only advice is this: Get out; they will not change. If the trading companies are to stay, right and honesty must perish; if right and honesty are to stay, the trading companies must perish. The bed is too narrow, says Isaiah, one must fall out, the covering is too small, it will not cover both [Isa. 28:20].

Now I know full well that this book of mine will be taken amiss;[63] perhaps they will toss it all to the winds and remain as they are. But it will not be my fault, for I have done my part to show how richly we have deserved it if God should come with his rod. If I have instructed a single soul and rescued it from the jaws of avarice, I have not labored in vain. Nevertheless, I hope (as I have said above)[64] that this thing has grown so high and so

---

in 1523 against certain of the merchants of Augsburg. They hastened to secure the favor of the princes but received their main support from the emperor in return for a large share in their profits. Smith, *op. cit.*, p. 530. Complicity between the merchants and the authorities was decried already at the Diet of Worms in 1521, and antedated the Fugger boast to having secured the election of Charles V as emperor. Kluckhohn, *op. cit.*, p. 672.

61 Wander (ed.), *Sprichwörter-Lexikon*, I, 589, "Dieb," No. 145.
62 Cf. Aulus Gellius, *Attic Nights* XI, xviii, 18.
63 *The Short Sermon on Usury* (WA 6, 3-8), published in the fall of 1519, had already made a bad impression in some circles. This is what led Luther in December of the same year to enlarge upon the same theme in order "that Christ's pure teaching may elicit further offense." WA 6, 33.
64 See p. 260.

top-heavy that it can no longer carry its own weight, and they will finally have to give it up.

Finally, let everyone look to himself. Let no one stop as a favor or service to me. Let no one begin or continue either, in order to spite and hurt me. This thing has to do with you, not me. May God enlighten us and strengthen us to do his good will. Amen.

USURY[65]

First. It should be known that in our times (which the Apostle Paul prophesied would be perilous [II Tim. 3:1]) avarice and usury have not only taken a mighty hold on the whole world, but have had the nerve to seek out certain subterfuges by which they might freely practice their wickedness under the guise of fair dealing. Besides, things have come almost to the point where we regard the holy gospel as having no value. Therefore, it is necessary in these perilous times for everyone to be alert, to use proper discretion in dealing with temporal goods, paying diligent attention to the holy gospel of Christ our Lord.

Second. It should be known that there are three different degrees or ways[66] of dealing fairly and righteously with temporal goods. The first [67] is that if anyone seizes some of our temporal property by force, we should not only permit it and relinquish that property, but be ready to let him take more if he wants to. Our dear Lord Jesus Christ says of this in Matthew 5 [:40], "If anyone would sue you in court to take your coat, let him have your cloak as well." This is the highest degree in this matter of dealing with temporal goods. It is not to be taken to mean, as some think, that we are to throw the cloak in with the coat. Rather,

---

[65] Usually called *The Long Sermon on Usury* to distinguish it from *The Short Sermon on Usury* of 1519 (see WA 6, 3-8) this treatise first appeared in 1520 and was incorporated—together with a brief supplement (see pp. 308-310)—into the present composite treatise in 1524. Our translation is based on the original given in WA 6, 36-60.
[66] Cf. Luther's 1524 list of "four Christian ways" on pp. 255-261.
[67] Cf. p. 256.

we are to let the cloak go also, and not resist or become impatient about it, or try to get it back. For he does not say, "Give him also the cloak," but, "Let him have the cloak too." This is what Christ did before Bishop Annas,[68] when He received a blow on the cheek [John 18:22]; he offered the other cheek, even both cheeks, and was ready to receive more such blows. Indeed, in his entire Passion we see that he never repays or returns an evil word or deed, but is always ready to endure more and more.

Third. It is indeed true that He said to the slave, Malchus, who struck Him,[69] "If I have spoken wrongly, bear witness to the wrong; but if I have spoken rightly, why do you strike me?" [John 18:23]. Some, even of the learned, stumble over these words, and think that Christ did not here offer the other cheek, as He had taught that men should do [Matt. 5:39]. But they do not view the words aright. For in these words Christ makes no threat; he does not avenge himself or strike back. Neither does he refuse the other cheek. Indeed, he does not even judge or condemn Malchus, but, as St. Peter writes of Him, He did not threaten or think to recompense evil, but committed it to God, the just Judge [I Pet. 2:23], as if to say, "Whether I have spoken rightly or you are right in striking me, God will find out, and the burden of proof is on you." This is what Zechariah said when they were about to kill him, "Videat dominus et judicet"; "God will see it and judge."[70] Christ did the same thing before Pilate, when He said, "He who delivered me to you has the greater sin" [John 19:11]. That is Christian and brotherly fidelity, to terrify him who does you wrong by holding up before him his wrongdoing and God's judgment. It is your duty to say to him, "Very well; you are taking my coat and this and that; if you are not doing right, you will have to answer for it." You must do this, not primarily because of your own loss, nor to threaten him, but to warn him

---

68 Annas was a high priest; there were of course no bishops then. Luther has simply fallen into the medieval habit of applying current titles to men of a former age.

69 The officer who did the striking is not identified in John 18:22 with the Malchus of John 18:10, the victim of Peter's sword.

70 In II Chron. 24:22 the Vulgate actually reads *requirat* rather than *judicet*. Luther turns the Latin optative (cf. the RSV, "May . . .") into a straight future.

and to remind him of his impending ruin. If this fails to change his purpose, let go what will, and do not demand its return. It is in this sense then that the words Christ uttered before the judgment seat of Annas are to be understood. It follows that, like Christ on the cross [Luke 23:34], you must pray for and do good to him who does evil to you [Luke 6:27-28]. But we will postpone this now until the proper time.

Fourth. Many think that this first degree is not commanded, and need not be observed by every Christian, but that it is a good counsel laid upon the perfect[71] if they wish to keep it, just as virginity and celibacy are recommended [I Cor. 7:25-28], not commanded. Therefore, they hold that it is all right for anyone to take back what is his, and to meet force with force to the best of his ability and knowledge. They deck out this opinion of theirs with pretty flowers,[72] and prove it with many (as they think) powerful arguments. In the first place, they point out that canon law (not to mention civil law) says, "Vim vi pellere jura sinunt;"[73] that is, the law allows that force be resisted with force. From this comes, in the second place, the common proverb about self-defense, that it is not punishable for what it does.[74] In the third place, they cite in addition some examples from Scripture, such as Abraham, David, and many more, of whom we read that they punished and repaid their enemies. In the fourth place, they bring in reason, and say, Solve istud ["explain this!"]: if this were a commandment, it would give the wicked permission to thieve and steal until no one had anything left, indeed no one could be sure of his own life. In the fifth place, in order that everything may be proved conclusively, they cite the words of

---

[71] See p. 256, especially n. 31.

[72] Flowery speech (cf. p. 277, ll. 14-15) was a special category within the rhetoric of that period to which Erasmus and the humanists, as well as Luther, objected. MA³ 5, 418, n. 135, 40.

[73] A gloss to Decret. Gratiani I, lxiv, 6, reads, "Vim vi repullere licet" ("It is permissible to repel force with force.") This gloss is found in Decretum Gratiani emendatum et notationibus illustratum una cum glossis (Paris, 1612), col. 365. See also WA, Br 5, 261 n. 10.

[74] Cf. Article 109 of the 1532 Constitutio criminalis Carolina quoted in MA³ 5, 419, n. 136, 4. The rabbis (Beruchoth 58 and Sanhedrin 72) say that even homicide is unpunishable if committed in self-defense. Wander (ed.), Sprichwörter-Lexikon, III, 1064, "Nothwehr," No. 3.

St. Augustine, who explains these words of Christ [Matt. 5:40] to mean that one must let the cloak go with the coat *secundum preparationem animi,*[75] that is, one should be ready in his heart to do it. This noble and clear explanation they interpret and obscure with another gloss, adding that it is not necessary for us to give it outwardly and in fact; it is enough, they say, that we be inwardly, in the heart, ready and prepared to do so. As though we were willing to do something that we were not willing to do, and yes and no were the same thing!

Fifth. See there, these are the masterpieces by which they have till now twisted, obscured, and entirely suppressed the doctrine and example of our dear Lord Jesus Christ, together with the holy gospel and all his martyrs and saints; so that nowadays those spiritual and temporal prelates and their subjects who follow these rules are the best Christians, though they resist Christ's life, teaching, and gospel. Hence it comes that lawsuits and litigations, magistrates, notaries, *officiales,*[76] jurists, and such fellows are as numerous as flies in summer. Hence it comes that there is so much war and bloodshed among Christians. And lawsuits must be taken on appeal to Rome,[77] for there a lot of money is the thing most needed; and the greatest, holiest, and most common occupation in all Christendom these days is suing and being sued, which means resistance to the holy and peaceful life and doctrine of Christ. This cruel game has finally come to the point where a poor man—but a Christian, whom God has redeemed with his blood—for the sake of the trifling sum of three or four groschen is not only cited to appear many miles[78] away, put under the ban, and driven away from wife, children, and

---

[75] In his *Commentary on the Lord's Sermon on the Mount,* I, 19, 59, Augustine says that Matt. 5:40 is to be rightly understood as a precept *"ad praeparationem cordis, non ad ostentationem operis"* ("with regard to the preparation of the heart, and not . . . in the visible performance of the deed"). MPL 34, 1260. Denis J. Kavanagh (trans.), *Saint Augustine: Commentary on the Lord's Sermon on the Mount.* FC 3, 85. On the heart's disposition called for by Augustine, see Karl Holl, *op. cit.,* pp. 166-167.
[76] *Officiales* were the judges in the bishops courts. PE 2, 103, n. 2.
[77] A few months later Luther discussed this common grievance at greater length in *An Open Letter to the Christian Nobility* (1520). PE 2, 103-104.
[78] A sixteenth-century German mile was the equivalent of about four and one-half modern English miles. LW 35, 292, n. 134.

family,[79] but the bright boys actually look upon this as a good thing to do, and even smile about it. So shall they fall who make a mockery of God's commandments; so shall God blind and put to shame those who turn the brightness of his holy word into darkness with their *"Vim vi repellere licet"* and their "letting the cloak go *secundum animi preparationem."* For to that extent the gospel is kept by the heathen also, indeed, even by wolves and all the unreasoning beasts; men do not have to be Christians to do that.

Sixth. Therefore, I want to do my part, and so far as I can warn everyone not to be led astray, no matter how learned, how mighty, how spiritual, or how numerous they all may be who have made and still make a counsel[80] of this first degree, and no matter how many may be the flowers and colors with which they decorate it. There is no evading it. This is simply a commandment that we are bound to obey, as Christ and his saints have confirmed and exemplified it for us in their lives. It is of no consequence to God that laws—be they canon or civil—permit force to be resisted with force. And what precious things the laws permit! They permit public brothels, although they are contrary to God's commandment, and many other evil things which God forbids; they necessarily permit also sins and wickedness. The things that human laws command and forbid matter little, not to mention the things they permit or do not punish. Thus, self-defense is not punishable under human law, but in the sight of God it has no merit. Suing in the courts is condemned neither by pope nor emperor, but it is condemned by Christ and his teaching. When some of the Old Testament fathers punished their enemies, it was never at their own discretion or without an express command from God, who punishes sinners at times by means of both good and bad angels and men. For this reason the

---

[79] At the 1521 Diet of Worms a list of 102 grievances against the abuses of ecclesiastical jurisdiction was presented to the emperor, in which there loomed large complaints against the church's judicial process whereby cases were transferred to Rome which should have been settled in Germany. See the text of the *Gravamina* in *Deutsche Reichstagsakten*, II, 671-704; and Bruno Gebhardt, *Die gravamina der Deutschen Nation gegen den römischen Hof* (2nd ed.; Breslau: Koebner, 1895), p. 113.

[80] See p. 82, n. 361.

277

fathers never sought their own revenge or profit therein, but only acted as obedient servants of God; just as Christ teaches in the gospel that at God's command we must act even against father and mother [Matt. 10:35-37; Luke 14:26], whom he has commanded us to honor [Exod. 20:12; Matt. 15:4]. Yet the two commandments are not contradictory, but the lower is governed by the higher. So when God commands you to take revenge or defend yourself, you shall do it; but not before then.

Seventh. Now it is true that God has instituted the temporal sword and in addition the spiritual power of the church, and has commanded both these authorities to punish the wicked and rescue the oppressed, as Paul teaches in Romans 13 [:3-4], and as is taught in many other places, such as Isaiah 1 [:23-26], and Psalm 82 [:2-4]. This should be done in such a way, however, that no one would be the complainant in his own case, but that others, in brotherly fidelity and care for one another, would inform the rulers that this man is right and that one wrong. Thus, the authorities would proceed to punish in a just and orderly way, on proof furnished by others. Indeed, the aggrieved party ought to request and insist that his case not be brought to trial; the others, in their turn, ought not to desist until the offense is punished. In this way affairs would be conducted in a friendly, Christian, and brotherly spirit, with more regard to the sin than to the injury. This is why St. Paul rebukes the Corinthians in I Corinthians 6 [:7] for going to law with one another instead of suffering themselves to be injured and defrauded, although because of their imperfection he allowed them to appoint the least among them[81] as judges. He did this to shame them [I Cor. 6:5] into a knowledge of their imperfection. In like manner we must tolerate those who sue and are sued for temporal goods as weak and immature Christians; we dare not cast them off, because there is hope for their improvement, as the same apostle teaches in many places.[82] We ought to tell them, however, that such conduct is neither

---

[81] While Luther interpreted I Cor. 6:4 in this sense in his 1522 New Testament (cf. the KJV, "least esteemed in the church"), from 1530 on his different understanding and rendering of the same verse was underscored by a marginal gloss referring the phrase to the heathen (cf. the RSV: "least esteemed by the church"). WA, DB 7, 100-101.

[82] Cf., e.g., Acts 20:35; Rom. 14:1; 15:1-2; I Cor. 9:22; I Thess. 5:14.

Christian nor praiseworthy but human and earthly, more of a hindrance to salvation than a help.

Eighth. Christ gave us this commandment [Matt. 5:40] in order to establish within us a peaceful, pure, and heavenly life. Now for everyone to demand what is his and be unwilling to endure wrong is not the way to peace, as those blind men think, of whom it is said in the fourteenth Psalm, "They do not know the way to peace."[83] That way passes only through suffering, as even the heathen know by reason,[84] and we by daily experience. If peace is to be kept, one party must remain quiet and suffer. Even though quarrels and litigation last for a long time, they must eventually come to an end—after the injuries and evils which would not otherwise have occurred, had the people kept this commandment of Christ from the start and not allowed the temptation with which God tries us to drive them from the commandment and overcome them. God has so arranged matters that he who will not let a little go for the sake of God's commandment, will have to lose a great deal, perhaps all, through lawsuits and war. It is no more than fair that a man who will not even for God's sake or his own eternal merit give up ten gulden or six to his neighbor, should be obliged in service of the devil to give to the judges, proctors, and clerks twenty, thirty, or forty gulden.

Thus, he loses both temporal and eternal goods where, had he been obedient to God, he might have had enough for both time and eternity. So too it must happen at times that great lords ruin an entire land through war, expending vast sums on the military, all for the sake of some small advantage or privilege. That is the perverted wisdom of the world; it fishes with golden nets,[85] and the cost is greater than the profit. Such fellows win little by squandering much.

Ninth. It would also be impossible for us to become cleansed

---

[83] Rom. 3:17 is a quotation from Isa. 59:8, a passage which was familiar to Luther from the Vulgate Bible where it had been included as a part of Ps. 13:3. The passage is correctly omitted from the corresponding English versions, even as Luther similarly omitted it from Ps. 14:3 in his German Psalter. *WA, DB* 10I, 138-139.

[84] On Luther's view of reason, see Holl, *op. cit.*, pp. 263-265.

[85] This proverbial expression is documented in Wander (ed.), *Sprichwörter-Lexikon*, III, 1005-1006, "*Netz*," Nos. 36, 607; and in Grimm, *Deutsches Wörterbuch*, VII, 636.

of our attachment to temporal goods if God did not ordain that we should suffer unjust losses, and thereby be trained to turn our hearts away from the false temporal goods of this world, letting them go in peace, and pinning our hopes on invisible and eternal goods. Hence, he who demands that which is his, and does not let the cloak go with the coat [Matt. 5:40], is resisting his own cleansing and the hope of eternal salvation, toward which God would train and drive him by means of such a command-ment and unjust treatment. And even though everything were taken from us, there is no reason to fear that God will forsake us and fail to provide for us even in temporal matters; as it is written in Psalm 37 [:25], "I have been young, and now am old; yet I have not seen the righteous forsaken or his children beg-ging bread." This is proven also in the case of Job, who in the end received much more than he had before, although all that was his had been taken from him [Job 42:10, 12]. In short, such commandments are intended to detach us from the world and make us desirous of heaven. Therefore, we ought freely and joy-fully to accept God's faithful counsel, for if he did not give it, and did not let us experience injustice and trouble, the human heart could not maintain itself; it becomes too deeply enmeshed in temporal things and too firmly attached to them. The result is satiety, and disregard of the eternal goods in heaven.

Tenth. So much for the first degree of dealing with temporal goods. It is also the foremost and greatest; but, alas! it has not only become the least, but has even come to nothing, quite un-known amid the fog and clouds of human laws, usages, habits, and customs.

Now comes the second degree.[86] It is that we are to give freely and without return to anyone who needs our goods or asks for them. Of this our Lord Jesus Christ says in Matthew 5 [:42], "Give to him who begs from you." Although this degree is much lower than the first, it is nevertheless hard and bitter to those who have more taste for temporal than eternal goods; they have not enough trust in God to believe that he can or will

---

[86] See p. 273, and cf. p. 256.

sustain them in this wretched life. They therefore fear that they would die of hunger or be ruined entirely if they were to obey God's command and give to everyone who asks of them. How then can they trust him to maintain them in eternity? As Christ says, "He who does not trust God in a little matter, will never trust him in something greater."[87] Nevertheless, they go ahead and suppose that God will save them eternally. They even think that in this regard they have perfect trust in him; yet they will not heed this commandment of his by which he would train and drive them to learn to trust him in things temporal and eternal. Hence, there is reason to fear that he who will not listen to this teaching and follow it will never acquire the art of trusting, and that those who will not trust God in little temporal things must at last despair also in those matters that are great and eternal.

Eleventh. This second degree is so small a thing that it was commanded even to the simple, imperfect Jewish people in the Old Testament, as it is written in Deuteronomy 15 [:11], "The poor will never cease out of your land; therefore I command you, You shall open wide your hand to your poor and needy brother and give to him." Moreover, in the same place he commanded them very strictly that they must allow no one to beg, saying in Deuteronomy 15 [:4], "There shall never be a beggar or starveling among you." Now since God gave this commandment in the Old Testament, how much more ought we Christians to be bound, not only to allow no one to starve or beg, but beyond that also to keep the first degree of this commandment and be prepared to let everything go that anyone would take from us by force. But now there is so much begging that it has even become an honor; it is not enough that men of the world beg, but even the spiritual estate of priests practices it as a precious thing.[88] I will not quarrel with anyone about it, but I think it would be more fitting if there were no more begging in Christendom under the New Testament than among the Jews under the Old Testament; I hold that the spiritual and temporal authorities would be dis-

---

87 Cf. Luke 16:10.
88 The chief mendicant orders were the Franciscans, Dominicans, Augustinian Hermits, and Carmelites. See p. 175, n. 15, and MA³ 2, 399, n. 130, 21.

charging their duty properly if they did away with all the beggars' sacks.[89]

Twelfth. There are three common practices or customs among men that stand in the way of this second degree. The first is that people give and present things to their friends, and to the rich and powerful who do not need them, but forget the needy. And if they thereby obtain the favor, reward, or friendship of these people, or are praised by them as good and upright, they go confidently along, satisfied with the praise, honor, favor, or reward of men; failing to observe, meanwhile, how much better it would be if they did these things for the needy, and obtained therein the favor, praise, and honor of God. Of such men Christ says in Luke 14 [:12-14], "When you give a dinner or a banquet, do not invite your friends or your brothers or your kinsmen or your neighbors or the rich, lest they also invite you in return, and you be repaid. But when you give a feast, invite the poor, the sick, the lame, the blind, and you will be blessed, because they cannot repay you. You will be repaid among the righteous when they arise from the dead." Although this precept is so clear and plain that everyone sees and knows well that it ought to be so, yet we never see an example of it among Christians any more. There is neither measure nor limit to the entertaining, the high living, the eating, drinking, giving, and presenting; and yet they are all called good people and Christians, and the only thing it accomplishes is that giving to the needy is forgotten. O what a horrible judgment will fall upon these carefree spirits, when at the Last Day they are asked to whom they have given and done good![90]

Thirteenth. The second custom is the refusal to extend this giving to enemies or opponents. It comes hard to our false nature to do good to them who have done evil to us. But there is no getting around it, the commandment has reference to all men, "Give to him who begs from you" [Matt. 5:42]; it is clearly expressed in Luke 6 [:30], "Give to everyone who begs from you." There is no exclusion here of enemies or opponents; indeed,

---

[89] See the Introduction to Luther's 1523 *Preface to an Ordinance of a Common Chest* in this volume, pp. 161-162, and 176, and in the *Ordinance* itself, pp. 185-186.
[90] Cf. Matt. 25:31-46.

they are included, as the Lord explains in the same passage where he says, "If you love only those who love you, what kind of goodness is that? Even the wicked love those who love them. And if you do good only to those who love you, what kind of goodness is that? Even the wicked do that. But you shall love your enemies, and do good to them; you shall lend to them, and expect nothing in return; and your merit will be great, and you will be sons of the Most High, for he is kind to the ungrateful and the wicked" [Luke 6:32-35].

These wholesome commandments of Christ have so fallen into disuse that men not only do not keep them, but have made of them a "counsel" which one is not bound to keep unconditionally, just as they have done with the first degree.[91] They have been helped in this by pernicious teachers who say that it is not necessary to lay aside the *signa rancoris*,[92] that is, the signs and outward tokens of wrath and bitterness toward one's enemy; it is enough, they say, that he is forgiven in your heart. Thus, they apply Christ's commandment about external acts to the thoughts alone, although he himself in clear words refers it to actions, saying, "You shall do good (not merely think good) to your enemies" [Luke 6:35]. Paul too in Romans 12 [:20], in agreement with King Solomon [Prov. 25:21-22], says the same thing, "If your enemy is hungry, feed him; if he is thirsty, give him drink; for by so doing you will heap burning coals upon his head." That is, you will load him with kindnesses so that, overcome with good [Rom. 12:21], he will be kindled with love for you. From the false doctrine has sprung the common saying, "I will forgive him, but I will not forget." Not so, dear Christian! You must forgive and forget, as you would that God should not only forgive you and forget, but also grant you even more kindnesses than before.

Fourteenth. The third custom has a beautiful, brilliant appearance, but it does the most harm to this giving. There is considerable risk involved in speaking of it, for it concerns those who are supposed to be teaching and ruling others; and these

---

[91] See p. 275.
[92] This was the position of Gabriel Biel, following Bonaventura. Holl, *op. cit.*, p. 167, n. 1.

are the very folk who from the beginning of the world to its end can never bear to hear the truth or suffer others to hear it. The way things are now, they bestow the lofty title of "alms" and of "giving for God's sake" solely on giving for churches, monasteries, chapels, altars, towers, bells, organs, paintings, images, silver and gold ornaments and vestments, and for masses, vigils, singing, reading, testamentary endowments, brotherhoods,[93] and the like. Giving has taken hold here, and the real stream of giving runs in the direction toward which men have guided it and where they wanted to have it. No wonder, then, that in the direction toward which Christ's word guides it things are so dry and desolate; where there are a hundred altars or vigils there is not a single person who feeds a tableful of poor people or in other respects assists a needy household.

Not what Christ has commanded, but what men have invented, is called "giving for God's sake"; not what one gives to the needy, the living members of Christ, but what one gives to stone, wood, and paint, is called "alms." And this giving has become so precious and noble that God himself is not enough to recompense it, but has to have the help of letters,[94] bulls, parchments, lead, plate, cords large and small, and wax in green, yellow, and white. If it makes no show, it has no value. It is all bought from Rome at great cost "for God's sake," and such great works are rewarded with indulgences here and there, over and above God's reward. But that miserable work of giving to the poor and needy according to Christ's commandment must be robbed of such splendid reward, and be content simply with the reward that God gives. The latter work is therefore pushed to the rear and the former is placed out in front, and the two when compared shine with unequal light.

This is why even St. Peter of Rome must now go through the whole world begging for the building of his church, gathering great heaps of "alms for God's sake" and paying for them dearly

---

[93] See p. 181, n. 39.
[94] Indulgence letters came into use about the turn of the fifteenth century. Elaborately ornamented with papal signatures and seals, they provided impressive tangible evidence of heavenly forgiveness and effectively boosted sales of the "sacred commodity." Schwiebert, *op. cit.*, p. 305.

and richly with indulgences.[95] This work suits him well, and he can easily attend to it, because he is dead; if he were alive he would have to preach Christ's commandments, and could not attend to indulgences. Following studiously after their faithful shepherd, his lambs strayed about in the land with indulgences; wherever there is a parish festival[96] or an annual fair[97] these beggars gather like flies in summer and all preach the same song, "Give to the new building, that God and the holy lord St. Nicholas[98] may reward you." Afterward they go to their beer or wine, also "for God's sake," and the commissioners are made rich from the indulgences, also "for God's sake." But neither commissioners nor legates[99] are necessary to tell us that we should give to the needy according to God's commandment.

Fifteenth. What are we to say to this? If we reject these works, the Holy See at Rome puts us under the ban,[100] and learned scholars promptly denounce us as heretics,[101] because the place toward which the stream of money is directed makes a tremendous difference. Now we would not disallow the building

---

[95] The sale of indulgences for the purpose of building St. Peter's basilica in Rome was the occasion for Luther's writing his *Ninety-five Theses*, and is specifically mentioned in Theses 50 and 86. *LW* 31, 21, 30, 33. See Schwiebert, *op. cit.*, p. 308.

[96] The *Kirchwey*, which was either the dedication of a church or the anniversary celebration of such event, usually drew great crowds and was observed in anything but a spiritual fashion. *PE* 2, 128, n. 1; *PE* 4, 47, n. 2.

[97] A *jarmarckt* was one of the numerous annual fairs held at stated times in various cities which drew merchants from great distances and accounted for a large portion of the year's wholesale trade. *PE* 2, 95, n. 2.

[98] The reference is probably to the fourth-century Bishop Nicholas of Myra in Lycia, patron of mariners, regarded in Germany as the secret purveyor of gifts to children on December 6, his feast day. *Catholic Encyclopedia*, XI, 63-64.

[99] *Commissarien* and *botschafften* were those authorized from above to publish and sell indulgences. In his *Vadiscus*, Hutten likened the legates in Germany to Vergil's Trojan horse (*Opera* 4, 230).

[100] Written already in December of 1519 and published at the beginning of 1520, this prophetic sentence anticipated by nearly six months the inevitable papal reaction to his attack on indulgences, which finally came in the form of the papal bull—*Exsurge, Domine*, signed June 15, 1520—threatening excommunication in sixty days if Luther did not recant his errors. For Luther's understanding of excommunication see his *Treatise Concerning the Ban*, written about the same time as this treatise. *PE* 2, 37-54.

[101] On August 29, 1519, the University of Cologne condemned Luther's writings as heretical; on November 9, 1519, fifteen members of the faculty of the University of Louvain did likewise. Schwiebert, *op. cit.*, pp. 427-431.

of suitable churches and their adornment; we cannot do without them. And public worship ought rightly to be conducted in the finest way.[102] But there should be a limit to this, and we should take care that the appurtenances of worship be pure, rather than costly. The pity—and the thing we are complaining about—is that we are diverted from God's commandments by such a stir and clamor, and that our attention is directed to things which God has not commanded, and without which his commandments can readily be kept. It would be satisfactory if we gave the smaller proportion to churches, altars, vigils, bequests, and the like, and let the main stream flow toward God's commandments, so that among Christians charitable deeds done to the poor would shine more brightly than all the churches of wood and stone.

To speak boldly, it is sheer trickery, dangerous, and deceptive to the simple-minded, when bulls, letters, seals, banners,[103] and the like are displayed for the sake of dead stone churches, and the same thing is not done a hundred times more for the sake of needy, living Christians. Beware, therefore, O man! God will not ask you at your death and at the Last Day how much you have left in your will, whether you have given so and so much to churches—although I do not condemn this—but he will say to you, "I was hungry, and you gave me no food; I was naked, and you did not clothe me" [Matt. 25:42-43]. Take these words to heart, dear man! The important thing is whether you have given to your neighbor and treated him well. Beware of show and glitter and color that draw you away from this!

Sixteenth. Pope, bishops, kings, princes, and lords ought to labor for the abolition of these intolerable burdens and impositions. It ought to be established and decreed, either by their own mandate or in a general council,[104] that every town and locality should build and furnish its own churches, towers, and bells, and make provision itself for its own poor. Then begging would

---

102 *Auff zierlichst.*
103 Banners were a part of the indulgence hawkers' paraphernalia. *CL* 1, 237, n. 5.
104 Luther's hope of reform through a general council was expressed more forcefully several months later in *An Open Letter to the Christian Nobility* (1520). *PE* 2, 76-79.

cease entirely,[105] or at least not be done according to the present unhappy custom whereby each locality begs for its churches and its poor in all the other towns. The Holy See at Rome should just be left in peace with its bulls; if it really wanted to attend to its duties it would have plenty of other things to do besides selling bulls and building churches, neither of which is its essential function. God has expressed it plainly in his law, Deuteronomy 15 [:11], "The poor will never cease out of your city." Thus, he has committed to every city its own poor; he will not have men running hither and yon with beggars' sacks, as men now run to St. James[106] and to Rome. Although I am too small a man to give advice to popes and to all the rulers of the world in this matter—and do not think myself that anything will come of it—nevertheless, men ought to know what the proper and needful course should be; it is the duty of the authorities to consider and to do what is necessary for the best government of the common people who are committed to their care.

Seventeenth. A clever little trick has been invented which teaches in a masterly way how this commandment can be evaded and the Holy Spirit deceived. It is this: No one is bound to give to the needy unless they are in extreme want.[107] In addition, they have reserved to themselves the right to discuss and determine what extreme want is. So we learn neither to help nor to give to the needy until they are perishing, starving, freezing to death, or fleeing because of poverty and debts. But this infamous gloss and supplement[108] is confounded by a single word, "What you wish another to do to you, do so to him."[109] No one is so foolish, however, as to be unwilling that anyone should give to him until

---

[105] See pp. 281-282.
[106] The shrine at Santiago de Compostela in Spain, supposed burial place of the apostle James, was one of the most popular pilgrim goals during the Middle Ages. LW 31, 198, n. 73; LW 35, 10, n. 5.
[107] This was the position taken by Johann Eck's 1518 Obelisks in which he had endeavored to refute Luther's Ninety-five Theses. Thomas had declared the giving of alms "in extrema necessitate" to be a matter of precept over against counsel (see p. 82, n. 6). Holl, op. cit., p. 166, n. 1.
[108] The reference is to the objectionable qualifying addition to Christ's command.
[109] Matt. 7:12 and Luke 6:31 are repeatedly cited by Luther as "natural law." See p. 127, n. 117.

such time as the soul is leaving the body or he has run away from his debts, and then help him when he is beyond help. But when it comes to churches, endowments, indulgences, and other things which God has not commanded, then no one is so keen or so diligent in figuring out whether we should give to the church before the tiles fall off the roof, the beams rot, the ceiling caves in, the letters of dispensation molder, or the indulgences rot with age; although all these things could wait more easily than people who are in need. In such matters every hour is instead one of "extreme want," even though all the coffers and storerooms are full, and the buildings in good repair. Indeed, here one must forever be gathering treasure, not to be given or lent to the needy on earth, but for the Holy Cross, for Our Dear Lady, and the Holy Patron, St. Peter, who are in heaven. All this must be done with more than ordinary foresight, so that if the Last Day were never to come the church would be taken care of for a couple hundred thousand years! Thus, in case of need, the canonization of a saint[110] or a bishop's pallium[111] or the like can be bought at the fair[112] in Rome.

---

[110] To possess the relics of a saint, or to have him as the local patron, gave a certain distinction and importance to a church, and proved a good drawing-card for attracting generous pilgrims. Hence, local ecclesiastical authorities were willing to pay a considerable sum for the canonization of a departed bishop or other local dignitary. See Luther's fuller treatment of the subject in his June, 1520, *Open Letter to the Christian Nobility* (*PE* 2, 131-132) and in Hutten's bitter dialogue against Rome, the *Vadiscus* of April, 1520 (*Opera* 4, 232).

[111] The pallium, a white scarf with black crosses, was the emblem of the archbishop's office; at least in theory it was woven from the wool of sheep pastured on the property of the Vatican in Rome, and was obtainable only from the pope. Bestowal of the pallium is a very ancient custom; Gregory I (590-604) referred to it already in his time as an "old custom." Canon 2. *Decreti Magistri Gratiani Prima Pars*, dist. C. *Corpus Iuris Canonici*, I, col. 352. Canon 1 prescribes that the archbishop-elect must secure the pallium from Rome within three months after his election; otherwise, he may not discharge any of the duties of his office. *Ibid.* In Luther's time huge fees, normally about ten thousand gulden for a German archbishop, were exacted for the bestowal of the pallium, which had originally been bestowed gratis. Archbishop Albert of Mainz was charged a much higher pallium fee, and the resulting bargain between Pope Leo X, Albert, and the Fugger banking house which financed him led directly to the sale which precipitated the indulgence controversy with Luther. *PE* 2, 89, n. 3. Schwiebert, *op. cit.*, pp. 306-308. Hutten refers also to the pallium and the role of the Fuggers in the purchase of benefices in his *Vadiscus* (*Opera* 4, 199 and 158).

[112] *Jarmarck* is used here sarcastically; see p. 285, n. 97. Luther frequently

I truly think that the Romans are indeed great fools not to sell canonization, pallia, bulls, and letters at an even higher price and get still more money for them, as long as these fat German fools come to their fair and obligate themselves to buy them; though, to be sure, no Antichrist[113] could collect these treasures on earth[114] more fittingly than the bottomless bag at Rome, into which they are all gathered and categorized. It would grieve me to the heart if these damned sums, taken from the needy to whom they properly belong, were spent for anything but Roman wares. St. Ambrose[115] and Paulinus[116] at one time melted down the chalices and everything that their churches had, and gave it to the poor. Turn over the page, and you will find how things are today. It is fortunate for you, dear Rome, that even though the Germans run short of money, they still have chalices, monstrances,[117] and images enough; and all of them are still yours!

Eighteenth. Now we come to the third degree[118] of dealing with temporal goods. It is this, that we should willingly and gladly lend without charge or zinss.[119] Of this our Lord Jesus Christ says in Matthew 5 [:42], "From him who would borrow from you, turn not away"; that is, do not refuse him. This degree is the lowest of all, and is commanded even in the Old Testament, where God says in Deuteronomy 15 [:7-8], "If any among your brothers in your town becomes poor, you shall not harden your heart or shut your hand against him, but you shall open your

---

uses the term in a derogatory sense to refer to deceitful trade practices. Grimm, *Deutsches Wörterbuch*, IV², 2246.

[113] On Luther's identification of the pope with Antichrist, see p. 60, n. 8.

[114] The allusion is to the treasures amassed by the Antichrist in Dan. 11: 43, 39.

[115] According to tradition, Ambrose (*ca.* 340-397), bishop of Milan, melted down gold vessels belonging to the church to redeem captives taken by the Goths. To the Arian reproach of sacrilege he answered, "If the Church possesses gold it is in order to use it for the needy, not to keep it." Herbert Thurston and Donald Attwater (eds.), *Butler's Lives of the Saints* (4 vols.; New York: Kenedy, 1956), IV, 510-511.

[116] Paulinus (*ca.* 354-431), bishop of Nola, was noted for his charity. He is supposed to have written "the life of Saint Ambrose . . . in a letter to Saint Augustine." *The Golden Legend of Jacobus de Voragine*, I, 25.

[117] The monstrance is a vessel in which the sacred host, i.e., the consecrated wafer, is exposed for the veneration of the faithful. LW 35, 97, n. 30.

[118] See p. 273 and cf. pp. 256-259.

[119] On *zinss* see pp. 234-238.

hand wide and lend him whatever he needs." They have allowed this degree to remain a commandment.[120] For all the doctors agree in this, that borrowing and lending shall be free, without charge or burden;[121] though they do not all agree on the question to whom we ought to lend. For, as was said about the previous degree of giving,[122] here too there are many who gladly lend to the rich or to good friends, more to seek their favor or because they are related to them than because God has commanded it, and especially if it is given the high title spoken of above,[123] namely, "for the worship of God," or, "for God's sake," etc. Everybody gladly lends to the Holy Cross and to Our Dear Lady and the Holy Patron. But there is always trouble and labor about those to whom God's command points; to them no one wants to lend, except in cases of extreme want where lending does no good, as was said above.[124]

Nineteenth. Christ, however, excluded no one from his commandment; indeed, he included all kinds of people, even one's enemies, when he said in Luke 6 [:34], "If you lend only to those from whom you expect a loan in return, what kind of goodness is that? Even wicked sinners lend to one another, to receive as much again." And again, "Lend, expecting nothing in return" [Luke 6:35]. I know very well that a good many doctors have interpreted these words as though Christ had therein commanded to lend in such a way as not to make any charge for it or seek any profit, but to lend gratis.[125] This opinion is doubtless not wrong, for he who makes a charge for lending is not lending, and neither is he selling; therefore, this must be usury, because lending is, in its very nature, nothing else than to offer another something without charge, on the condition that one eventually get back the same thing or its equivalent, and nothing more.

---

[120] See p. 82, n. 6.
[121] The scholastics unanimously condemned loans at interest as usury. They differed in their analysis of the various contracts devised to circumvent the unusual prohibition against usury, but generally came to regard many of them as something other than loans, often sales.
[122] See p. 282.
[123] See pp. 284-285.
[124] See pp. 287-288.
[125] Augustine, Ambrose, and Jerome so interpreted Luke 6:35. Neumann, *op. cit.*, p. 5.

But if we examine the word of Christ closely, it does not teach that we are to lend without charge. There is no need for such teaching, since there is no other kind of lending except that which is without charge; if a charge is made, it is not a loan.[126] What He wants is that we should lend not only to friends, to the rich, and to those we like, who can repay us again by returning the loan, or by lending to us, or some other favor; but that we lend also to those who are unable or unwilling to repay us, such as the needy and our enemies. Just as in his teaching about loving and giving,[127] so also our lending is to be done without personal gain or advantage. This does not happen unless we lend to our enemies and to the needy. For all that He says is aimed to teach us to do good to everyone, that is, not only to those who do good to us, but also to those who treat us ill or cannot do us good in return.

That is what he means when he says, "Lend, expecting nothing in return" [Luke 6:35], that is, you should lend to those who are neither willing nor able to lend to you in return. He who lends expects to receive back the same thing that he lent; if he expects nothing, then, according to their interpretation, it would be a gift and not a loan. It is such a little thing to lend to one who is a friend, or rich, or who may render some service in return, that even sinners who are not Christians do this. Christians therefore ought to do more, and lend to those who do not reciprocate, that is, to enemies and to the needy. And so that doctrine again falls to the ground which says that we are not bound to lay aside the *signa rancoris*, as has been said above.[128] Even though they speak aright concerning lending, they still turn this commandment into a counsel, and teach us that we are not bound to lend to our enemies or to the needy unless they are in extreme want.[129] Beware of this!

Twentieth. From this it follows that they are all usurers who lend their neighbor wine, grain, money, or whatever it may be on such terms that they obligate him to pay *zinssen* on it after

---

126 Cf. the similar statement of Gabriel Biel quoted in *MA*³ 5, 421, n. 146, 9.
127 See Matt. 5:44, 42; Luke 6:27-35.
128 See p. 283, especially n. 92.
129 See pp. 282-283, 287-288.

a year or a specified time interval; or burden or overload him with the obligation of paying back more than he has borrowed, or something else that is better than what he borrowed. In order that these men may themselves perceive how wrong their practice is—despite the fact that it has, unfortunately, become common —we will set before them three laws.

First: This present passage in the gospel [Luke 6:35] which commands us to lend. Now lending is not lending unless it is done without charge and without any advantage to the lender, as has been said. Crafty avarice, to be sure, sometimes camouflages itself beautifully and pretends to accept the surplus as a gift,[130] but this is of no help if that gift is a basis for the loan, or if the borrower would rather not make the gift provided he could borrow gratis. The gift is particularly suspicious if it is the borrower who presents it to the lender—one who lacks to the one who has—for it is not natural to suppose that a needy person would present a gift to a wealthy man of his own free will; it is necessity that forces him to do so.

Second: Charging for a loan is contrary to natural law. The Lord points this out in Luke 6 [:31] and Matthew 7 [:12], "As you wish that men would do to you, do so to them."[131] Now beyond any doubt, there is no one who wants a man to lend him rye to be repaid with wheat, bad money to be repaid with good, or inferior wares to be repaid with good wares. Indeed, he would much rather that a man should lend him good wares to be repaid with bad, or at most with goods of like quality and without additional charge. Therefore, it is clear that such lenders are acting contrary to nature, are guilty of mortal sin, are usurers, and are seeking in their own profit their neighbor's loss; they do not want to be treated this way in return by others, and are therefore dealing unfairly with their neighbor.

Third: It is also against the Old and the New Law, which commands, "You shall love your neighbor as yourself" [Lev. 19:18;

---

130 In the Middle Ages many payments for loans, especially in the case of kings and states, were made as gifts to free the recipient from public odium or prosecution for usury. The scholastics held acceptance of the gift to be licit if it was not hoped for by the creditor, and not given by the debtor for the purpose of obtaining favors. Noonan, op. cit., pp. 104-105.
131 See p. 287, n. 109.

Matt. 22:39]. Such lenders love themselves alone and seek only their own;[132] they do not love and look out for their neighbor with the same fidelity as they love and look out for themselves.

Twenty-first. No better or briefer instruction can therefore be given in this and in any other matters where dealing with temporal goods is concerned, than that everyone who is to have any dealings with his neighbor should keep in mind these commandments: "What you wish another to do to you, do so to him" [Luke 6:31; Matt. 7:12], and, "Love your neighbor as yourself" [Lev. 19:18; Matt. 22:39]; he should consider in addition what he would wish to have for himself if he were in his neighbor's place. If he were to do this he would discover for himself all that he needs to know. There would be no need for lawbooks or courts or complaints; all cases would be decided quickly and simply, since everyone's heart and conscience would tell him how he would like to be dealt with, what he would like to have remitted, what given, and what forgiven. From this he would have to conclude that he ought to do the same for everyone else.

Because we fail to keep our eyes on these commandments, however, and look only at the business deal and its profit or loss, we are bound to have innumerable books, laws, courts, lawsuits, blood, and all sorts of misery. From violation of God's commandments must follow the destruction of God's kingdom, which is peace and unity in brotherly love and faith.[133] And yet these wicked men go about, sometimes praying and fasting, sometimes giving alms; but in this matter, on which salvation depends, they are altogether heedless and carefree, as if this commandment did not apply to them at all, although without it they cannot be saved even if they performed all the other works of all the saints.

Twenty-second. Here we are met with two objections. The first is this: If lending were to be done in this way, the *interesse*[134] would be lost; that is, the profit that could have been made meanwhile from the goods that are loaned. The second is the extensive precedent: everywhere in the world it has become the custom to lend for profit, especially since scholars, priests, clergy, and the

---

132 Cf. I Cor. 13:5.
133 Cf. Rom. 14:17.
134 See p. 298, n. 145.

churches do it with a view to seeking to improve the churches, ecclesiastical property, and divine worship; there would otherwise be very few Christians in the world, and everyone would be reluctant to lend.

Answer: There is nothing to this. In the first place, you have to lose the *interesse* and the profit anyway if the sum is taken from you, or if you give to someone outright.[135] Why, then, do you seek to keep it in the matter of lending? He who decides to give or lend must waive the *interesse* in advance, or it is neither giving nor lending. In the second place, whether the practice be custom or not, it is not Christian or godly or natural, and no precedent can change that fact. For it is written, "You shall not follow a multitude to do evil [Exod. 23:2], but honor God and his commandments above all things."[136] That the clergy and churches do this is so much the worse, for ecclesiastical property and churches have neither authority nor freedom to break God's commandments, rob their neighbor, practice usury, and do wrong; by such means divine worship is not improved, but corrupted. The way to improve divine worship is to keep God's commandments; even notorious scoundrels can improve church property. And even if the whole world had the custom of lending at such charges, the churches and the clergy should do the opposite; the more spiritual their possessions, the more Christian —in accordance with Christ's command—should be the manner in which they lend them, give them, and let them go. He who does otherwise is doing so not to improve the churches or ecclesiastical property but for his own usury-loving greed, which decks itself out with such fine names.

It is no wonder, then, that Christians are few, for here we see who are practicing really good works, although many blind and deceive themselves with their own self-chosen good works, which God has not commanded them to do. If anyone finds, however that these conditions make it hard for him to lend to his neighbor, it is a sign of his great unbelief; he despises the comforting assurance of Christ, who says, "If we lend and give, we are sons of the Most High, and our reward will be great" [Luke

---

135 See pp. 256, 273, 280.
136 Cf. Deut. 5:29; 6:2; Eccles. 12:13; I John 5:2.

6:35]. He who does not believe this comforting promise and make it a guide for his works, is not worthy of it.

Part Two

First. Beneath these three degrees[137] are other degrees and ways[138] of transferring[139] temporal goods, such as buying, bequeathing, conveying, and the like, which are governed by temporal and spiritual law. By these methods no one becomes better or worse in the sight of God, for there is no Christian merit in buying anything, receiving it by inheritance, or acquiring it in some other honest way; since heathen, Turk, and Jew can be equally upright. Christian dealing, however, and the right use of temporal goods consist in the three degrees or ways mentioned above—giving them away, lending them without charge, and calmly letting them go when they are taken by force.

Let us now leave out of consideration all other ways of dealing, and devote our attention to the matter of buying [*den kauff*], in particular the *zinss kauff*[140] since this involves a pretty pretense by which a man can—seemingly without sin—burden others and get rich without worry or effort. In the other ways of dealing each person obviously knows for himself if he is selling too dear, offering inferior wares, securing a legacy by fraud, or trafficking in counterfeit goods. But this slippery and newly-invented business[141] very frequently makes itself an upright and loyal protector of damnable greed and usury.

Second. Although the *zinss* contract is now established as a proper and admissible operation, it is nevertheless an odious and

---

[137] See p. 273.
[138] Cf. pp. 259-261.
[139] *Handeln* here means *überweisen*. CL 3, 35, n. 31.
[140] For an explanation of this term, *Zinskauf*, see the Introduction to this treatise, pp. 234-238.
[141] The *Zinskauf* had developed gradually in the fourteenth and fifteenth centuries out of the earlier practice of *Rentenkauff*, which dated from the twelfth and thirteenth centuries. Neumann, *op. cit.*, pp. 212-292. See below, p. 307, and *An Open Letter to the Christian Nobility* (1520), PE 2, 159, where Luther's figure of "one hundred years" probably has reference to the 1425 bull of Pope Martin V, sanctioning the *Rentenkauff*. Walter E. Köhler, *Die Quellen zu Luthers Schrift 'An den christlichen Adel deutscher Nation'* (Halle: Waisenhaus, 1895), p. 238.

hateful practice for many reasons. In the first place,[142] it is a new and slippery invention, especially in these recent perilous times when nothing good is invented any more, and the thoughts and minds of all men are bent upon wealth and honor and luxury without restraint. We can find no example of this particular contract in olden times, and St. Paul says of these later times that many new, wicked practices will be invented [I Tim. 4:1; II Tim. 3:1-9].

In the second place—as they themselves will have to admit —however legitimate the thing may be, it looks bad and has an offensive appearance. And in I Thessalonians 5 [:22] St. Paul bids us abstain from every evil and offensive appearance, even though the thing itself be right and proper: *Ab omni specie mala abstinete vos;* Avoid every appearance of evil. Now in this contract the advantage of the buyer, or the receiver of *zinss*, is invariably looked upon as greater and better and more desirable than that of the seller, or the payer of *zinss*. This is a sign that the transaction is never made for the sake of the seller, but always for the sake of the buyer; for every man's conscience suspects that it may not be right to buy *zinss*, but no one has any doubt that he can give away or sell what is his own at any risk he cares to take. So perilously close does this purchase contract come to the conscience!

In the third place, even if the transaction involved no usury, it can scarcely be made without violating natural law and the law of Christian love. For it may be assumed that with his purchase the buyer is seldom if ever seeking and desiring the welfare and advantage of his neighbor—the seller—as much as or more than his own, especially when the buyer is the richer of the two and has no need for such a contract. Yet natural law says that what we wish and desire for ourselves, we shall wish and desire for our neighbor also and it is the nature of love (as St. Paul says in I Corinthians 13 [:5]) not to seek its own benefit or advantage, but that of others. Who is to believe that in this business anyone buys *zinss* (unless he absolutely needs it) with a view to giving his neighbor—the seller—a profit and advantage equal to

---

142 This is the first of five minor points made under the second of twelve major points.

his own? Why, in all likelihood the buyer would not want to be in the seller's place at all, as in the case of other purchase transactions.

In the fourth place, everyone will have to admit that whether this contract is usury or not, it accomplishes exactly the same thing that usury accomplishes, that is, it lays burdens upon all lands, cities, lords, and people, sucks them dry, and brings them to ruin as no usury could have done. We see this plainly in many a city and principality. Now the Lord taught not that the fruit is known by its tree but that the tree is known by its fruit [Matt. 7:16-20]. I cannot possibly think you are a sweet fig tree when you bear nothing but sharp thorns; and I cannot reconcile the claim that *zinss kauff* of this sort is right with the fact that land and people are ruined by it.

In the fifth place, let us for the sake of argument imagine, or dream, or force ourselves to think that this contract as presently practiced, is right and proper. Even so, it deserves that the effort be made by pope, bishops, emperor, princes, and everybody else to have it abolished; and it is the duty of everyone who can prevent it to do so because of its evil and damnable fruits, which burden and ruin the whole world.

Third. It is not enough that this contract should be rescued by canon law from the taint of usury,[143] for that does not free it or protect it from greed and self-love; and from canon law we learn that it is not directed toward love, but toward self-seeking. Money won by gambling is not usury either; yet it is not won without self-seeking, self-love, and sin. The profits of prostitution are not usury either; yet they are earned by sin. And wealth that is acquired by cursing, swearing, and slander is not usury either; yet it is acquired by sin. Therefore, I cannot conclude that *zinss* purchasers who have no real need for such *zinss*

---

[143] The formal recognition by Pope Martin V (see p. 295, n. 141) of the legality of interest charges in contracts of sale was reaffirmed by Pope Calixtus III in 1455. Both bulls were incorporated into the canon law: *Extrav. comm.* lib. iii, tit. V, 1-2. *Corpus Iuris Canonici*, II, cols. 1269-1272. Pope Martin's decretal related to a specific case arising in the Breslau diocese; it sanctioned a *Zins* contract secured by a specifically-named property and carrying the privilege of full redemption at any time at the discretion of the debtor, a *contractus emptionis et venditionis*. *MA*[3] 5, 422, n. 151, 1.

are acting rightly and properly. Indeed, I make bold to say and give warning that the rich, who use this contract only to increase their incomes and their wealth despite the fact that it places a burden upon others, are in grave danger. Nor do I think it is permissible for them to do what some greedy-bloated fellows[144] do: they collect their *zinss* at stated times and immediately reinvest it in more *zinss,* so that one *zinss* is always driving the other along, as water drives the mill wheel. This is such open and unashamed greed that no one, however stupid, can deny that it is greed; yet it is all held to be right and proper. If there were no other reason to regard the *zinss kauff* as usury, or at least as a crooked business, especially in a case like this, this one reason would be enough, namely, that it cloaks open and shameless greed and lets it function with impunity. Whatever is of God checks sin and all manner of evil. But this transaction gives free rein to avarice; therefore, it cannot, as presently practiced, be of God.

Fourth. Now we will take a look at the arguments by which this dainty business is justified. There is in Latin a little word called *interesse.*[145] This noble, precious, tender little word may be translated into German this way, "I have a hundred gulden with which I could go into business and by my care and effort make five or six gulden or more a year. Instead, I place it with

---

[144] *Geytzige blassen.* Cf. p. 85, n. 15.

[145] Roman jurists, followed by the early canonists, held that *quod interest* (literally, "that which is the difference")—the single substantive *interesse* introduced by Laurentius Hispanus became standard from about 1220 on—was distinct from *usura* in kind rather than degree. *Usura* was prohibited as a special payment on a loan. *Interesse* was allowed on the injured party's damages on any contract due to the other party's default, i.e., something purely compensatory. Noonan, *op. cit.,* p. 106.

Interest as understood today—as due from the beginning of a loan—came very gradually to be defended by some canonists and theologians in the fourteenth century under the titles of *damnum emergens* ("loss or damage incurred") and *lucrum cessans* ("profit ceasing or lost") as a result of lending; chief cause of the new attitude was the need to justify the financial practices of the Italian city states. *Ibid.,* pp. 115, 121.

A long step toward the formal approval of interest was taken by Pope Leo X's bull *Inter multiplices* at the Fifth Lateran Council of 1516. Over Dominican and Augustinian objection, it sanctioned the *montes pietatis* ("mounts of piety") which were in effect low interest-charging public pawn shops, championed and fostered by Franciscans to protect poor Christians against the high-interest charging, truly usurious moneylenders. *Ibid.,* pp. 299-300.

someone else on a productive property, so that not I but he can put it to work there. In return for doing this I take from him five gulden, the amount which I might otherwise have earned. Thus, he is selling me the *zinss*—five gulden for a hundred—and I am the buyer and he the seller." Here they now say that the *zinss* contract is proper because, with the same money, I might perhaps have made more in a year; and the *interesse* is just and satisfactory. All this seems so pretty that no one can find fault with it at any point. But it is also true that this kind of *interesse* is not possible on earth because there is another kind which runs counter to it, like this: If I have a hundred gulden with which to do business, I may run into a hundred kinds of risks. I may make no profits at all, or even lose four times as much to boot in trying to save my original investment. Or on account of illness I may not be able to work. Or there may be no wares or goods available. Hindrances of this sort are innumerable, as we see. The result is failures, losses, and damages greater than any profits. Thus the "interest" in the losses is as great or greater than the "interest" in the profits.

Fifth. Now if *zinss* is bought solely on the interest of profit, whereby no risk or effort is entailed and the buyer can never lose more than he invests—and thus the money is invested as though it could be wholly and always free from the interest of loss—it is clear that the contract has no actual basis. This kind of *interesse* simply does not exist and cannot be found. In a transaction of this sort the buyer finds goods always on hand; he can do business if he is sitting down or is sick, whether he be a child or a woman, and no matter how incompetent he may be—none of which is possible in business. You cannot make money just with money.[146] For this reason those who are seeking to do busi-

---

[146] The sterility of money, proposed by Aristotle (see p. 233, n. 1) and espoused in Roman law, had first become a canon of the church when in about 1180 the fifth century *Palea, Ejiciens,* was incorporated in the *Decreti Gratiani.* See the text in Noonan, *op. cit.,* pp. 38-39 and in *Decreti Prima Pars,* dist. LXXXVIII, can. 11. *Corpus Iuris Canonici,* I, col. 309. Along with the criterion of the incidence of risk (see p. 304, n. 150), it was one of the two great pillars of usury theory. Noonan, *op. cit.,* p. 202. It was accepted by Aquinas on the theory that "the use of money is not other than its substance"; money was thus juridically, though not economically, sterile in a loan. *Ibid.,* pp. 54-56. The notion that money might at times be a source

ness only in this one kind of interest are worse than usurers: for they are buying the interest of profit and paying for it with the interest of loss, and thus making their gains at the expense of other people's losses.

Again, since it is not possible to define, compute, and calculate this other *interesse*, which is not within the power of man, I do not see how the *zinss* contract can stand up. For who would not rather invest a hundred gulden at *zinss* than do business with it. In business he might lose twenty gulden in a year and his capital besides, while in the *zinss* contract he cannot lose more than five, and still keeps his capital. Moreover, in business his money must often lie idle for lack of goods or markets or because of physical infirmity, while in the *zinss* contract it is active and earning all the time.

Is it any wonder, then, that a man gathers in the wealth of the whole world when at no cost he has goods always on hand, and enjoys constant security and less risk, with his capital fully protected from the outset? Time is bound to reward heavily him who has an unfailing supply of goods, just as it penalizes heavily him who can neither procure goods nor market them. Hence, money engaged in business and money put out at *zinss* are two different things, and the one cannot be compared with the other. The latter has a base which is constantly growing and producing profit out of the earth without any fear of capital losses; while there is nothing certain about the former, and the only interest it yields is accidental and cannot be counted on.

Here they will perhaps say that because they are investing money on land as a base there is an interest of loss as well as an interest of profit, inasmuch as the *zinss* stands or falls with the stability of the base on which it rests. This is all true, and we shall hear more about it below. But the fact remains that money invested with land as a base appreciates with respect to the interest of profit and depreciates with respect to the interest of loss far more than money employed directly in a business, for, as was said

---

of gain, while implicit in Thomas' *Summa* and in his commentary on the *Sentences,* did not receive clear statement until Cajetan's conditional defense of *lucrum cessans* in the sixteenth century. *Ibid.,* pp. 110, 252-255. Luther called money a "sterile thing" in his *Table Talk* of 1542. WA, TR 5, 146.

above, there is far more risk involved in trade than in land. Since with the same money one cannot always buy an identical plot of ground, so with the same money one cannot always purchase the same *zinss*. Therefore, it is not enough to say, "With so much money I could earn so much income from a piece of land, and therefore, it is proper for me to take so much *zinss* instead and let someone else look after the land"; for in that way one would be equating a particular sum of money with a fixed land value, which is impossible. The result would necessarily be great hardship for land and people.

Sixth. No wonder that the *zinss* contractors quickly become richer than other people. The others keep their money tied up in business and hence subject to both kinds of interest, while the *zinss* contractors by this little device extricate themselves from the interest of loss and enter into the first interest of profit, where their risk is greatly reduced and their security increased. For this reason there should be a prohibition against the purchase of *zinss* with money alone, without specific indication and definition of the land on which it is based, as is now the custom among the big merchants who go ahead and put out money on a base which is general and undefined. By so doing they ascribe to the very nature of money something which is only accidental to it, and a matter of chance. It is not in the nature of money to buy land. It is simply that a piece of land may happen to become saleable for *zinss* just at the time when there is some money available for use. That does not happen with all land, or with all money. Therefore, the piece of land ought to be specified and exactly defined. If that were done, it would become clearly evident that much money would have to remain in business or in the coffers without *zinss*, money which today is producing *zinss* without any other right or pretext than that they say in general, "With this amount I can contract for so much *zinss* on a piece of land." And that is supposed to be called *interesse!* Yes, my dear fellow, my money can buy my neighbor's house; but if it is not for sale, the power of my money and its interest is worthless. In the same way, it is not the luck of all money to buy *zinss* on a piece of land. Yet some people want to buy *zinss* on everything that can be used; they are usurers, thieves, and robbers, for they are selling the money's luck, which is not theirs or within their power.

"But," you say, "money is capable of buying *zinss* on a piece of land." Answer: It is not doing so yet, and perhaps it will never be able to do so. Hans is capable of taking a Gretchen, but if he does not yet have her he is not yet married. Your money is capable of buying *zinss;* that is half of the matter. But the deal depends on the rest of it—the acceptance and the other half. I do not take a half for the whole. Yet the rich merchants are now trying to sell their money's good fortune—wholly divorced from any bad fortune—and along with it the will and intentions of other people, on which their desire to sell depends. That is what you call selling the thirteenth bearskin.[147]

Seventh. I say further that it is not enough that the base of the contract actually exist and be named, but it must be clearly indicated, item by item, and the money and *zinss* specifically related to each piece, as for example the house, the garden, the field, the pond, the cattle—all still free, unsold, unencumbered. They must not play the blind cow in general and encumber the property in its entirety. For where this itemizing is not done, there a poor man or a city[148] is inevitably sold in the same package and utterly ruined by the indiscriminate contract, as we see happening today in many a city and domain.

The reason is this: A city's trade may decline, citizens become fewer, houses burn down, farms, fields, and all its land be dissipated; the goods and cattle of every householder may diminish while his children become more numerous; or he may be burdened with some other misfortune. Thus, the wealth slips away, but the indiscriminate contract, based on the entire property in general, remains. And so the property left over, small and poor as it is, must bear the burden and expense formerly borne by the whole

---

[147] This colloquial expression refers to selling what you do not possess.

[148] Between the *zinss* contract founded on a real estate base and tied to specific property, on the one hand, and the personal *zinss* contract founded on the returns of the debtor's own labor, on the other hand, there was the *zinss* contract founded not on any particular goods but on all the goods—indiscriminately considered—of the seller, who could be either an individual or a community; the latter, e.g., could found a *zinss* contract on its tax revenues. It was a decision of Pope Nicholas V in 1452 which first legitimized this kind of a *zinss* contract. Noonan, *op. cit.,* pp. 159-161.

lot in its entirety. This of necessity can never be right. The buyer is then assured of his *zinss* and takes no risk, which is contrary to the nature of any purchase transaction. This would not be the case if the property were itemized; the *zinss* would then fluctuate or remain constant with its respective base, as is right.

Eighth. The only way of defending this contract against the charge of usury—a way that would accomplish more than all the talk about *interesse*—would be that the *zinss* contractor should have the same risk and uncertainty with respect to his *zinss* as he has with respect to all his other property. For as regards his other property the *zinss* buyer is subject to the power of God—death, illness, flood, fire, wind, hail, lightning, rain, wolves, wild beasts, and the manifold losses inflicted by wicked men. All these risks should apply to the receiver of *zinss*, for upon this kind of base and no other does his *zinss* rest. Neither has he any right to receive *zinss* for his money unless the payer of the *zinss*—the seller of the property—specifically agrees, and can have free, adequate, and unhindered use of his own labor.

This is verified from reason, nature, and all laws, which unanimously affirm that in any sale transaction the risk lies with the buyer,[149] for the seller is not under obligation to guarantee his wares to the buyer. Thus, when I buy *zinss* on a specified piece of land, I buy not the land but the *zinss* payer's toil and effort on that land, by which he is to bring me my *zinss*. Hence, I am involved in all the risks by which his labor may be hindered—insofar as they do not occur through his own fault or negligence—whether they be the elements, beasts, men, sickness, or anything else. In these matters the seller of the *zinss* has just as great "interest" as the buyer, so that if, after exercising due diligence, his labor is unprofitable, he can and ought to say frankly to the buyer, "This year I owe you nothing, for I sold you my toil and effort for the production of income from such and such property; I have not succeeded. The loss is yours, not mine; for if you want to have an interest in my profits you must also have an interest in my losses, as the nature of every transaction requires." Any *zinss* buyers who will not put up with that are as righteous

---

[149] This is the ancient principle of *caveat emptor*.

THE CHRISTIAN IN SOCIETY

as robbers and murderers, wresting from the poor man his property and living. Woe to them!

Ninth. From this it follows that the indiscriminate *zinss* contract which is not founded upon an existent and itemized base but on a lot of properties in general all taken together is wrong. For since it cannot be shown on which items the contract is based, the buyer also assumes no risk but always collects; whether or not the income fails here and there, he wants to be assured of his *zinss*.

Perhaps you will say, "If it were to be done this way, who would ever contract for *zinss*?" See there! I knew perfectly well that human nature would turn up its nose at doing what is right. Now it comes out that in this *zinss* contract nothing is sought but security, greed, and usury. O how many cities, lands, and people are having to pay *zinss*, whose debts ought long since to have been forgiven! If this matter of risk is excluded from the *zinss* contract it is plain and simple usury.[150] They just go on endowing churches, monasteries, altars, and this and that, and yet there is no end or limit to this buying of *zinss*; just as if it were possible for property, persons, luck, production, and labor to be the same every year—no matter how they fluctuate, the *zinss* must go on at the same rate! Is this not going to ruin land and people? I am amazed that with this boundless usury the world still stands! The world has really progressed: what was formerly called an enfeoffment has now been changed into a *zinss kauff!*[151]

Tenth. This *zinss* contract at times involves purchase from those who really need to have something loaned or given to them instead. Then it is fundamentally null and void, for God's commandment stands in the way and directs that the needy shall be helped by loans and gifts. At other times it happens that both buyer and seller need their property and can therefore neither

---

[150] Along with the sterility of money (see p. 299, n. 146), the incidence of risk—risk and ownership were usually identified—was one of the two great pillars of the scholastic theory of usury. Noonan, *op. cit.*, pp. 202-203. Acceptance of insurance and the triple contract (see p. 252, n. 22) meant the definitive rejection of the theses that any temporary riskless transfer of property was usury and that the incidence of risk was the criterion of ownership. Noonan, *op. cit.*, pp. 81, 151-152, 229.

[151] See pp. 234-238.

lend nor give, but have to help themselves by means of the *kauff* transaction. If this can be done without violating canon law, which provides for the payment of four, five, or six gulden on the hundred,[152] it may be tolerated. But they should always have the fear of God in mind, and be afraid of taking too much rather than too little, so that greed may not become a factor in addition to the security of a reasonable purchase contract. The smaller the percentage the more godly and Christian the contract.

It is not my task, however, to point out when one ought to pay 5, 4, or 6 per cent.[153] I leave it to the law to determine when the property is so good and so rich that one may charge 6 per cent. It is my opinion, however, that if we tried to keep Christ's commandment in the first three degrees,[154] the *zinss* contract would not be so common or so necessary, except in cases where the amounts were very considerable and the properties large. But it has made its way into the groschen and pfennings, and deals with insignificant sums that could easily be dispensed by gifts or loans in accordance with Christ's command. Yet it refuses to be called greed!

Eleventh. There are some who not only deal in insignificant properties but also charge too high a rate:[155] 7, 8, 9, or 10 per cent. The rulers ought to look into this. Here the poor common folk are secretly fleeced and severely oppressed. This is also why these robbers and usurers often die an unnatural and sudden

---

[152] While public usurers generally charged from 32½ to 43½ per cent in Italy —as in the small loan business in modern America—the *montes pietatis* (see p. 298, n. 145) were customarily charging 6 per cent at the time they began to receive papal approval, beginning with Pope Paul II in 1467. Their payments of from 4 to 6 per cent on deposits as a means of supplementing their capital was first formally approved by Pope Paul III in 1542. Noonan, *op. cit.*, pp. 295, 258 and 34, n. 83. The remarkable thing here is that Luther, who was a sworn enemy of the canon law and would soon consign it to the flames (see *LW* 31, 381), was led by his keen sense of justice to a vigorous assertion of the canonical determinations on usury in opposition to the casuists' hair-splitting attempts to circumvent the very laws they were pledged to uphold. *BG* 7, 501.

[153] The contract most common in Germany, defended by Johann Eck, was currently bearing 5 per cent, a fact from which it derived its name. See p. 252, n. 22.

[154] See Luther's interpretation of Matt. 5:40 and 42 on pp. 273-295 and 255-261.

[155] In a *Table Talk* of June 14, 1542 Luther allowed interest up to 7 per cent because of the general price increase. *WA*, TR 5, 147.

death,[156] or come to some other terrible end, as tyrants and robbers deserve; for God is a judge for the poor and needy, as he says frequently in the Old Law.

But then they advance this argument, "The churches and the clergy do this and have done it, because this money is used in the service of God." If this is the best thing that can be cited in justification of usury, it is also true that nothing worse could ever be said of it. For it is an effort to bracket the innocent church and clergy in sin with usury, and drag them down to the devil. Leave the name of the church out of it, and say: It is usury-seeking greed that does it, or the indolent Old Adam that does not like to work to earn its bread, and makes the name of the church a cloak for idleness.

And what sort of "service of God" are you talking about? To serve God is to keep his commandment and not steal, rob, take increase, and the like, but give and lend to the needy. You would tear down this genuine service of God in order to build churches, endow altars, have masses chanted, and prayers read, none of which God has commanded; thus, with your "service of God" you bring the true service of God to naught. Let the service that God has commanded take precedence, and that which you have chosen bring up the rear. As I have said above, even if everybody were to charge 10 per cent, ecclesiastical institutions should still keep strictly to the law and—with fear—take 4 or 5 per cent. For they are supposed to shine [Matt. 5:16] and give a good example to the worldly. But they turn things around and want to be free to ignore the commandments and service of God in order to do evil and practice usury. If you want to serve God your way, then serve him without injuring your neighbor, and by keeping God's commandments. For he says in Isa. 61 [:8]: "I am a God who loves justice; I hate robbery for burnt offering." And the Wise Man says: "Give alms of that which is thine." [157] But such overcharges are a theft from your neighbor, contrary to God's commandment.

---

156 See p. 255.
157 See Luther's later (1524) quotation of Luke 11:41 on p. 259; cf. n. 38. His ascription of the verse to Solomon is in error, though he might have been thinking of the apocryphal passage in Tob. 4:7.

Twelfth. If anyone fears that the churches and their institutions would retrogress if this view were to be implemented, I say it is better to make of ten institutions one that is in accord with God's will, than to keep many that contravene his commandment. What good does the service of God do you, which you hear to be contrary to God, his commandment, and the true service of God? You cannot serve one God with two contradictory kinds of service any more than you can serve two masters [Matt. 6:24].

There are also some who are so utterly simple that they sell this *zinss* apart from any land or other security, or they sell more than the land can produce, which leads to evident ruin. This is a serious problem, so widespread that one can scarcely say enough about it. The best thing would be to turn back to the gospel, follow it, and deal with property in the Christian manner we have described.[158]

Moreover, there is in this contract a perilous intention,[159] from which I fear none of the *zinss* buyers, or at least very few of them, are free, and that is the desire that their *zinss* and property be secure and assured. This is why they invest their money with others instead of keeping it and taking risks. They much prefer to have others do the work and take the risks, so they themselves can be lazy and idle, and yet remain or become rich. If that is not usury, it is mighty close to it. Briefly put, it is against God. For if you seek to take an advantage of your neighbor which you would not want him to take of you, then love is gone and natural law broken. I am afraid that in *zinss* contracts we pay precious little heed to our neighbor's welfare,

---

[158] See pp. 255–61, 273–95.

[159] Intention was always a significant criterion in scholastic theology. In the early period only loans made from charity or under compulsion, without hope of gain, were recognized as licit; mental usury in itself was sin quite apart from any overt act. The motive of charity as opposed to profit was essential in the scholastic analyses which ultimately justified the various circumventions of the usury prohibition, such as the *lucrum cessans* (see p. 298, n. 145, and p. 299, n. 146). Summenhart justified the *zinss* contract if the purchaser intended to buy not money but the right to money. Beginning with Cajetan, the early sixteenth century scholastics began to reject the necessity of a charitable intention and simply presume that the investor or lender had the intention to gain a contract which in itself was honest and nonusurious. Hence, the existent economic contracts, which on their face might have been considered loans at usury, were justified on the grounds of implicit contracts and intentions. Noonan, *op. cit.*, pp. 32–33, 233–234, 252–255, 269–279.

if only our own *zinss* and our own property are secure, though this is the very thing we ought not to seek. This is certainly a sign of greed or laziness which, although it does not make the contract worse, is still a sin in the eyes of God.[160]

Back in Saxony, Lüneberg, and Holstein, the business is conducted so crudely that one would scarcely be surprised if one man devoured another. There they not only take 9 or 10 per cent or as much as they can get, but they have hitched onto it a special device, namely this: If a man lets me have a thousand gulden for *zinss*, I have to take instead of hard cash so many horses and cows, or so much bacon, wheat, etc. (that he cannot get rid of otherwise, or cannot sell for so high a price). So the money I get amounts to scarcely half the sum named, say about five hundred gulden in hard cash. Still I must pay *zinss* on a thousand gulden, although the goods and cattle are of no use to me, and may bring in scarcely one or two hundred gulden. Ei, these fellows are not highway robbers or swivel-chair robbers,[161] but common house thieves and rustlers. What shall we say about this? They are not men at all, but wolves and irrational beasts, who do not believe there is a God.

In a word, there is no better advice for all this usury and unjust *zinss* than to hark back to the law and example of Moses.[162] We ought to bring all these interest charges again under the ordinance that the amount to be charged, sold, put up, or given

---

[160] Luther's 1520 treatise, *Usury*, originally ended at this point. What follows is the supplement appended to it in 1524 when it was published as a part of our present composite treatise, *Trade and Usury*. See p. 273, n. 65. The translation of this supplement is a revision of that given in PE 4, 67-69, on the basis of the original given in WA 15, 321-322.

[161] Luther applies the term *stul reuber* to usurers, as those who perpetrate their robbery while seated on an office stool. In his *Large Catechism* of 1529 (see Tappert, *op. cit.*, p. 396, n. 9) and again in his 1540 *Admonition to the Clergy, That They Preach Against Usury* (WA 51, 361) Luther derives the term from "*Stuhl*" ("stool") and "*Räuber*" ("robber"). Dr. Pietsch, WA editor of the present treatise, holds that Luther is mistaken, however; that the term derives rather from the Middle Low German "*Stôl*," meaning capital that is loaned out at interest, and that a "*Stôlrover*" is simply a usurer who carries on his robbery by exacting (exorbitant) interest. WA 15, 321, n. 1.

[162] Cf. Luther's statement of about a year later describing *How Christians Should Regard Moses* (1525), in which the tithe and the jubilee year are praised as fine examples which Christians would be wise—though they are not bound—to follow. LW 35, 166-167.

shall be the tithe; or (in the case of need) the ninth, or eighth, or sixth. Then everything would be perfectly consistent, and all would depend on the grace and blessing of God. If the tithe turned out well in any year, it would bring the recipient of *zinss* a good sum; if it turned out badly, it would bring in but little. The creditor would thus have to bear both risk and good fortune as well as the debtor, and both of them would have to look to God. In this way the amount of the *zinss* could not be fixed, nor would that be necessary. Instead, it would always remain uncertain how much the tithe would yield, and yet the tithe itself would be certain.

The tithe is, therefore, the best *zinss* of all. It has been in use since the beginning of the world, and in the Old Law is praised and confirmed as the fairest of all arrangements according to divine and natural law. Following that, if the tithe ran short or were not enough, one could take the ninth, and sell or pledge and encumber it according as a land or house is able. Joseph required the taking of the fifth in Egypt, or found it to have been both required and customary from of old [Gen. 41:34; 47:24, 26]. By this arrangement the divine law of equity always prevails, that the lender take the risk. If things turn out well, the fifth is a goodly amount; if things turn out badly, it is proportionately less, according as God gives; it is not a fixed and certain sum.

Now that the *zinss* purchase is predicated on a fixed and certain amount—all years reckoned the same, good and bad alike —both land and people must necessarily be ruined. For the *zinss* contract changes and buys unequal years for equal years, and poor years for prosperous years. In fact, for something already given it buys a blessing that God has not yet given. That can never be right, for by that means one sucks up the other's blood and sweat. It is no wonder that in these few years that the *zinskauff* has been in operation, say about a hundred years,[163] all principalities and lands have been impoverished and mortgaged and ruined.

But if the contract or the *zinss* were based not on crops but on houses or places where manual labor is done, the purchase

---

[163] See p. 295, n. 141.

could once more be governed in accordance with the law of Moses by having a jubilee year in such cases, and not selling things in perpetuity. I think that since this business is in such a disorganized state we could have no better precedent or laws than the laws which God provided for his people and by which he governed them [Lev. 25:10ff.]. He is certainly as wise as human reason can be, and we need not be ashamed to keep and follow the law of the Jews in this matter, since it is useful and good.

Emperor, kings, princes, and lords ought to watch over this matter, look after their lands and people, and help and rescue them from the gaping jaws of usury; it would make things that much better for them, too. The diets should be dealing with this as one of the most pressing matters; instead, they just let it lie,[164] and in the meantime serve the papal tyranny, burdening lands and people more and more heavily as time goes on. But they will necessarily go to destruction themselves one day, when the land can no longer endure them but has to spew them out. God give them his light and grace. Amen.

---

[164] The failure of the diets of Nürnberg in 1522 and 1524 to take any effective action against the monopolies was one of the factors which led Luther to publish this 1524 treatise. See the Introduction, pp. 241-242.

EXPOSITION OF PSALM 127, FOR THE CHRISTIANS AT RIGA IN LIVONIA

1524

Translated by Walther I. Brandt

INTRODUCTION

At the opening of the sixteenth century Livonia, the territory which in modern times includes the Baltic lands of Latvia, Lithuania, and Esthonia,[1] was ruled by a branch of the Teutonic Order.[2] Ecclesiastical authority was exercised by the archbishop of Riga and his suffragan bishops in Dorpat and Reval.[3] Lutheran ideas began to seep into Livonia quite early,[4] especially among the German burghers in the towns, who eagerly read Luther's pamphlets. The impulse toward constructive reform work in Livonia came from Pomerania, indirectly through Johann Bugenhagen,[5] and directly through his colleague, Andreas Knopken.[6]

[1] Otto Pohrt, *Reformationsgeschichte Livlands* ("Schriften des Vereins für Reformationsgeschichte," Jahrgang 46, Heft 2, No. 124 [Leipzig: Heinsius, 1928]), p. 1.
[2] On the Teutonic Order, see in this volume, pp. 133-134.
[3] During the events leading up to the publication of the present treatise the archbishop of Riga was Jasper Linde (1509-1524); Dorpat and Reval were administered by a single bishop, Johann Blankenfeld (d. 1527), who succeeded Archbishop Linde in 1524. The Livonian Master of the Teutonic Knights from 1494 to 1535 was Walter von Plettenberg.
[4] For a brief survey covering the introduction of the Reformation into Livonia see Pohrt, *op. cit.* A more detailed account is given in L. Arbusov, *Die Einführung der Reformation in Liv-, Est-, und Kurland* ("Quellen und Forschungen zur Reformationsgeschichte," vol. 3 [Leipzig, 1921]).
[5] Bugenhagen (1485-1558) attended the University of Greifswald, where he came under the influence of the humanist Hermann von Busch (Latinized to Buschius). From 1504 to 1521 he was master of the Latin school at Treptow in northern Pomerania, which drew students from Livonia. In 1518 he published a history of Pomerania in which he took occasion to attack indulgence abuses and to uphold the sole authority of the Bible. Chancing to receive a copy of Luther's *Babylonian Captivity of the Church* (1520) which had been sent to the local pastor by a Leipzig friend, he was first shocked but then became enthused over its contents; he soon won over the pastor, the abbot of the local monastery, and his colleague and former pupil Andreas Knopken. In 1521 he went to Wittenberg, where he joined the university faculty. He succeeded Luther in the pulpit in 1523, a position which he held until a year before his death. It was Bugenhagen who performed Luther's wedding ceremony in 1525, and who preached his funeral sermon in 1546.
[6] Knopken (*ca.* 1468-1539) studied at Treptow and from 1514 to 1517 was Bugenhagen's assistant in the Latin school. His brother Jakob went to Riga soon after 1509 and became a canon at St. Peter's Church. About 1517 Andreas went to Riga to be his brother's chaplain; preaching in St. Peter's for two years, he had occasion to observe conditions which seemed to call

When Knopken had to leave Pomerania for Riga in 1521, he began to preach reformed doctrines, and succeeded in winning the support of some influential citizens. Archbishop Linde, a mild and now elderly man, does not appear to have offered any strong opposition. On June 12, 1522, under the burgomaster's protection, Knopken disputed with the Catholic clergy in St. Peter's Church before the whole congregation;[7] a few months later the Riga city council appointed him archdeacon of St. Peter's where his inaugural sermon was preached on October 23, 1522.

Bishop Blankenfeld of Dorpat and Reval, younger and more aggressive than his ecclesiastical superior, had the Edict of Worms (1521) proclaimed in his territories. The city council of Reval protested against this, apparently on political grounds, for at that time none of the councilmen seems to have been a follower of Luther. At the Landtag in Wolmar in June, 1522, the prelates tried to persuade the assembly to condemn Luther's doctrines, but the knighthood and burghers insisted that such legislation should await the pronouncement of a general council. They declared that they would tolerate no mandate or ban in this or any other matter, since Livonia had been won by the secular sword, not by the ban.[8] The order maintained strict neutrality in the dispute between the people and the prelates.[9]

Johann Lohmüller,[10] who as secretary to the Wolmar Landtag was influential in blocking the prelates' effort to have Luther's doctrines condemned, wrote Luther on August 20, 1522, saying that Livonia was a candidate for the word of faith, that a good many of Luther's writings were known there and eagerly read, and that Riga was taking the lead. He concluded by requesting

---

for reform. In 1519 he was back at Treptow, and in the following year, through Bugenhagen's influence, was won over to Lutheranism. Under pressure from the civil and ecclesiastical authorities he left for Riga in 1521 where he remained until his death. Pohrt, *op. cit.*, pp. 20-25; *Allgemeine deutsche Biographie*, XVI, 324. See also D. F. Hoerschelmann, *Andreas Knopken, der Reformator Rigas* (Leipzig, 1896).

[7] See Knopken's twenty-four theses in Pohrt, *op. cit.*, pp. 114-125.

[8] *WA* 12, 143-144.

[9] Pohrt, *op. cit.*, p. 27.

[10] The place and date of Lohmüller's birth are unknown. He became chancellor to Archbishop Linde in 1517 and secretary of the Riga city council in 1520, and was from the beginning a strong supporter of Knopken. *Allgemeine deutsche Biographie*, XIX, 126-129.

Luther to encourage the brethren in Livonia by sending them a letter, mentioning them in his writing, or dedicating to them some devotional treatise.[11] Luther apparently delayed his reply, for Lohmüller wrote him again in the fall of 1523,[12] stating that he had waited more than a year for a reply, and feared that his first letter must have failed to reach Luther; he therefore renewed his request for a "godly treatise."

Luther's long-delayed reply to Lohmüller's first letter took the form of a brief address *To the Christians in Riga, Reval, and Dorpat*,[13] written probably in September of 1523, in which there is no mention of Lohmüller. It was sent to Riga in printed form as a sort of "open letter," and was received on November 11. Luther speaks of having learned of affairs in Livonia "from letters and by word of mouth." "Letters" presumably refers to Lohmüller's first letter; "by word of mouth" may refer to the messenger who delivered that letter, or it may refer to two students from Livonia who are listed in the Wittenberg University records as being in attendance in the spring and summer of 1523.[14] The burgomaster and the Riga council replied promptly on the same day, thanking Luther for his letter to the Livonian Christians, mentioning that Lohmüller had previously written to him, and repeating Lohmüller's request.[15]

Luther received the letter of November 11 from the Riga council shortly before February 1, 1524, and he replied by dedicating to them the present treatise on the 127th Psalm, which was probably composed in the latter half of 1524, and came from the press before the end of the year. The choice of this particular psalm probably was not dictated by anything connected with the situation in Riga—at least nothing of that sort is mentioned in the treatise—but by Luther's general concern about the covetousness which was everywhere manifesting itself in the inadequate support

---

[11] See the text of Lohmüller's letter in WA, Br 2, 591-592.

[12] See the truncated text of this second letter in WA, Br 3, 189-190. It must have been written before November 11, the date on which the Riga council finally received Luther's reply to Lohmüller's first letter. If this second letter was ever completed and sent it must have crossed Luther's letter to the Riga council.

[13] See the text in WA 12, 147-150, and in S-J 2, 199-202.

[14] WA 12, 146.

[15] See the text in WA, Br 3, 192-194.

being given to schools and pastors, about which Luther was constantly complaining about this time.[16]

Luther had already dealt with Psalm 127 in his *Dictata super Psalterium* 1513-1516.[17] In 1534 he published a more extensive and learned interpretation of it in Latin;[18] this reawakened interest in the more popular treatise of 1524, for in that year a new edition appeared which included a new translation of the psalm based upon the complete German Bible published in 1534, and a hymn— probably by Lazarus Spengler[19]—based on the psalm, which we have here omitted though it is included in WA 15, 378-379.

The following translation, the first into English, is based on the original Wittenberg printing of Lucas Cranach, *Der hundert und Sieben und zwentzigst psalm ausgelegt an die Christen zu Rigen ynn Liffland*, as that has been reprinted with annotations in WA 15, (348) 360-378.

---

[16] WA 15, 348-349, and Otto Albrecht, *Studien zu Luthers "Sendschreiben an die Christen zu Riga und in Liefland vom Jahre 1524"* ("Zeitschrift für Kirchengeschichte," Vol. XVII [Gotha: Perthes, 1897]), pp. 406-409.

[17] WA 4, 414-416, 523.

[18] EA (Latin series) 20, 48-109.

[19] See Albrecht, *Studien zu . . . "die Christen zu Riga,"* p. 403.

EXPOSITION OF PSALM 127,
FOR THE CHRISTIANS AT RIGA
IN LIVONIA[1]

Martin Luther to all his dear friends in Christ at Riga and in Livonia.

Grace and peace from God our Father through our Lord Jesus Christ. Some time ago, dear friends, I was asked to write you something in a Christian vein.[2] I would gladly have done so, as was my duty, but all manner of distractions prevented me. Also, I knew of nothing special to write, since God our Father has so richly blessed you with his holy word that you yourselves can both teach and admonish, strengthen and comfort one another perhaps even better than we. However, since this has been asked of me, I have stolen time enough to quicken my own spirit and yours with a spiritual, godly song, and have undertaken an exposition of the 127th Psalm.

I selected this psalm because it so beautifully turns the heart away from covetousness and concern for temporal livelihood and possessions toward faith in God, and in a few words teaches us how Christians are to act with respect to the accumulation and ownership of this world's goods. It is hardly to be expected that the gospel, which has now again come to the fore, will fare any better among us and among you than it did at the time of Christ and the apostles, indeed, since the beginning of the world. For not only the evangelists, but all the prophets as well, complain that covetousness and concern for this world's goods hinder the gospel greatly from bearing fruit. Indeed, the precious word of

---

[1] Livonia embraced roughly the territory covered in modern times by the Baltic states of Latvia, Lithuania, and Esthonia. See the Introduction, p. 313.
[2] Luther is referring to the Riga council's letter of November 11, 1523, which he now answers in the spirit of Lohmüller's earlier request, to which they made reference, that he "dedicate something" to them. See the Introduction, pp. 314-316.

God sometimes falls among thorns and is choked [Matt. 13:22] so that it proves unfruitful; sadly enough, our daily experience shows us this only too well. And Paul also complains that all seek their own interests, not those of Jesus Christ [Phil. 2:21].

Now I have preached and written a great deal urging that good schools should be established in the cities[3] in order that we might produce educated men and women, whence good Christian pastors and preachers might come forth so that the word of God might continue to flourish richly. But people take such an indifferent attitude toward the matter, pretending that it might cost them their whole livelihood and temporal possessions, that I fear the time will come when schoolmasters, pastors, and preachers alike will have to quit, let the word go, and turn to a trade or some other means of stilling the pangs of hunger; just as the Levites had to abandon the worship of God to till the fields, as Nehemiah writes [Neh. 13:10].

Isn't it a crying shame? Up to now, a town with four or five hundred population could turn over to the mendicant monks[4] alone the equivalent of five, six, or seven hundred gulden, besides what bishops, officials,[5] and other bloodsuckers,[6] together with beggars and relic hawkers,[7] have already wrung from them. In addition, such a town will today probably be contributing annually

---

[3] Luther was a consistent proponent of popular education. See, e.g., *An Open Letter to the Christian Nobility* (1520). PE 2, 151-152. See also Luther's 1523 *Ordinance of a Common Chest*, in this volume, pp. 175, 188-189. The numerous comments on the subject scattered through his earlier writings culminated in the address *To the Councilmen of All Cities in Germany*, which was published very early in this same year of 1524, just about the time Luther received the Riga council's letter; see the text in this volume, pp. 347-378. See further Luther's letter of April 25, 1524, to Jacob Strauss (De Wette, *Dr. Martin Luthers Briefe*, II, 505; Margaret A. Currie [trans.], *The Letters of Martin Luther* [London: Macmillan, 1909], p. 125) and his letter of July 4, 1524, to Johann Briesmann (De Wette, *op. cit.*, III, 258).

[4] See p. 175, n. 88.

[5] *Official*; see p. 276, n. 76.

[6] *Schinder*, literally, "flayer" or "knacker," one who skinned butchered animals, was a common—and strong—term for an oppressor or tormentor. Grimm, *Deutsches Wörterbuch*, IX, 195-196.

[7] *Stationirer*. See p. 69, n. 34. In his famous 1494 satire, *The Ship of Fools* (63, 12), the humanist Sebastian Brant (1457-1521) similarly lumped the *Stationirer* together with the beggars.

five or six hundred gulden just for a biretta.[8] I will not even mention the sums expended on spices, silks, gold, jewels, and similar vanities; yes, and what is squandered on beer and wine. When you lump all these together, such a town throws far more than a thousand gulden down the drain every year. Such is the miserable, wretched, hopeless state of affairs in the German lands today! But when they are asked to contribute one or two hundred gulden toward good schools and pulpits, they cry, "You would reduce us to rags and make beggars of us! We would have nothing left"; then covetousness and concern for livelihood take over, and the people think they will die of hunger.

But what will God finally say about this? He will say, "What the wicked dreads will come upon him" [Prov. 10:24]. We fear hunger; hunger will come upon us, and all our concern will not help. Like unbelieving heathen, we are so needlessly anxious that we fail to advance God's word and work with the very means he has given us for that purpose. He will therefore allow a time to come in which we shall have plenty to worry about and our worry will nevertheless avail us nothing. Should this happen, as well it might, that there should be a terrible famine, it would serve us right; we're asking for it.

Take those seducers, the priests and monks, who have disgraced our mothers, wives, daughters, and sisters, and made harlots of them;[9] who have so oppressed us with their insolence and violence that we have to pant as if hounded by devils; who in addition have slain our bodies and souls with their poisonous doctrines, and herded them into hell. These are the very ones to whom we have in the past not only given more than enough, but we have even given them lands and people, cities and castles, and made of them greater lords than any among us.

Now that God is sending us upright, trustworthy, and learned men, who by word and deed encourage us toward self-discipline and chastity, who by godly marriage reduce the pre-

---

[8] The *Parret* was the peaked cap worn by the higher clergy, whose tenure in office depended upon the regular payment of stipulated sums to Rome according to several established practices, which Luther vigorously denounced in *An Open Letter to the Christian Nobility* (1520). PE 2, 84-101.

[9] See p. 142, n. 4.

valence of fornication, and who in addition zealously serve us in body and soul and direct us on the right path to heaven, we simply ignore them. Those whom we should be securing at whatever expense even from the ends of the earth, we are supporting about as well as the rich man supported poor Lazarus [Luke 16:19-21]. Now we find it impossible to support three upright, learned, married preachers, where formerly we maintained in splendor a hundred of those whoremasters.

Very well; we shall soon find out how this pleases God. Nobody can tell us anything. So God in turn will stop up his ears too and refuse to listen. Just watch how things turn out once certain persons now living are gone. I can foresee nothing better than the establishment of another papacy worse than before which will do us even greater harm (if that were possible) than this one has. This must and undoubtedly will happen, unless the Last Day intervenes. After all, we want to be betrayed, seduced, disgraced, and despoiled. As Wisdom complains in Proverbs 1, "I called, and you refused to listen; I stretched out my hand, and no one heeded; you have ignored all my counsel, and would have none of my reproof. I will therefore laugh at your destruction, and mock when that which you feared comes upon you. Then they will call upon me, but I will not hear. Therefore they shall eat the fruit of their way, and be sated with their own devices." [10]

For this reason I want yet to sing one little song for the benefit of such covetousness, that some might still be roused to help us ward off the wrath of God a bit longer. And that shall be this psalm which carries the superscription, "A song of Solomon in alt." [11]

Why this psalm and certain others are inscribed, "Songs in alt," I do not know. Some think it is because the priests and Levites chanted these psalms while going up the steps or stairs

---

[10] Prov. 1:24-26, 28, 31 (Vulgate).

[11] *Eyn lied Salomo in der höhe*, which was also Luther's rendering in his 1524 Psalter (*WA*, DB 10I, 536), became *Eyn lied Salomo im höhern Chor* in the Psalters of 1531 and 1545 (*WA*, DB 10I, 537) and in some later editions of the treatise published from 1534 on (*WA* 15, 362, n. 27). Luther's rendering of the Hebrew superscription for Psalms 120–134 (*shir hammaaloth*)—rendered "A Song of Ascents" in the RSV and "A Song of degrees" in the KJV—is here rendered in a manner consonant with his suggested interpretation of the phrase.

into the temple; therefore, they refer to them as "Graduals" or "Songs of Ascent."[12] But that is not right, for Scripture contains no evidence or suggestion of this. Moreover, they did their singing within the temple, not on the stairs. If conjecture or opinion is worth anything, my guess is that these psalms were chanted in a higher pitch, just as children's and women's voices are pitched higher than male voices. The meaning is the same as where some psalms are called *lamnazeah,* that is, "chanted in high pitch,"[13] etc. Since the Levites' style of chanting no longer exists, however, anything we might say of it is tentative. It makes little difference anyway, so long as we have a proper understanding of the psalm.

Solomon composed this psalm.[14] Not only was he enlightened by the Holy Spirit, but as he daily exercised his administrative functions and mingled with people, he learned from frequent experience how vainly unbelief burdens itself with worries about feeding the belly, when in fact everything depends on God's blessing and protection. For where God withholds his blessing, we

---

[12] Historically, a variety of interpretations have been offered for this phrase. Luther is likely referring to the view set forth by Nicholas of Lyra (d. 1340) in his *Postillae*—suggested already by Jerome's rendering in the Vulgate: *Canticum graduum;* and developed by later Jewish exegetes, though rather incorrectly, from the Talmud (*Middoth* ii, 5; *Succa,* 51b)—that these psalms were sung one at a time by the Levites as they stood on each of the fifteen steps going up from the women's court to the men's court in the temple. See Franz Delitzsch, *Biblischer Commentar über die Psalmen* (4th ed.; Leipzig: Dorffling and Franke, 1883), pp. 778-781, especially n. 3; see also *LW* 12, 200.

[13] The Hebrew superscription, *lamnatseach,* found in Psalm 4 and in fifty-four other psalms, was already a puzzle to the early translators (Targum: "to praise"; Septuagint and Vulgate: "unto the end"; other Greek versions connected it with "victory"). In a marginal note to his 1524 Psalter, Luther explained his understanding of "high" in terms of one voice being above another in a duet (*WA,* DB 10I, 112). In 1531 he changed his rendering from *"hoch* ("high") *zu singen"* to *"vor* ("before") *zu singen,"* and added a different gloss explaining the word in terms of the antiphon which precedes a response. In his 1532 exposition of Psalm 45 Luther interpreted the word as "choirmaster" or "director of song"; see *LW* 12, 198-200.

[14] With few exceptions, tradition had generally assumed Solomonic authorship, the ancient title seemingly finding corroboration in the Hebrew word for "his beloved" in verse 2 which so nearly approximated the name given to Solomon in II Sam. 12:25, Jedidiah, "beloved of Jah." The "sleep" of verse 2 was referred to Solomon's dream in I Kings 3:5-15, and the "house" of verse 1 to Solomon's temple.

labor in vain; where God does not protect, our worry is futile. And he speaks thus:[15]

1a. *Unless the Lord builds the house,*
those who build it labor in vain.
1b. *Unless the Lord watches over the city,*
the watchman stays awake in vain.
2. *It is vain that you rise up early,*
sit up late,
and eat the bread of sorrow;
for to him who enjoys his favor,
he gives while he sleeps.
3. *Lo, children are a heritage from the Lord,*
the fruit of the womb is a reward.[16]
4. *Like arrows in the hand of a warrior,*
so are the children of youth.
5. *Happy is the man who has*
his quiver full of them;
They shall not be put to shame
when they speak with their enemies in the gate.

First we must understand that "building the house" does not refer simply to the construction of walls and roof, rooms and chambers, out of wood and stone. It refers rather to everything that goes on inside the house, which in German we call "managing the household" [*haushallten*]; just as Aristotle writes, "*Oeconomia*,"[17] that, is pertaining to the household economy which comprises wife and child, servant and maid, livestock and fodder. The same term is used by Moses in Exodus 1 [:20-21], where he

---

15 Luther did not number the verses; they are numbered here for the reader's convenience. See the note on scriptural references in the Introduction to this volume, pp. xv-xvi.

16 *Lohn* ("reward") here and in the 1524 Psalter became *geschenck* ("gift") in the 1531 Psalter and the later reprints of this treatise. WA, DB 10I, 536-537, WA 15, 364, l. 16.

17 Household economy—the Greek term is *Oikonomia*—includes three parts according to Aristotle, the relation of master to slave, of husband to wife, and of father to children. In addition to these personal relationships which are primary, the term also has reference secondarily to property and wealth-getting. *Politics* I, 3-13.

writes that God dealt well with the two midwives and "built them houses"[18] because they feared him and did not strangle the children of the Israelites; that is, he helped them to obtain husbands, sons and daughters, and enough of whatever goes along with keeping a family. Solomon's purpose is to describe a Christian marriage; he is instructing everyone how to conduct himself as a Christian husband and head of a household.

Reason and the world think that married life and the making of a home ought to proceed as they intend; they try to determine things by their own decisions and actions, as if their work could take care of everything. To this Solomon says No! He points us instead to God, and teaches us with a firm faith to seek and expect all such things from God. We see this in experience too. Frequently two people will marry who have hardly a shirt to their name, and yet they support themselves so quietly and well that it is a pleasure to behold. On the other hand, some bring great wealth into their marriage; yet it slips out of their hands till they can barely get along.

Again, two people marry out of passionate love; their choice and desire are realized, yet their days together are not happy. Some are very eager and anxious to have children, but they do not conceive, while others who have given the matter little thought get a house full of children. Again, some try to run the house and its servants smoothly, and it turns out that they have nothing but misfortune. And so it goes in this world; the strangest things happen.

Who is it that so disrupts marriage and household management, and turns them so strangely topsy-turvy? It is he of whom Solomon says: Unless the Lord keeps the house, household management there is a lost cause. He wishes to buttress this passage [Ps. 127:1a] and confirm its truth. This is why he permits such situations to arise in this world, as an assault on unbelief, to bring to shame the arrogance of reason with all works and cleverness, and to constrain them to believe.

---

[18] The Hebrew word for "house," *bayith*, occurs in both Ps. 127:1 and Exod. 1:21. Luther's rendering is paralleled in the literal KJV ("made them houses"), while his interpretation is paralleled in the freer RSV ("gave them families").

This passage alone should be enough to attract people to marriage, comfort all who are now married, and sap the strength of covetousness. Young people are scared away from marriage when they see how strangely it turns out. They say, "It takes a lot to make a home";[19] or, "You learn a lot living with a woman." This is because they fail to see who does this, and why He does it; and since human ingenuity and strength know no recourse and can provide no help, they hesitate to marry. As a result they fall into unchastity if they do not marry, and into covetousness and worry if they do. But here is the needed consolation: Let the Lord build the house and keep it, and do not encroach upon his work; the concern for these matters is his, not yours. For whoever is the head of the house and maintains it should be allowed to bear the burden of care. Does it take a lot to make a house? So what! God is greater than any house. He who fills heaven and earth will surely also be able to supply a house, especially since he takes the responsibility upon himself and causes it to be sung to his praise.

Why should we think it strange that it takes so much to make a home where God is not the head of the house? Because you do not see Him who is supposed to fill the house, naturally every corner must seem empty. But if you look upon Him, you will never notice whether a corner is bare; everything will appear to you to be full, and will indeed be full. And if it is not full, it is your vision which is at fault; just as it is the blind man's fault if he fails to see the sun. For him who sees rightly, God turns the saying around and says not, "It takes a lot to make a home," but, "How much a home contributes!" So we see that the managing of a household should and must be done in faith—then there will be enough[20]—so that men come to acknowledge that everything depends not on our doing, but on God's blessing and support.

We are not to understand from this that God forbids us to work. Man must and ought to work, ascribing his sustenance and the fulness of his house, however, not to his own labor but solely

---

[19] See Wander (ed.), *Sprichwörter-Lexikon*, I, 1440, *"Gehören,"* No. 15.
[20] On the problem of syntax with respect to this clause, which could be construed either with what precedes it or with what follows it, see Albrecht, *Studien zu . . . "die Christen zu Riga,"* p. 402.

to the goodness and blessing of God. For where men ascribe these things to their own labor, there covetousness and anxiety quickly arise, and they hope by much labor to acquire much. But then there is this contradiction, namely, that some people labor prodigiously, yet scarcely have enough to eat, while others are slower and more relaxed in their work, and wealth pours in on them.[21] All this is because God wants the glory, as the one who alone gives the growth [I Cor. 3:6-7]. For if you should till the soil faithfully for a hundred years and do all the work in the world, you couldn't bring forth from the earth even a single stalk; but God without any of your labor, while you sleep, produces from that tiny kernel a stalk with as many kernels on it as he wills.

Solomon here wishes to sanction work, but to reject worry and covetousness. He does not say, "The Lord builds the house, so no one need labor at it." He does say, "Unless the Lord builds the house, those who build it labor in vain" [Ps. 127:1a]. This is as if he were to say: Man must work, but that work is in vain if it stands alone and thinks it can sustain itself. Work cannot do this; God must do it. Therefore work in such manner that your labor is not in vain. Your labor is in vain when you worry, and rely on your own efforts to sustain yourself. It behooves you to labor, but your sustenance and the maintenance of your household belong to God alone. Therefore, you must keep these two things far apart: "to labor," and "to maintain a household" or "to sustain"; keep them as far apart from one another as heaven and earth, or God and man.

In the Proverbs of Solomon we often read how the lazy are punished because they will not work.[22] Solomon says, "A slack hand causes poverty, but industrious hands bring riches" [Prov. 10:4]. This and similar sayings sound as if our sustenance depended on our labor; though he says in the same passage [Prov. 10:22], as also in this psalm [127:1], that it depends on God's blessing; or, as we say in German, "God bestows, God provides."[23]

---

[21] Cf. Eccles. 11:11-13.
[22] See, e.g., Prov. 6:6-11; 10:4; 12:24, 27; 13:4; 20:4; 24:30-34.
[23] *"Gott bescheret, Gott beredt."* See Wander (ed.), *Sprichwörter-Lexikon*, II, 16, *"Gott,"* No. 316.

Thus, the meaning is this: God commanded Adam to eat his bread in the sweat of his face [Gen. 3:19]. God wills that man should work, and without work He will give him nothing. Conversely, God will not give him anything because of his labor, but solely out of His own goodness and blessing. Man's labor is to be his discipline in this life, by which he may keep his flesh in subjection. To him who is obedient in this matter, God will give plenty, and sustain him well.

God sustains man in the same way he sustains all other living creatures. As the psalm [147:9] says, "He gives to all flesh their food, and to the young ravens which cry unto him." Again, in Psalm 104,[24] "The eyes of all look to thee, O Lord, and thou givest them their food in due season. Thou openest thy hand, and fillest every living creature with blessings," that is, with fulness and sufficiency. Now no animal works for its living, but each has its own task to perform, after which it seeks and finds its food. The little birds fly about and warble, make nests, and hatch their young. That is their task. But they do not gain their living from it. Oxen plow, horses carry their riders and have a share in battle; sheep furnish wool, milk, cheese, etc. That is their task. But they do not gain their living from it. It is the earth which produces grass and nourishes them through God's blessing. Christ himself, in Matthew 6 [:26], bids us look at the birds: how they neither sow, nor reap, nor gather into barns; yet they are fed by God. That is, they perform their tasks all right, but they do no work from which they gain sustenance.

Similarly, man must necessarily work and busy himself at something. At the same time, however, he must know that it is something other than his labor which furnishes him sustenance; it is the divine blessing. Because God gives him nothing unless he works, it may seem as if it is his labor which sustains him; just as the little birds neither sow nor reap, but they would certainly die of hunger if they did not fly about to seek their food. The fact that they find food, however, is not due to their own labor, but to God's goodness. For who placed their food there where they can find it? Beyond all doubt it is God alone, as he

---

[24] Ps. 145:15-16; cf. 104:27-28.

says in Genesis 1 [:29-30], "Behold, I have given to you and to all creatures every growing plant for food." In short, even if Scripture did not teach this directly, experience would prove it to be so. For where God has not laid up a supply no one will find anything, even though they all work themselves to death searching. We can see this with our eyes, and grasp it with our hands; yet we will not believe. Again, where God does not uphold and preserve, nothing can last, even though a hundred thousand fortresses were thrown up to defend it; it will be shattered and ground to dust till no one knows what has become of it.

Tell me: who puts silver and gold in the mountains so that man might find them there? Who puts into the field that great wealth which issues in grain, wine, and all kinds of produce, from which all creatures live Does the labor of man do this? To be sure, labor no doubt finds it, but God has first to bestow it and put it there if labor is to find it. Who puts into the flesh the power to bring forth young and fill the earth with birds, beasts, fish, etc.? Is this accomplished by our labor and care? By no means. God is there first, secretly laying his blessing therein; then all things are brought forth in abundance. And so we find that all our labor is nothing more than the finding and collecting of God's gifts; it is quite unable to create or preserve anything.

Here then we see how Solomon, in this one little verse [Ps. 127:1], has solved in short order the greatest of all problems among the children of men, about which so many books have been written, so many proverbs and approaches devised, namely, how to feed our poor stomachs. Solomon rejects them all in a body, wraps the whole matter up in faith, and says: You labor in vain when you labor for the purpose of sustaining yourself and building your own house. Indeed, you make for yourself a lot of worry and trouble. At the same time by such arrogance and wicked unbelief you kindle God's wrath, so that you only become all the poorer and are ruined completely because you undertook to do what is his alone to do. And if with such unbelief you should succeed anyway in attaining wealth in all things, it would only bring greater ruin to you soul eternally when God lets you go blindly on in your unbelief.

327

If you want to earn your livelihood honorably, quietly, and well, and rightly maintain your household, give heed: Take up some occupation that will keep you busy in order that you can eat your bread in the sweat of your face [Gen. 3:19]. Then do not worry about how you will be sustained and how such labor will build and maintain your house. Place everything in God's keeping; let him do the worrying and the building. Entrust these things to him; he will lay before you richly and well the things which your labor is to find and bring to you. If he does not put them there, you will labor in vain and find nothing.

Thus, this wholly evangelical verse in masterful fashion sets forth faith, as against that accursed covetousness and concern for the belly which today, alas! everywhere hinders the fruit of the gospel. When this verse is fully understood, the rest of the psalm is easy. We will now briefly run through the other verses.

Unless the Lord keeps the city,
the watchman guards in vain.

In the first verse he rebuked covetousness, worry, and unbelief in every household in particular. In this verse[25] he does the same thing for a whole community. For a whole community is nothing other than many households combined. By this term we comprehend all manner of principalities, dominions, and kingdoms, or any other grouping of people.

Now the blind world, because it does not know God and his work, concludes that it is owing to its own cleverness, reason, and strength that a community or dominion endures and thrives. Accordingly, they gather together great treasures, stuff their coffers, construct mighty towers and walls, provide suits of armor and vast supplies of provisions, enact wise laws, and conduct their affairs with courage and prudence. They just go ahead in their arrogance without even consulting God about any of it, like those who built the Tower of Babel [Gen. 11:1-9].

Meanwhile, God sits above and watches how cleverly and boldly the children of men proceed, and he causes the psalmist to

---

25 The German *Vers*, like the Latin *Versus*, means one line, in poetry a metrically measured unit. The reference here is to Ps. 127:1b.

sing in his praise, "God brings the counsel of the nations to naught" [Ps. 33:10]. Again, "God knows the thoughts of man, that they are vain" [Ps. 94:11]. And yet again, "He takes away the spirit of princes, and deals strongly with the kings of the earth" [Ps. 76:12]. He allows such cities and dominions to arise and to gain the ascendancy, for a little while. But before they can look around he strikes them down; and in general the greater the kingdom, the sooner. Even though they flourish for a short time, that is in the sight of God little more than a beginning. Never does one of them arrive at the point it strives to reach.

If you will look at the history of the kingdoms of Assyria, Babylon, Persia, Greece, Rome,[26] and all the rest, you will find there exactly what this verse says. All their splendor is nothing more than God's little puppet show. He has allowed them to rise for a time, but he has invariably overthrown them, one after the other. As they gained a brief ascendancy, through human wit and arrogance, so much the more quickly did they fall again; not because they lacked manpower, money, goods, and all manner of resources, but because the true watchman had ceased to uphold them, and caused them to see what human wit and power could accomplish without his watchful care and protection. So it turned out that their cause was nothing but vain counsel and a futile undertaking which they could neither uphold nor carry out.

They themselves have felt and acknowledged this. The pagan Vergil wrote of Troy that the slain Hector appeared before Aeneas in a dream and said, "If Troy could have been defended, it would have been defended by my hand."[27] And Lucan wrote, "*Magnisque negatum Stare diu*"; "It is not given great kingdoms to long endure."[28] So utterly apparent is God's work; yet men will not acknowledge him even though they bump their heads against it. Soldiers, too, acknowledge that victory does not depend on the numbers or strength of the army, but, as they say, on luck. But Scripture says it depends on God, as Psalm 24 [:8] reads, "The Lord mighty in battle." And Psalm [147:10 and] 33 [:17], "His

---

26 Cf. Luther's later detailed discussion of these histories in connection with his 1530 interpretation of Daniel. *LW* 35, 295-316.
27 See the *Aeneid* (II, 291-292) of the Roman poet Vergil (70-19 B.C.).
28 See the *Pharsalia* (I, 70-71) of the Latin poet Lucan (A.D. 39-65).

delight is not in the strength of the horse, and the horse is a vain hope for victory and by its great might it cannot save," etc. And Ecclesiastes 9 [:11], "I saw that the race is not to the swift, nor the battle to the strong," etc.

Thus, by this verse Solomon would briefly instruct all kings, princes, councilmen, and everyone in authority how to conduct and maintain a good, peaceful, and blessed government which functions well. In the first place, they should be watchful and diligent in the performance of their official duties. He does not say that they should not be watchful and diligent, just as in the preceding verse he does not forbid them to work (St. Paul, too, says in Romans 12[29] that those who are in authority over others should be careful or diligent). He wants rather that their watchfulness be not fruitless and in vain, but beneficial and worth while.

In the second place, he wants them in faith to entrust such watchful care to God and let him worry about how the watching is to be done, so they do not arrogantly presume that their own solicitude and diligence preserves the city, but are assured that God will preserve the city and protect land and people. Just take the arrogance and worry out of the watchfulness, and let it proceed in faith. For although God will preserve nothing unless we exercise diligence and care, still he does not want us to get the idea that it is our own solicitude and diligence which accomplishes that which is done by his goodness and mercy alone.

One of two things must necessarily follow when we rely on our own watchfulness: either arrogance or worry. If all goes well and is secure, we pride ourselves on our watchfulness; if things go wrong and are about to fail, we worry, lose heart, and become doubtful. Now God will tolerate neither of these, neither arrogance nor worry. We should neither worry when we are insecure, nor be proud when we are secure, but in free and true faith do our watching and perform the duties of our calling. We should no more be anxious when things go wrong than be proud when things go well.

Now none but a believing heart acts in this way. As David

---

[29] Rom. 12:8 (Vulgate); cf. the KJV, "He that ruleth with diligence."

says when he speaks out against worry in Psalm 3 [:6], "I will not be afraid though many thousands set themselves against me round about." Again, in Psalm 27 [:1, 3], "The Lord protects me; whom shall I fear? Though war arise against me, in him will I be confident." He speaks again against arrogance in Psalm 44 [:6], "I will not trust in my bow, neither shall my sword save me."

Why, then, does he urge us to labor and watch, and want us to have walls, armor, and all manner of supplies, just as he commanded the children of Israel to put on their armor and fight against the Canaanites? Are we to provide no supplies, leave our gates and windows open, make no effort to defend ourselves but allow ourselves to be pierced through and become lifeless corpses as they did in the book of Maccabees? [I Macc. 2:34-38]. By no means. You have just heard that those in authority should be watchful and diligent, and perform all the duties of their office: bar the gates, defend the towers and walls, put on armor, and procure supplies. In general, they should proceed as if there were no God and they had to rescue themselves and manage their own affairs; just as the head of a household is supposed to work as if he were trying to sustain himself by his own labors.

But he must watch out that his heart does not come to rely on these deeds of his, and get arrogant when things go well or worried when things go wrong. He should regard all such preparation and equipment as being the work of our Lord God under a mask, as it were, beneath which he himself alone effects and accomplishes what we desire. He commands us so to equip ourselves for this reason also, that he might conceal his own work under this disguise, and allow those who boast to go their way, and strengthen those who are worried, so that men will not tempt him. In this way he conducted all the wars of King David and of the whole people of Israel in the Old Testament. He does the same thing today, wherever the authorities have such faith. In like manner, through their own labor he made Abraham, Isaac, and Jacob wealthy, etc. Indeed, one could very well say that the course of the world, and especially the doing of his saints, are God's mask, under which he conceals himself and so marvelously exercises dominion and introduces disorder in the world.

It is vain that you rise up early
and go to bed late,
and eat the bread of sorrow;
for so he gives to his beloved in sleep.

This whole verse [Ps. 127:2] is directed against arrogance and anxiety, as if he were to say: It is futile for you to rise up early and go to bed late, and think that the more you labor the more you will have. For that is something that the blessing of God has to accomplish. And even if you do succeed in acquiring more than others who are not so concerned about getting things and keeping them, still your earnings will not go as far as those of the carefree, but will slip through your fingers and disappear, as Psalm 37 [:16] says, "It is better for the righteous to have a little than to have the great riches of the wicked." And Solomon says in the Proverbs, "Better is a dinner of herbs where love is, than a fatted ox and hatred with it" [Prov. 15:17].

That this is his meaning, and that it is not his intent to prohibit labor or diligence, is clear from his phrase, "and eat the bread of sorrow." This says in effect: You are making your bread and sustenance harsh and bitter; and this is not the fault of your labor, but of your anxious and unbelieving heart. It refuses to believe that God will nourish you; instead, it is importunate and demanding, wanting to fill coffers, purses, cellars, and storehouses, and refusing to rest until it is assured of having more supplies on hand than it could consume in many years. He who has faith in God, however, is not anxious about tomorrow but is content with today. He does his work with joy and with a quiet heart, and lives in accord with Christ's injunction in the gospel, "Do not be anxious about tomorrow, for tomorrow will have its own troubles. It is enough that each day has its own evil."[30] Lo, the livelihood of such believers will not be harsh and bitter; for although they too eat their bread in the sweat of their faces out-

---

[30] In a gloss on Matt. 6:34 in his 1522 New Testament, retained later in his German Bible, Luther explains the last three words of the passage thus, "That is, daily labor; the meaning is that it is sufficient for us to work each day, but we should have no cares or worries beyond that. WA, DB 6, 34-35.

wardly [Gen. 3:19], they do it with faith and a joyful conscience inwardly.

Thereupon, he concludes by showing how God gives all such things, saying: *Sic dabit dilectis suis somno;* All such things (both the building of the house and the keeping of the city) he gives to his beloved as in their sleep [Ps. 127:2]. That is, he lets them work hard and be diligent, in such a way, however, that they are neither anxious nor arrogant, but go happily along, assuming no burden of care, and committing everything to Him. They live a calm and untroubled life with tranquil hearts, as one who sleeps sweetly and securely, letting nothing trouble him, and yet continues to live and be well cared for. They have enough; indeed, they must be well supplied and protected because they have committed all to God in accordance with Psalm 55 [:22], "Cast your burden on the Lord, and he will sustain you"; and I Peter 5 [:7], "Cast all your anxieties on him, and know that he cares for you." At issue is not the matter of work, but only the matter of pernicious worry, covetousness, and unbelief.

Lo, children are a heritage from the Lord,
the fruit of the womb a reward.

All of this is spoken in typical Hebrew fashion. "Heritage from the Lord" and "reward" are one and the same thing, just as "children" and "fruit of the womb" are one and the same thing. Thus it means to say: What good does it do you to be so deeply concerned and anxious about how to procure and protect your possessions? Why even children, and whatever is born of woman, are not within your power; although they are a part of household and city alike, for if there were no children and "fruit of the womb" neither household nor city would endure. So the very reward and "heritage from the Lord," about which you are so terribly anxious, are actually the gift and boon of God. (Even if all the whole world were to combine forces, they could not bring about the conception of a single child in any woman's womb nor cause it to be born; that is wholly the work of God alone.) Why, then, are you concerned and anxious about acquiring and securing goods, when you do not even possess that for which you seek them? A lord, then, and the head of a household ought rightfully to say to himself: I will labor and perform my allotted tasks; but He who creates children in the home and inhabitants in the city (all of whom are "fruit of the womb") will also sustain and preserve them. Lo, this one's labor and that one's watching would then not be bitter to him, but would proceed aright in faith.

Christ touched upon this (to which virtually the whole psalm is devoted) when he said in Matthew 6 [:25], "Is not the body more than clothing, and the soul more than food?" It is as if he were to say: Since children and "the fruit of the womb" are not for you to worry about, why then do you worry about the matter of securing and keeping possessions? For who can ever explain how it is that all the children of men are brought forth out of the flesh of women? Who has hidden such a multitude of men in that poor flesh, and who brings them forth in such marvelous fashion? None other than He alone, who gives children as a heritage and the fruit of the womb as a reward to his beloved [Ps. 127:3] as in sleep [Ps. 127:2]. God bestows his gifts overnight, they say; and that is literally true.

> *Like arrows in the hand of a warrior,*
> *so are the children of one's youth.*

Here he compares children and people with the arrows in the hand of a mighty hero, who shoots his arrows whenever and withersoever he wills. Thus, we also see how God deals with us. Just look at how amazingly he matches husband and wife, in a way no one would expect; and how they attain to extraordinary stations in life for which they have not striven, so that men marvel at it. Generally, things turn out quite differently from what father, and mother, and even the person himself, had envisioned. It is as if God would confess this verse [Ps. 127:4] in deeds and say: I will bring to naught all the counsels of men and deal with the children of men according to my own will, that they may be in my hand as the arrows of a powerful giant. Of what use is a lot of worrying and planning for our future when that future will be nothing other than what he wills? The best thing to do then is to work, and let him worry about the future.

He mentions especially "the children of youth," meaning those who are not yet householders or guardians of the city, those whom we regard as being committed solely to the care of our own cleverness. He still guides them in their homes and in the city as he wills, and does with them what he wills, to show us that he cares for all things, and never leaves anything to us but our labor, that we may not think God governs only infants in the cradle and allows grown-ups to use their reason and free will. Indeed, he directs the grown-ups (he says here[31]) just as much as he does the small children; they are arrows in his hand, and must come and go as and wherever he wills. To God they are all the same: rationality and irrationality, heaven and earth, the young and those who are old, wise, and experienced.

Indeed, he deals even more strangely with those who are wise and possessed of reason. He has much more to do with them in that he turns their counsels and reason into foolishness, and directs them otherwise than they intend. Therefore, according to this verse [Ps. 127:4] it is not the children and "the fruit of the womb"—whom he calls God's heritage and gift[32]—but the children of youth, who have now grown up and reached the age of discretion, whom he holds in his hand as a giant holds his arrows; though to all appearances he seems to have these in his hand least of all, allowing their reason and wit to rule them while he devotes his attention to the little children. His whole purpose is to check and take from us the whole matter of our governing and caring for ourselves, in order that we may know it is he himself who alone rules over us and cares for us, and so lets[33] us go about our business and do our work.

---

[31] The fact that Luther apparently takes Ps. 127:4 to refer to people considerably older than the infants intended in the preceding verse may serve as a guide to interpreting the obscure syntactical relationship between this parenthetical clause and the phrase in the sentence which precedes it, "that we may not think." See Albrecht, *Studien zu . . . "die Christen zu Riga,"* pp. 402-403.

[32] Luther substituted *gabe* ("gift") for *erbe* ("heritage") in his rendering of Ps. 127:3 from 1531 on; at the same time he changed *lohn* ("reward") to *geschenck* ("gift" or "present"). WA, DB 10I, 536-537.

[33] We have followed the preference of Albrecht (*Studien zu . . . "die Christen zu Riga,"* p. 400) over that of Paul Pietsch (WA 15, 377, n. 1) for construing

Happy is the man who has
his quiver full of them;
They shall not be put to shame
when they speak with their enemies in the gate.

He desires that such youth, given by God, and recognized as such, may be many, for then the world would be well off. That is very true. If all manner of problems are to be dealt with successfully, then the young people who are to live and govern on this earth after us must be trained and guided accordingly. Just as the giant who has his quiver full of arrows is well prepared and equipped, so the householder and the city to whom God has granted an abundance of such youth are well supplied. For there it is God himself who keeps the house and watches over the city.

Such a great blessing however, will not be without persecution, for where things go according to God's will there must also be onslaughts of the devil. The unbelief and covetousness of this world cannot tolerate godly life and teaching; therefore, such householders and cities will not be without enemies to revile and abuse them. But over against such attacks there stands this comfort, that they will ultimately emerge with honor and put their enemies to shame in the gate (that is, publicly) [Ps. 127:5]. He mentions no armor or weapons but only the word, saying that "they will speak with their enemies in the gate," as if to say: By their teaching they will stand, because it is true, no matter how sharply their opponents attack it.

I wanted to write this to you, my dear friends in Christ, for your encouragement, that your hearts and ours may be yet more diligent, in order that the gospel may become rich and fruitful among us all in all manner of understanding and of good works, against which covetousness, the fruit of pernicious unbelief, fights so vigorously. Our dear Lord Jesus Christ strengthen and help us. For if we are still so weak that we cannot leave off worrying about the needs of our bellies, how shall we be able to bear the

---

the syntax of this last clause, and have accordingly supplied the missing *lasse* after the fashion of two early editions and of the Wittenberg and Jena collections of Luther's works.

world's fury, death, opprobrium, and all other misfortune? Yes, how shall we stand firm when the false spirits come upon us, who just now are beginning to rise? May God, the Father of all mercy, who has introduced his word and begun his work among you, preserve your minds and hearts in the simple and pure knowledge of Jesus Christ our Saviour, to whom be praise and thanks in all eternity. Amen.[34]

---

[34] Editions of 1534 and following added here a hymn, probably composed by Lazarus Spengler, based on this psalm, with musical notation. See the Introduction, p. 316.

TO THE COUNCILMEN
OF ALL CITIES IN GERMANY
THAT THEY ESTABLISH AND
MAINTAIN CHRISTIAN SCHOOLS

1524

Translated by Albert T. W. Steinhaeuser

Revised by Walther I. Brandt

INTRODUCTION

During the early Middle Ages the principal means of obtaining an education was the monastic school.[1] The growth of an urban society in the twelfth and thirteenth centuries brought a demand for a somewhat broader curriculum, a demand which was met by the cathedral schools. A third type, which developed during the later Middle Ages, was the chantry school.[2] A fourth type was the guild school. It was a common practice for the merchant and craft guilds to support priests for the performance of all manner of religious services for the members. Often this included conducting a school for the children of guild members. As urban society grew more self-conscious and municipal governments became more firmly established, some of these guild schools, together with the parish schools, became burgher schools, largely supported and controlled by the secular authorities. Instruction was still mainly carried on by members of the clergy, but lay teachers became increasingly numerous.[3]

All these schools were directly or indirectly under the domination of ecclesiastical authorities committed to the theological system of the Church. The appearance of humanism in Germany in the fifteenth century added a new and sometimes discordant note. The humanists sought to revive the conception of a liberal education as developed by the ancient Greeks. Hostile toward scholasticism, the humanists sometimes succeeded in introducing humanist subjects into the curriculum of existing schools; occasionally they founded new schools in which their ideas of education prevailed.[4]

---

[1] See p. 175, n. 17.

[2] Chantry foundations were income-producing property granted by an individual to support a priest in return for prayers and masses for the souls of the grantor and his family. The chantry priest's duties occupied but little of his time, and it became customary to stipulate that he should teach the children of the community. Such stipulations varied widely. Frank Pierrepont Graves, *A History of Education During the Middle Ages and the Transition to Modern Times* (New York: Macmillan, 1920), p. 98.

[3] Graves, *op. cit.*, pp. 97-99.

[4] Mention should be made here of the schools of the Brethren of the Common

The impact of the events of the early sixteenth century on Germany was by no means favorable to schools and education. The economic prosperity brought about in the age of discovery by increased trade and the influx of Spanish gold gave rise to a spirit of materialism. If a youth were not destined for the church or for one of the learned professions—theology, law, or medicine— why should he waste his time in acquiring an education which had no direct relationship to the world of trade and industry? Let him rather learn a trade at an early age and thus insure his livelihood. Such an attitude was expressed in the current saying, "*Gelehrte sind verkehrte,*" which may be freely translated, "The learned are daft." The course of study advocated by the humanists tended toward an aristocracy of letters, and held little appeal for the common man.

The Reformation, too, had in the beginning a disastrous effect on the existing church-dominated schools. If, as the reformers contended, many of the current doctrines and practices of the church were erroneous and dangerous to salvation, surely parents ought not to send their children to schools where these doctrines were inculcated. Princes, nobles, and municipal authorities, doubtless motivated by greed as much as by their theological principles, confiscated the endowments by which schools were supported. Luther, although a consistent advocate of what he considered to be the right kind of education,[5] attacked existing schools in the harshest terms. He referred to the monastic and cathedral schools as "devil's training centers," and stigmatized their textbooks as "asses' dung." He went so far as to say that rather than send a boy to such a school he would prefer that he received no schooling at all.[6]

When Luther preached the spiritual priesthood of all be-

Life, a lay religious order active in the Low Countries. These schools—one of which Luther attended in Magdeburg in 1497—offered an enriched curriculum, including the Latin classics. Virtually every German humanist of the fifteenth and early sixteenth centuries either attended or came under the influence of these schools. See Albert Hyma, *The Christian Renaissance: A History of the "devotio moderna"* (New York: Century, 1925), pp. 122-135.
[5] See, for example, his remarks in his 1520 *Open Letter to the Christian Nobility* (*PE* 2, 151-153) and in his 1523 *Adoration of the Sacrament* (*LW* 36, 304).
[6] See pp. 352, 374.

lievers, some took it to mean that no formal training was necessary as a preparation for the priesthood.[7] Others went even further, holding that God speaks directly to the human heart; there must be an inner word supplementing the written word. This inner word, this prompting of the Holy Spirit within, wholly independent of any formal education, makes it possible to understand the written word. For this reason Karlstadt and Münzer were opposed to learning of any kind, even declaring it to be sinful and devilish.[8]

Small wonder that schools and education declined sharply in the areas where these ideas penetrated. At Wittenberg, where Karlstadt dominated the scene during Luther's enforced exile at the Wartburg, attendance at the university fell off markedly, to be restored later through the combined efforts of Luther and Bugenhagen. Matters were still worse at Erfurt, where the activities of a small group of the Karlstadt-Münzer persuasion were instrumental in reducing the university enrolment to less than fifty students. Why should one study Latin, Greek, and Hebrew? Had not Luther himself urged the use of the vernacular, and had he not just published a German translation of the New Testament?

Since these opponents of education could and did cite Luther's words in support of their position, he felt impelled to speak out.[9] The treatise which follows, addressed to the councilmen of all German cities, was composed probably in January or early in February, 1524, and came from the press in February.[10] It does not outline a complete system of education; that task was achieved later by Melanchthon, who justly earned the sobriquet, "Praeceptor Germaniae."[11] What Luther does here is to offer practical advice to the responsible authorities in the cities of Germany, and answer the anti-educational arguments summarized above.

He maintains that education is necessary for the spiritual

---

[7] See his 1520 Open Letter to the Christian Nobility. PE 2, 73-76.

[8] WA 15, 10.

[9] Luther was just then deeply concerned over the difficulties encountered by the parish of Leisnig in its attempt to set up a system of local control over its church and school. See in this volume, pp. 188-189.

[10] WA 15, 9, cites an unpublished letter of February 28, 1524, from the humanist Michael Hummelberg of Ravensburg to Joachim Vadian of St. Gall, which mentions the recent appearance of the treatise.

[11] See Karl Hartfelder, Philipp Melanchthon als Praeceptor Germaniae ("Monumenta Germaniae Paedagogica," Vol. VII [Berlin: Hofmann, 1889]).

growth of both boys and girls,[12] and equally essential if they are to become useful citizens. To the argument that parents cannot spare their children from domestic duties, he suggests that they attend school an hour a day. On the matter of languages he becomes positively eloquent in his argument that they are essential for the study and exposition of Scripture, and also for the training of good citizens.

The influence of humanism is clearly evident in the treatise, but Luther has in mind more than a humanist education. He would combine the best features of humanist education with history, literature, and the other liberal arts, and, above all, a thorough Christian training. Beyond anything even the humanists had considered before, the Reformation set as its goal universal, even compulsory, public education for everyone.[13] Luther also advocates that municipalities found public libraries, and suggests principles for the selection of books to be placed on their shelves.

The schools he advocated would lie somewhere above the elementary schools and below the universities. Yet because of the very fact that his proposals did not comprise a complete system of schools, the influence of his ideas was felt both in the elementary schools and in the universities. That he did not speak in vain is evident from the school reforms adopted that very year in Magdeburg, Nordhausen, Halberstadt, and Gotha; Eisleben adopted similar reforms in 1525, and Nürnberg followed suit in 1526.

The best source for Luther's ideas on education is his own writings, especially the present treatise and his *Sermon on Keeping Children in School* (1530).[14] There is an excellent introduction, together with the text of the two treatises, in F. V. N. Painter, *Luther on Education* (St. Louis: Concordia, 1889). Brief general treatments may be found in histories of education, such as Frank

---

[12] The education of girls as a general principle, while not unheard-of, was essentially something new. That Luther was in earnest about his suggestion of establishing girls' schools—first made in 1520 (*PE* 2, 151)—is evident from his letter of August 22, 1527, to one Else von Kanitz, inviting her to open a school for girls in Wittenberg, and offering her board and room in his home. *WA*, Br 4, 236; Currie, *Letters of Martin Luther*, p. 160.

[13] Karl and Barbara Hertz and John H. Lichtblau (trans.), Karl Holl's *Cultural Significance of the Reformation* ("Living Age Books" [New York: Meridian, 1959]), pp. 110-111.

[14] *WA* 30^II, (508) 517-588; *PE* 4, 135-178.

Pierrepont Graves, *A History of Education During the Middle Ages and the Transition to Modern Times;* R. Freeman Butts, *A Cultural History of Western Education* (2nd ed.; New York: McGraw-Hill, 1955); William Boyd, *The History of Western Education* (6th ed.; London: Black, 1952). More extended treatments are available in Georg Karl Mertz, *Das Schulwesen der deutschen Reformationszeit im 16. jahrhundert* (Heidelberg: Winter, 1902); Karl Hartfelder, *Philipp Melanchthon als Praeceptor Germaniae.*

The following translation is a revision of that which appeared in *PE* 4, 103-130, and is based on the original printing of Lucas Cranach in Wittenberg, *An die Radherrn aller Stedte deutsches lands: dass sie Christliche schulen auffrichten und halten sollen,* as that has been reprinted with annotations in *WA* 15, (9) 27-53.

TO THE COUNCILMEN
OF ALL CITIES IN GERMANY
THAT THEY ESTABLISH AND
MAINTAIN CHRISTIAN SCHOOLS

Grace and peace from God our Father and the Lord Jesus Christ. Honorable, wise, and dear sirs: Had I feared the command of men more than God[1] I should have remained silent on this subject, for it is now some three years since I was put under the ban and declared an outlaw,[2] and there are in Germany many of both high and low degree who on that account attack whatever I say and write, and shed much blood over it.[3] But God has opened my mouth and bidden me speak, and he supports me mightily. The more they rage against me, the more he strengthens and extends my cause—without any help or advice from me—as if he were laughing and holding their rage in derision, as it says in Psalm 2 [:4]. By this fact alone anyone whose mind is not hardened can see that this cause must be God's own, for it plainly bears the mark of a divine word and work; they always thrive best when men are most determined to persecute and suppress them.

Therefore, I will speak and (as Isaiah says) not keep silent as long as I live,[4] until Christ's righteousness goes forth as brightness, and his saving grace is lighted as a lamp [Isa. 62:1]. I beg of you now, all my dear sirs and friends, to receive this letter

---

[1] Cf. Acts 5:29.

[2] Pope Leo X's formal bull of excommunication against Luther, the *Decet Romanum pontificem*, was published January 3, 1521. On May 26 Emperor Charles V signed the Edict of Worms putting Luther under the ban of the empire. Schwiebert, *Luther and His Times*, pp. 492, 511-512.

[3] The earliest martyrs to the cause of Lutheranism were Henry Vos and Johann van den Esschen, who were burned at Brussels July 1, 1523. *LW* 32, 263.

[4] In a letter to Spalatin November 30, 1524, Luther remarked, "I daily expect the death decreed to the heretic." *S-J* 2, 264; *WA, Br* 3, 394.

kindly and take to heart my admonition. For no matter what I may be personally, still I can boast before God with a good conscience that in this matter I am not seeking my own advantage—which I could more readily attain by keeping silent—but am dealing sincerely and faithfully with you, and with the whole German nation into which God has placed me, whether men believe it or not. And I wish to assure you and declare to you frankly and openly that he who heeds me in this matter is most certainly heeding not me, but Christ; and he who gives me no heed is despising not me, but Christ [Luke 10:16]. For I know very well and am quite certain of the content and thrust of what I say and teach; and anyone who will rightly consider my teaching will also discover it for himself.

First of all, we are today experiencing in all the German lands how schools are everywhere being left to go to wrack and ruin. The universities are growing weak, and monasteries are declining. The grass withers and the flower fades, as Isaiah [40:7-8] says, because the breath of the Lord blows upon it through his word and shines upon it so hot through the gospel. For now it is becoming known through God's word how un-Christian these institutions are, and how they are devoted only to men's bellies. The carnal-minded masses are beginning to realize that they no longer have either the obligation or the opportunity to thrust their sons, daughters, and relatives into cloisters and foundations, and to turn them out of their own homes and property and establish them in others' property. For this reason no one is any longer willing to have his children get an education. "Why," they say, "should we bother to have them go to school if they are not to become priests, monks, or nuns? 'Twere better they should learn a livelihood to earn." [5]

---

[5] *Man las sie so mehr leren, da mit sie sich erneren.* The precise connection and meaning of this last sentence—a rhyming couplet—is obscure. We have been guided in our rendering by the arguments of Albrecht who construes the sentence as the concluding part of the protest of the opponents of education (hence included within the quotation marks) rather than as a quick rejoinder by Luther to their protest ("all the more then do they need a practical education"). "Studien zu Luther's Schrift 'An die Ratsherren aller Städte deutschen Lands, dass sie christliche Schulen aufrichten und halten sollen, 1524,'" *Theologische Studien und Kritiken,* Jahrgang 70, I[1] (Gotha: Perthes, 1897) pp. 696-698, 725-726.

The thoughts and purposes of such people are plainly evident from this confession of theirs. If in the cloisters and foundations, or the spiritual estate, they had been seeking not only the belly and the temporal welfare of their children but were earnestly concerned for their children's salvation and eternal bliss, they would not thus fold their hands and relapse into indifference, saying, "If the spiritual estate is no longer to be of any account, we can just as well let education go and not bother our heads about it." Instead, they would say, "If it be true, as the gospel teaches, that this estate is a perilous one for our children, then, dear sirs, show us some other way which will be pleasing to God and of benefit to them. For we certainly want to provide not only for our children's bellies, but for their souls as well." At least that is what truly Christian parents would say about it.

It is not surprising that the wicked devil takes a position in this matter and induces carnal and worldly hearts thus to neglect the children and young people. Who can blame him for it? He is the ruler and god of this world [John 14:30]; how can he possibly be pleased to see the gospel destroy his nests, the monasteries and the clerical gangs, in which he corrupts above all the young folks who mean so much, in fact everything, to him? How can we expect him to permit or promote the proper training of the young? He would indeed be a fool to allow and promote the establishment in his kingdom of the very thing by which that kingdom must be most speedily overthrown, which would happen if he were to lose that choice morsel—our dear young people—and have to suffer them to be supported at his own expense and by means of his own resources for the service of God.

Therefore, he acted most adroitly at the time when Christians were having their children trained and taught in a Christian manner. The young crowd bade fair to escape him entirely and to establish within his kingdom something that was quite intolerable. So he went to work, spread his nets, and set up such monasteries, schools, and estates that it was impossible for any lad to escape him, apart from a special miracle of God. But now that he sees his snares exposed through the word of God, he goes to the other extreme and will permit no learning at all.

Again he does the right and smart thing to preserve his kingdom and by all means retain his hold on the young crowd. If he can hold them, and they grow up under him and remain his, who can take anything from him? He then maintains undisputed possession of the world. For if he is to be dealt a blow that really hurts, it must be done through young people who have come to maturity in the knowledge of God, and who spread His word and teach it to others.

No one, positively no one, realizes that this is a despicable trick of the devil. It proceeds so unobtrusively that no one notices it, and the damage is done before one can take steps to prevent and remedy it. We are on the alert against Turks,[6] wars, and floods, because in such matters we can see what is harmful and what is beneficial. But no one is aware of the devil's wily purpose. No one is on the alert, but just goes quietly along. Even though only a single boy could thereby be trained to become a real Christian, we ought properly to give a hundred gulden to this cause for every gulden we would give to fight the Turk, even if he were breathing down our necks. For one real Christian is better and can do more good than all the men on earth.

Therefore, I beg all of you, my dear sirs and friends, for the sake of God and our poor young people, not to treat this matter as lightly as many do, who fail to realize what the ruler of this world [John 14:30] is up to. For it is a grave and important matter, and one which is of vital concern both to Christ and the world at large, that we take steps to help the youth. By so doing we will be taking steps to help also ourselves and everybody else. Bear in mind that such insidious, subtle, and crafty attacks of the devil must be met with great Christian determination. My dear sirs, if we have to spend such large sums every year on guns, roads, bridges, dams, and countless similar items to insure the temporal peace and prosperity of a city, why should not much more be devoted to the poor neglected youth—at least enough to engage one or two competent men to teach school?

Moreover, every citizen should be influenced by the following consideration. Formerly he was obliged to waste a great deal of

---

[6] See p. 44, n. 44; p. 116, n. 91; p. 352, n. 12.

money and property on indulgences, masses, vigils,[7] endowments, bequests, anniversaries,[8] mendicant friars, brotherhoods,[9] pilgrimages, and similar nonsense. Now that he is, by the grace of God, rid of such pillage and compulsory giving, he ought henceforth, out of gratitude to God and for his glory, to contribute a part of that amount toward schools for the training of the poor children. That would be an excellent investment. If the light of the gospel had not dawned and set him free, he would have had to continue indefinitely giving up to the above-mentioned robbers ten times that sum and more, without hope of return. Know also that where there arise hindrances, objections, impediments, and opposition to this proposal, there the devil is surely at work, the devil who voiced no such objection when men gave their money for monasteries and masses, pouring it out in a veritable stream; for he senses that this kind of giving is not to his advantage. Let this, then, my dear sirs and friends, be the first consideration to influence you, namely, that herein we are fighting against the devil as the most dangerous and subtle enemy of all.

A second consideration is, as St. Paul says in II Corinthians 6 [:1-2], that we should not accept the grace of God in vain and neglect the time of salvation. Almighty God has indeed graciously visited us Germans and proclaimed a true year of jubilee.[10] We have today the finest and most learned group of men, adorned with languages and all the arts, who could also render real service if only we would make use of them as instructors of the young people. Is it not evident that we are now able to prepare a boy in three years, so that at the age of fifteen or eighteen he will know more than all the universities and monasteries have known before? Indeed, what have men been learning till now in the universities and monasteries except to become asses, blockheads,

---

[7] *Vigilien* were services held in the cloisters at night. *LW* 36, 198, n. 59.

[8] On the *jartagen*, see p. 180, n. 37.

[9] On the *bruderschafften*, see p. 181, n. 39.

[10] *Ein recht gülden jar* means literally, "a truly golden year." Luther is alluding to the papal practice of proclaiming from time to time a jubilee year, which in Germany was popularly called a *"Güldenjahr."* During such a year throngs of pilgrims would visit Rome to earn the promised papal indulgence; their substantial gifts made it literally a "golden" year indeed for the church. *PE* 4, 107, n. 1. The reference, of course, is to the recent advances in humanistic education. See the Introduction, pp. 341-345.

and numbskulls? For twenty, even forty, years they pored over their books, and still failed to master either Latin or German, to say nothing of the scandalous and immoral life there in which many a fine young fellow was shamefully corrupted.

It is perfectly true that if universities and monasteries were to continue as they have been in the past, and there were no other place available where youth could study and live, then I could wish that no boy would ever study at all, but just remain dumb. For it is my earnest purpose, prayer, and desire that these asses' stalls and devil's training centers should either sink into the abyss or be converted into Christian schools. Now that God has so richly blessed us, however, and provided us with so many men able to instruct and train our youth aright, it is surely imperative that we not throw his blessing to the winds and let him knock in vain. He is standing at the door;[11] happy are we who open to him! He is calling us; blessed is he who answers him! If we turn a deaf ear and he should pass us by, who will bring him back again?

Let us remember our former misery, and the darkness in which we dwelt. Germany, I am sure, has never before heard so much of God's word as it is hearing today; certainly we read nothing of it in history. If we let it just slip by without thanks and honor, I fear we shall suffer a still more dreadful darkness and plague. O my beloved Germans, buy while the market is at your door; gather in the harvest while there is sunshine and fair weather; make use of God's grace and word while it is there! For you should know that God's word and grace is like a passing shower of rain which does not return where it has once been. It has been with the Jews, but when it's gone it's gone, and now they have nothing. Paul brought it to the Greeks; but again when it's gone it's gone, and now they have the Turk.[12] Rome and the Latins also had it; but when it's gone it's gone, and now they have the pope. And you Germans need not think that you will have it forever, for ingratitude and contempt will not make

---

[11] Cf. Rev. 3:20.
[12] From the conquest of Syria beginning in 635 until the fall of Constantinople in 1453 the Byzantines were constantly pressed by Islam, and the Greek church gradually lost its best territories to the Turks.

TO THE COUNCILMEN OF GERMANY

it stay. Therefore, seize it and hold it fast, whoever can; for lazy hands are bound to have a lean year.[13]

The third consideration is by far the most important of all, namely, the command of God, who through Moses urges and enjoins parents so often to instruct their children that Psalm 78 says: How earnestly he commanded our fathers to teach their children and to instruct their children's children [Ps. 78:5-6]. This is also evident in God's fourth commandment, in which the injunction that children shall obey their parents is so stern that he would even have rebellious children sentenced to death [Deut. 21:18-21]. Indeed, for what purpose do we older folks exist, other than to care for, instruct, and bring up the young? It is utterly impossible for these foolish young people to instruct and protect themselves. This is why God has entrusted them to us who are older and know from experience what is best for them. And God will hold us strictly accountable for them. This is also why Moses commands in Deuteronomy 32 [:7], "Ask your father and he will tell you; your elders, and they will show you."

It is a sin and a shame that matters have come to such a pass that we have to urge and be urged to educate our children and young people and to seek their best interests, when nature itself should drive us to do this and even the heathen afford us abundant examples of it. There is not a dumb animal which fails to care for its young and teach them what they need to know; the only exception is the ostrich, of which God says in Job 31 [39:16, 14] that she deals cruelly with her young as if they were not hers, and leaves her eggs upon the ground. What would it profit us to possess and perform everything else and be like pure saints, if we meanwhile neglected our chief purpose in life, namely, the care of the young? I also think that in the sight of God none among the outward sins so heavily burdens the world and merits such severe punishment as this very sin which we commit against the children by not educating them.

When I was a lad they had this maxim in school: *"Non minus est negligere scholarem quam corrumpere virginem"*; "It is just as bad to neglect a pupil as to despoil a virgin." The purpose

---

[13] *Faule haende müssen eyn bösses jar haben.* Wander (ed.), *Sprichwörter-Lexikon*, II, 300, *"Hand,"* No. 153.

of this maxim was to keep the schoolmasters on their toes, for in those days no greater sin was known that that of despoiling a virgin. But, dear Lord God, how light a sin it is to despoil virgins or wives (which, being a bodily and recognized sin, may be atoned for) in comparison with this sin of neglecting and despoiling precious souls, for the latter sin is not even recognized or acknowledged and is never atoned for.[14] O woe unto the world for ever and ever! Children are born every day and grow up in our midst, but, alas! there is no one to take charge of the youngsters and direct them. We just let matters take their own course. The monasteries and foundations should have seen to it; therefore, they are the very ones of whom Christ says, "Woe unto the world because of offenses! Whoever causes one of these little ones who believe in me to sin, it would be better for him to have a millstone fastened round his neck, and to be drowned in the depth of the sea" (Matt. 18:7, 6). They are nothing but devourers and destroyers of children.

Ah, you say, but all that is spoken to the parents; what business is it of councilmen and the authorities? Yes, that is true; but what if the parents fail to do their duty? Who then is to do it? Is it for this reason to be left undone, and the children neglected? How will the authorities and council then justify their position, that such matters are not their responsibility?

There are various reasons why parents neglect this duty. In

---

[14] Our rendering of the several ambiguous words in this sentence is based on considerations advanced by Albrecht, op. cit., pp. 698-702. Luther does not mean to say that a light sin—one against the body—because it is acknowledged can be atoned for, while a grave sin—one against the soul—even if acknowledged cannot be atoned for. His purpose is not to diminish the gravity of sexual sin, which was universally recognized, but by way of comparison to assert the generally unrecognized gravity of the sin of omission in matters of education. His assessment of the seriousness of a sin in terms of its detriment to body or to soul must be seen in the light of the fact that it derives from a proverb not of his own coinage which he is exploiting by way of hyperbole for his own purpose. It certainly runs in the direction of such biblical estimates of sin as those found in Matt. 21:31-32, Rom. 14:23, and Luke 18:9-13, where the chief sins are defined in terms of unbelief, a view utterly remote from the current Roman teaching and practice regarding confession. Cf. Luther's distinction between open sins and unbelief of the heart in his 1522 sermon on the Pharisee and the publican (WA 10III, 301) and in his later expositions of Galatians (WA 40I, 221) and Isaiah (WA 25, 121).

the first place, there are some who lack the goodness and decency to do it, even if they had the ability. Instead, like the ostrich [Job 39:14-16], they deal cruelly with their young. They are content to have laid the eggs and brought children into the world; beyond this they will do nothing more. But these children are supposed to live among us and with us in the community. How then can reason, and especially Christian charity, allow that they grow up uneducated, to poison and pollute the other children until at last the whole city is ruined, as happened in Sodom and Gomorrah [Gen. 19:1-25], and Gibeah [Judges 19–20], and a number of other cities?

In the second place, the great majority of parents unfortunately are wholly unfitted for this task. They do not know how children should be brought up and taught, for they themselves have learned nothing but how to care for their bellies. It takes extraordinary people to bring children up right and teach them well.

In the third place, even if parents had the ability and desire to do it themselves, they have neither the time nor the opportunity for it, what with their other duties and the care of the household. Necessity compels us, therefore, to engage public schoolteachers for the children—unless each one were willing to engage his own private tutor. But that would be too heavy a burden for the common man, and many a promising boy would again be neglected on account of poverty. Besides, many parents die, leaving orphans, and if we do not know from experience how they are cared for by their guardians it should be quite clear from the fact that God calls himself Father of the fatherless [Ps 68:5], of those who are neglected by everyone else. Then too there are others who have no children of their own, and therefore take no interest in the training of children.

It therefore behooves the council and the authorities to devote the greatest care and attention to the young. Since the property, honor, and life of the whole city have been committed to their faithful keeping, they would be remiss in their duty before God and man if they did not seek its welfare and improvement day and night with all the means at their command. Now the welfare of a city does not consist solely in accumulating vast treasures, building mighty walls and magnificent buildings, and producing a goodly supply of guns and armor. Indeed, where such things are plentiful, and reckless fools get control of them, it is so much the worse and the city suffers even greater loss. A city's best and greatest welfare, safety, and strength consist rather in its having many able, learned, wise, honorable, and well-educated citizens. They can then readily gather, protect, and properly use treasure and all manner of property.

So it was done in ancient Rome. There boys were so taught that by the time they reached their fifteenth, eighteenth, or twentieth year they were well versed in Latin, Greek, and all the liberal arts[15] (as they are called), and then immediately entered upon a political or military career. Their system produced intelligent, wise, and competent men, so skilled in every art and rich in experience that if all the bishops, priests, and monks in the whole of Germany today were rolled into one, you would not have the equal of a single Roman soldier. As a result their country prospered; they had capable and trained men for every position. So at all times throughout the world simple necessity has forced men, even among the heathen, to maintain pedagogues and schoolmasters if their nation was to be brought to a high standard. Hence, the word "schoolmaster" is used by Paul in Galatians 4[16] as a word taken from the common usage and practice of mankind, where he says, "The law was our schoolmaster."

Since a city should and must have [educated] people, and since there is a universal dearth of them and complaint that they are nowhere to be found, we dare not wait until they grow up of themselves; neither can we carve them out of stone nor hew them out of wood. Nor will God perform miracles as long as men can solve their problems by means of the other gifts he has

---

[15] The liberal arts were traditionally seven in number. Grammar, rhetoric, and dialectic comprised the trivium of the medieval elementary schools; music, arithmetic, geometry, and astronomy comprised the quadrivium of the secondary schools. *BG* 3, 32, n. 6. Luther's description has reference to Roman education in the shape it took after the end of the republic, as he had come to know it through his own reading of Cicero, Quintilian, and others. Albrecht, *Studien zu . . . "die Ratsherren,"* p. 710.

[16] Luther consistently rendered the *paidagōgos* of Gal. 3:24 (literally, "attendant" or "custodian"; cf. RSV) as *Zuchtmeyster* (literally, one who educates, trains, or disciplines in home, court, or school; cf. KJV). *WA, DB* 7, 182-183; Grimm, *Deutsches Wörterbuch*, VII, 275.

already granted them. Therefore, we must do our part and spare no labor or expense to produce and train such people ourselves. For whose fault is it that today our cities have so few capable people? Whose fault, if not that of authorities, who have left the young people to grow up like saplings in the forest, and have given no thought to their instruction and training? This is also why they have grown to maturity so misshapen that they cannot be used for building purposes, but are mere brushwood, fit only for kindling fires.[17]

After all, temporal government has to continue.[18] Are we then to permit none but louts and boors to rule, when we can do better than that? That would certainly be a crude and senseless policy. We might as well make lords out of swine and wolves, and set them to rule over those who refuse to give any thought to how they are ruled by men. Moreover, it is barbarous wickedness to think no further than this: We will rule now; what concern is it of ours how they will fare who come after us? Not over human beings, but over swine and dogs should such persons rule who in ruling seek only their own profit or glory. Even if we took the utmost pains to develop a group of able, learned, and skilled people for positions in government, there would still be plenty of labor and anxious care involved in seeing that things went well. What then is to happen if we take no pains at all?

"All right," you say again,[19] "suppose we do have to have schools; what is the use of teaching Latin, Greek, and Hebrew, and the other liberal arts? We could just as well use German for teaching the Bible and God's word, which is enough for our salvation."[20] I reply: Alas! I am only too well aware that we Germans must always be and remain brutes and stupid beasts, as the neighboring nations call us, epithets which we richly de-

---

[17] Cf. Matt. 13:30.

[18] On Luther's view of temporal government as an abiding divine institution, see his 1523 treatise on *Temporal Authority*, in this volume, pp. 85-87.

[19] *Aber mal* refers back to the last four lines of p. 348. Having discussed the need for education, Luther now considers its content.

[20] This was the position of the ex-monks at Erfurt, who disparaged higher education in the name of their new evangelical religion. See the Introduction, pp. 342-344, and Albrecht, *Studien zu . . . "die Ratsherren,"* pp. 733-745.

serve.[21] But I wonder why we never ask, "What is the use of silks, wine, spices, and other strange foreign wares[22] when we ourselves have in Germany wine, grain, wool, flax, wood, and stone not only in quantities sufficient for our needs, but also of the best and choicest quality for our glory and ornament?" Languages and the arts, which can do us no harm, but are actually a greater ornament, profit, glory, and benefit, both for the understanding of Holy Scripture and the conduct of temporal government—these we despise. But foreign wares, which are neither necessary nor useful, and in addition strip us down to a mere skeleton—these we cannot do without. Are not we Germans justly dubbed fools and beasts?

Truly, if there were no other benefit connected with the languages, this should be enough to delight and inspire us, namely, that they are so fine and noble a gift of God, with which he is now so richly visiting and blessing us Germans above all other lands. We do not see many instances where the devil has allowed them to flourish by means of the universities and monasteries; indeed, these have always raged against languages and are even now raging. For the devil smelled a rat, and perceived that if the languages were revived a hole would be knocked in his kingdom which he could not easily stop up again. Since he found he could not prevent their revival, he now aims to keep them on such slender rations that they will of themselves decline and pass away. They are not a welcome guest in his house, so he plans to offer them such meager entertainment that they will not prolong their stay. Very few of us, my dear sirs, see through this evil design of the devil.

Therefore, my beloved Germans, let us get our eyes open, thank God for this precious treasure, and guard it well, lest the devil vent his spite and it be taken away from us again. Although the gospel came and still comes to us through the Holy Spirit alone, we cannot deny that it came through the medium of languages, was spread abroad by that means, and must be preserved

---

21 Luther is alluding to the common sneers of the Italian humanists at German crudities. WA 15, 36, n. 3.
22 On Luther's opposition to foreign wares, see his 1524 treatise on *Trade*, in this volume, pp. 246-247.

by the same means. For just when God wanted to spread the gospel throughout the world by means of the apostles he gave the tongues for that purpose [Acts 2:1-11]. Even before that, by means of the Roman Empire he had spread the Latin and Greek languages widely in every land in order that his gospel might the more speedily bear fruit far and wide. He has done the same thing now as well. Formerly no one knew why God had the languages revived, but now for the first time we see that it was done for the sake of the gospel, which he intended to bring to light and use in exposing and destroying the kingdom of Antichrist.[23] To this end he gave over Greece to the Turk in order that the Greeks, driven out and scattered, might disseminate their language and provide an incentive to the study of other languages as well.

In proportion then as we value the gospel, let us zealously hold to the languages. For it was not without purpose that God caused his Scriptures to be set down in these two languages alone—the Old Testament in Hebrew, the New in Greek. Now if God did not despise them but chose them above all others for his word, then we too ought to honor them above all others. St. Paul declared it to be the peculiar glory and distinction of Hebrew that God's word was given in that language, when he said in Romans 3 [:1-2], "What advantage or profit have those who are circumcised? Much indeed. To begin with, God's speech[24] is entrusted to them." King David too boasts in Psalm 147 [:19-20], "He declares his word to Jacob, his statutes and ordinances to Israel. He has not dealt thus with any other nation or revealed to them his ordinances." Hence, too, the Hebrew language is called sacred. And St. Paul, in Romans 1 [:2], calls it "the holy scriptures," doubtless on account of the holy word of God which is comprehended [verfasset] therein. Similarly, the Greek language too may be called sacred, because it was chosen above all others as the language in which the New Testament was to be written, and because by it other languages too have been sanctified as it

[23] On Luther's identification of the pope with Antichrist, see p. 60, n. 8.
[24] *Gottes rede* was rendered as *was Gott gered hat* (literally, "what God has spoken") in Luther's 1522 New Testament and in subsequent editions until the complete Bible of 1546 where it was rendered as *Gotteswort* (literally, "God's Word"). WA, DB 7, 36-37.

spilled over into them like a fountain through the medium of translation.[25]

And let us be sure of this: we will not long preserve the gospel without the languages. The languages are the sheath in which this sword of the Spirit [Eph. 6:17] is contained; they are the casket in which this jewel is enshrined; they are the vessel in which this wine is held; they are the larder in which this food is stored; and, as the gospel itself points out [Matt. 14:20], they are the baskets in which are kept these loaves and fishes and fragments. If through our neglect we let the languages go (which God forbid!), we shall not only lose the gospel, but the time will come when we shall be unable either to speak or write a correct Latin or German. As proof and warning of this, let us take the deplorable and dreadful example of the universities and monasteries, in which men have not only unlearned the gospel, but have in addition so corrupted the Latin and German languages that the miserable folk have been fairly turned into beasts, unable to speak or write a correct German or Latin, and have wellnigh lost their natural reason to boot.

For this reason even the apostles themselves considered it necessary to set down the New Testament and hold it fast in the Greek language, doubtless in order to preserve it for us there safe and sound as in a sacred ark. For they foresaw all that was to come, and now has come to pass; they knew that if it was left exclusively to men's memory, wild and fearful disorder and confusion and a host of varied interpretations, fancies, and doctrines would arise in the Christian church, and that this could not be prevented and the simple folk protected unless the New Testament were set down with certainty in written language. Hence, it is inevitable that unless the languages remain, the gospel must finally perish.

Experience too has proved this and still gives evidence of it. For as soon as the languages declined to the vanishing point, after the apostolic age, the gospel and faith and Christianity itself declined more and more until under the pope they disappeared entirely. After the decline of the languages Christianity witnessed

---

[25] Our rendering of the difficult sentence is based on the suggestions of Albrecht, *Studien zu . . . "die Ratsherren,"* pp. 702-703.

little that was worth anything; instead, a great many dreadful abominations arose because of ignorance of the languages. On the other hand, now that the languages have been revived, they are bringing with them so bright a light and accomplishing such great things that the whole world stands amazed and has to acknowledge that we have the gospel just as pure and undefiled as the apostles had it, that it has been wholly restored to its original purity, far beyond what it was in the days of St. Jerome and St. Augustine. In short, the Holy Spirit is no fool. He does not busy himself with inconsequential or useless matters. He regarded the languages as so useful and necessary to Christianity that he ofttimes brought them down with him from heaven.[26] This alone should be a sufficient motive for us to pursue them with diligence and reverence and not to despise them, for he himself has now revived them again upon the earth.

Yes, you say, but many of the fathers were saved and even became teachers without the languages. That is true. But how do you account for the fact that they so often erred in the Scriptures? How often does not St. Augustine err in the Psalms and in his other expositions, and Hilary[27] too—in fact, all those who have undertaken to expound Scripture without a knowledge of the languages? Even though what they said about a subject at times was perfectly true, they were never quite sure whether it really was present there in the passage where by their interpretation they thought to find it. Let me give you an example: It is rightly said that Christ is the Son of God; but how ridiculous it must have sounded to the ears of their adversaries when they attempted to prove this by citing from Psalm 110: *"Tecum principium in die virtutis tuae,"*[28] though in the Hebrew there is not a word about the

---

26 Acts 2:4; 10:46; I Cor. 12:10; 14:2-19.
27 Hilary (*ca.* 315-367), the Bishop of Poitiers, was important to Luther primarily because of his commentaries on the psalms. See, e.g., *LW* 14, 285.
28 This Vulgate version of Ps. 110:3 (translated literally, "With thee is sovereignty in the day of thy strength") is derived in part from the Septuagint text (*meta sou* . . .), which itself rests upon a misunderstanding of the Hebrew text whereby "your people" (cf. RSV) was read as "with you" through the simple change of one vowel point. The error of course could never be discovered without renewed examination of the Hebrew original. Luther was critical of the Vulgate rendering already in his earliest (1513-1516) commentary on the Psalms (see *WA* 4, 227, 233, 516-517). Au-

Deity in this passage! When men attempt to defend the faith with such uncertain arguments and mistaken proof texts, are not Christians put to shame and made a laughingstock in the eyes of adversaries who know the language? The adversaries only become more stiff-necked in their error and have an excellent pretext for regarding our faith as a mere human delusion.

When our faith is thus held up to ridicule, where does the fault lie? It lies in our ignorance of the languages; and there is no other way out than to learn the languages. Was not St. Jerome compelled to translate the Psalter anew from the Hebrew[29] because, when we quoted our [Latin] Psalter in disputes with the Jews, they sneered at us, pointing out that our texts did not read that way in the original Hebrew? Now the expositions of all the early fathers who dealt with Scripture apart from a knowledge of the languages (even when their teaching is not in error) are such that they often employ uncertain, indefensible, and inappropriate expressions. They grope their way like a blind man along the wall, frequently missing the sense of the text and twisting it to suit their fancy, as in the case of the verse mentioned above, *"Tecum principium,"* etc. Even St. Augustine himself is obliged to confess, as he does in his *Christian Instruction,*[30]

gustine had interpreted *principium* not in terms of spontaneity or voluntariness as did Luther (WA 4, 233; see also his constant rendering of the Psalter from 1524 on—*williglich*—in WA, DB 10¹, 476-477), but in terms of God the Father. See Albrecht, *Studien zu . . . "die Ratsherren,"* pp. 713-714.

[29] Jerome's first revision of the Old Latin Psalter, done in 383 at Rome and known as the *Psalterium Romanum,* was based on the Septuagint. His second revision, done in Palestine about four years later and known as the Gallican Psalter was also based on the Septuagint; it became the current version in the Latin Church and is still printed in most Vulgate Bibles. Finally, at the suggestion of Sophronius about 392, Jerome translated the Psalms from the Hebrew. Luther is probably thinking of the exchange of letters between Augustine and Jerome in which the former placed great confidence in the accuracy of the Septuagint—over against the great diversity of Latin Scriptures—while the latter's purpose was "not so much . . . to do away with the old texts, which, with their emendations, I translated from Greek into Latin for men of my own tongue, but rather to bring out that evidence which was passed over or corrupted by the Jews, so that our people might know what the Hebrew text really contained." See Sister Wilfrid Parsons (trans.), *Saint Augustine: Letters, I.* FC 9, 95, 325-328, 363-367, especially p. 365.

[30] "Men who know the Latin language . . . have need of two others in order to understand the sacred Scriptures. These are Hebrew and Greek, by which they may turn back to the originals if the infinite variance of Latin translators cause any uncertainty." John J. Gavigan (trans.), "Christian Instruc-

that a Christian teacher who is to expound the Scriptures must know Greek and Hebrew in addition to Latin. Otherwise, it is impossible to avoid constant stumbling; indeed, there are plenty of problems to work out even when one is well versed in the languages.

There is a vast difference therefore between a simple preacher of the faith and a person who expounds Scripture, or, as St. Paul puts it [I Cor. 12:28-30; 14:26-32], a prophet. A simple preacher (it is true) has so many clear passages and texts available through translations that he can know and teach Christ, lead a holy life, and preach to others. But when it comes to interpreting Scripture, and working with it on your own, and disputing with those who cite it incorrectly, he is unequal to the task; that cannot be done without languages. Now there must always be such prophets in the Christian church who can dig into Scripture, expound it, and carry on disputations. A saintly life and right doctrine are not enough. Hence, languages are absolutely and altogether necessary in the Christian church, as are the prophets or interpreters; although it is not necessary that every Christian or every preacher be such a prophet, as St. Paul points out in I Corinthians 12 [:4-30] and Ephesians 4 [:11].

Thus, it has come about that since the days of the apostles Scripture has remained so obscure, and no sure and trustworthy expositions of it have ever been written. For even the holy fathers (as we have said) frequently erred. And because of their ignorance of the languages they seldom agree; one says this, another that. St. Bernard[31] was a man so lofty in spirit that I almost venture to set him above all other celebrated teachers both ancient and modern. But note how often he plays (spiritually to be sure) with the Scriptures and twists them out of their true sense. This is also why the sophists[32] have contended that Scripture is obscure; they have held that God's word by its very nature is obscure and

---

tion" (*De doctrina Christiana* II, 11), *Writings of Saint Augustine*. FC 4, 73. *MPL* 34, 42.

[31] Bernard (1090-1153), abbot of Clairvaux, foremost leader of the rigorist Cistercian order and founder of one hundred sixty-three Cistercian monasteries, was a prominent mystic renowned for his preaching. For an example of Luther's critique of Bernard's exegesis, see *LW* 35, 217, n. 25.

[32] See p. 82, n. 5.

employs a peculiar style of speech. But they fail to realize that the whole trouble lies in the languages. If we understood the languages nothing clearer would ever have been spoken than God's word. A Turk's speech must needs be obscure to me—because I do not know the language—while a Turkish child of seven would understand him easily.

Hence, it is also a stupid undertaking to attempt to gain an understanding of Scripture by laboring through the commentaries of the fathers and a multitude of books and glosses.[33] Instead of this, men should have devoted themselves to the languages. Because they were ignorant of languages, the dear fathers at times expended many words in dealing with a text. Yet when they were all done they had scarcely taken its measure; they were half right and half wrong. Still, you continue to pore over them with immense labor even though, if you knew the languages, you could get further with the passage than they whom you are following. As sunshine is to shadow, so is the language itself compared to all the glosses of the fathers.

Since it becomes Christians then to make good use of the Holy Scriptures as their one and only book and it is a sin and a shame not to know our own book or to understand the speech and words of our God, it is a still greater sin and loss that we do not study languages, especially in these days when God is offering and giving us men and books and every facility and inducement to this study, and desires his Bible to be an open book. O how happy the dear fathers would have been if they had had our opportunity to study the languages and come thus prepared to the Holy Scriptures! What great toil and effort it cost them to gather up a few crumbs, while we with half the labor—yes, almost without any labor at all—can acquire the whole loaf! O how their effort puts our indolence to shame! Yes, how sternly God will judge our lethargy and ingratitude!

---

[33] Having finally read the Bible along with the *glossa ordinaria* as a monk at Erfurt and carefully taken into account the exegesis of the fathers in his own early lectures, Luther did not sharply distinguish between the authority of Scripture and that of the fathers, traditionally set alongside or above Scripture in the common scholastic method of studying theology, until his 1520 *Assertio omnium articulorum* (cf. *LW* 32, 11-12, which is based on the German version) and his 1521 controversy with Emser (see *PE* 3, 332-353). Albrecht, *Studien zu . . . "die Ratsherren,"* pp. 743-745.

Here belongs also what St. Paul calls for in I Corinthians 14
[:27, 29], namely, that in the Christian church all teachings must
be judged. For this a knowledge of the language is needful above
all else. The preacher or teacher can expound the Bible from
beginning to end as he pleases, accurately or inaccurately, if there
is no one there to judge whether he is doing it right or wrong.
But in order to judge, one must have a knowledge of the languages; it cannot be done in any other way. Therefore, although
faith and the gospel may indeed be proclaimed by simple preachers
without a knowledge of languages, such preaching is flat and
tame; people finally become weary and bored with it, and it falls
to the ground. But where the preacher is versed in the languages,
there is a freshness and vigor in his preaching, Scripture is treated
in its entirety, and faith finds itself constantly renewed by a
continual variety of words and illustrations. Hence, Psalm 129[34]
likens such scriptural studies to a hunt, saying: to the deer God
opens the dense forests; and Psalm 1 [:3] likens them to a tree
with a plentiful supply of water, whose leaves are always green.

We should not be led astray because some boast of the Spirit
and consider Scripture of little worth,[35] and others, such as the
Waldensian Brethren,[36] think the languages are unnecessary. Dear
friend, say what you will about the Spirit, I too have been in

---

[34] Ps. 29:9; Luther, or his printer, by mistake slipped in another digit. His
understanding of the verse is based on the Vulgate, whose obscurity is
compounded by Luther's reading of *cervas* ("deer") for *cervos* ("forked
stakes"; Douay: "oaks"). This understanding, including the interpretation
of "forests" in terms of "the obscure books of the Old Testament," goes back
to Luther's earliest commentary of 1513-1516 on the psalms. WA 3, 157.
Actually, both psalm passages are here interpreted allegorically.
[35] This is an allusion to zealots and fanatics such as Karlstadt, Münzer, and
the Zwickau prophets. Luther had begun to warn against Münzer already
in 1523 and was soon to publish further writings culminating in his *Against
the Heavenly Prophets* of 1525. See LW 40, 47-223.
[36] Luther commonly referred to the Bohemian Brethren as "Waldensians,"
as in his treatise of less than a year earlier, *The Adoration of the Sacrament*
(1523), the treatise in which he also urged them not to "neglect the languages." See LW 36, 271-276 and 304. Paul Speratus, who had originally
established the relationship between Luther and the Brethren was at the
time of this writing a guest in Luther's house, having been driven out of
Moravia. Luther's incidental reference to the Bohemians may be significant
for an understanding of the various other groups inimical to education;
Albrecht suggests the possibility of their being influenced directly by the
radical Taborites. *Studien zu . . . "die Ratsherren,"* pp. 727-728.

the Spirit and have seen the Spirit, perhaps even more of it (if it comes to boasting of one's own flesh[37]) than those fellows with all their boasting will see in a year. Moreover, my spirit has given some account of itself, while theirs sits quietly in its corner and does little more than brag about itself. I know full well that while it is the Spirit alone who accomplishes everything, I would surely have never flushed a covey[38] if the languages had not helped me and given me a sure and certain knowledge of Scripture. I too could have lived uprightly and preached the truth in seclusion; but then I should have left undisturbed the pope, the sophists, and the whole anti-Christian regime. The devil does not respect my spirit as highly as he does my speech and pen when they deal with Scripture. For my spirit takes from him nothing but myself alone; but Holy Scripture and the languages leave him little room on earth, and wreak havoc in his kingdom.

So I can by no means commend the Waldensian Brethren for their neglect of the languages. For even though they may teach the truth, they inevitably often miss the true meaning of the text, and thus are neither equipped nor fit for defending the faith against error. Moreover, their teaching is so obscure and couched in such peculiar terms, differing from the language of Scripture, that I fear it is not or will not remain pure. For there is great danger in speaking of things of God in a different manner and in different terms than God himself employs. In short, they may lead saintly lives and teach sacred things among themselves, but so long as they remain without the languages they cannot but lack what all the rest lack, namely, the ability to treat Scripture with certainty and thoroughness and to be useful to other nations. Because they could do this, but will not, they have to figure out for themselves how they will answer for it to God.

To this point we have been speaking about the necessity and

---

37 Cf. II Cor. 12:1-6 and Phil. 3:4.
38 *Were ich doch allen püsschen zu ferne gewest.* We have been guided in the rendering of this difficult clause, and in the construing of its obscure syntactical relationship to the clauses preceding it, by the suggestions of Albrecht, *Studien zu . . . "die Ratsherren,"* pp. 703-705. It seems clearly to have reference to the matter of success, and to be derived in all likelihood from some proverbial expression, perhaps one connected with the hunt to which Luther had just alluded in connection with Ps. 29:9.

value of languages and Christian schools for the spiritual realm and the salvation of souls. Now let us consider also the body. Let us suppose that there were no soul, no heaven or hell, and that we were to consider solely the temporal government from the standpoint of its worldly functions. Does it not need good schools and educated persons even more than the spiritual realm? Hitherto, the sophists have shown no concern whatever for the temporal government, and have designed their schools so exclusively for the spiritual estate that it has become almost a disgrace for an educated man to marry. He has had to hear such remarks as, "Well! so he is turning worldly and does not want to become spiritual," just as if their spiritual estate alone were pleasing to God, and the worldly estate (as they call it) were altogether of the devil and un-Christian. But in the sight of God it is they themselves who are meanwhile becoming the devil's own (as happened to the nation of Israel during the Babylonian Captivity [II Kings 24:14]); only the despised rabble has remained in the land and in the right estate, while the better class of people and the leaders are carried off with tonsure and cowl to the devil in Babylon.[39]

It is not necessary to repeat here that the temporal government is a divinely ordained estate (I have elsewhere[40] treated this subject so fully that I trust no one has any doubt about it). The question is rather: How are we to get good and capable men into it? Here we are excelled and put to shame by the pagans of old, especially the Romans and the Greeks. Although they had no idea of whether this estate were pleasing to God or not, they were so earnest and diligent in educating and training their young boys and girls to fit them for the task, that when I call it to mind I am forced to blush for us Christians, and especially for us Germans. We are such utter blockheads and beasts that we dare to say, "Pray, why have schools for people who are not going to become spiritual?" Yet we know, or at least we ought to know, how essential and beneficial it is—and pleasing to God—that a

---

[39] Luther had used this same illustration in his 1520 *The Babylonian Captivity of the Church. LW* 36, 78.
[40] See Luther's *Temporal Authority: To What Extent it Should be Obeyed* (1523), in this volume, pp. 85-104.

prince, lord, councilman, or other person in a position of authority be educated and qualified to perform the functions of his office as a Christian should.

Now if (as we have assumed) there were no souls, and there were no need at all of schools and languages for the sake of the Scriptures and of God, this one consideration alone would be sufficient to justify the establishment everywhere of the very best schools for both boys and girls, namely, that in order to maintain its temporal estate outwardly the world must have good and capable men and women, men able to rule well over land and people, women able to manage the household and train children and servants aright. Now such men must come from our boys, and such women from our girls. Therefore, it is a matter of properly educating and training our boys and girls to that end. I have pointed out above that the common man is doing nothing about it; he is incapable of it, unwilling, and ignorant of what to do. Princes and lords ought to be doing it, but they must needs be sleigh riding, drinking, and parading about in masquerades.[41] They are burdened with high and important functions in cellar, kitchen, and bedroom. And the few who might want to do it must stand in fear of the rest lest they be taken for fools or heretics. Therefore, dear councilmen, it rests with you alone; you have a better authority and occasion to do it than princes and lords.

But, you say, everyone may teach his sons and daughters himself, or at least train them in proper discipline. Answer: Yes, we can readily see what such teaching and training amount to. Even when the training is done to perfection and succeeds, the net result is little more than a certain enforced outward respectability; underneath, they are nothing but the same old blockheads, unable to converse intelligently on any subject, or to assist or counsel anyone. But if children were instructed and trained in schools, or wherever learned and well-trained schoolmasters and schoolmistresses were available to teach the languages, the other arts, and history, they would then hear of the doings and sayings of the entire world, and how things went with various cities, kingdoms, princes, men, and women. Thus, they could in a short time set

[41] See Luther's criticism of the rulers' preoccupation with amusements to the neglect of their office elsewhere in this volume, pp. 120-121 and 249-250.

before themselves as in a mirror the character, life, counsels, and purposes—successful and unsuccessful—of the whole world from the beginning; on the basis of which they could then draw the proper inferences and in the fear of God take their own place in the stream of human events. In addition, they could gain from history the knowledge and understanding of what to seek and what to avoid in this outward life, and be able to advise and direct others accordingly. The training we undertake at home, apart from such schools, is intended to make us wise through our own experience. Before that can be accomplished we will be dead a hundred times over, and will have acted rashly throughout our mortal life, for it takes a long time to acquire personal experience.

Now since the young must always be hopping and skipping, or at least doing something that they enjoy, and since one cannot very well forbid this—nor would it be wise to forbid them everything—why then should we not set up such schools for them and introduce them to such studies? By the grace of God it is now possible for children to study with pleasure and in play languages, or other arts, or history. Today, schools are not what they once were, a hell and purgatory in which we were tormented with *casualibus* and *temporalibus*,[42] and yet learned less than nothing despite all the flogging, trembling, anguish, and misery. If we take so much time and trouble to teach children card-playing, singing, and dancing, why do we not take as much time to teach them reading and other disciplines while they are young and have the time, and are apt and eager to learn? For my part, if I had children[43] and could manage it, I would have them study not only languages and history, but also singing and music together with the whole of mathematics.[44] For what is all this but

---

[42] Luther did not object to "cases" and "tenses" as such but to the perverted methods whereby declining and conjugating were made disciplinary exercises in the classroom. Albrecht, *Studien zu . . . "die Ratsherren,"* p. 709.

[43] Luther, still a bachelor, married Katherine von Bora some sixteen months later on June 13, 1525, and eventually became the father of three sons and three daughters.

[44] Luther here distinguishes between the practical art of singing and the theoretical discipline of music, the latter being, with arithmetic, geometry, and astronomy, a part of the quadrivium, generally termed the mathematical disciplines in the Middle Ages. See p. 356, n. 15, and Albrecht, *ibid.*

mere child's play? The ancient Greeks trained their children in these disciplines; yet they grew up to be people of wondrous ability, subsequently fit for everything. How I regret now that I did not read more poets and historians, and that no one taught me them! Instead, I was obliged to read at great cost, toil, and detriment to myself, that devil's dung, the philosophers and sophists, from which I have all I can do to purge myself.

So you say, "But who can thus spare his children and train them all to be young gentlemen? There is work for them to do at home," etc. Answer: It is not my intention either to have such schools established as we have had heretofore, where a boy slaved away at his Donatus[45] and Alexander[46] for twenty or thirty years and still learned nothing. Today we are living in a different world, and things are being done differently. My idea is to have the boys attend such a school for one or two hours during the day, and spend the remainder of the time working at home, learning a trade, or doing whatever is expected of them. In this way, study and work will go hand-in-hand while the boys are young and able to do both. Otherwise, they spend at least ten times as much time anyway with their pea shooters, ballplaying, racing, and tussling.

In like manner, a girl can surely find time enough to attend school for an hour a day, and still take care of her duties at home. She spends much more time than that anyway in sleeping, dancing, and playing. Only one thing is lacking, the earnest desire to train the young and to benefit and serve the world with

---

[45] Aelius Donatus, teacher of St. Jerome at Rome about the year 355, wrote the elementary Latin grammar which bears his name. It was originally in two parts, the *Ars minor* and *Ars grammatica*. The latter soon fell into disuse, but the former remained for more than a thousand years the chief textbook for teaching the rudiments of Latin grammar. It was among the earliest products of Gutenberg's press. See the English translation by Wayland Johnson Chase, *The Ars minor of Donatus* ("Wisconsin Studies in the Social Sciences and History," No. 11 [Madison, Wis., 1926]).

[46] Alexander de Villa-Dei, a Franciscan in Normandy, in 1199 composed the *Doctrinale puerorum,* a grammatical treatise in hexameters designed to help pupils memorize the necessary rules; it became immensely popular for over three hundred years. Alexander drew his illustrations from the later Christian poets rather than from the ancient classics, and is largely responsible for the decadence of Latin style in the later Middle Ages. See the text in Dietrich Reichling (ed.), *Doctrinale* ("Monumenta Germaniae Paedagogica," Vol. XII [Berlin: Hofmann, 1893]). See Henry Osborn Taylor, *The Medieval Mind* (3rd American ed., 2 vols.; New York: Macmillan, 1919), II, 152-154.

able men and women. The devil very much prefers coarse blockheads and ne'er-do-wells, lest men get along too well on earth.

The exceptional pupils, who give promise of becoming skilled teachers, preachers, or holders of other ecclesiastical positions, should be allowed to continue in school longer, or even be dedicated to a life of study, as we read of [those who trained][47] the holy martyrs SS. Agnes, Agatha, Lucy,[48] and others. That is how the monasteries and foundations originated; they have since been wholly perverted to a different and damnable use. There is great need of such advanced study, for the tonsured crowd is fast dwindling. Besides, most of them are unfit to teach or to rule, for all they know is to care for their bellies, which is indeed all they have been taught. We must certainly have men to administer God's word and sacraments and to be shepherds of souls. But where shall we get them if we let our schools go by the board, and fail to replace them with others that are Christian? The schools that have been maintained hitherto, even though they do not die out entirely, can produce nothing but lost and pernicious deceivers.

It is highly necessary, therefore, that we take some positive action in this matter before it is too late; not only on account of the young people, but also in order to preserve both our spiritual and temporal estates. If we miss this opportunity, we

---

[47] The text itself actually speaks of the training imparted by, rather than given to, the martyrs. Albrecht (*op. cit.*, pp. 693-694), however, suggests that our present rendering may have been intended. Parallels for this line of thought are to be found elsewhere in Luther, particularly in his 1520 *Open Letter to the Christian Nobility* (*PE* 2, 118 and 152), his 1521 *Against Latomus* (*LW* 32, 258), and his 1523 *Ordering of Divine Worship* (*PE* 6, 61). Several early manuscripts as well as the Latin translation of Obsopoeus so construe the meaning. *The Golden Legend of Jacobus de Voragine* affords no evidence of the teaching activity of these women. Paul Pietsch, on the other hand, thinks that Luther may perhaps have used a different source, or been himself in error, but that it is distinctly possible that Luther actually intended to speak of instruction imparted by, rather than received by, the martyrs; he cites the ambiguity of *PE* 2, 152, in this regard, and might have cited the 1521 *De votis monasticis* (*WA* 8, 615) as well.

[48] The Roman maiden Agnes, traditionally esteemed for her youthful chastity and innocence, was martyred under Diocletian, *ca.* A.D. 304. Both born in Sicily, Agatha was martyred under Decius, *ca.* A.D. 250, and Lucy (see p. 25, n. 16) was martyred under Diocletian, *ca.* A.D. 304. All three names occur in the litany of the saints in the canon of the mass (see the text in *LW* 36, 322).

may perhaps find our hands tied later on when we would gladly attend to it, and ever after have to suffer in vain the pangs of remorse. God is offering us ample help; he stretches forth his hand and gives us all things needful for this task. If we disdain his offer we are already judged with the people of Israel, of whom Isaiah says [65:2], "I spread out my hand all the day to an unbelieving and rebellious people"; and in Proverbs 1 [:24-26] we read, "I have stretched out my hand, and no one has heeded; you have ignored all my counsel. Very well, then I will also laugh at your calamity, and will mock when your misfortune overtakes you," etc. Of this let us beware! Consider, for example, what a great effort King Solomon made in this matter; so deeply was he concerned for the young that in the midst of his royal duties he wrote for them a book called Proverbs. Consider Christ himself, how he draws little children to him, how urgently in Matthew 18 [:5, 10] he commends them to us and praises the angels who wait upon them, in order to show us how great a service it is when we train the young properly. On the other hand, how terrible is his wrath when we offend them and suffer them to perish! [Matt. 18:6].

Therefore, dear sirs, take this task to heart which God so earnestly requires of you, which your office imposes upon you, which is so necessary for our youth, and with which neither church [geyst] nor world can dispense. Alas! we have lain idle and rotting in the darkness long enough; we have been German beasts all too long. Let us for once make use of our reason, that God may perceive our thankfulness for his benefits, and other nations see that we too are human beings, able either to learn something useful from others or to teach them in order that even through us the world may be made better. I have done my part. It has truly been my purpose to counsel and assist the German nation. If there be some who despise me for this and refuse to listen to my sincere advice because they think they know better, I cannot help it. I know full well that others could have done this better; since they keep silent, I am doing it as well as I can. It is surely better to have spoken out on the subject, however inadequately, than to have remained altogether silent about it. It is my hope that God will awaken some of you, so that my well-meant advice may not be offered in vain, and instead of having regard for the one who utters it you will rather be stirred by the cause itself to do something about it.

Finally, one thing more merits serious consideration by all those who earnestly desire to have such schools and languages established and maintained in Germany. It is this: no effort or expense should be spared to provide good libraries or book repositories, especially in the larger cities which can well afford it. For if the gospel and all the arts are to be preserved, they must be set down and held fast in books and writings (as was done by the prophets and apostles themselves, as I have said above).[49] This is essential, not only that those who are to be our spiritual and temporal leaders may have books to read and study, but also that the good books may be preserved and not lost, together with the arts and languages which we now have by the grace of God. St. Paul too was concerned about this when he charged Timothy to give attention to reading [I Tim. 4:13], and bade him bring with him the parchments from Troas [II Tim. 4:13].

Indeed, all the kingdoms which ever amounted to anything gave careful attention to this matter. This is especially true of the people of Israel, among whom Moses was the first to begin the practice when he had the book of the law kept in the ark of God [Deut. 31:25-26]. He put it in charge of the Levites so that whoever needed a copy might obtain one from them. He even commanded the king to procure from them a copy of this book [Deut. 17:18]. Thus, we see how God directed the Levitical priesthood, among its other duties, to watch over and care for the books. Later this library was added to and improved by Joshua, then by Samuel, David, Solomon, Isaiah, and by many other kings and prophets. Thence have come the Holy Scriptures of the Old Testament, which would never have been collected or preserved had God not required such care to be bestowed upon them.

Following this example, the monasteries and foundations of old also established libraries, although there were few good books among them. What a loss it was that they neglected to

---

[49] See pp. 356-370.

acquire books and good libraries at that time, when the books and men for it were available, became painfully evident later when, as time went on, unfortunately all the arts and languages declined. Instead of worthwhile books, the stupid, useless, and harmful books of the monks, such as *Catholicon, Florista, Grecista, Labyrinthus, Dormi secure,*[50] and the like asses' dung were introduced by the devil. Because of such books the Latin language was ruined, and there remained nowhere a decent school, course of instruction, or method of study. This situation lasted until, as we have experienced and observed, the languages and arts were laboriously recovered—although imperfectly—from bits and fragments of old books hidden among dust and worms. Men are still painfully searching for them every day, just as people poke through the ashes of a ruined city seeking the treasures and jewels.

This served us right; God has properly repaid us for our ingratitude in not considering his kindness toward us and failing to provide for a constant supply of good books and learned men while we had the time and opportunity. When we neglected this, as though it were no concern of ours, he in turn did the same; instead of Holy Scripture and good books, he suffered Aristotle[51]

---

[50] The Latin lexicon *Summa grammaticalis,* commonly known as *Catholicon,* was compiled about 1286 by the Dominican John of Genoa, sometimes called Balbi or de Balbis (d. *ca.* 1298) comprising treatises on orthography, etymology, grammar, prosody, rhetoric, and an etymological dictionary of the Latin language, it appeared in a number of printed editions before 1500.

A rhymed Latin syntax, composed in 1317 by Ludolf von Luchow of Hildesheim, the *Flores grammaticae* gave its author the nickname "Florista," and the book itself subsequently came to be called by that name. The *Graecismus,* a grammatical treatise in hexameters, interposed with elegiacs, ascribed to Eberhard of Bethune (*fl.* 1212), got its name from the tenth chapter, which takes up Greek etymologies; this book too came to be called by the nickname it had won for its author.

The *Labyrinthus* was an early thirteenth-century poem, *De miseriis rectorum scholarum,* also by Eberhard of Bethune.

The *Dormi secure* was a collection of seventy-one sermons for the church year and holy days, compiled ostensibly by the Franciscan, Johann von Werden (*ca.* 1450); the title implies that it was for the benefit of preachers too ignorant or too lazy to compose their own sermons. Luther attributes to the bad Latin of these books the medieval decline of the language. See Albrecht, *Studien zu . . . "die Ratsherren,"* pp. 705-707.

[51] On Luther's view of Aristotle, the ancient Greek philosopher whose ideas became basic for scholastic theology, and for a bibliography on the subject see Peter Petersen, *Geschichte der aristotelischen Philosophie im protestantischen*

to come in, together with countless harmful books which drew us farther from the Bible. In addition to these he let in those devil's masks, the monks, and those phantoms which are the universities, which we endowed with vast properties. We have taken upon ourselves the support of a host of doctors, preaching friars, masters, priests, and monks; that is to say, great, coarse, fat asses decked out in red and brown birettas, looking like a sow bedecked with a gold chain and jewels. They taught us nothing good, but only made us all the more blind and stupid. In return, they devoured all our goods and filled every monastery, indeed every nook and cranny, with the filth and dung of their foul and poisonous books, until it is appalling to think of it.

Isn't it a crying shame that heretofore a boy was obliged to study for twenty years or even longer merely to learn enough bad Latin to become a priest and mumble through the mass? Whoever got that far was accounted blessed, and blessed was the mother who bore such a child! And yet he remained all his life a poor ignoramus, unable either to cackle or to lay an egg.[52] Everywhere we were obliged to put up with teachers and masters who knew nothing themselves, and were incapable of teaching anything good or worthwhile. In fact, they did not even know how to study or teach. Where does the fault lie? There were no other books available than the stupid books of the monks and the sophists. What else could come out of them but pupils and teachers as stupid as the books they used? A jackdaw hatches no doves,[53] and a fool cannot produce a sage. That is the reward of our ingratitude, that men failed to found libraries but let the good books perish and kept the poor ones.

My advice is not to heap together all manner of books indiscriminately and think only of the number and size of the collection. I would make a judicious selection, for it is not necessary

---

Deutschland (Leipzig: Meiner, 1921), pp. 31-38. Cf. also Luther's own judgment of Aristotle's several works in his 1520 *Open Letter to the Christian Nobility*. *PE* 2, 146-147.

[52] Cackling (*Glucken*) was said to be easier than laying an egg; Wander (ed.), *Sprichwörter-Lexikon*, I, 1774. Whoever could do neither the harder nor the easier was presumably pretty worthless. *WA* 15, 51, n. 1

[53] See Wander (ed.), *Sprichwörter-Lexikon*, I, 671, "*Dohle*," No. 4.

to have all the commentaries of the jurists, all the sentences[54] of the theologians, all the *quaestiones*[55] of the philosophers, and all the sermons of the monks. Indeed, I would discard all such dung, and furnish my library with the right sort of books, consulting with scholars as to my choice.

First of all, there would be the Holy Scriptures, in Latin, Greek, Hebrew, and German, and any other language in which they might be found. Next, the best commentaries, and, if I could find them, the most ancient, in Greek, Hebrew, and Latin. Then, books that would be helpful in learning the languages, such as the poets and orators, regardless of whether they were pagan or Christian, Greek or Latin, for it is from such books that one must learn grammar.[56] After that would come books on the liberal arts,[57] and all the other arts. Finally, there would be books of law and medicine; here too there should be careful choice among commentaries.

Among the foremost would be the chronicles and histories, in whatever languages they are to be had. For they are a wonderful help in understanding and guiding the course of events, and especially for observing the marvelous works of God.[58] How many fine tales and sayings we should have today of things that took place and were current in German lands, not one of which is known to us, simply because there was no one to write them down, and no one to preserve the books had they been written. That is why nothing is known in other lands about us

[54] The term should properly be "books of sentences." "Sentences" was a common title for dogmatic-theological treatises of the Middle Ages. Luther probably had in mind the countless commentaries on the *Sentences* compiled *ca.* 1150 by Peter Lombard (d. 1160), for centuries the most influential textbook of theology.

[55] Scholastic philosophers, in dealing with almost any subject, customarily split it up into *quaestiones,* i.e., specific topics to be discussed in the form of question and **answer.**

[56] *Grammatica,* the most basic of the liberal arts, included much more than we understand by the term "grammar" today. Perhaps "English" would be the closest modern equivalent, for it included besides the rules of a language such things as vocabulary, reading, interpretation, and creative expression. Albrecht, *Studien zu . . . "die Ratsherren,"* p. 711.

[57] See p. 356, n. 15.

[58] Luther set forth his ideas on the value of history at greater length in his 1538 preface to Wenceslaus Link's translation of Capella's history of Francesco Sforza. WA 50, 383-385.

Germans, and we must be content to have the rest of the world refer to us as German beasts who know only how to fight, gorge, and guzzle.[59] The Greeks and Latins, however, and even the Hebrews, wrote their things down so accurately and diligently that if even a woman or a child said or did something out of the ordinary the whole world must read of it and know it. Meanwhile, we Germans are nothing but Germans, and will remain Germans.

Now that God has today so graciously bestowed upon us an abundance of arts, scholars, and books, it is time to reap and gather in the best as well as we can, and lay up treasure in order to preserve for the future something from these years of jubilee,[60] and not lose this bountiful harvest. For it is to be feared—and the beginning of it is already apparent—that men will go on writing new and different books until finally, because of the devil's activity, we will come to the point where the good books which are now being produced and printed will again be suppressed, and the worthless and harmful books with their useless and senseless rubbish will swarm back and litter every nook and corner. The devil certainly intends that we shall again be burdened and plagued as before with nothing but *Catholicons, Floristae,* Modernists,[61] and the accursed dung of monks and sophists, forever studying but never learning anything.

Therefore, I beseech you, my dear sirs, to let this sincere effort of mine bear fruit among you. Should there be any who think me too insignificant to profit by my advice, or who despise me as one condemned by the tyrants,[62] I pray them to consider that I am not seeking my own advantage, but the welfare and

---

[59] On the bitter comments especially of the Italians, who frequently characterized the Germans as uncultured barbarians, see Albrecht, *Studien zu* . . . *"die Ratsherren,"* p. 712.

[60] See p. 351, n. 10.

[61] The *Moderni* were the followers of Occam and opponents of the *Antiqui* who adhered strictly to the interpretation of Aristotle as delivered by Albertus Magnus, Thomas Aquinas, and Duns Scotus. Their quarrel over the best methods of introducing young students to logic and dialectics became bitter enough to split faculties and require intervention by authorities. While the former called themselves nominalists and the latter realists, the controversy was essentially not that which divided the two great systems of scholastic thought going by the same names. Albrecht, *Studien zu* . . . *"die Ratsherren,"* p. 708.

[62] See p. 347, n. 2.

salvation of all Germany. Even if I were a fool and had hit upon a good idea, surely no wise man would think it a disgrace to follow me. And if I were a very Turk or a heathen, and my plan were nevertheless seen to benefit not myself but the Christians, they ought not in fairness to spurn my offer. It has happened before that a fool gave better advice than a whole council of wise men.[63] Moses was obliged to take advice from Jethro [Exod. 18:17-24].

Herewith I commend all of you to the grace of God. May he soften and kindle your hearts that they may be deeply concerned for the poor, miserable, and neglected youth, and with the help of God aid and assist them, to the end that there may be a blessed and Christian government in the German lands with respect to both body and soul, with all plenty and abundance, to the glory and honor of God the Father, through our Savior Jesus Christ. Amen.

---

[63] See Luther's similar statement in the address to Amsdorf with which he began his 1520 *Open Letter to the Christian Nobility. PE* 2, 62.

THAT PARENTS SHOULD
NEITHER COMPEL NOR HINDER
THE MARRIAGE OF
THEIR CHILDREN,
AND THAT CHILDREN SHOULD
NOT BECOME ENGAGED WITHOUT
THEIR PARENTS' CONSENT

1524

Translated by Walther I. Brandt

INTRODUCTION

Luther had predicted in 1522 that the discussion of marriage problems would come to occupy much of his time and attention.[1] One of these problems was the question of the extent of parental authority.[2] The current position of canon law, later confirmed by the Council of Trent, was that the consent of the two persons directly concerned constituted the "form" of the sacrament of marriage; parental consent was not necessary for a valid marriage.[3] Luther, on the other hand, denied that marriage was a sacrament,[4] and relied on the Mosaic law and practice which emphasized parental authority. This raised several questions: Did a parent have the authority (1) to prevent his child from marrying a particular person? (2) to forbid his marrying at all? (3) to force him into a marriage distasteful to him? In the present tract Luther answered the first question in the affirmative, pointing out that Scripture records no instance of an engagement entered into without the parents' consent, expressed or implied. To the second question he gave an emphatic negative. The third question, as he said, was "the knottiest problem." On the basis of certain Old Testament examples[5] he concluded that in principle the child is bound to obey his parents. At the same time, on the basis of Gen. 24:57, he held that the consent of the child was necessary under the law of Christian love, and that the child might with a good conscience act contrary to the will of a tyrannical and obstinate parent.

Evidently, Luther had for some time been considering a full

---

[1] See *The Estate of Marriage* in this volume, p. 25.
[2] In commenting on the gospel of the three kings (Matt. 2:1-12) in his 1522 *Kirchenpostille,* Luther had discussed the question whether a father had the authority to break up a marriage which his child had contracted without the father's knowledge or against his will. *WA* 10I, 1, 642-645.
[3] See *WA* 10I, 1, 643, n. 1.
[4] See his 1520 *Babylonian Captivity of the Church. LW* 36, 92-96
[5] E.g., Abraham and Isaac found wives for their sons; Jacob accepted Leah, although she was given him by a trick and against his will.

expression of his views on these questions. Early in 1524 Spalatin called Melanchthon's attention to an instance of marriage brought about by parental coercion. Melanchthon replied on April 11 by citing Luther's argument from the examples of Adam and Eve, and of Rebekah, that mutual consent was essential, adding the remark, "I think that Dr. Luther is going to explain all this fully."[6]

We have some undated remarks by Luther in 1524 on the validity of a forced engagement,[7] in which he includes the illustration of Adam and Eve, of Rebekah, and also of Samson, as proof that by the law of Christian love the agreement of the parties directly concerned must be added to the will of the parents. Since these brief remarks can scarcely be the full explanation to which Melanchthon referred, it is to be presumed that the present tract addressed to Hans Schott[8] must be.

The immediate occasion for writing the tract seems to have been a story of the abuse of parental authority told to Luther by Hans Schott.[9] What the story was, we do not know. It may possibly have had some relation to Schott's own marital troubles. It appears that one Anna Auerbach married a Torgau burgher, Jakob Hufener. He proved to be a philanderer, and discord developed. Anna finally left him, and sought Schott's protection. In the course of time Anna and Schott decided to marry. They first consulted Gabriel Zwilling,[10] the parish priest at Torgau, who interposed no objection. The matter later came to the attention of Elector John of Saxony, who in April, 1526, directed a letter of inquiry to Schott.[11] The elector also asked Luther

---

[6] *C.R.* 1, 653. Melanchthon was expressing an inference he had drawn from a conversation with Luther.

[7] De Wette, *Dr. Martin Luthers Briefe*, II, 594-595; Enders, *Briefwechsel*, V, 97.

[8] Hans Schott of Oberlind was knighted on July 22, 1517, before the Holy Sepulcher while on a pilgrimage to the Holy Land. In 1521 he had offered lodging to Luther on the latter's arrival at Worms for his hearing. WA, Br 4, 68, n. 1.

[9] This may have been communicated to Luther by word of mouth; at least no such letter from Schott is extant.

[10] On Zwilling (*ca.* 1487-1558), see p. 13.

[11] See the letters from both Schott and Hufener to the elector in WA, Br 4, 66-68.

for an opinion on the grounds that Luther "had previously dealt with the problem," presumably in the present treatise.[12]

The tract probably appeared in printed form toward the end of April, 1524, or soon thereafter. In the conclusion of his sermon on divorce of May 8, 1524,[13] Luther discusses the same material in such close accord with the present tract that both tract and sermon must have been composed at about the same time, or else Luther had one in front of him while he wrote the other.

The following translation, the first into English, is based on the first Wittenberg edition of Lucas Cranach, *Das Elltern die Kinder zur Ehe nicht zwingen noch hyndern, Und die kinder on der elltern willen sich nicht verloben sollen,* as that has been reprinted with annotations in WA 15, (155) 163-169.

---

[12] *MA*³ 5, 413. See the Elector's letter of May 1, 1526, to Luther in *WA,* Br 4, 65.
[13] See the text of the sermon in *WA* 15, 558-562.

THAT PARENTS SHOULD NEITHER COMPEL NOR HINDER THE MARRIAGE OF THEIR CHILDREN, AND THAT CHILDREN SHOULD NOT BECOME ENGAGED WITHOUT THEIR PARENTS' CONSENT

To the formidable and valiant Hans Schott, knight, etc., my dear lord and friend, from Martin Luther:

Grace and peace in Christ, our Lord and Savior. Honorable dear lord and friend. When I began writing on the estate of marriage, I was afraid that things would turn out as they now have, that I would be kept busier with this one topic than with my entire cause apart from it.[1] If there were nothing else to suggest that the estate of marriage is a godly estate this fact alone should be enough to convince you, namely, that the prince of this world—the devil—sets himself against it in so many ways to resist it with hand and foot and all his strength; indeed, that fornication is not diminishing but on the increase.

Previously I wrote that obedience to parents is so important that a child should not become engaged or marry without their knowledge and consent, and that if this does occur the parents

---

[1] See the opening paragraph of *The Estate of Marriage* (1522), in this volume, p. 17. Luther's earliest extant sermon *On the Estate of Marriage* was delivered in 1519; see the text in *WA* 2, 166-171. He had also dealt with the subject in *The Babylonian Captivity of the Church* (*LW* 36, 92-106), in the "winter" postils of 1522 (*WA* 10^I, 1, 642-645), in his 1523 *Exhortation to the Knights of the Teutonic Order* (in this volume, pp. 143-145), and on other occasions (see in this volume p. 14); and was to treat of it again in his 1530 *Of Matrimonial Matters* (*WA* 30^{III}, [198] 205-248).

have the authority to dissolve such a union.[2] But now the parents are going too far in this direction. They are beginning arbitrarily to hinder and prevent their children from getting married and, according to the incident you recently told me about, to compel them to marry someone they do not love. Therefore, I am once more compelled to offer my opinion and advice for the sake of those who might wish to be guided and comforted by it. Herewith I commend you to God's grace. Amen.

First, that parents have neither the right nor the authority
to compel their children to marry

To hinder or prevent a marriage is something quite different from compelling or forcing a marriage. Even if parents had the right and authority to do the first, that is, to prevent a marriage, it does not follow that they also have the authority to compel a marriage. It is more tolerable that the love which two have for one another be hindered and broken up, than that two be forced together who have no love for one another. In the first instance the grief is but temporary. It is to be feared that the second, however, involves an eternal hell and a lifetime of misery. Now Paul says in I Corinthians 16[3] that even the very highest authority, namely, to preach the gospel and govern souls, was granted by God for building up and not for destroying. How much less, then, should the authority of parents, or any other authority, have been given for destroying rather than exclusively for building up.

It is quite certain therefore that parental authority is strictly limited; it does not extend to the point where it can wreak damage and destruction to the child, especially to its soul. If then a father forces his child into a marriage without love, he oversteps and exceeds his authority. He ceases to be a father and becomes a tyrant who uses his authority not for building up—which is why God gave it to him—but for destroying. He is taking authority into his own hands without God, indeed, against God.

---

[2] See *The Estate of Marriage* (1522), in this volume, p. 29, and the 1522 Postil (*WA* 10^I, 1, 642-645), where parental authority is described as absolute except in case the parents demand something contrary to God's command or God requires something contrary to the wishes of the parents.
[3] II Cor. 10:8.

The same principle holds good when a father hinders his child's marriage, or lets the child go ahead on his own, without any intention of helping him in the matter (as often happens in the case of step-parents and their children, or orphans and their guardians, where covetousness has its eye more on what the child has than on what the child needs). In such a case the child is truly free and may act as if his parent or guardian were dead; mindful of what is best for himself,[4] he may become engaged in God's name, and look after himself as best he can.

The child may take this course only if he has previously besought his father, or had him besought and admonished, so that the fact may be established that the father or relative refuses to do anything about it, or repeatedly puts him off with empty words. In such a case the father is failing to do his duty and live up to the obligations of his authority, and is jeopardizing his child's honor and soul. It is only right therefore—it is what he deserves—that you give no heed to him who gives no heed to your honor and soul. This is particularly true in cases where relatives refuse, as they are doing today,[5] to assist poor nuns in obtaining husbands; they give heed neither to the honor nor to the soul of their kinfolk. In such case it is enough if these former nuns give them notice, and then go ahead and marry in God's name whether the relatives like it or not.

But the knottiest problem in the matter is this: Is a child obligated to render obedience to a father who is forcing him into marriage, or compelling him to marry someone whom he does not love? It is easy enough to understand and conclude that the father is wrong, and that he is acting like a devil or a tyrant rather than a father. But where the shoe pinches[6] is on the question whether the child should bow to this authority and injustice and obey the tyrant. For in Matthew 5 Christ clearly and bluntly commands us not to resist evil but to go two miles with whoever

---

[4] See p. 125, n. 111.
[5] This was written at about the time Luther was busily trying to secure husbands for those nuns—including Katharine von Bora who was to become Mrs. Luther—who about a year earlier had fled from the convent at Nimbschen. See Schwiebert, *Luther and His Times*, pp. 585-588; also Luther's letter to Spalatin of April 10, 1523. WA, Br 3, 54-55; S-J 2, 179-181.
[6] *Da stösset es sich.*

forces you to go one, let your cloak go with your coat, and turn the other cheek also.[7] From this it would follow that a child should and must obey, and accept the injustice which such a tyrannical and unpaternal father forces upon him.

To this I reply: Where it is Christians who are dealing with a case of this sort, the problem is quickly resolved. For a true Christian, one who complies with the gospel (because he is prepared to suffer injustice and oppression even though it touch body, goods, or honor; and whether it be brief or lasting, or even forever, if God wills it), would by all means neither refuse nor resist such a forced marriage. He would act as one who had fallen into the hand of the Turks or of some other enemy, and accept whatever the Turk or enemy might thrust upon him, even though it meant languishing forever in a dungeon or being chained to a galley. We have an excellent example of this in the holy patriarch Jacob, who contrary to all justice had Leah forced upon him against his will and kept her nevertheless. Although in the eyes of mankind he was under no obligation, since he had lain with her unwittingly,[8] yet he tolerated and endured the injustice, and kept her contrary to his own desire [Gen. 29:21-28].

But where are there such Christians? And if there be any such, where are there any hardy enough, like Jacob, to reconcile themselves to such injustice? It certainly is not my job to suggest or to teach anything but what is Christian, in this matter or any other. If anyone finds himself unable to follow this advice, let him confess his weakness to God and pray for grace and help, just as the person does who dreads and shrinks from dying or suffering anything else for the sake of God (as he is obligated to do) and feels that he is too weak to accomplish it. There is no alternative; the word of Christ must stand, "Agree with your adversary while you are in the way with him" [Matt. 5:25].

It is of no use to offer the excuse that such a forced marriage will engender hatred, jealousy, murder, and all manner of mis-

---

[7] See Luther's earlier interpretation of Matthew 5:39-41 in his 1523 treatise on *Temporal Authority*, in this volume, pp. 87-104 passim; and in his 1520 treatise on *Usury*, in this volume, pp. 273-274.

[8] Luther cited the same example in discussing the impediment of "error" in his 1522 *The Estate of Marriage*, in this volume, p. 27.

fortune. For Christ has the ready answer: Let that be my concern; why do you have no faith in me? Obey my command, and I can so govern events that none of the misfortunes you foresee will occur, and all will be good fortune and happiness. Would you transgress my certain and blessed commandment on account of an uncertain future misfortune? Or would you do evil, that good might result? Paul condemns this in Romans 3 [:8]. And even though misfortune were certain for the future, indeed already at hand, should you on that account disregard my commandment, when you are in duty bound to hazard body and soul temporally and eternally for my sake?

Yet, I would also advise those weak Christians who may be unable to comply with Christ's command to seek and gain the good offices of princes, burghermasters, or other authorities, that they may put a stop to such outrageous injustice, deprive the father of his devilish power, rescue the child from him, and restrict him to the proper use of his parental authority. Although a Christian is in duty bound to tolerate injustice, the temporal authority is also under obligation to punish and prevent such injustice and to guard and uphold the right.

Should the government too prove to be negligent or tyrannical, as a last resort the child might flee to another land and abandon both parent and government, just as in former times certain weak Christians[9] fled from tyrants into the wilderness. Uriah the prophet too fled to Egypt before King Jehoiakim [Jer. 26:21-23]. And there were the hundred prophets [I Kings 18:4], and Elijah himself who fled before Queen Jezebel [I Kings 19:2-3].

Except for these three items, I know of no other advice to give a Christian. As for those who are not Christians, in this matter I leave them to do what they can, within the temporal laws.

Second, that a child should not marry or become engaged without the knowledge and consent of his parents.

Although I have spoken of this also in the Postil,[10] I must

---

9 See p. 200, n. 7.
10 On the Postils, see p. 90, n. 29. For Luther's specific reference here, see the Introduction, p. 381, n. 2.

repeat it here. The fourth commandment here stands strong and firm, "Honor and obey your father and your mother."[11] This is why in all of Scripture we find not a single example of two young people entering into an engagement of their own accord. Instead, it is everywhere written of the parents, "Give husbands to your daughters and wives to your sons," Jeremiah 29 [:6]; and Moses says in Exodus 21 [:9], "If a father gives a wife to his son," etc. Thus, Isaac and Jacob took wives at the behest of their parents [Gen. 24:1-4; 28:1-2].

From this the custom has spread throughout the world that weddings and the establishment of new households are celebrated publicly with festivity and rejoicing. Thereby these secret engagements are condemned, and the marriage entered into with the knowledge and consent of both families is confirmed and honored. Even Adam, the very first bridegroom, did not himself select Eve as his bride. Instead, as the text [Gen. 2:22-23] clearly states, God first brought her to him; thus did he receive her.

Now all this is said with reference to parents who treat their child in a fatherly manner, as was pointed out above.[12] Those who treat their children otherwise are to be regarded as if they were not parents at all, or were dead; their child is free to become engaged and to marry whomsoever he fancies. Parents are guilty of unparental conduct when they see that their child is grown up and is fit for and inclined toward marriage, and yet are unwilling to assist and counsel him thereto; when they let him remain a bachelor all his days, or even urge and compel him to become a religious celibate. This is how the nobility has hitherto dealt with their daughters, tucking them away in the cloisters.

Parents should understand that a man is created for marriage, to beget fruit of his body (just as a tree is created to bear apples or pears), unless his nature is altered or hindered by God's supreme grace and special miracle.[13] Therefore, they are in duty bound to assist their children to marry, removing them from the

---

[11] Exod. 20:12; cf. Eph. 6:1-2.
[12] See p. 386.
[13] On God's creation and those who are exempted from it, see *The Estate of Marriage*, in this volume, pp. 11-49, especially pp. 19-22.

perils of unchastity. If they fail to do so they are no longer parents, and it behooves the child to enter into an engagement on his own account (though not without first giving notice to his parents and voicing complaint against their slothfulness), take steps on his own to avoid the perils of unchastity, and enter that estate for which he was created, whether or not this meets with the approval of his father and mother, his friends or his enemies.

Where matters have gone beyond mere engagement, and the two have secretly become one flesh, it is right to allow them to remain united and to withhold the hand of parental authority; though in the law of Moses God, even in such circumstances, reserved the child to the father, as we read in Exodus 22 [:16-17], "If a man lies with a maiden, he shall endow her and make her his wife; but if her father refuses this, he shall provide for her the dowry," etc. At that time, however, there was not so much stress laid on virginity. In our day there is a strong aversion to marrying a despoiled woman; such a marriage is regarded as disgraceful. As a result the second part of this law of Moses, with respect to parental authority over the despoiled virgin, is harmful and a source of peril to the child. For this reason it is right that the first part remain in force, namely, that he who despoiled her shall retain her.

Now someone may protest: If the father has the authority to break off his child's engagement and disrupt his marriage, then he must also have the authority to forbid his child to marry at all, and to force him into celibacy, etc. I answer: Not so. I have said above that man is created—not by his father, but by God— to eat, drink, produce fruit of his body, sleep, and respond to other calls of nature. It is not within the power of any man to alter this. Therefore, it is one thing to hinder a child's marriage to this or that particular person, and quite another thing to forbid marriage entirely. A father may lay down the rule that his child must not eat or drink this or that, or sleep here or there; but he cannot rule that the child abstain entirely from food, drink, and sleep. On the contrary, he is duty bound to provide his child with food, drink, clothing, sleep, and whatever else is needful for his well-being. If he fails to do this, he is no father at all, and the child will have to do it himself.

In like manner, the father also has the authority to prevent his child from marrying this one or that one; but he does not have the authority to forbid him to marry altogether. On the contrary, he is duty bound to get his child a good mate who will be just right for him, or who seems to be just right for him. If he fails to do this, the child should and must provide for the matter himself. Again, the father can without sin forego his right and authority; when he has faithfully counseled his child and voiced his objections, he can let him have his own way and marry whomsoever he will even without his father's consent. For who can possibly ward off all evil when good advice and sound judgment are ignored? Thus, Isaac and Rebekah allowed their son Esau to do as he pleased and take wives whom they did not favor, Genesis 27.[14] In such a case the father has sufficiently met his obligation and fulfilled his parental duty. It is not necessary for him to restrain the child with sword and spear. God will surely see and deal with the child's disobedience and wilfulness.

To sum it all up, these things transpire according to two kinds of law, either Christian or human. Where they proceed in Christian fashion there will be knowledge and consent on both sides: the father will not bestow his child without the child's knowledge and consent (as it is written in Genesis 24 [:57-58], where Rebekah was asked beforehand and freely consented to become the wife of Isaac); the child in turn will not bestow himself without the father's knowledge and consent. But if the thing is to be done simply in human fashion, strictly according to the law, the father may arbitrarily bestow his child, and the child is bound to comply. Further, the father has the authority to break off an engagement into which his child has entered, and the child does not have the right to enter into an engagement behind the father's back.

But if one of the parties, namely, the father, wishes to conduct himself as a Christian should, he may forego his rights and permit the child to be governed by his own wilfulness and disobedience. Having voiced his sincere and paternal objections, warning, and counsel, the father may put his own conscience at

---

14 See Gen. 26:34-35; 27:46—28:9.

ease and let the child's conscience bear the burden; just as many holy fathers have doubtless many times borne patiently, against their will, even greater disobedience on the part of their children, and committed the matter to God.

If the thing is done, however, in a fashion that is neither human nor Christian, but devilish, as when a father forcibly compels his child to marry when he has no heart for it, that child may consider himself as one who is captured by the Turk and compelled to do the enemy's will; or, if he can, he may take refuge in flight, as we have said.[15]

Let this now be enough for one letter. The matter itself will perhaps necessitate further discussion as to how one is to act in keeping with the temporal laws, and not simply in keeping with the gospel.

---

[15] See p. 389.

INDEXES

Prepared by Frederick C. Ahrens

INDEX OF NAMES AND SUBJECTS

407

INDEX TO SCRIPTURE PASSAGES

Type used in this book
Body, 10 on 13 Caledonia
Display, Bulmer and Caledonia
Paper: Standard White Antique "RRR"